NINE MEN

NINE
MEN

*A Political History
of the Supreme Court
from 1790 to 1955*

by FRED RODELL

RANDOM HOUSE · NEW YORK

Second Printing

FOR Janet and Mike
with thanks and love

Contents

Foreword

THIS BOOK is the oh-hell-I-might-as-well-try-it-myself result of many years of wishing someone else would write it. Reviewing a couple of contemporary works about the Supreme Court, not quite two decades ago, I said: "Somewhere between these two books a really first-rate job has yet to be done on the Supreme Court. It would not spare personalities, yet it would not be content to give its readers the cheap thrill of vicariously peeping through keyholes at undressed Justices. It would not skimp the past history of the Court, but would use that history to point up an incisive inspection of the Court's place in our scheme of government today." This is not to imply by any means that mine is a "first-rate job"; but it is at least an A-for-effort attempt to do what I have so long hoped some other, abler soul might do—and to do it so that any halfway literate non-lawyer can understand it. My chief editor of words and phrases has been my fourteen-year-old son, Mike; my chief editor of ideas has been my wife, Janet, who knows as little about law as I do about her field, child psychology.

If people cannot understand this book, it will be because Janet and Mike are too bright for her skirts and his breeches.

It may be that lawyers will not understand it, because it is not written down to them. I have done my best not to use the easy slang (once you have learned it) of long-worded legal language, which too often lets off-the-real-point thinking become a habit. More than that, I have kept completely away from matters that would interest only lawyers —from Supreme Court cases that deal with anything other than the part the Court plays in the way this nation is run; Erie *v.* Tompkins, "a great legal landmark," (what it said was that federal judges, when handling private legal squabbles, should use a different set of rules from those they had used before) is not even mentioned—except here. My interest and, I think, most people's interest in the Court is in what it—or rather the men who man it—have done on the (dirty word) political scene for 165 years.

This book has no footnotes, no here's-where-to-look-it-up lists of cases or sources. It is meant for reading, not for easy reference by lazy scholars. Of course, the quotations and facts have been checked and are accurate—in so far as a fallible human, meaning me, can make them accurate— though on matters of opinion, as opposed to fact, I hope I make it clear that the views I express are mine. Moreover, it would be impossible, literally, for me to list where all the stuff came from that stuck in my head throughout more than a quarter-century of reading and hearing—with intent fascination, but with nary a filing-cabinet except the universal filing-cabinet of the mind—about the Court and its past and present Justices. I dare say the reading has

included all or parts of over a thousand books and over ten
thousand articles, not counting the daily newspapers and
the Court's own official reports. And bits of the whole that
is here between covers have been filched, with their faces
washed and lifted, from the fifty-odd pieces I have written
myself, about the Court and the Justices, in the rather
recent past.

Beyond that, I am prejudiced, as all men are prejudiced,
by my own ideas and ideals. But I like to think that my
slant toward people, especially those I know or have
known (and Supreme Court Justices are people), is based
on those ideas and ideals, not on petty, personal things. If
Justice Holmes is one of the major heroes of this book, it is
not because I once spent in his home an intellectually exciting afternoon; if Justice McReynolds appears as one of
the book's near-villains, it is not because my visit with him
was far less pleasant; the reasons come closer to running
the other way round. I once took law-school courses from
both Justice Douglas and Justice Frankfurter, when they
were mere professors of law—and Professor Frankfurter
gave me the higher grade and made the more of me, then
and for some years after. If Justice Douglas is today my
friend, and is also rated in this book considerably above
Justice Frankfurter, *both* facts are by my choice and *both*
stem from my estimate of them as Justices, as government-
serving men.

The ideas and ideals—or prejudices—by which I judge
men in public life (or in private life) are mainly two. As
even he who reads on the run will easily discover, I am one
of that great and unlike group that is fuzzily labeled
"liberal"—so I tend, of course, to admire liberals or

lookers-after-the-other-fellow more than I admire conservatives; yet awareness of my own leaning has led me,
throughout this book, to try to give the devils their more
than due. My other ideal or prejudice is more important. I
confess an almost fanatical devotion to that kind of personal
integrity that combines intellectual honesty with courage.
"Better a plain-speaking conservative than a weak and
weaseling liberal" might well be my motto in appraising
men. The man who says what he means, and means and
acts what he says, can almost always win me—which goes,
of course, for Supreme Court Justices.

All this is by way of what the lawyers (and how did
they creep in?) call "full disclosure." No one who goes
beyond these words can now say he wasn't warned. Happy
reading.

F. R.

Bethany, Connecticut
March, 1955

NINE MEN

CHAPTER 1

Powerful, Irresponsible, and Human

AT THE TOP LEVELS of the three branches of the civilian government of the United States sit the Congress, the President plus his Cabinet, and the Supreme Court. Of these three—in this unmilitary, unclerical nation—only one wears a uniform. Only one carries on its most important business in utter secret behind locked doors—and indeed never reports, even after death, what really went on there. Only one, its members holding office for life if they choose, is completely irresponsible to anyone or anything but themselves and their own consciences. Only one depends for much of its immense influence on its prestige as a semi-sacred institution and preserves that prestige with the trappings and show of superficial dignity rather than earning it, year after working year, by the dignity and wisdom of what it is and does. Under our otherwise democratic form of government, only one top ruling group uses ceremony and secrecy, robes and ritual, as instruments of its *official* policy, as wellsprings of its power.

The nine men who are the Supreme Court of the United States are at once the most powerful and the most irresponsible of all the men in the world who govern other men. Not even the bosses of the Kremlin, each held back by fear of losing his head should he ever offend his fellows, wield such loose and long-ranging and acountable-to-no-one power as do the nine or five-out-of-nine Justices who can give orders to any other governing official in the United States—from the members of a village school board who would force their young charges to salute the flag, to a President who would take over the steel industry to keep production going—and can make those orders stick. Ours may be, for puffing purposes, a "government of checks and balances," but there is no check at all on what the Supreme Court does—save only three that are as pretty in theory as they are pointless in practice. (These are the Senate's power to reject a newly named Justice, used only once this century, and in the past usually unwisely; the power to impeach a Justice, only once tried and never carried through; the power of the people to reverse a Supreme Court decision by amending the Constitution, as they have done just three times in our whole history.) The nine Justices sit secure and stand supreme over Congress, President, governors, state legislatures, commissions, administrators, lesser judges, mayors, city councils, and dog-catchers—with none to say them nay.

Lest these words sound like arrant overstatement, here are what three of the most thoughtful men who ever held high national office said about the Supreme Court's flat and final power of government. Thomas Jefferson, who was President when the Court first fully used this power, exploded, prophetically but futilely: "Our Constitution . . . intending to establish three departments, coordinate and independent, that they might check and balance one another, . . . has given, according to this opinion, to one of them alone the right to prescribe rules for the government of the others, and to that one, too, which is unelected by and independent of the nation. . . . The Constitution, on this hypothesis, is a mere thing of wax in the hands of the judiciary which they may twist and shape into any form they please." Jefferson was talking of the Court's then brand-newly wielded power to override Congress and the President. More than a century later, Justice Holmes, revealingly in dissent, berated his brethren for freely using their judicial power to upset *state* laws: "As the decisions now stand I see hardly any limit but the sky to the invalidating of those rights ['*the constitutional rights of the states*'] if they happen to strike a majority of this Court as for any reason undesirable. I cannot believe that the [Fourteenth] Amendment was intended to give us carte blanche to embody our economic or moral beliefs in its prohibitions." And a few years after, Justice Stone, he too in dissent, exclaimed: "The only check upon our own exercise of power is our own sense of self-restraint."

In Stone's same angry protest against the Court's six-

to-three veto of the first Agricultural Adjustment Act—a
protest that helped spark Franklin Roosevelt's "Court-
packing" plan and later led FDR to reward its author with
the Chief Justiceship—he also said: "Courts are not the
only agency of government that must be assumed to have
capacity to govern." This statement, while true on its face,
is essentially and subtly—though of course not deliberately
—misleading. No "agency of government" governs; no
"court" governs; only the men who run the agency of
government or the court or the Supreme Court do the
governing. The power is theirs because the decisions are
theirs; decisions are not made by abstractions like agencies
or courts. Justice Stone, who knew what he meant, might a
little better have said: "Five or six of the nine men who
make up this Court are not the only men in our government
who must be assumed to have the capacity to govern." And
he might have added: "Nor are they necessarily the wisest
in their judgments; I work with them and have reason to
know."

For the old saw, beloved of history textbooks and political speeches, that "ours is a government of laws, not of
men," is an insult and an undemocratic canard. Laws are
words, nothing more. Laws do not write or enforce or
interpret themselves. Even constitutions are no more than
words except as men give them flesh and muscle and meaning in action; then the flesh and muscle are molded and the
meaning in action is directed by men. The words of the
Soviet constitution are in many ways more democratic
than those of ours—as are the words of the constitutions of
several Latin-American countries now run by dictators.
And the cold truth about "laws, not men" was never better

put than by one of the Founding Fathers, John Mercer of Maryland, who said what all of them were wise enough to know as they hammered out the U.S. Constitution back in 1787: "It is a great mistake to suppose that the paper we are to propose will govern the United States. It is the men whom it will bring into the government and interest in maintaining it."

Among those men, and most powerful of all of them for the past century and a half, are the Justices of the U.S. Supreme Court. They may say—and often do—that it is not *they* who make the decisions, lay down the rules, give orders to every other governing official in the land; they may say they do nothing but "interpret" the laws, including the Constitution; they may talk at times as though they neither had nor need human minds, as though they might almost as well be a nine-headed calculating machine, intricately adjusted to the words of the Constitution and of lesser laws, and ready to give automatic answers to any attorneys who drop their briefs in the proper slot and push the button. But even non-lawyers have come to find a trifle naïve and unconvincing the old fantasy that our government, especially its judicial branch, is mechanically controlled by laws, not by men. If it were, how explain split Supreme Court decisions (5–4, 6–3, 7–2, even 8–1); how explain dissenting opinions that too often make more sense than the majority "opinions of the Court"; how explain the "overruling" of past decisions—a term which means that the same question, decided one way before, is now decided exactly the opposite way? There was more truth than lawyerly discretion in the comment of Charles Evans Hughes, before he became Chief Justice of the United

States: "We are under a Constitution, but the Constitution is what the judges say it is."

The judges who say what the Constitution is have ranged throughout our history from the wise to the stupid, from the broad and brilliant to the narrow-minded and uninformed. No more than election to Congress or the Presidency ensures the ability of the man who is elected, does appointment to the Supreme Court ensure an able judge. For every Marshall, for every Holmes—who comes along sadly seldom, as does a Jefferson or a Lincoln—there will be scores of merely competent or middling or quite inept Justices, who can often outweigh by numbers alone, if not by depth of insight or clarity of vision, their more capable colleagues. It is a telling and disturbing fact that no Supreme Court Justice in the past half-century, save only Hughes, has achieved a generally acknowledged greatness except in dissent.

When a lame-duck Senator is named to the Court to pay off a party's political debt to him, or a querulous Attorney-General is kicked upstairs to the Court, or a lawyer-politician attains the Court because the President, by happenstance, knows and likes him personally, he does not become, by the process of donning a black gown and a solemn mien, a different man. He retains the same mind, the same personality, the same political perspectives and prejudices—plus the same ability or inability to govern wisely. But he has now been entrusted with tremendous governmental power, untrammeled by anyone except his own colleagues, who may be as unable—or as able—as he. Warren G. Harding is not widely regarded as one of our first-rate presidents, but most people assume that his influence on national policy ended when death cut short his term of office. What is too easily forgotten is that the four mediocre or worse-than-mediocre Justices whom he appointed dominated the Court and, through it, the country for years after his death. It has been said that the good a President does is oft interred with his bones but his choice of Supreme Court Justices lives after him. It has also been said that "the Supreme Court follows the election returns" —although Mr. Dooley might have added "of ten or twelve years before." The truth implicit in both these remarks is that the nine Justices are not judicial automatons but highly human and hence inevitably political men.

Being men, the Justices sometimes seem to change their more lightly or expediently held political opinions after they have achieved the security of the Court. McReynolds and Jackson, both of them rampagingly liberal Attorneys-General under crusading Presidents, became eloquent spokesmen of conservatism as Justices; Calvin Coolidge caught a Tartar when he named his old friend, Harlan Stone, a former corporation lawyer and hence a presumably safe and solid Republican choice; Theodore Roosevelt was outraged when Justice Holmes, in a touted trust-busting case, voted against the administration on what was one of T.R.'s pet projects, shortly after T.R. appointed Holmes; and Franklin Roosevelt would doubtless be outraged today at many of the votes and views of two of his New Deal appointees—Frankfurter and Reed. Yet none of these men—nor any other—changed his true colors by the act of ascending the bench, although a few may have been sailing under false colors before. The Presidents who chose them merely misjudged them—as men often misjudge other men. And ever since the time when John Adams put John Marshall in a position, as Chief Justice, to carry on Federalist policies long after the Federalists had been voted out of power, the history of the Court has been replete with the picking of Justices who stuck precisely, permanently, and often stubbornly to the policies and politics that their appointing Presidents expected them to stick to.

If there is anything sinister or wrong about the system whereby every President naturally tries to appoint Justices whose slant toward the big problems of government follows and fits with the appointing President's slant, the wrongness does not lie in the fact that Justices are still men—and that the men are still themselves. The wrongness lies rather in the fact that these men—remaining themselves, attaining the power of Justices, and retaining that power for sometimes more than thirty years—inevitably act as a check, a lag, on the forward momentum of government and on the democratic directing of national policy by other men who are perpetually responsible to the voters (as the Justices are not responsible) for what they don't and what they do. Especially in times of crisis and change, a reluctant and backward-looking Supreme Court, dominated by a man or group of men who owe their power to a repudiated President or party, can create at least friction, at most chaos, in the running of a nation.

Just as John Marshall's Federalist Court slowed down the operations of Andrew Jackson's popular administration thirty-odd years after reactionary John Adams named Marshall Chief Justice, so Roger Taney's pro-Southern Court, in its fateful Dred Scott decision, bucked the shifted

popular will and helped bring on the Civil War, twenty
years after Andrew Jackson appointed Taney. That the
voters, in 1892, elected a Democratic President and a
Democratic-Populist Congress, dedicated to the passage of
an income tax, did not stop five hangover Supreme Court
Justices from throwing out that income tax after it was
enacted. And in the 1930's, a high bench top-heavy with
the Four Horsemen of the Old Deal brought the Court, as
an institution, to one of its lowest ebbs and greatest crises
when it flouted the nation's voters by vetoing much of
Franklin Roosevelt's New Deal. In each of these instances,
as so often in our history, a majority of the Justices were
behind the political times.

In a sense, it is inevitable that the Court, if it be anything, should be a brake on the rest of our machinery of
government. By the very nature of the way it works, the
Court, for all the power its members hold, is only a negative—never an affirmative—force. It cannot create, it
cannot initiate, it cannot put into action any government
policy of any kind (except in the governmental sideline
dealing with the mechanics of how the Court itself, and
lesser courts, carry on their job). All the Justices can do is
to say Yes or No to a policy or a program or a part of a
policy or program that has been started by someone else
in some other branch of government. All they can do is to
approve or disapprove—after they are asked to do so—a
law passed by a legislature, an order given by an executive,
a ruling made by a commission, an effort made by a law-
enforcing official to fine somebody or put somebody in
jail.

In the course of saying Yes or No—though the Justices

never say it that briefly—or in the course of explaining, in legal language and commonly for the exclusive edification of lawyers, just why they are saying Yes or No, they may suggest, wittingly or unwittingly, a shift or an extension or perhaps a detour in the policies or programs of men in the affirmative branches of government. A decision throwing out a newly written law may hint to the lawmakers how to get the same thing done in a different way which the Justices will then approve. A decision that OK's the disputed act of some official—be it under some federal law on patents or monopolies or labor relations, or under, say, a state regulation of automobiles, or under a city ordinance about public meetings—may contain signposts telling the official he can go still farther along the same road if he chooses. Or a decision that forbids an official to act as he is now acting may outline to the official, in the very detailing of what he may not do, precisely what he may do.

Yet in every such instance—and there are scores of them—the Justices can do nothing but impotently point toward future action after Yessing or Noing past action by men in a position to act. And this very lack of capacity to go forward, this easy if inevitable isolation from all the choice-making, chance-taking responsibility that goes with governing actively and affirmatively, makes even more undemocratically dangerous the Justices' almost cavalier power to keep the nation and its government standing still.

If the Court is irresponsible—as it is—in the sense of being beyond all discipline, all direction, all effective censure, by the voters or by any other governing group, and if it is also irresponsible—as it is—in the sense of sitting in final judgment without ever facing the far tougher task of making first judgments (imagine a President who had nothing to do but veto or not veto), the Court is irresponsible in yet a third sense. For the Justices, by their own sole choice, can even duck, whenever they please, the secondary responsibility of merely giving a Yes or a No. They can shuck off any issue, no matter how important, which somebody asks them to settle finally with the final power they hold, by simply refusing to hear or to decide the issue— by saying, in effect: "This isn't our business; we can't be bothered."

One of the ways the Justices retreat from making decisions is to label a problem "political" rather than "legal" and announce that therefore it is not up to them to solve it. This is the word game the Court used, for instance, to get out of deciding whether Illinois, under the Constitution, had to change its voting districts to fit its shifts in population; one set of Illinois politicians wanted the change and one set did not, but both sets put their claims before the Court; the Justices listened and bowed themselves out —"political," not "legal." In the light of the hundreds of political issues the Justices have not even hesitated, much less balked, at wading into whenever *they* wished, over the past 150 years—issues ranging from segregation of Negroes in the South to strikes in wartime and loyalty programs and state-against-federal claims to tidelands oil— the political-not-legal excuse would be farcical if it were not so essentially shocking in its underlining of judicial irresponsibility.

Another system the Justices use to turn away from uncomfortable questions is to find and inflate some petty point of technical legal procedure—a minor flaw in the

way the case was argued or the briefs written, a lawyer's
slip—and hide behind that as a device for postponing or
evading a meaningful decision on the real issue. Many a
major government problem, many a queer and questionable criminal conviction, has been left hanging unresolved,
literally for years, while the lawyers ran the gauntlet of
the lower courts for the second, sometimes the third, time
—because the Justices had ordered them to start all over
and mind their methods and their legal manners. And after
the gauntlets and the years, the Court may dismiss the case
as "moot" or too-late-for-an-effective-decision (a protested ruling may meanwhile have been varied or someone
in the case may have died)—and small wonder. This purposeful putting off making up their minds about a thorny
problem, on a legalistic procedural excuse, is one of the
Justices' favorite self-protections.

Yet the political-not-legal evasion and the procedural-
error evasion, where the Justices listen and run away, are
as nothing compared to the Court's chief refuge of irresponsibility. For, as few non-lawyers are at all aware,
the Court is its own exclusive judge of which problems,
whose disputes—and how many or how few—it will deign
to decide. With a couple of rare exceptions, required by
the Constitution, the Justices for the past thirty years have
enjoyed—and the verb is accurate—the power to refuse to
hear any case that anybody, railroaded convict or President
of the United States, tries to bring before them. Reasonably and responsibly used, this power would protect the
Justices from wasting their time on trivial or patently
futile and desperate appeals, and would let them devote
their minds and energies to important matters only. But

this power, since it is absolute, is a free ticket to open abuse, an invitation to laziness, incompetence, even cowardice, and it has been precisely so abused in the recent past.

Chief Justice Vinson's take-it-easy Court heard about half as many cases a year as did Chief Justice Hughes' hustling Court a mere decade before. Nor was this for lack of critical cases, of urgent issues begging for a hearing, and turned down. The question whether a city-helped housing project may discriminate against a Negro war veteran (which split the top court of New York state, four to three); the question whether a radio station is "obstructing justice" when it broadcasts a defendant's alleged out-of-court confession during a murder trial (which pits one civil liberty against another—the guarantee of a fair trial against the guarantee of free speech and press); the question whether a fugitive from a Georgia chain gang must be sent back from his hard-won asylum in another state to what the Constitution calls "cruel and unusual punishment"; the question whether movies, like newspapers and books, are protected from narrow local censorship by freedom of the press: all these questions and dozens like them, within the short space of two Court terms, were deemed by Vinson and company not worthy of decision—or perhaps too hot to handle. Nor could any power on earth then force the unjudging Justices to handle them.

Along with this we-won't-even-take-the-case facet of Supreme Court irresponsibility, there goes an attitude so autocratic as to be looked at askance even by many people who otherwise approve of the Court's autocracy. When the

Justices hear and decide a case, though they do their actual deciding in forever secret conference, they at least write opinions which explain—or try to explain or purport to explain—why they are saying Yes or No. But when they simply refuse to take a case, no reason is ever given for that refusal. True, the Justices have let it be known that, by their own self-made rule, if four of them vote—in secret, of course—to hear a case, that case will be heard. And increasingly, in recent years, a couple of the more industrious and courageous Justices, Douglas and Black, have gone to the unusual extreme of recording their protests, time after time, not against a decision by their brethren (which would be a regular dissent) but against the refusal of their brethren to so much as hear and handle many an important issue. Yet even these often disgusted, often angry protestants, bound by the rules of the lodge, never tell—if indeed they always know—why at least six of their fellows have voted themselves out of doing a job that the protestants think ought to be done. Here, in the Court's unwillingness to explain its own seemingly indiscriminate, and perhaps inexplicable, refusals to act, is the ultimate of undemocratic power abused to a point akin to arrogance.

This arrogance is further compounded by a strange fiction, a judicial fairy tale which many Justices mouth and maybe believe, about what their turning down of a case or problem means. The fiction is that the Court, in *not* taking and *not* deciding a case, which it has the power to take and decide, is actually deciding absolutely nothing. As Justice Frankfurter, the most persistent of recent Justices in flaunting this fiction, put it not long ago: "All that a denial of a petition for a writ of certiorari means [*that being lawyers' language for the commonest way of refusing to hear a case*] is that fewer than four members of the Court thought it should be granted." But ignored by this pseudo-explanation, which (Frankfurter again speaking) "the Court has stated again and again," is the plain fact that no case, no problem, vanishes into the blue with the Court's refusal to hear it.

Technically, what happens is that the judgment of some lower court stands just as inexorably, just as finally, as if the Supreme Court had heard the case and affirmed—or said Yes to—the lower court's decision. Practically, what happens is that the Negro war veteran does not get an apartment in the Stuyvesant Town housing project in New York City; that certain movies, offensive to city censors, can *not* be shown in Atlanta, Georgia; that the Baltimore murder suspect whose supposed confession, bought or cajoled from him without legal safeguards and broadcast for all the jurors—or their friends and families—to hear, may be hanged. When the Justices downed their thumbs against listening to Alger Hiss's appeal from his conviction for perjury, none other than Richard Nixon, a lawyer who was then a U.S. Senator and is now Vice-President of the United States, remarked: "Now that the Supreme Court has finally *written the decision* [*italics added*] in the case of Alger Hiss, I should like to take this opportunity to give due credit . . ." But according to the Justices themselves and their insistent fairy story, they had done nothing, much less "write the decision," in the case of Alger Hiss. They had only denied a petition for a writ of certiorari—and: "All that a denial of a petition for a writ of certiorari means is that fewer than four members of the Court thought it should be granted."

If a law—say on uniform rules for divorce throughout the forty-eight states—should be proposed in Congress (as it has been) and the proposed law should never be brought to vote, perhaps by the device of letting it be buried in committee, it is hard to imagine that any voter, any newspaper, any pressure group that had backed such a law, would accept the bland explanation that Congress had made no decision whatever about it. If such a law should be passed by Congress, and then the President, by simply doing nothing—by failing to sign or to veto it for ten days—should let it go into effect, it is inconceivable that anyone, pro or con, would swallow a White House statement that the President had made no decision. But if such a law should go into effect, after passage by Congress and no veto by the President, and a case should be taken to court by someone who claimed the law was unconstitutional, and the case should go through the lower courts until the Supreme Court was asked to decide it, and the Justices should "deny certiorari" or refuse to hear the case —then the third branch of our tripartite federal government would officially announce, and expect both lawyers and non-lawyers to believe, that it had made no decision at all as to whether the new national divorce law was valid or invalid, good or bad.

Of course this is patent poppycock—and the reason why it is poppycock, even when intoned by a spokesman for the solemn and black-robed nine, is that wherever the power to govern, to make decisions on policy, indubitably exists, it is used every bit as effectively by a deliberate refusal to use it as by its firm and forthright use. Practically speaking, Calvin Coolidge governed just as surely by the near non-exercise of his Presidential power, by *letting* things be done that he wanted done, as did Franklin Roosevelt by the active exercise of the same power, by *getting* things done that he wanted done. Practically speaking, a Supreme Court that lets issues be decided by turning its collective head away from them decides them just as surely as does a Court that meets them head-on. Failure to use the power to govern is one way of governing.

Throughout the whole history of the Court as a governing power and not just as a final forum for lawyers arguing points of private law about contracts and torts and procedure and property and the rest of the stuff that lawyers argue about—that is, ever since John Marshall boldly annexed for the Court a top political spot in the running of the nation—political theorists, from thesis-writing seekers for Ph.D.'s to college professors to the Justices themselves, have worried the problem of an active Court as against a passive Court, of a set of Justices that grabs the reins as against one that lets things roll, or slide. In the current jargon, one set is praised or damned as "judicial activists" and the other set praised or damned as apostles of "judicial self-denial." But the so-called split between the two is a silly circular self-deception on the part of those who worry and debate it. So long as the passivists, the judicial-self-denial boys, the alleged advocates of non-interference in legislative or executive decisions, refuse to go so far as to say that the Court has no *power* to interfere, refuse to urge abdication by the Justices of the role that Marshall won for them, the Court will continue to interfere, and continue to govern, merely by the imminent omnipresence of that power.

Those Justices, after the Civil War, who struck down *state* efforts to regulate business because they wanted a national economy to thrive were no more activists, in so acting, than were Franklin Roosevelt's New Deal Justices when they passively failed to strike down *federal* efforts to regulate business—because they too wanted a national economy to thrive. Those Justices who bow today to whatever lawmakers or law-enforcers may do to cut down our ancient constitutional liberties are no more passivists than are other Justices who would *act* to return to the people's Bill of Rights—despite its legislative or executive disregard. No matter whether a majority of the Justices answer Yes or No, or by shunning a case answer nothing, to a government problem brought before them, their action or inaction settles that case, decides that problem. A genuine judicial passivist, on or off the Court, would urge that the Constitution be amended to take from the Justices all power to make political decisions. No Justice, self-denying or not, has ever so urged (although Holmes once said that he scarcely thought the nation would fall apart if the Court were deprived of its right to veto the rest of the *federal* government). Men, for all their sometime talk of pious self-denial, rarely want to really relinquish power.

Yet to say that the power of the nine Justices—as cannot be said too strongly—is essentially an autocratic and irresponsible power which is quite as potent when not used as when used, *because it is there*, is not necessarily to condemn that power; or at least is not to condemn it altogether. Our government is far from being a genuine

democracy, New England town-meeting fashion, or even a
democracy only diluted in so far as final decisions are made
not by the people but by their elected representatives in
their stead. For in such a democracy a constitution saying
that certain things may not be done by government, or
must only be done in certain ways, as does our Constitution, would be a senseless superfluity, a mere piece of
paper—as indeed, though for different and scarcely
democratic reasons, is the constitution of the U.S.S.R. In
such a democracy the people, by majority vote of themselves or their elected representatives, could make or
change any laws or rules they pleased, constitution or no.
And one of the oldest dilemmas of all political thinkers who
approve of constitutions, but also favor democracy, is the
question *who* is then to decide whether the act of a lawmaker or law-enforcer goes against a written constitution.
Whatever men are entrusted with that ultimate decision,
especially if they are not elected to that position of trust,
their power cannot but be an autocratic power—for it lets
them reverse the choice of a contemporary majority and so
defeat the democratic will.

The defeat of the democratic will of a contemporary
majority by some sort of autocratic decision—the holding
back of the many by a few—is called for, under our Constitution, in one especial and many-faceted field of government. That field of government—or, more accurately,
of non-government—is the protection of the civil liberties
of all the people from infringement *by* their government.
It is the protection, in particular, of unpopular people and
groups of people, of suspected criminals and suspected
Communists, of religious and racial and noisy political

minorities, from the excesses of mob rule and the little-less-than-lynching that are all too often aimed at them, nationally, statewise, or locally, under the guise of law.

The Constitution guarantees, against any muzzling by Congress, the rights of free speech and a free press, those basic means of free political expression. That guarantee is flatly stated and altogether unqualified: "Congress shall make no law . . . abridging the freedom of speech, or of the press"; if Congress then passes such a law, in defiance of the Constitution—as it did within the first ten years of the nation's life and has done sporadically ever since—what but an autocratic power can defend, not so much the Jacobins of 1799 or the Communists of 1949 as the very Constitution itself, against the lawmakers' disregard of its words? The Constitution guarantees, against unequal treatment by any state, the right of every citizen to be given the same legal privileges and protection that are given to every other citizen. If a democratically chosen state government then passes and puts in force a law that treats citizens of African or Mexican or Japanese ancestry less well than it treats "white" citizens—as many states have done—what but an autocratic power can order that the Constitution be obeyed? The Constitution guarantees to everyone accused of crime the right of fair treatment and a fair trial—and does it in considerable detail. If, as probably happens daily somewhere in the U.S., a confession is wrung from a suspect by third-degree methods, or his home is searched without a search-warrant, or his so-called trial, as in an espionage or kidnapping case, with public opinion inflamed for revenge and a prejudiced judge and jury, more nearly resembles a formalized lynching—what but an autocratic power can reverse, in the name of the Constitution, the popularly approved acts of overzealous law-enforcing officials? In short, if there is any place in a near-democracy for the proper use of ultimate political power by an autocratic group like the nine Justices, that place is in protecting the few against the legalized tyrannies, major or minor, of the many. It is in giving man-backed meaning and force to the civil liberties that our parchment Constitution can "guarantee" only with wishful words.

Yet the one field of government in which the Supreme Court's majority, throughout the whole history of the Court, have been most bumblingly bashful, most reluctant to assert the autocratic power they hold, is precisely in the realm of civil liberties. Justices who do not hesitate to strike down duly enacted economic laws—laws regulating business or taxing wealth—will meekly "defer to the legislative will" when laws come before them which restrict the personal freedom of individuals in ways more important than the making or keeping of money. Justices may, without blinking, distort the constitutional stop-sign against any state's depriving anyone of "life, liberty, or property without due process of law" in order to veto the will of a majority that sweatshops for women be abolished, or that bakers not cheat housewives with short-weight loaves of bread, or that life insurance rates be kept reasonable; but the same Justices will turn away from using the same admonition against taking "life, liberty, or property without due process of law" to achieve the original meaning of the phrase—which was, quite simply, that nobody should be executed (deprived of life), jailed (deprived of liberty), or fined (deprived of property) without proper legal procedure including a fair trial. And over the years, the Justices have not hesitated to overturn federal laws that—to list a few examples out of scores—limited the extension of slavery into the western territories, imposed a graduated income tax, put an end to almost all child labor, brought help to the nation's farmers hard hit by depression, and regulated the chaotic coal industry—while letting the federal government do as it pleased, and the Constitution be damned, to browbeat unpopular political minorities all the way from the infamous Alien and Sedition Acts at the end of the eighteenth century to the strikingly similar Smith and McCarran Acts today.

Indeed, the bald record of the Court's use of its autocratic power to overturn federal, not state or local, laws is perhaps the most telling single fact about the kind of part it has played in U.S. political history. On the state and local level, the Justices have acted often to uphold civil liberties against their official restriction—though not nearly so often as they might well have acted, and not nearly so often as they have acted to slap down laws that were stepping on someone's financial interests, not on someone's personal freedoms. That Chief Justice Vinson and his confreres, despite some of the most formidable and far-reaching anti-libertarian decisions in the Court's whole life, won a reputation as a civil-liberties Court, largely by upholding against state and local abuses the rights of a comparatively few Negroes and of a tiny religious sect called Jehovah's Witnesses, merely illustrates how very little has come to be expected of the Justices as champions of civil liberties. But the Court's over-all freedom-defending record *below* the national level of government towers majestic and impressive next to its score as the people's constitutional watchdog against abuses by, or with the approval of, the Congress of the United States.

Since Marshall made of the Court a sort of super-legislature, back in 1803, thousands upon thousands of people and companies have sought the Court's help in protesting, under the Constitution, against some law passed by Congress and (if not re-passed over his veto) signed by the President. Most of these thousands of pleas have been turned away by the Justices—most, although far from all of them, properly. Of the hundreds left that the Court has heard, perhaps half, at a calculated guess, dealt exclusively with money matters and half with one or another facet of civil liberties (granted no black-and-white line divides the two: a slavery question, pre-Civil War, touched one man's wealth and another man's freedom; a low-wage employer, banned by the Wagner Act from anti-union appeals to his workers, could reasonably claim infringement of his freedom of speech). In the hundreds of cases the Court has heard where a federal law was attacked as unconstitutional for either a money reason or a civil-liberties reason, the Justices have held less than eighty times that that law—or a part of it or the way it was working in action—did violate the Constitution. But of those seventy-eight decisions overruling the Congress, and usually the President too, practically all the untrivial ones threw out a law or part of a law that hurt some person or company in the pocketbook or the bank account alone. Only three of those seventy-eight decisions in 150 years could conceivably be classed as significant, if still small-scale, protections of personal, not financial, freedoms. Only three notable times in the Court's entire history have a majority of the Justices, in defense of civil liberties, declared an Act or part of an Act of Congress unconstitutional.

Here, then, are nine non-elected and often haphazardly chosen men wielding the top political power in an otherwise democratic national government, and using that autocratic and triply irresponsible power in a strange and onesided manner. For they use it nearly exclusively to stymie the majority will where the two elected branches of government have acted to control or affect the business life of the nation in ways that five or more of the nine happen to disapprove. They use it almost never toward the kind of end that would thoroughly justify the place of an autocratic group in a constitutional democracy—that is, as a final defender *against* the majority will of unpopular minorities, under the Constitution. Indeed, the only minority in whose behalf the Justices have regularly and effectively used their power, to block the majority will as expressed in federal laws, is the minority of the well-to-do.

How come? How have the Justices managed to maintain their political supremacy so long despite the misuse—and the frequent and maybe frightened non-use—of their power? Why did most of the nation, not just the lawyers of bench and bar, rise in indignant protest when Franklin Roosevelt proposed to add six new Justices—to make a Supreme Court of fifteen men, and also to help outvote, he hoped, the majority of the Nine Old Men who were then judicially murdering the New Deal, which most of the nation applauded? Why the popular championing of a government institution whose members were making unpopular decisions—in order to defeat the countermove of a popular President, which move not one lawyer in all the nation could, or did, brand as unconstitutional? Part of the answer, and a large part, lies in the ceremony and the ritual of the Court, the robes and the secrecy and the solemn pronouncements in lumbering legal language, the whole panoply of a surface-deep dignity that is deliberately donned to impress its audience and that has invested the Court, in the popular mind, with a symbolic sacredness, an aura of being above such petty and temporal things as the making of political decisions and the wielding of political power. Most U.S. citizens regard the Court with much the same automatic respect and reverence that British citizens feel for their royalty—and for much the same reasons.

But beyond the hypnotic effects of the show that the Court puts on to look and sound and seem so awe-inspiring, no matter how weak or unwise may be the things it does or fails to do, there are two interrelated reasons, both of them basically myths, that mainly account for the Court's continuing political power. The first myth is that the Court is a sort of single force, an integrated institution, a collective mind that operates as a *unit* of government instead of as nine distinct and disparate human beings. This myth is nurtured by the odd notion that the Justices do not *make* law when they make decisions but merely get together to discover what the law is, and was all along. It feeds on the Court's official ukases which always announce "the opinion of the Court"—although "the opinion of the Court" has more than once been the opinion of the Justice who wrote it and his alone, with the other Justices who voted the same way writing separate or "concurring" opinions to explain their reasons why. (One Justice recently rebuked a lawyer who referred, in argument, to "your former opinion, Mr. Justice," by snapping: "You don't mean *my* opinion; you mean the opinion of the *Court.*") The myth has also been fostered by almost all legal scholars who write about the Court; the more naïve discuss "the Court's" work, "its" philosophy, "its" shifting points of view, as though "it" were a strange creature with eighteen legs and one brain; the more sophisticated deplore, particularly of late, the Court's failure to act as they think "it" ought to act—that is, as a single-purposed, predictable, and perforce mono-minded institution, for all its being made up of nine men. Yet neither scholars nor ordinary citizens expect the Senate or the House or, for that matter, any town council to behave other than as a collection of individuals who react to, think about, vote on different government problems in their own individual ways. So too, despite the myth, do Supreme Court Justices.

The second and related myth, even more deeply imbedded in our folklore of government, has it that the men who become Justices become simultaneously—or ought to become if they don't—politically sterile; that they put on, or should put on, with their robes a complete impartiality or indifference toward the nation's social and economic problems; that they switch, or should switch, their minds to neutral in dealing with every issue outside the verbal needlework of the law. A lawyer who has spent his professional life in the service of corporate clients, to whose interests he has been sincerely sympathetic, is supposed, by the myth, to forget it all, to turn it off like a faucet on appointment to the Court. A legislator who has spent his political life in behalf of liberal measures, in which he has deeply believed, is supposed to take the veil, politically, on becoming a Justice; so goes the myth.

This myth, which extends to the whole judiciary, not just the Supreme Court, is further illustrated by the condemnation of any judge who indulges in any remotely political activity—except the deciding of cases. When Justice Douglas, a few years back, made a series of public speeches urging that the Constitution's Bill of Rights be zealously followed and jealously guarded, especially in explosive times like these—a sentiment scarcely out of keeping with the duties or office of a high judge sworn to uphold the Constitution—he was bitterly criticized by much of the press and most of the bar for stooping to political partisanship and so sullying his judicial robes and judicial integrity. Although not yet deprived of their right, as citizens, to cast their votes every November, Supreme Court Justices—off the bench as well as on it—are deemed by the myth to be, properly, apolitical persons, unaffected by what goes on in the nation outside their marble temple, aloof and remote from the workaday world.

Like the other myth which helps uphold the power of the Justices, no matter how they use, abuse, or fail to use that power, this myth is of course arrant nonsense. The idea that a human being, by a conscious act of will, can rid his mind of the preferences and prejudices and political slants or values that his whole past life has accumulated in him, and so manage to think in the rarefied atmosphere of simon-pure objectivity, is simply a psychological absurdity. Granted, a wise Justice like Holmes, out of tolerance for the views of others, may try to temper those of his private biases of which he himself is aware. But only a dull-witted Justice would suppose, and only an intellectually dishonest one pretend—and the Court has been manned by far too many of both—that he could ever purge his thinking processes, for the purpose of making decisions, of all his personal predilections even of the conscious kind, much less the unconscious and unrecognized. Myths or no myths, solemn show or no solemn show, the Supreme Court is nothing other than nine sometimes wise, sometimes unwise, but always human, men.

And so it is superficial, however technically true, to say, for example, that "the Supreme Court," in 1935, declared unconstitutional the New Deal's railroad retirement act (under which all railroads would have had to chip in to a compulsory insurance fund to pay annuities to retired railroad workers over the age of 65). It is somewhat more accurate, more meaningful, and more revealing to say that five Supreme Court Justices—one of whom made the legal reputation that led to his Justiceship as a lawyer for the Great Northern, the Northern Pacific, and the Chicago, Burlington, and Quincy railroads (Butler); one of whom was kicked upstairs to the Court because of his cantankerousness as Attorney-General, including his reluctance to prosecute the New York, New Haven, and Hartford Railroad on anti-trust charges (McReynolds); one of whom had made a small fortune and a large legal name for himself by representing, in government and out, the Union Pacific Railroad (Van Devanter); one of whom had been a close Senate friend of a certain Senator Harding who later, as President, named him to the Court, after the voters of Utah had refused to re-elect him because of his reactionary Senate record in behalf of corporations, including railroads (Sutherland); and one of whom, as a former Philadelphia lawyer, had counted among his several large corporate clients the Pennsylvania Railroad plus its affiliates (Roberts)—that these five Justices outvoted their four considerably abler colleagues (Hughes, Brandeis, Cardozo, and Stone—who dissented) and thus negated the will of Congress, the will of the Administration, and presumably the will of the people of the country, as well as, quite coincidentally of course, saving money for the railroads. Not all of the Supreme Court's constitutional decisions are as easy to explain as this one, or as crystal-clear in meaning and in motive. But none of those decisions can be explained or analyzed or understood on any other than a sheerly superficial, legalistic level, except in terms of the Justices, the *men*, who made them.

Hence any attempt to explore and evaluate the Court's role in our national history—past, present, and future—must stem from and come constantly back to the men who really play that role in the Court's name. It must cut through all the falderol of ceremony and sanctimony; it must not be taken in by the quaint notion that words, whether of constitution or statute, can govern, without men to use the words as the men see fit to use them; it must kept straight that the so-called reasons the Justices give for what they do, in their long and legal-languaged opinions, are as often self-justifying excuses, wittingly or unwittingly made, as they are genuine sources of decision.

Any such attempt must recognize too, in a realistic way, that the overwhelming political power held by the Justices is triply an irresponsible power—in that they are accountable to no one but themselves; in that they never take, nor can they take, responsibility for affirmative government action; and in that they can either use or refuse to use their power as they please, without ever so much as telling why. And last—and first—any such attempt must consider the proper part, if any, to be played by a small and autocratic group of men who make authoritarian decisions within the framework of a constitutional democracy.

Only so can the Court as a political institution be seen in its true colors and in perspective. Only so can a light be shined on what the Justices, over the years—good and bad Justices, wise and less than wise, farsighted and astigmatic—have done for the nation and done to the nation. Only so can a long look at the Supreme Court of the United States make sense.

CHAPTER 2

From the Gleam in the Founding Fathers' Eyes to the Birth of Supreme Court Power

IN NO OTHER NATION on earth does a group of judges hold the sweeping political power—the privilege in practice, not just in theory, of saying the last governmental word—that is held by the nine U.S. Supreme Court Justices. Whence came this unique judicial supremacy over all other branches and levels of government? What is its source; did it spring, like Minerva, fullblown from the foreheads of the Founding Fathers, or did it, like Topsy, just grow? The answer is neither so black-or-white simple nor yet so difficult, nor even so important, as the scholarly squabbles of historians and political scientists would sometimes make it seem. In brief summary, the Supreme Court's political power was conceived, if furtively, during the drafting of the Constitution; it was carefully nourished prenatally by the Federalist Party during the early years of the nation's life while that Party controlled the entire federal government; it was skillfully and timely midwived by Chief Justice John Marshall soon after the Federalists had lost the Congress and the Presidency; and, with only a few short lapses, it has gradually grown in strength and stature ever since.

The origins of Supreme Court power are of little real import today save to academicians and antiquarians simply because that power indubitably exists. No delving into its roots, no research into its legitimacy in history or in logic, can refute or reverse its stark presence as a political force. Only in a rather negative way—in exploding misconceptions about what the Court "should" be today, based on misconceptions about what it was at its birth, in dispelling illusions about the Court being any other than an essentially political body, and being so intended, from its very creation—only so may a look at the earliest sources and uses of its power carry some current bite. If the Founding Fathers, or many of them, meant the Court to wield a sort of superlegislative shillelagh to protect the rights of property against laws that would chip away those rights, perhaps the conservative Four Horsemen who were the judicial bane of the New Deal were scarcely abusing their *historic* function, as so many New Dealers claimed. If so high-minded a President as George Washington could staff the first Court exclusively with fellow Federalists, passing over such anti-Federalist brilliants as patriot Patrick Henry, maybe Franklin Roosevelt can be forgiven —or better understood—for naming only Democrats to the Court; and if one of Washington's appointees, the legally quite undistinguished James Iredell, was so honored largely to pay off a political debt, perhaps Harry Truman should not be too severely censured for making Tom Clark a Justice.

Those who see the past through the rosy glow of fable with which time tends to fog the facts too readily misapprehend the present. For the last quarter-century, the Court as a whole and each of its separate Justices have been bitterly criticized—now from the left, now from the right, now from the left—and the bulk of that criticism has flayed the intrusion of downright partisan politics, now conservative, now liberal, into the judicial process, while urging the Court to go back to being above partisanship, disinterested, politically numb, "as it was and was meant to be in the beginning." It never was. From its very inception—in its nascent and then surgent governmental strength, in the choosing of its personnel, in its practices and policies and declarations and decisions—the Court has been an instrument, as the Justices have been both agents and exercisers, of sheer political power.

Most palaver about the governmental power of the Justices, be it scholarly or more mundane, by lawyers or by laymen, centers solely on one aspect of that power, the right of judicial review, which is what the lawyers and scholars call the Justices' now accepted authority to veto any law—national, state, or local—or anything done under any such law, by saying that it is forbidden by the

U.S. Constitution. This right of judicial review is indeed the most potent and pregnant facet of Supreme Court power; and its most dramatic and controversial manifestation is in the vetoing by the Justices of things done by the other two supposedly equal branches of the national government, the Congress and the President. It is this ultimate supremacy of the judiciary within the federal government itself—plus the uses to which it has been put and the motives behind those uses—that is so widely misunderstood today as being, originally and properly, remote from the realm of ordinary political affairs. Because it is thus misunderstood, a look at its sources and its history may help bring its present into sharper perspective.

But before going briefly back to the Founding Fathers for a preview of judicial review, it should be clear that the Justices hold and have always held yet another political weapon, as generally underrated as it has been commonly overlooked in judicial review's long shadow. That weapon is their unquestioned right—and more than that, their duty—to "interpret" the laws passed by Congress, to tell what the words of a law mean whenever that meaning is in dispute. And lest this sound like a trivial source or a piddling type of power, be it remembered—in Mr. Dooley's phrase—that a statute which reads like a stone wall to a layman can become in the hands of a lawyer a triumphal arch—and that the Justices are lawyers.

The Justices, with Taft as their Chief, wielded pure political power when they "interpreted" the Clayton Act's famous Section 20—which was called, when passed, "labor's Magna Charta" because its words seemed so clearly to restrict court injunctions against unions—as *not* restricting court injunctions against unions and not so intended. And so, on the other side, did the New Deal Justices wield political power twenty years later when they "interpreted" the anti-trust laws as almost never applying to labor unions at all. As in countless other cases of mere "interpretation," each of these decisions, one conservative, one liberal, carried a political punch far greater than many a Court ruling declaring a law unconstitutional. And much of the Justices' influence over the nation has always come from reading federal tax laws, labor laws, patent laws, business-regulating laws one way or another way, for business or against business, for or against the other two branches of the federal government.

The chief difference between this kind of Supreme Court power and the judicial-review variety is that here the Justices' decision, however potent, is not necessarily final. Congress, if sufficiently displeased by judicial "interpretation" of any of its laws, can if it wishes amend or rewrite that law more plainly and more specifically to get done what it wants done. In fact, Congress once revised the wording of part of the federal estate tax statute the very day after the Court had handed down a political "interpretation" of the old wording so patently incorrect as to be absurd. But when the Justices brand an act of Congress unconstitutional, there is nothing further Congress can do —save perhaps try to achieve the same end in a different and devious way or else hope for a radical shift in the Court's membership. Here is judicial supremacy at its supremest; and it does indeed stem from the work of the Founding Fathers.

But not from their words—or at least, not from the

words of the U.S. Constitution which they drafted in the
famous Convention of 1787. Nowhere in that document,
nor anywhere in any of its amendments, is there so much
as a mention of the right of judicial review. Article III
sets up a Supreme Court, lists the kinds of cases it is to
handle, *not* including those where a law is said to violate
the Constitution, and leaves the rest to "such regulations
as the Congress shall make." Endless and pointless controversy has raged ever since about whether the founders
meant the right of judicial review to be implied from between the lines of the written Constitution.

Those who say No point to the meticulous care with
which the machinery of a federal government was detailed
in the document and scoff at the notion that anything so
important, if intended, should have been omitted. Those
who say Yes claim that the right of judicial review was so
widely accepted and practiced at the time that it did not
need to be specified and was simply taken for granted by
the founders. Actually, neither argument holds water.
The founders might well have wanted judicial review and
still not dared to say so in black and white for fear that the
open grant of such power to the courts might keep the
people, who trusted their legislatures more than they
trusted judges, from ratifying the Constitution. As for the
claim that judicial review was the regular order of the day,
quite the contrary was the case, with the British Parliament
dominant over the British judiciary, just as it still remains,
and with early American legislatures overturning court
decisions far more frequently than the one or two instances
where an early American court boldly balked at applying a
duly enacted law. Only in the striking down by King

George's Privy Council of laws passed by colonial legislatures had there been anything resembling widespread
judicial review—and that had been one of the causes of the
Revolution.

The fact is that some of the men who drafted the Constitution clearly favored judicial review, some clearly opposed
it, and some had no strong opinion either way. Those who
favored it, though well aware it would be a governmental
innovation, were the most forthright conservative and
property-minded members of the Convention like Alexander Hamilton, James Wilson (later a Supreme Court
Justice), and Oliver Ellsworth (later a Supreme Court
Chief Justice). They feared that an unchecked Congress
might run riot in passing, even over the President's veto,
the sort of "leveling laws," as they called them, that
helped the poor at the expense of the wealthy, just as
many state legislatures had done; and they feared too the
domination of the new federal judiciary by the legislature,
as had also happened in the states. The founders who
opposed judicial review, perhaps with pre-Revolutionary
repression of self-government more vividly in their minds,
feared rule by the people's representatives less and rule
by an oligarchy, whether of His Majesty's agents or of
home-grown judges, more; as Benjamin Franklin plainly
stated this side of the case, it would be "improper to put
it in the power of any man to negative a law passed by the
legislature because it would give him the control of the
legislature."

Actually, the right of judicial review never became an
issue at the Constitutional Convention because even those
who hoped the judges would use it did not propose that it

be designated in the document. References to it were incidental to discussion of a "council of revision"—to be made up of the President and two Supreme Court Justices, with a partial power to veto acts of Congress—which *was* proposed and was voted down. Reports of the Convention record only eleven members of the fifty-five as taking a stand either way on judicial review, and of these, six were for and five against—scarcely a score to warrant a confident conclusion about "what the Founding Fathers intended." And even though other members expressed themselves outside the Convention at other times, no count has ever put those who spoke in favor of judicial review higher than twenty-five, or three less than a majority, and no count has ever put those who spoke against it nearly that high.

But if wrangles over "the intent of the founders" with respect to judicial review are then futile, as they are, and this largely because the founders never made it an issue they had to face officially at the Convention, judicial review nevertheless became a very live and important issue when they presented the finished Constitution to the people of the then-sovereign states for ratification. As all but devotees of the Parson Weems approach to American history are aware, the question of ratifying or not ratifying the new Constitution—of creating or not creating a real United States—set off one of the bitterest, no-holds-barred political battles in all our history. By and large, the Constitution-backers were the men of wealth and substance, the creditors or well-propertied class, the commercial traders of the North and the slave-holding plantation owners of the South. Suspicious or hostile were the small farmers and mechanics, the debtor class, the men who, from the fishermen on the coast to the frontiersmen clearing the Western wilderness, did their day's work with their hands. And one of the most suspect, if still implicit, wrinkles of the proposed new Constitution was the threat, perceived by many, that a national judiciary topped by a Supreme Court might try to overturn laws passed by the people's legislatures, including Congress.

In countering these suspicions, the more active and articulate of the Federalists—as the pro-Constitution party came to be called—did not deny the possibility of judicial review. Instead, they cleverly claimed that such review would be used mainly to protect the whole of the people, not the propertied class, against unfair laws like "bills of attainder" (by which individuals are picked out and punished by a legislature without court trial). As historian J. Allen Smith once described this shrewd campaign, overstating it only slightly: "The advocates of judicial supremacy were careful to support it not as a conservative safeguard but as a means—assumed to be necessary—of protecting popular rights and enforcing the constitutional checks on public officials. Every effort was made to create the impression that the Supreme Court of the United States was designed to protect the people. . . . There is probably no other instance in the whole history of constitutional development where public opinion has been so misled as to the fundamental nature of a political arrangement. . . . The real purpose was to centralize political authority largely in the Supreme Court of the United States, and through the power of final interpretation, to make the Constitution an adequate bulwark of conservatism."

Though the Constitution did not in so many words set up the right of judicial review, though the overt intent of the founders was inconclusively hazy, though the high hopes in this respect of the pro-ratification spokesmen were stated with strategic indirection, it took little time to translate those Federalist hopes into substantial action, once the Constitution was adopted and the brand-new U.S. government had taken over. That government was, of course, a Federalist government, with George Washington, who had chairmanned the constitutional convention, as its President, and with a Congress, chosen in quick elections by a small fraction of America's adult males, overweighted with ardent Federalists. And one of the very first things done by this very first of U.S. Congresses, early in 1789, was to write a system of national courts, plus a set of rules for those courts to follow, into a law much more pointed and meaningful and far-reaching than the Constitution specified or required.

The Judiciary Act of 1789, which remains even today the foundation of the whole federal court system, was one of the most remarkable statutes ever enacted by any legislative body in the world. That it set up a Supreme Court—then composed of only six Justices—and two kinds of lower federal courts was not so remarkable. Nor was the staffing of these courts with marshals, U.S. attorneys, and all the personal paraphernalia needed to try cases and enforce decisions. What was remarkable was the listing of the kinds of cases—in addition to those named in the Constitution itself—which the Supreme Court was to hear on appeal. For in the course of that listing, a national legislature, by its own voluntary act, deliberately made itself subordinate to and reversible by a national judiciary.

Even here, the Supreme Court's right of judicial review was not written out plain and bold for all to read. But Section 25 of the Judiciary Act would have made no sense at all unless understood as bestowing on the Justices the right of judicial review. What Section 25 did was to give the Supreme Court the flat power to affirm or reverse, on appeal, any decision by the highest court of a state holding that a *state* law was valid, constitutional, good, or that a *federal* law was bad. At the extreme of technical strictness, this would only allow the Supreme Court to overrule *Congress* after a state court had done so first—though the Justices' full supremacy over *state* legislatures is bluntly stated. But to suppose that so nation-minded a political assemblage as the first Congress meant to concede, as does Section 25, to the courts of the states a power to veto Congress, subject to Supreme Court approval, and *not* give that same power to the Supreme Court, acting initially or in review of lower federal courts, would be the depth of absurdity. No member of Congress, when the Section was debated (and judicial supremacy over Congress, not the states, was flayed by a militant minority) so supposed.

Why this strange renunciation of power by men in a position to keep that top power in their own hands—a renunciation which, incidentally, has never been reversed or retracted by any Congress since (though the right to renounce power by passing a law embodies the right to reclaim it by repealing that law)? Why this gift to the judges, as on a platter, of a king-of-the-castle role among the three supposedly equal branches of federal government?

Because the Federalists were political realists. Because the Federalist Congress and the Federalist President knew that *they* were not renouncing *their* power in any but an abstract and theoretical way. To future Congresses and future Presidents, the renunciation might—as it did—become meaningful. But no Federalist-appointed judiciary was going to balk the Congress that created it nor the President that named its members; the notion of a truly independent and apolitical batch of judges, despite the high-flown falderol that had helped sell the Constitution to the people, would have brought snickers from all but the least sophisticated Federalists.

More than that, these men were aware that the Congressmen among them held office for only two years and then had to be re-elected—or rejected—by the people; that the Senators among them held office, at most, for six years and then had to be re-chosen—or not—by state legislatures elected by the people; that the President held office for four years and then had to be given—or denied—a second term by electors picked by the people. They had not forgotten, these Federalists, by how close a squeak their Constitution had run the gauntlet of ratification in the face of potent popular opposition (two of the thirteen "original" states had still not joined the union when the Judiciary Act was drafted); and they also foresaw that many of the measures and policies of the new government would not be calculated to add to its, or their, widespread popular support. In short, they and their Federalist Party could not count on staying in office, and in control, for more than four years, much less forever.

But federal judges, including Supreme Court Justices,

were to be appointed, not elected—and moreover, appointed for life. What could a Federalist Congress lose by blessing with ultimate national power the men who were sure to wield that power longest? The Judiciary Act of 1789, with its Section 25, was no renunciation of any sort of power that the practical men of the first Congress cared about. It was rather a foresighted extension of Federalist domination into a future when the Party might lose—as it did—the executive and the legislature, and only the judges would be left to hold the fort of Federalist policies.

Implicit in all of this, of course, and essential to an understanding of otherwise inexplicable Section 25, was the assumption that President Washington would choose his judges and Justices in much the same manner that he picked his Cabinet, and for much the same reason—to assure that the new government, its judicial branch not excepted, would be exclusively in the hands of its friends, of the political leaders who wrote the Constitution and fought to get it ratified, of the Federalists. The assumption was warranted; President Washington did not fail them.

No President since Washington has had the chance to pack the entire federal judiciary with men of his own political persuasion and no President since Washington ever did a more thorough job with whatever chance he had to fill federal judgeships with party bedfellows. Indeed, Washington seemed to rate the courts as of greater political importance than the Cabinet; to his Cabinet he at least named Thomas Jefferson, who had looked askance at the Constitution from the beginning and was soon to become the anti-Federalists' leader; but every judgeship, high and low and without exception, went to a full-blown Federalist faithful. Rarely has any statesman of comparable stature demonstrated more pointedly his awareness that the men, not the laws, control and direct even the judicial branch of government.

To the first Supreme Court Washington appointed three Northerners and three Southerners, thus initiating the rather ridiculous practice of roughly equal geographical representation on a *national* tribunal which has, ever since, kept many first-rate men off the Court and helped put less able Justices on. All six were, of course, ardent Federalists, wealth-conscious and conservative in the extreme, and although three or perhaps four of them could be said to have merited their Justiceships on the basis of ability and legal reputation, the others could not hold a lawyer's candle to many well-known but less politically appealing luminaries, of whom Patrick Henry was only one. (Some years later, when age and illness had softened the "give me liberty or give me death" patriot to comparative conservatism, Washington did offer him a vacant Justice-ship, which Henry declined.)

As first Chief Justice of the United States, Washington chose land-rich John Jay of New York, experienced as a judge and diplomat and main draftsman of his state's first constitution. His slant toward matters governmental is hinted by his opposition to the Declaration of Independ-ence, though he afterward supported the Revolution, and is shouted by his credo that "those who own the country ought to govern it." Able, aloof, aristocratic, a high-minded right-winger, Jay somewhat resembled in political and personal temperament a subsequent Chief Justice from the same state, Charles Evans Hughes.

That Washington picked Jay over his two top rivals for the post, James Wilson and John Rutledge, was either fortuitous or inspired—for it would scarcely have added to the fledgling Supreme Court's popular prestige to have its Chief Justice go insane, as Rutledge later did, or spend his last days jumping from one state to another to avoid being arrested for debt, as did Wilson. But both Wilson, who had literally applied for the Chiefship, and Rutledge, whose friends had campaigned for him, were named Associate Justices. Both were learned and practiced in the law, both were wealthy and belligerently tough-minded about the protection of wealth by government, both had helped draft and put across the Constitution, and each was largely responsible for a provision in it that looked to the financial welfare of himself and his friends—Rutledge, from South Carolina, for the legalizing of the slave trade for twenty more years, and Wilson for the tricky little phrase forbidding any state to pass a law "impairing the obligation of contracts." (Such a law would almost always favor debtors at the expense of creditors; Wilson was not to become a debtor himself until years later.) In short, both men were naturals for the kind of Court the Federalists contemplated and wanted.

Yet neither man contributed, in net, to the Court as a government institution; Washington was only the first of many Presidents to pre-misjudge men named as Justices. Rutledge for two years never attended a session of the Court (he did have the farthest to travel and the Court had almost no business at the start); he then resigned to take what seemed to him the more important post of chief justice of South Carolina. Appointed U.S. Chief Justice at his own oblique request when Jay resigned in 1795, he presided over the Court for one term until the Senate refused to confirm him—the only nominee for Chief Justice ever so dishonored—simply because he had recently made a political speech that sounded anti-Federalist; at which point Rutledge went crazy.

Wilson, by contrast, carried more than his share of the Court's work for the nine years from his appointment until his death, and faithfully followed on the bench the Federalists' political line. But Wilson's penchant for land speculation and other get-rich-quick—or rather, get-richer-quick—schemes of a questionable character brought him into increasing disrepute even before the failure of one of his biggest plunges set the sheriffs after him with arrest warrants. He might have been named Chief Justice, after the Senate rejected Rutledge, had not his recent major participation in the smelly Yazoo land frauds—which involved the open bribing of the Georgia legislature—outweighed on the minus side, in terms of the Court's influence and integrity, the plus of his substantial judicial record. As John Jay's personal rectitude made him a Court asset, so the comparative personal frailty of the deeper-thinking, harder-working Wilson (Justices are human beings) made him an ultimate liability.

Compared to Jay, Rutledge, and Wilson, their three colleagues on the first Supreme Court were mental lightweights—although William Cushing, who had served the creditor class well as chief justice of Massachusetts, was rather highly regarded in concentric legal circles, partly because of his judicial ancestry, partly because of the surface dignity which he affected, as in insisting on wearing a full wig after all other American judges had discarded it. Cushing's chief claim to fame is that, by refusing to retire from the Court even after senility had rendered him quite incompetent, he managed to extend his undistinguished career there to twenty years, or more than twice as long as any of the other original Justices.

The remaining two members of the first Court were appointed as so many too many second- or third-rate Justices have been appointed since. Gentleman John Blair, who was later to get rich by gambling heavily in government securities, had played an inconsequential part in the Constitutional Convention and had also, as a minor judge in Virginia, early proclaimed the right of judicial review, but neither of these facts accounts for his appointment; he was George Washington's close personal friend. Young James Iredell had been a mediocre minor judge in North Carolina but he was named to the Court because, as militant head of the North Carolina Federalists, he had just succeeded in getting that reluctant state to join the Union—a sheer political reward. The only thing of note in either man's career as a Justice came when Iredell was presiding in a lower federal court, as the Justices then did regularly, and the Federalist Party was on its way out of power; dealing with a farmer named Fries who had resisted a federal tax collector, Iredell actually urged and upheld Fries' indictment and conviction for treason against the United States. (After re-conviction in a second trial and sentence by equally vindictive, equally Federalist Justice Chase that he be hanged, Fries got a Presidential pardon.)

Here, then, was the first Supreme Court of the United

States, made up of six men all of whose appointments
were, in whole or in part, politically inspired and motivated
—and in the most partisan sense of the word "politically."
A distinguished and decent, but neither profound nor brilliant, Chief Justice whose conception of the importance of
his post, and of an independent judiciary, was soon to be
indicated by his twice running for governor of New York
without resigning from the Court, and then resigning when
he was elected; two extremely able Associate Justices, one
of whom did not deign to waste an iota of his ability on
the Court's work until, after resigning, he later served a
brief term as Chief Justice, and one of whom served the
Court arduously but also came to disgrace it with his
personal financial peccadilloes; an Associate Justice of
considerable narrowly legalistic competence who, when
age and illness put an end to this competence, became and
remained for years a drag on the Court and a hindrance to
its work; and two Associate Justices who had no business
being on the Court at all, and could scarcely have achieved
such eminence save for the happenstance of Presidential
friendship or gratitude. If so great a President as Washington could choose no more wisely than this—and his
subsequent appointments were of much the same stripe—
it may be that later Presidents should rather be praised for
their sometime selection of good Justices than damned for
their designation of so-so or bad ones.

The first official meeting of the now high-and-mighty
Supreme Court of the United States, held in the Wall Street
section of New York City early in 1790, must have been
a singularly unimpressive affair. Only three Justices both-

ered to attend, the Southern trio apparently not rating the trip worth the trouble. The half-Court stayed in session for a few days, admitting lawyers to practice before it, obviously in the future, and then adjourned. Indeed, the Court did not hear a single case during the first two years of its existence, the only case brought before it in that period being summarily dismissed on a legal technicality. Thus it might be said that the very first precedent established by the Court—a precedent still in robust health today—was the tossing out of cases for "procedural error," the delaying of substantial decisions and the penalizing of litigants for their attorneys' technical mistakes.

Seen in the light of the Court's initial inactivity, Rutledge's resignation to head the supreme court of South Carolina—a resignation also sparked by pique at not having been named Chief Justice—does not seem too surprising. Nor does it seem surprising that Washington had to offer the vacant post to three men, including Rutledge's nephew, before he got an acceptance from an insignificant Maryland judge named Johnson—who in turn resigned two years later, to be replaced by William Paterson of New Jersey, a wealthy former Founding Father who knew far less of law than he did of business and politics, the latter being, of course, of the Federalist brand.

Yet to say that the *Court* did almost nothing for the first few years of its life does not mean that the Justices themselves were idle. For under the Judiciary Act they had to ride circuit—and riding meant just that in the eighteenth century—in order to sit in the lower federal courts, called Circuit Courts, which regularly met in each section of the nation. Each Circuit Court, at the start, required the presence of two Justices, but the number was soon reduced to one to lighten their literally physical burden—and the requirement was eventually eliminated save for rare occasions when, even today, Supreme Court members sit with their judicial inferiors in a few types of cases. Except as unrealism would distinguish an abstract institution from the human beings who man it, most of the Supreme Court's work and its most important work, for the first decade of its existence, was performed by the Justices, not as a six-man team at the top of the judicial heap but in pairs or singly as they ran the show in a lower technical echelon of the federal judiciary.

It was here in the Circuit Courts that Justices of the Supreme Court first dared to brand an Act of Congress unconstitutional—eleven years before John Marshall, in his most famous decision, proclaimed the same judicial supremacy for the Supreme Court itself. The law that four of the original Justices, in two separate cases, called bad in 1792, a scant two years after the federal judiciary first began to operate, was peculiarly wide open to the *effective* flaunting of the right of judicial review, even over Congress. Had these early Justices been so bold as to order anyone in the legislative or executive branches of the government not to obey a Congressional mandate, their decisions might well have been flouted or ignored. But the law in question ordered federal judges, including the Justices themselves, to act as commissioners in awarding pensions to disabled veterans of the Revolution. So when the Justices held this unconstitutional in giving to the judiciary a job that was not properly a judicial job (and so offending the famous "separation of powers" between the three branches of government), they had only to say, in effect, *We* refuse to take it on—and how and by whom could they be forced to do it? Actually, most of the Justices offered to do the work voluntarily, but in a private capacity, not as members of the Supreme Court—a distinction to delight the devious legal mind. This absurdity was brought full circle when a case came up later, questioning the validity of the pension awards made by the Justices acting voluntarily, whereupon the same Justices, sitting now as the Supreme Court, held that they had had no authority to do what they had done. Thus the disabled veterans were left holding an empty bag; the nonsense was doubly promulgated that a man is not the same man when he is a judge as when he is not a judge; and judicial supremacy over Congress was tentatively but officially written into the law reports for the first time.

It was in the Circuit Courts too that the Justices began to assert their dominance of state legislatures and their right to veto state laws under the U.S. Constitution. In 1792, the same year when they first balked at taking orders from Congress, two Justices held that a Rhode Island statute, relieving a hard-pressed debtor, violated the little "obligation of contracts" clause that had been thoughtfully inserted into the Constitution by Justice, then-Founding-Father, James Wilson. Then a Georgia statute went the same way for the same reason, then a South Carolina statute, then a Pennsylvania one. The Justices, on circuit, had started in earnest to slap down the "leveling laws" that the founders had, with property-minded near-unanimity, deplored and that the Federalists had counted on *their* judges to take care of.

Meanwhile, a few cases had finally trickled into the Supreme Court itself, most of them suits by people who claimed that different states owed them money and who knew they could never collect in the state courts. This was an especially touchy matter because, although some of the words of the Constitution could be read as contemplating suits of this sort, the Federalists, during the fight over ratification, had given solemn assurance that no such slur on state sovereignty as letting a state be sued by a citizen in a federal court had been intended or would ever be tolerated; the point had seemed so important at the time that, without this assurance, the Constitution would probably not have been ratified.

Nevertheless, old assurances or no, the Federalist Supreme Court set out to uphold these claims against the states—and, in so doing, got itself embroiled in its first big political brawl. One of these claims was against the then truculently democratic and proud state of Georgia, and Georgia refused to so much as dignify the suit by appearing in court to defend against it. Content to hear only one side of the case, the Court held against Georgia, with Chief Justice Jay, who had personally participated in the pledges that nothing like this would ever happen, leading the pack, and only Iredell registering the first Supreme Court dissent. The immediate result throughout the country was a shock of resentment and indignation at so blatant a breaking of faith; in Georgia, one house of the legislature passed a bill—which never became law—that any federal marshal who tried to carry out the Supreme Court's decision would be hanged "without benefit of clergy," and actually the decision was never enforced. The ultimate result was the quick adoption of the Eleventh Amendment to the Constitution, specifically banning suits of this kind in all federal courts. The Justices had lost their first open battle with the people—but the Court was young, and it was not often to lose again.

Nor did it lose its next political set-to, though this was no tempestuous and publicized issue but only a mild little family disagreement between the Court and the Washington Administration. Its repercussions, nonetheless, have echoed down the intervening years with a significance far greater than the semi-sentimental stuff involved in suits against the states. Out of the French Revolution, of the war it spawned between France and England, and of the old defensive alliance between the U.S. and France, arose a cluster of knotty problems in international law, as applied especially to the capture of American ships, to the service of U.S. citizens on warring foreign vessels, and to the setting up of so-called "prize-courts" to handle conflicting claims about the captured "prizes." President Washington, bent on keeping this country out of war, sent to the Supreme Court a series of legal questions about the technical aspects of neutrality, foreign treaties, and like matters—asking the Justices for their professional advice just as a President today would consult his Attorney-General. The Justices politely replied that it was none of their business to hand out legal opinions of this sort, even to a President, even to help keep the U.S. out of war; their only responsibility was deciding cases properly brought before them.

Soon after this mannerly putting-in-his-place of a U.S. President (plus telling him what they thought *their* place to be) the Justices did get a case that covered most of the major questions Washington had asked, and decided those questions just as Washington would have liked them decided. (In brief, U.S. national sovereignty was upheld and foreign nations, at war or not, were warned to respect it.) But the long-term significance of all this lay not so much in the Court's first venture into international law, nor even in the judicial upholding of Administration policy in foreign relations. The long-term significance lay rather in the Justices' firm refusal to sully or jeopardize what they conceived to be their judicial independence by ruling on concededly legal problems—though of vast and vital national import, though bound to be brought before them eventually—in any other than the conventional, dilatory way of waiting for an actual case to arise and reach them. For all the Justices might have cared, their refusal could have helped put the nation at war before the case arose; at least, *they* would not have overstepped the bounds of judicial propriety.

This apparently self-abnegating attitude of we-won't-touch-it-unless-it-comes-to-us-in-the-correct-and-ortho-dox-manner, religiously adhered to by the Supreme Court ever since, has been lavishly lauded by almost all lawyers and most political scientists as a hallmark of the federal judiciary's proud freedom from contamination by the other branches of government, as a living testament to the separation of powers. It is, of course, nothing of the sort. Supreme Court Justices can be just as influenced by, or just as servile to, a Congress or a President when they make their politically consequential decisions in actual cases, a year or five years later, as if they had given the legislature or the executive preliminary legal advice. George Washington got the decision he wanted even though he had to wait for it—and so have Presidents, and Congresses, since.

Moreover, though this insistence on real litigation, on the militant lining-up for the Court of the arguments on both sides in an actual lawsuit, has some excuse as applied to little private legal squabbles (for all its being, at bottom, a hangover from medieval trial by battle), it has virtually no excuse at all as applied to the big problems of government that the Court handles. Rarely, at best, does the eloquence or cogency of an attorney switch a Justice's mind as to whether a minimum-wage law is constitutional, or whether insurance companies or the baseball business are covered by the anti-trust acts. If full-fledged fighting litigation were needed to get the right decision, the Justices would have to throw out of Court, as they do not, the many "friendly suits," dressed up to resemble the genuine article, that are staged to get important problems decided less slowly. And if live political issues with legal overtones required real cases in order to be properly solved —or to preserve judicial independence—then the systems of justice of the several states which *do* authorize *their* supreme courts to give "advisory opinions" to other government branches, without benefit of lawsuits, should long since have broken down. Massachusetts, for one, had been indulging in this practice back in the eighteenth century, even before its former chief justice, Cushing, joined with his Supreme Court brethren in self-righteously refusing an advisory opinion to President Washington.

What the Supreme Court's 160-year-old tradition—of

never giving advice and never laying down the law except in a formal "case or controversy"—really adds up to is not nearly so admirable as the safeguarding of an independent federal judiciary or the assurance that every issue will be decided on its well-argued merits. What it adds up to is mainly a trio of practical and quite unadmirable consequences. The first is the entrenching of delay, sometimes interminable delay, in the federal judicial process, regardless of the impact or the immediacy of the political problem that cries for a solution. If Congress had been forewarned that the Missouri Compromise would be tossed aside by the Court as unconstitutional thirty-odd years later, other means might have been found to deal with the extension or non-extension of slavery to the Western territories; the inflammatory Dred Scott decision would never have been handed down, fantastically late, from on high; and the Civil War might conceivably have been averted. The National Industrial Recovery Act, bulwark of the original New Deal, was vigorously—and presumably illegally—enforced throughout half of Franklin Roosevelt's first Administration before a unanimous Supreme Court got around to proclaiming that the NRA, blue eagle and all, had been unconstitutional, improper, void, from the beginning. Countless people and companies have paid all sorts of federal taxes for years before being informed by the Justices, after a formal protest against this or that tax came to the Court's attention in the accepted, leisurely manner, that the taxes were invalid and need never have been paid at all (and in most instances—insult on injury—that it was too late to recover them). None of these injustices or worse would likely have occurred or could normally occur, as they still do, today if the Court would deign to be consulted initially, and officially, instead of still following the too-proud-to-advise lead of George Washington's early Justices.

The second and more subtle consequence of the Court's unwillingness to give out governmental advice except by deciding cases is that it thus retains its dominant position, its precious power to say the last word in political affairs. If the Justices had counseled Washington as to what they deemed his proper conduct according to international law, he might have discarded their counsel or accepted it only in part, for the decision would still have been his to make. If any set of Justices should ever consent to advise any President or Congress about a contemplated law or a planned course of government action, even from a strictly legal angle—which is all that could be asked or expected— the failure of the executive or the legislature to take this advice would mean the partial subordination of the judiciary to them, instead of vice versa. Only so long as the Justices insist on speaking last, after the other two branches have decided and acted, can they surely and automatically retain their supremacy.

And herein lies the third unadmirable consequence of the Court's old hands-off-until-we-get-a-case habit. By always speaking last, by always waiting for a case to come before them in which they need only say Yes or No to something already done, the Justices guarantee and underscore their freedom from all responsibility for the *affirmative* operations of government. It is not the independence of the federal judiciary but rather one facet of its irresponsibility that is made secure by its rigid refusal to speak or act except in the course of deciding litigated cases. Here was perhaps the most telling contribution to future federal jurisprudence—and to the nation's political picture, seen in long-term perspective—of the young Supreme Court under the Chief Justiceship of John Jay.

Jay remained Chief Justice for only five years and spent one of those years on a diplomatic mission to Great Britain —a service to the President which scarcely stressed the alleged independence of the judiciary and which subjected Jay to considerable criticism, much like that leveled at Justice Robert Jackson a century and a half later, when he took a year off from the Court to help prosecute the Nazis at Nuremberg after World War II. But Jay was little criticized for running twice for governor of New York without resigning his judicial post—an act which would bring a storm of protest, and probable impeachment, today, when Justices are supposed to keep clean of all politics. Barely missing election the first time, Jay made it on his second try and quit the Court.

John Rutledge had written Washington, just before Jay resigned, that he had shared his friends' feeling, five years before, that "my pretensions to the office of Chief Justice were at least equal to Mr. Jay's in point of law-knowledge, with the additional weight of much longer experience and much greater practice." Washington took the hint, and the man who had never honored the Court with his presence during his two earlier years as an Associate Justice presided over it for one short term until the Senate refused to confirm him—not because the Senators disagreed with Rutledge's less than modest self-estimate but simply because he had recently pulled a political boner that hurt and irked the Federalist Party. The job was then offered, too late, to no-longer-fiery Patrick Henry and next to the oldest sitting Justice, Cushing—both of whom rejected it; it was rather conspicuously not offered to able Justice Wilson, who was already embarrassing his brethren and the Administration with his financial follies. Finally, the begging Chiefship fell to proper and well-propertied Oliver Ellsworth of Connecticut, a shrewdly successful lawyer-politician-banker who had cut an influential figure at the Constitutional Convention and had once suggested, out of his aristocratic Anglophilia, that the U.S. President be called "His Highness."

Meanwhile, mild Justice Blair had resigned and Washington had replaced him with his exact temperamental opposite—a huge, rude, choleric Marylander named Samuel Chase, a man of indubitable and explosive intellectual capacity who almost immediately took over the leadership of the Court from his seniors and his Chief, and went on to become the most unabashedly active political partisan in the Court's whole history. Chase had once been a fire-eating rebel, a rioting member of the "Sons of Liberty," a signer of the Declaration of Independence, and— paradoxically, in the light of what was to come—a violent advocate of freedom of the press. But his subsequent conversion into a dedicated Federalist—as when a Communist today turns Catholic—had been complete and unqualified; and his unjudicial crusading, on and off the bench, for the cause he now espoused was to make him the only Supreme Court Justice ever impeached, although he was not convicted.

The Court which Ellsworth formally headed and Chase

dominated for the five final years of the eighteenth century could easily be rated the worst in U.S. history, but could also contend for honors as the most honest; its members pulled no verbal punches and made no polite bones about being active agents of the fast-fading Federalist Party. Cushing and Paterson remained Justices throughout this period. Wilson died in the middle of it and was replaced, President John Adams now doing the appointing, by the ex-President's nephew, Bushrod Washington—sloppy, snuff-sniffing, slight of build and slight of mentality—whose chief qualification was obviously his name and who was to stick on the Court for thirty-one years, dully mouthing old Federalist doctrine to the very end. Later, Iredell died and his seat went to another North Carolinian, Alfred Moore, who at least had the grace to retire after four years of judicial ineptitude. Shifting personnel did not vary the Court's caliber, except slightly for the worse, and Justice Chase continued throughout to run the show.

That the show Chase ran was a garish sideshow to the final Federalist Administration, fighting tooth and nail to save the Party from defeat and extinction, was not, by realistic standards, the reason why the Chase-Ellsworth Court was a fourth-rate Court. Fourth-rateness lay not in political forthrightness—for a Court less openly, more cleverly dedicated to the same ends would have been worse—but in the Justices' flagrant perversion of the plainest words of the Constitution, to try to thwart the popular will. Where an autocratic super-legislature might justify its place in a democracy by defending the civil liberties of a *minority* under the Constitution, the Chase-Ellsworth crew managed to be doubly undemocratic in trampling on the civil liberties of a *majority* whose political views they despised and sought to kill. And once more the bulk of the Justices' work—now political party work—was done not with the imprimatur of the Supreme Court itself but instead by its separate members, sitting in lower federal courts and laying down punitive, Federalist Party law.

The transatlantic reverberations of the French Revolution plus the eloquent home-grown pamphleteering of Thomas Paine in behalf of the "Rights of Man" had for some years been deepening the political-financial-emotional breach between the "rich and well-born" Federalists and their less favored but increasingly more numerous domestic opponents, at the time when Associate Justice Chase took effective command of the Supreme Court. As the Federalists had grown more and more pro-British, once independence was assured, so the anti-Federalists had grown pro-French—to the point where they now called themselves Republicans, a title then tinged with overtones of the French revolutionaries. What the Federalists called them was "Jacobins," after the ruthless French extremists —and they used the word with the same combination of hatred, contempt, and horror that "Communists" evokes in twentieth-century America, and with the same implication of treason. But by contrast to the dwindling number and political puniness of U.S. Communists today, the Jacobin-Republicans elected their leader, Thomas Jefferson, to the Vice-Presidency in 1796 and continued to grow in influence and power. In a last desperate effort to stifle the Republican Party by muzzling it, the frightened Federalists, against the advice of their wiser adherents, enacted the infamous Alien and Sedition Laws—and so gave Chase and his fellow Justices a chance to show their mettle as guardians of the rights guaranteed by the Constitution.

Though the Alien Act was never enforced, the Sedition Act was soon filling the federal courts with defendants. Under its terms, among other things, it was made a crime, punishable by fine and imprisonment, to "write, print, utter or publish any false, scandalous and malicious writing . . . against the government of the United States, or either house of the Congress . . . or the President of the United States, with intent . . . to bring them . . . into contempt or disrepute. . . ." To a Federalist judge —and all federal judges were Federalists—almost any mild criticism of his Party's leaders was, *per se*, "false, scandalous and malicious"—so not only Republican political speakers but bystanders at Federalist meetings who booed or made spontaneous Republican cracks were hauled into court and convicted of sedition. And, as might be expected, the most vicious enforcement of the Act was visited on editors of Republican papers—though their criminal remarks were often less intemperate than the castigations of Franklin Roosevelt by this century's quite different Republicans, in print, or of the Eightieth Congress by this century's Trumanite Democrats.

In the forefront of this vindictive campaign against anti-Federalist editors were the Justices of the Supreme Court —presiding almost gleefully over Sedition Act trials, charging juries with angry righteousness to bring in convictions, sentencing respectable men who had published

Republican sentiments (a U.S. Congressman, Matthew Lyons, or a well-known philosopher, Dr. Cooper) to long terms in jail. It did not bother the Justices that Jefferson, aided and backed by James Madison, "the father of the Constitution," got the legislatures of Kentucky and Virginia to pass resolutions condemning the Sedition Act as unconstitutional and urging other states to join in defying it. Nor, far more significantly, did it bother the Justices that the First Amendment to the Constitution forbids Congress to pass any law "abridging the freedom of speech, or of the press." To them, the uncertain future of the Federalist Party was more important than the upholding of the Constitution.

In Northern, Middle, and Southern states, in Vermont and Massachusetts and Pennsylvania and Virginia, the Justices sent editors to jail. Moreover, without so much as Congressional sanction, non-editing friends and confederates sometimes went to prison with, or in place of, the offending editors—by an early use of the doctrine of guilt by association. A group who started to raise money with a lottery to pay the fine of an impoverished editor, and so get him out of jail a little sooner, found that they too were therefore guilty of sedition; and so was the editor of a neighboring paper for merely printing a paid advertisement of the lottery. To prison, elsewhere, went one editor's brother who had nothing to do with the "seditious" published remarks, except that he ran the printing-press; since the editor was dying and unable to stand trial, the brother was convicted in his stead. But the low-water mark of this American Inquisition was undoubtedly the double conviction of farmer Fries—first

under Iredell, then under Chase, who ordered him hanged
—on the ground that resistance to a federal tax collector
amounted not just to sedition but to treason. President
Adams, in pardoning Fries, showed that he at least respected the Constitution's rigid definition of treason more
than did two Supreme Court Justices—although no more
than they did he respect its guarantee of free speech and
a free press.

Before the Sedition Act was repealed, its prisoners
pardoned, and almost all the fines imposed under it re-
funded—as happened shortly after Jefferson rode to the
Presidency, thanks in part to popular revolt against this
Federalist indecency—how did the Supreme Court manage, even in legal language, to square the Act with its
patent prohibition by the plain words of the First Amendment? By what reasoning did the Court call the Act constitutional? The answer is that it never had to try; no case
asserting that the Act was unconstitutional ever reached
the high Court itself—and small wonder, since not even
from behind bars was any of the Act's victims fool enough
to suppose that the Justices, *en masse*, would react differently than they had been reacting, and with enthusiastic
vigor, on their own. Such efforts as were made to argue
the unconstitutionality of the Act during the actual lower-
court trials of its hapless defendants were either ignored
or shouted down from the bench as quite irrelevant to the
issue at hand. Not by the Supreme Court but by its separate members, not by head-on meeting of the legal problem but by taking for granted of the political answer, was
the Sedition Act upheld. Here was a judiciary performing,

without shame and without pretense, a partisan political role.

Nor can it be convincingly contended that perhaps the Justices were a little leery still of matching their judgment against Congress's judgment, of using to the ultimate the right of judicial review. For, despite the active part they played in the lower federal courts during the dark years at the close of the eighteenth century—a part that smacked more of prosecutor than of judge—the Justices found time to hear and decide a few cases as the Supreme Court of the United States. And one of the cases they took on demanded a decision whether a new federal tax on carriages was or was not constitutional. With only three Justices sitting—and these the most politically minded and motivated of the six—and with Chase writing the chief opinion for himself and Paterson and Iredell, the tax was upheld; which fact was not nearly so important as that the Supreme Court, for the first time as a Supreme Court, undertook without so much as blinking to pass on the validity of an Act of Congress. Since the Act was held valid, the practical result was precisely the same as though the Court had never heard the case, and the decision, however historic in theory and in retrospect, created no stir at the time.

But even a Federalist Court, which was now well on its way toward declaring itself the supreme and final interpreter of the U.S. Constitution, did not dare go so far as to assert a similar protective domination over the constitutions of the states. In another of the few cases heard by the Chase-Ellsworth Court, the Justices bowed themselves out of deciding whether a *state* law offended that

state's constitution—though in the course of doing so
Chase and Iredell took separate pains to point out in
windy and wide-of-the-point opinions that the U.S. Constitution was their ward, even if the state constitutions
were not. That the meaning of state constitutions belongs
to state courts to determine is still the Supreme Court's
rule today; it might not have been had not the Justices of
1798—who were scarcely shrinking violets in claiming
government power for themselves—realized in full that a
contrary ruling in those explosive times could well have
sparked a real revolt of the state-proud national populace
against the federal judiciary, and perhaps the whole of the
federal Administration.

The revolt, when it came, was peaceful but it did not
include the judiciary in its sweep, simply because judges
could not be voted out of office—as were Congressmen,
Senators, and a President in the elections of 1800 that
brought Thomas Jefferson to the brand-new White House.
Despite their personal lifetime tenure, the Justices did their
best to avert this Federalist catastrophe. Iredell, Cushing,
Paterson, and of course Chase had for some years been
making straight political speeches from the bench, and
these had been faithfully circulated by the Federalist press.
In the last Supreme Court term before the election, Chase
never sat at all because he was out stumping the state of
Maryland for Adams's re-election. Since Cushing was sick
throughout that term and Chief Justice Ellsworth was
away doing his Federalist bit on a diplomatic mission to
prevent a war with France—not that the ineffectual Chief's
absence made much of a dent in the Court—only three
Justices were left to carry on the Court's official business.

The only decision of any note they handed down was based on their finding that the U.S. was then engaged in a sort of cold war—"limited, partial war" they called it—with France, a finding that did not exactly jibe with what their Chief was at that moment trying to accomplish abroad, but that warmed some stubbornly Francophobian Federalist hearts. None of these activities, not even Chase's callously unjudicial campaigning, could stem the Republican tide.

Routed at the polls, the lame-duck Federalists still had time to set booby-traps for their incoming Republican enemies, and the obvious place to set them was around the one branch of government destined to stay Federalist. In the Judiciary Act of 1801, the outgoing Party made its big bid for retention of power, through the courts. This Act provided, by way of the first Court-packing, or perhaps Court-unpacking, plan, that at the death of the first sitting Justice (Cushing was inaccurately expected to die soon) the number of Justices on the Supreme Court should be reduced to five—which would patently deprive Jefferson of his first Court appointment. In a more maliciously clever move, the Act also relieved Supreme Court Justices of their circuit-riding duties and set up sixteen new federal circuit courts, complete with new judges who would, of course, be appointed by President Adams and confirmed by the Federalist Senate before the Republicans took over.

The cleverness of this last provision was two-edged. Except for the timing, which advertised its partisan motivation, this step would have been a wise and widely applauded revision of the federal judiciary. For more than a decade the Justices had been griping, quite justifiably, about their circuit duties (Iredell once dubbed himself "a travelling post boy"); these duties were the reason or excuse for several Court declinations or resignations, including Rutledge's, and also for the comparatively little work done by the Justices as a Supreme Court; had the move been made ten, or two, years earlier it would have won even Republican support. Now, it was damned by Republicans as everything from "a bill for providing sinecure places and pensions for thorough-going Federalist partisans" to the establishment of "an army of Judges . . . [who] . . . may deprive us of our liberties . . . for we cannot remove them."

And herein lay the second edge of the 1801 Judiciary Act's sword. The Federalists well knew that the Republicans could and probably would (as they did) repeal the Act as soon as the government changed hands. But how about the flat mandate of the Constitution that federal judges were to hold office "during good behavior"— meaning for life, short of impeachment? The Republicans might abolish the circuit courts, but what could they do about lifetime-appointed circuit judges who, if jettisoned, could appeal to the still-Federalist Supreme Court, under the Constitution, to keep their jobs? What eventually happened was that none of these judges had sense, courage, or perhaps money enough to make such an appeal—a fact which detracts nothing from the ingenuity of the Federalists' last-ditch scheme to enlarge their hold on the federal judiciary by simply enlarging the judiciary that they held.

Yet the midnight move that *did* work, and that was destined to save for the Federalists the upper hand—not just for a few years but for thirty-four years, not just over

the judiciary but over the government of the entire nation
—went strangely unheralded when it was made; the newspapers of the day barely reported it. Ellsworth, sick and
tired, had resigned his Chief Justiceship just before Jefferson's election; John Jay had refused reappointment to his
old position. President Adams, brushing aside the strong
claims of Paterson for the post, named to the Chiefship a
well-respected and powerful forty-five-year-old Virginia
politician who had had almost no formal education, legal
or otherwise (he was actually born and reared in a log
cabin), and no judicial experience whatsoever, and whose
government slant was revealed in a casual comment on
Jefferson's election to the Presidency: "The Republicans
are divided into speculative theorists and absolute ter-
rorists. With the latter, I am disposed to class Mr.
Jefferson."

This new Chief Justice took over the Supreme Court
just one month before the Republicans took over, for
twenty-four solid years, the rest of the federal government. He outlasted them by a decade. His name was John
Marshall

CHAPTER 3

Government by John Marshall, the Great Chief Justice

BY EVERY SENSIBLE STANDARD, John Marshall deserves superbly his sobriquet of "the great Chief Justice." He deserves it, that is, by every standard save only the mincing and squeamish view of a "proper" judicial attitude that prevails in these milk-toast times. For, almost all that the man believed and lived and brought to life would be sheer anathema to those who honor his name in happy ignorance as they damn any current Justice who dares to do his current job with the same contempt for legalism, the same concern for the end product, the same

conception of the Court as a stark political instrument,
that marked the work of Marshall. Marshall was great
because he saw the law as a servant, not as a master, of
the functions and goals of government—and because he
used the Court as a means to achieve the goals he was
after, however he had to bend or twist the law to achieve
them. Scorning past legal precedents to fabricate his own,
turning tiny technical points into ringing and far-reaching
political principles, making a mockery of the nice-Nelly
notion of "judicial self-restraint" that contemporary scholars hold in such high esteem, he ran his Court with a
realistic gusto as refreshing in retrospect as it would be
deemed improper, even indecent, today. If ever a figure
in U.S. history embodied in his career clear proof that
ours is a government of men, not of laws, that figure is
John Marshall, the great Chief Justice.

To say that a man was great is not to say that he was
always wise, for greatness does not perforce imply wisdom. There are many who still question the wisdom of
much that Franklin Roosevelt did; there are few who
would deny him a place among the great Presidents. The
point is that Roosevelt used the powers of his high office
to the full and, in doing so, greatly affected—for good or
ill—the course of the nation. So did John Marshall. Looking at Marshall's greatness from another angle, there are
many who would rate Holmes above him as the wisest
Justice who ever sat on the Court. But Holmes was wise
almost exclusively in dissent, where present ineffectiveness
coupled with indignation often makes comparatively easy
the eloquent expression of wisdom; by contrast, Marshall
spoke almost exclusively with the authority of the Court

behind him, so that his words were not merely something he *said* but official statements of what he and his Court—whether wisely or unwisely—effectively did.

What Marshall did, and well-nigh single-handed—for the force and warmth of his personality swung even his political adversaries on the Court to his side—was to mold the government of a new nation to his own ideas of how that nation ought to be run. More than any other man, more than Washington or Jefferson or Lincoln, he put flesh on the skeletal structure, the bare bones of the Founding Fathers' Constitution—and put it there to stay. Most of what he did to steer for his own times and chart for the future the main course of the country's development, economically, socially, politically, is with us yet, 150 years later, courtesy of the precedents he set and the respect in which they are still held, and in this fact lies the real mark and monument of Marshall's greatness.

Marshall thought the nation ought to be run by a strong central government to which the states played strictly second fiddle. So the bulk of his most momentous decisions either enlarged the powers of the federal government—over finance, commerce, business affairs—by what is commonly called a "broad construction" of those words of the Constitution that list what the federal government may do, or else restricted and cut down, by a narrow interpretation of other constitutional language, the similar and sometimes conflicting powers of the states. From banking to bankruptcy, from higher education to inland waterways, Marshall slapped down state attempts to control or regulate or supervise, and upheld, at least by inference, the hand of the central government. Yet strangely—and this

has gone little noted—Marshall's passionate attachment
to national supremacy sometimes faded slightly when it
came to supporting federal Administration acts or policies
which failed to win his personal approval.

For Marshall not only thought the nation should be run
by a strong central government; he also thought the nation
and its government should be run by and for his kind, his
political and economic class—meaning, of course, the
creditor-capitalists, the Federalists, the financial conservatives. And so, although most of his significant decisions can be read—and usually are—as sparked primarily
by a disinterested preference for federal, as against state,
control of national affairs, not one of those significant
decisions fails to fit the pattern of protecting and fostering
the long-range or short-run security of private property.
From the wholesale endowing of corporations with the
property rights of individuals to the repeated upholding
of land claims or money claims clearly based, originally,
on bribery or flagrant fraud, Marshall served not only
honest investors but less scrupulous speculators well.
Practically all his anti-state and pro-federal-government
rulings were as welcome to the well-to-do as they were
deplored and denounced by the relatively poor, the "common men" of the time.

Thus an entertaining poser arises as to what John
Marshall's political views and his legal leanings would
have been had he lived and served on the Court in the
middle of the twentieth century instead of at the beginning
of the nineteenth. For in Marshall's day the states were
still the chief citadels of a "liberal" or "leveling" political
philosophy, controlled by and responsive to the mass of

the people, whereas the central government, even under Jefferson and his followers, was more respectful of property rights. In recent times the situation has been the precise reverse, so that solid citizens are now states'-righters and liberals put greater faith in the federal government, even under conservative auspices. Where, then, would Marshall stand, faced with a New Deal, a Fair Deal, or even a New Look, and unable to champion simultaneously a strong central authority and the interests of the creditor class? Would he love national power more or leveling laws less? The probable answer must stem from the ineluctable fact that Marshall, like the Founding Fathers, was an eminently practical man, far more concerned with down-to-earth political realities than with the abstractions of government theory, more bent on achieving results than expounding principles. So, paradoxical as it may sound, there is little doubt that John Marshall, for all the tremendous part he played in giving the federal government strength and supremacy back in the early nineteenth century, would be a states' rights advocate today. Except — and quite an exception—in one regard:

Just as Marshall, for practical reasons, wanted the federal government dominant over the states and worked successfully to make it so, he also wanted one branch of that government dominant over the other two branches— and for identical practical reasons. Nor would Marshall, if he were living now, have any cause to regret what is generally rated his greatest, and was surely his most complete and spectacular, political achievement. In establishing unshakably the supremacy of the judiciary over both the legislature and the executive—and this in the face of a

series of Congresses and Presidents who were either ex-
plosively or seethingly hostile—Marshall built a bastion
for the rights of property, no matter how careless of those
rights the rest of the federal government might come to
be, that has stood secure and firm through all the intervening years and that a contemporary Marshall would still
approve, with pardonable pride. For it was under Marshall
that the Supreme Court, officially and as a whole Court,
first proclaimed and exercised the right of judicial review
in its ultimate and most radical sense—by holding a part
of an Act of Congress unconstitutional. And from that
most famous of all the famous Marshall decisions, in the
case of Marbury *v.* Madison—a decision that drew the
battle lines between the new Chief Justice and his bitter
antagonist, President Jefferson—until, toward the close
of his career, Marshall made the ruling that brought forth
President Andrew Jackson's perhaps apocryphal but essentially accurate snort: "Well, John Marshall has made
his decision; now let him enforce it" (and the decision was
reluctantly obeyed nonetheless), Marshall forced on his
foes and flaunted to the nation the doctrine of judicial
supremacy.

It was an extraordinary hierarchy of pyramided political
power that Marshall built, with himself at its apex. The
pyramid encompassed the entire governmental structure
of the nation, and at every level Marshall had to drive or
win his way to the top against massed majority opposition. Beginning at the bottom, there was the basic issue
whether, under a system of "dual sovereignty," the
centralized federal government or the proudly separate
states should prevail; the climate of opinion backed by the

weight of popular pressure was strongly with the states at the time; Marshall won supremacy for the union. At the next level up, the question was which branch of the federal government would hold sway over the other two; Marshall for over thirty years contended and coped with Presidents and Congresses who wanted the last word for themselves; he won conclusive supremacy for the judiciary. (Within the judiciary the Supreme Court was already, and naturally, dominant; it was easy for Marshall to rivet this supremacy over lower federal courts—and over top state courts as well.) As the final step, Marshall had to assert and maintain his own personal authority over his colleagues on the Supreme Court itself; as his Court was early infiltrated, and later numerically overweighted, by Justices whose political slant ran counter to his own, it was no simple task to line them up behind him; but until, shortly before his death, he was barely defeated on a big decision—and wrote one of the nine dissents he ever had to express in this thirty-four years on the high bench— Marshall never faltered and never importantly failed in keeping himself supreme over his fellow Justices.

Thus the great Chief Justice, by dominating the Supreme Court which dominated the judiciary which dominated the federal government which dominated the states —and with each of these steps substantially his own indomitable doing—himself effectively dominated the nation for a third of a century, and left it a lasting legacy in the conduct of its government. His accomplishment is all the more fabulous considered in the light of the personal and institutional statuses from which Marshall raised first himself, then the Court, to glory.

The likely key to Marshall's unyielding economic conservatism, and perhaps to his dynamic drive as well, is the fact that, in the common phrase, he was a self-made man who came up the hard way. Like so many who fight their way to the top against original odds, he had scant sympathy for those less able or less fortunate or less determined whom he left behind and beneath; successful, respected, well-to-do by dint of his own efforts, he identified himself completely with the class to which he had climbed. His was a primitive, frontier childhood; his was the meagerest of formal educations, later supplemented by a couple of months of law lectures at William and Mary; his was the suffering through the awful winter at Valley Forge as a soldier in the Revolution. By persistence and native brilliance, he rose in both law and politics, hewing straighter and straighter, the farther he rose, to the Federalist line. As a young Virginia assemblyman and as a middle-aged U.S. Congressman, he developed an impatient mistrust of legislatures, with their inefficiencies and their bending to the winds of popular will. As one of the trio of envoys to France who were offered French bribes, in the so-called XYZ Affair, he developed a contempt for revolutionary democracy, which had there run riot. Outstanding among the few whole-hog Congressional supporters of President Adams's save-the-Federalist-Party policies, he was named Secretary of State (he had earlier turned down a Supreme Court Associate Justiceship) until Ellsworth's timely resignation gave Adams the chance to choose as Chief Justice the man who was to prove the doughtiest Federalist of them all.

The Court of which Marshall took command, a Court

which had been depreciated even below its original lowly status by Ellsworth's why-bother indifference to its operations and by Chase's rambunctious extra-judicial politicking, was regarded by most citizens with either apathy or scorn. The important thing was that Jefferson had been elected, the Republicans were in the saddle, and those federal judges who used to go around putting decent people in jail just for speaking their minds about politics would soon find out who was running the country now. Symbolic—and quite incredible today when the Court, in all its majestic dignity, meets in a marble temple that is one of the showplaces of Washington—was the fact that the architect of the new Capitol building had completely forgotten, or maybe deliberately failed, to provide a place for the Court to do its business. The great Chief Justice was sworn into office in a twenty-four-by-thirty-foot committee room in the Capitol basement, politely furnished by the Senate for the Court's use. In that tiny chamber, Marshall and his five associates began to hear the cases that wore to raise the Court to prestige and preeminence.

Marshall's associates, at the start, were of course all fellow Federalists. But within a few years, deaths plus the addition of a seventh Justice gave the Republicans an expanding beachhead on the high tribunal; and by 1811, a decade after Marshall took charge, five of the seven Justices were Republican-appointed, with only Bushrod Washington, due to last another eighteen years, hanging on with his Chief from the old Federalist days. Still, the gradual filling of the Court with presumable opponents of Marshall's political and legal views did not shift, until near the very end of Marshall's long tenure, the course of

Supreme Court decisions. Indeed, except for William
Johnson, the vastly underrated Justice who was Jefferson's
first appointee and whose continuous if futile disagreement
with many of Marshall's rulings made him the first great
Court dissenter, and Joseph Story, the nominal Republican
who immediately became Marshall's right-hand man, the
other Justices of the Marshall era—forgotten names like
Brockholst Livingston, Robert Trimble, Gabriel Duval—
deserve scarcely so much as a passing mention in an account of the Court's history. Marshall *was* the Court—and
they were his pawns, his puppets.

Stark statistics tell part of the story. During Marshall's
whole incumbency, his Court gave the full treatment,
meaning a decision plus an opinion explaining it, to 1,106
cases; in 519, or almost half of these, Marshall wrote the
Court's opinion; (a Chief Justice does well today to write
one-eighth of the Court's opinions, and Vinson, for instance, did not come close to this fraction). Of the 1,106
cases, 62 dealt with the "meaning" of the Constitution,
thus embodying, one way or another, the most important
facet of judicial review—and Marshall spoke for the Court
36 of the 62 times. How completely he guided his colleagues, even when he did not himself speak for them, is
shown by the fact that he dissented from only 9 of all the
1,106 decisions—or in less than one per cent of the cases,
a figure incredibly low when viewed against the habitually
split Supreme Court of the mid-twentieth century.

Nor did Marshall waste any time taking full command
over his seniors in service. Through the first four years
of his Chief Justiceship, the Court, gathering momentum
slowly, honored with formal opinions just twenty-six

cases, and Marshall, who did not sit in two of them, delivered the Court's opinion in all of the other twenty-four—with not a single Justice dissenting from any of them. This, of course, was while the Court was still staffed, or stuffed, with hangover Federalists, only too glad to follow the lead of their new dynamic Chief and to let him do the dirty work of opinion-writing for them. As the first (and best) Republican Justice, Johnson, in a later letter to Jefferson, explained Marshall's monopoly as Court spokesman at the time Johnson joined the Court: "Cushing was incompetent, Chase could not be got to think or write—Paterson was a slow man and willingly declined the trouble, and the other two judges [*meaning Marshall himself and Bushrod Washington*] you know are commonly estimated as one judge."

But if it was a cinch for Marshall, at the beginning, to make a one-man show of a fully Federalist and either-unfit-or-lazy crew of colleagues, how did he manage to maintain effectively the same I-*am*-the-Court role in the face of the Court's early dilution and subsequent flooding with Republican appointees? By what Marshall magic did Federalist doctrine not wither but flourish as the law of the land, long after the electoral interment of the Federalist Party and the eventual extension of this shifted political sentiment to the judiciary? The answer lies partly—strange as it may sound—in the cozy living arrangements whereby the Justices, under an almost sacred ritual established by Marshall, were together not only at work but before and after working hours, in a pleasant routine that discouraged deep disagreement (Justices are human beings) and put a premium on friendly capitulation to the views of the most cogently articulate. The answer lies partly in the skill with which Marshall took advantage of this day-after-day intimacy to exploit, now patiently, now pointedly, his persuasive personality. The answer lies largely in that personality.

For Marshall made of his Court a sort of close-knit men's club, whose members lived and dined and wined with each other in the same Washington boarding house, wifeless while the Court was in session; and trudged together, through muddy or dusty streets, to and from their little courtroom in the Capitol basement; and did their most decisive work away from their official site of business, as legal discussion blended into political commentary or sheer social gossip and then drifted back to the cases, around the cogenial board. In such close and common quarters, even more than in the stiffness of the formal consultation chamber, Marshall's easy eloquence was at its best. Republicans might come and Federalists go, but Marshall stayed king of the cloister.

He did not stay king by throwing his weight around, by parading his Chiefship to his officially slightly inferiors, nor by sternness and severity of manner. By contrast to the oft-imagined picture of Marshall as austere, autocratic, coldly impressive—as a stronger John Jay, a tougher Charles Evans Huges—the man was a thoroughly likeable, approachable, outgoing and easy-going figure in his relationships with people, blessed with a gangling, rough-cut charm that made personal friends out of political enemies. Like so many innately powerful leaders, he wore his leadership casually and it needed no putting on of surface dignity. He could, as occasion called for, be shrewd or forthright, soft or bold, for the mind of a master strategist was always at work behind the genial front to achieve and secure, by whatever means, the ambitious aims to which his whole career was dedicated. In the intimate theater of the Court, his strategic talents masked by his effortless magnetism served to win to his purposes, one by one, almost every new Justice who was sent up to do him battle. On the larger stage of national politics, the same strategic genius came into play at a different level. He needed every ounce of it to wage successful war against his most outspoken major antagonist, President Jefferson—to whom, by the irony of events, he had administered the oath of office.

It was Jefferson who threw down the gauntlet in his first Presidential message, where he off-handedly presented "to the contemplation of Congress" the existing federal court system "and especially that portion of it recently enacted"—meaning, as was apparent to all, the Federalists' Judiciary Act of 1801, under which the new circuit judgeships had been hastily set up and manned with Federalist judges. Not that the Republican Congress needed any such reminder; they not only repealed the Act but, slightly worried that Marshall's Court would declare the repeal unconstitutional (because of the guarantee of lifetime tenure for all federal judges) they actually closed down the Supreme Court for a year under their constitutional power to make "such regulations." Marshall obeyed this edict and bided his time; his first big chance, or challenge, had come to him a short while before.

This challenge stemmed from another last-minute move of Adams's outgoing Administration, in which he had

appointed no less than forty-two new justices of the peace
for the District of Columbia but had done it so late that he
had no time to make out their formal commissions. Jefferson, right after his inauguration, ordered his Secretary of
State, James Madison, to withhold a batch of these commissions, and four of the would-be J.P.'s—headed by a
William Marbury who thus made his name a byword in
Supreme Court annals—asked the Court to order or, in
the legal term, "mandamus" Madison to deliver their
commissions to them. A preliminary order of Marshall's
was contemptuously ignored by Madison, and when
Congress shut down the Court for a year the whole affair
was still unfinished business, waiting to be settled when
the Justices reconvened.

The case of Marbury *v.* Madison, seen in retrospect,
ranks as the most important decision in all Supreme Court
history—judged by its potency as a legal precedent, a
guiding authority, a basis for linking new decisions to old.
Yet the actual ruling was of practically no contemporary
consequence, since the term for which President Adams
had named Mr. Marbury a D.C. J.P. (D.C. J.P.'s are no
lifetime federal judges) had just about expired by the time
the ruling was made. This fact did not stop Marshall—
who thoroughly understood the implicitly fundamental
challenge to the judiciary which fairly bristled from the
Jefferson-Madison course of action—from turning a tiny
and almost academic immediate issue into a mighty and
abiding principle of constitutional law. To do so, however,
he had to face and hurdle a dilemma which would have
stymied a man less imaginatively bold.

Marshall was well aware that if the Court ordered the

delivery of the commissions to the Marbury quartet, the Administration would disregard this mandamus, leaving the Court helpless to enforce it and hence humiliated. He was also aware that if the Court bowed to the Administration by simply saying that Madison was within his rights in refusing the commissions, the judiciary would be publicly confessing its ignominious and perhaps irreparable submission to the executive. What Marshall did was a stroke of political genius, salted with lawyerly adroitness. He declared in ringing tones that Marbury and the rest were clearly entitled to their commissions; he excoriated Madison and especially Jefferson for not handing the commissions over; and then, in his master thrust, he held that the Supreme Court technically did not have the power to order the commissions delivered. To so hold, he had to make the audacious step that made Marbury *v.* Madison a milestone in the nation's history (though some might call it a millstone around the nation's neck). Speaking for a unanimous Court, he ruled that the section of the old, original Judiciary Act of 1789 (not of 1801) which said the Supreme Court could issue such orders or "writs of mandamus"—and which had stood unchallenged and been used regularly for years—was a violation of the Constitution and therefore completely void.

Here was the first exercise by the Supreme Court as a whole of its controversial veto power over Congress, of its full right of judicial review. John Marshall, by fastening on a petty point of proper legal procedure in an essentially insignificant case, by attacking a harmless bit of a statute that had been enacted not by Republicans but by Federalists, by handing his political opponents, with magnificent opportunism, a strictly Pyrrhic victory (Marbury never got his commission), established the supremacy of the judiciary over the rest of the federal government. That supremacy still holds today.

In touting Marshall's eloquent defense, in Marbury *v.* Madison, of constitutions *as read by judges* against laws passed by legislatures, the customary adulatory accounts frequently overlook a few other interesting facts:

In the first place, his argument was not precisely puncture-proof; with no authoritative precedent to fall back on (he was creating it, not following it) he had to resort to theory and logic to prove his point; his theory was often quite onesidedly inaccurate, as in his bland claim of universal agreement that constitutional words could automatically void legislative acts, a subject only recently hotly debated in the U.S. Congress; and his logic conveniently skipped the basic question whether judges were any better qualified than legislators or executives to interpret constitutions.

In the second place, Marshall's sincerity—or at least the depth of his conviction—was somewhat open to question. Only seven years earlier, in the course of arguing before the Supreme Court in defense of a Virginia statute which was under attack, he had insisted that "the judicial authority can have no right to question the validity of a law, unless such a jurisdiction is expressly given by the constitution"—and of course the U.S. Constitution nowhere expressly gives such a right. It can at least be doubted whether Marshall, a practical and politically knowledgeable man, would have asserted the right of judicial review as strongly as he did in Marbury *v.* Madi son if a Federalist Congress and Administration had just taken over and the judiciary had been overwhelmingly Republican.

In the third place, Marshall's decision in Marbury *v.* Madison, for all its doctrinal boldness, was actually, when considered in its context, quite cautious and not terribly courageous. Marshall did not say to Congress: *You* may not do something yourselves—such as set up an income tax or prohibit child labor. All he said was: You may not authorize *us*, the Supreme Court, to do something— namely, issue writs of mandamus. Just as when the Justices of pre-Marshall days, acting then separately and not in a body, told Congress it could not turn them even temporarily into pension commissioners for veterans of the Revolution, so here, how could the Justices, now speaking through Marshall as a solid Court, be forced to do what they disowned the power to do? In this sense, Marshall's action was as safe as it was sensational—which merely adds another facet to its strategic brilliance.

Moreover, the less-than-bravery of Marbury *v.* Madison was underlined in a decision handed down within a week after the disposal of that celebrated case. The other case, Stuart *v.* Laird by name, gave the Court a wide-open opportunity to call the Republican repeal of the Federalists' 1801 Judiciary Act unconstitutional; indeed the Federalist press had been crowing, a bit prematurely, that this was precisely what Marshall's Court would do. Instead, the Court—with Marshall not sitting officially but clearly commanding his colleagues—decorously ducked the question of the repeal Act's constitutionality, in ruling that Supreme Court Justices could be made to sit in lower federal courts (the 1801 Judiciary Act had relieved them of this duty and the repeal Act had restored it) simply because they had been doing it for some fourteen previous years. Had precisely the same reasoning been used in Marbury *v.* Madison about the Court's power to issue writs of mandamus—which the Court had also been doing for several years—Marshall's most famous decision would have had to go the other way.

Thus, from every standpoint except immediate political expediency plus perhaps long-range political foresight, the great decision that nailed down Supreme Court dominance of the national government was a legal cripple. Lacking, perforce, any solid basis in precedent, vulnerable in theory and in logic, its central core of reasoning reversed within a week by another Court decision, Marbury *v.* Madison may seem scarcely worthy of the plaudits that have been heaped on it or the deference that has been paid it in the intervening century and a half. But both the plaudits and the deference, like the decision itself, and like every significant Supreme Court decision since, were and are rooted in politics, not in law. This only the ignorant would deny and only the naïve deplore.

Shortly after Marshall had clipped Jefferson from behind in Marbury *v.* Madison—with no official in a position to call any infraction of the rules—politics came even more pointedly to the Court in the impeachment of that old Federalist war-horse, Justice Chase. Although Chase's star had been eclipsed, as Court captain, by the luminosity of his new Chief, his open animosity to all things anti Federalist had not abated but burgeoned with the advent of the Republicans to power. One angry harangue against the Administration which Chase delivered before a grand jury—of a sort that would have led him to ship its author off to jail, had it been directed at President Adams's regime a few years before—sparked the high-riding Republicans into an effort to get Chase and thus teach the rest of the Federalist judges a lesson. The House duly voted Chase's impeachment (comparable to an indictment in an ordinary case) but an intra-Party split among his prosecutors, plus doubt whether the Constitution's "good behavior" requirement called for criminal or merely un-judicious conduct to unseat a judge, kept the Senate from convicting him. Backhandedly vindicated, Chase kept his seat—though he lost most of his influence—until his death seven years later.

The most salient thing about the Chase impeachment episode was the conduct of the great Chief Justice. Marshall, though in full sympathy with Chase's political views, had never approved his slam-bang way of expressing them; his attitude was much like that of many mid-twentieth-century Republicans toward Senator McCarthy. Aware of the threat to the Court's power and prestige that was embodied in Chase's impeachment, concerned for the future of the whole federal judiciary as a top force in the nation's government if Chase should be convicted, Marshall, for once in his triumphant career, was frightened into ineffective ineptitude. Not only did he make a poor and halting witness when called in Chase's behalf; he went so far as to suggest, while the trial was in progress, that the judiciary, to protect its personnel, should even give up its governmental supremacy. "A reversal of those legal opinions deemed unsound by the legislature," he wrote

to Chase, "would certainly better comport with the mild-
ness of our character than a removal of the judge who has
rendered them. . . . "

Whether or not Marshall was mainly worried about his
own judicial skin in making this astonishing suggestion
that Congress be empowered to overrule the Court, it
stands in stark contrast to the so recent swagger of his
Marbury v. Madison opinion. Once Chase was acquitted,
Marshall regained his old confidence, and in newly refreshed and strengthened measure. (If so blatantly unjudicial a Justice as Chase could not be convicted, how
could any other? Nor, in fact, has any other Justice ever
been so much as impeached.) But it is interesting to
speculate that, if Chase had been convicted, the man chiefly
responsible for judicial supremacy might also have been
chiefly responsible—through his judge-protecting proposal to let Congress reverse Court decisions—for killing
it shortly after it was born. Had this happened, the whole
of U.S. history, from the Dred Scott decision right up until
today, might have taken a quite different course.

Marshall's refurbished confidence soon led him into another patently political battle with Jefferson in the trial of
Aaron Burr for treason, over which trial Marshall presided
in person. Burr, though a nominal Republican who had
come close to wangling the Presidency away from Jefferson when they were elected together in 1800 (the confusion of equal votes for President and Vice-President
with no preference stated, was cleared up afterward by the
Twelfth Amendment to the Constitution), had of late been
flirting with the Federalists, who were quite willing to
make the most of his personal pique against Jefferson

When Burr was caught with an armed force, apparently preparing to start a revolt against the U.S. government with help from abroad, the Jefferson-hating Federalists tended to wink at this abortive undertaking and to side with Burr. Marshall sided with him in such a partisan way at his trial—tossing out evidence that might have convicted him, practically demanding his acquittal—that so conservative a Senator as John Quincy Adams more than hinted, in a later Senate report on the case, that Marshall ought to be impeached. But Marshall, after the Chase fiasco, was safely beyond any possibility of impeachment. His handling of the Burr case was in the nature of a cocky you-can't-touch-me-now gesture of contempt toward Jefferson.

Throughout these years, and especially after the Burr trial, all sorts of schemes were proposed in Congress with Administration backing to curb the power of the Justices— schemes ranging from an easy machinery for the removal of Justices without impeaching them to a limitation of their terms of office. None of these came to anything. Marshall, once he had survived the Chase impeachment scare, clearly bested Jefferson in their intra-governmental duel over judicial supremacy. But more than a decade after he left the White House, Jefferson—still smarting over his defeat at Marshall's hands, outraged that most of the Justices he had appointed had gone over to the enemy, battling away for his lifetime conviction that a last-word judicial autocracy was improper and evil—was still taking pot shots at the Court in general and John Marshall in particular. "An opinion," he wrote to a friend in 1820, "is huddled up in conclave, perhaps by a majority of one, delivered as if unanimous, and with the silent acquiescence of lazy or timid associates, by a crafty chief judge, who sophisticates the law to his mind, by the turn of his own reasoning."

But by this time the "crafty chief judge" and his Court —no longer the prime target of Presidential attack under the mild Administrations of Madison and Monroe—had turned their main attention to other matters. Outstanding among these was the slapping down of the sometimes rambunctiously democratic states—in the protection, as always, of the rights of private property.

Though important decisions dotted the whole of Marshall's Chief Justiceship, spreading across the Administrations of five U.S. Presidents, the three cases usually deemed the most momentous, after Marbury v. Madison, were bunched within a five-year span from 1819 to 1824. Each of the three threw out as unconstitutional an act of a state legislature. Each, either directly or by the broad grounds on which it was based, was a boon to commercial and financial interests, a shot in the arm to expanding U.S. capitalism. Each was essentially political; each still stands as good law today; and each in its own way has had a major effect on the nation's development. The three cases are known as the Dartmouth College case, Mc-Culloch v. Maryland, and Gibbons v. Ogden or, as it is sometimes called, the steamboat case.

Many who have heard the almost tearfully emotional peroration of Daniel Webster's plea to the Court in the Dartmouth College case ("It is . . . a small college— and yet there are those who love it") have no notion what the crying was all about nor what the subsequent shouting was all about after Webster's pathos, far more than his legal arguments, won the decision for his client. Yet historian Charles Beard called the Dartmouth College decision "a spectacular event more important in American educational history than the founding of any single institution of higher learning"—including, presumably, Harvard and Yale. And the legal ripples of Marshall's ruling, which rested in part on making an imaginary individual out of a corporation, spread far beyond the educational world.

Dartmouth, under a charter granted by King George III in the mid-eighteenth century, was run—as were and are so many colleges and universities—by a self-perpetuating board of trustees. Being self-perpetuating, the board was still heavily overweighted with rather old-fogy Federalists long after the nation, and the state of New Hampshire, had gone Republican. Sparked by an insurgent Republican group within the college, the New Hampshire legislature passed a law to pack the board with new, politically appointed members, and so turn Dartmouth into a sort of state university. It was to stymie this purely political move that the equally political old trustees hired the spellbinding Webster to take their case to the Supreme Court.

In order to sustain his academic fellow Federalists, John Marshall had to rule that a charter was the same as a contract (this was brand-new legal doctrine); that the promises made by the British Crown in granting the charter were still binding, despite the Revolution, on the state of New Hampshire (this was also new); and that therefore the New Hampshire statute was unconstitutional because it "impaired the obligation of contracts." By such tortuous and unprecedented legal argumentation, with an assist from Webster's sentimentality, Marshall managed to hold the fort for Dartmouth's Federalist trustees. In doing so, he also set the stage for the permanent and practically unregulated control of U.S. higher education, especially in the East, by private "corporations"—and thus gave a tremendous boost both to academic conservatism on one side (only the wealthy can afford to endow colleges) and to academic freedom-from-direct-political-pressures on the other.

Furthermore, Marshall's new doctrines, once proclaimed as the law of the land, could scarcely be limited—and were not meant to be limited—to corporations that ran colleges. Many types of business corporations, especially transportation companies with their canals and turnpikes and ferries and bridges, operated under government-granted charters, which now became inviolable contracts. As Marshall's biographer, Beveridge, put it, the decision in the Dartmouth College case gave new hope and confidence to "investors in corporate securities" and to the whole of "the business world." And so did McCulloch v. Maryland, decided at the same Supreme Court term.

As a piece of political oratory turned by legal logic into enduring government principle, McCulloch v. Maryland is Marshall's most impressive opinion. It was here that he made his famous statement, whose appeal lies more in its sound than its sense: "We must never forget that it is a constitution we are expounding." It was here, too, that he simultaneously enlarged the power of the federal government to help private business, cut down the power of the states to interfere with such help, and created in almost off-hand fashion a tax-free sanctuary for wealthy investors which still gapes open, thanks to the broad strokes of Marshall's logic, in even more inviting measure than it did in Marshall's day.

The Bank of the United States, set up by Congress (for the second time) just after the War of 1812 to try to bring financial order out of the chaos of state-run banks, had been loaning money high-wide-and-handsomely to favored businesses and businessmen and then, as a depression came on, acting tough with smaller borrowers. Annoyed at this uneven-handedness, several states slapped heavy taxes on the branches of the U.S. Bank within their borders—taxes meant to drive the branches out, or out of business—and among these states was Maryland. The U.S. Bank's Baltimore branch, with a cashier named Mc-Culloch, refused to pay the tax and Maryland sued to collect it. (McCulloch's name, like Marbury's, was thus legally immortalized; forgotten is the incidental fact that Mr. McCulloch was later convicted of misappropriating over $3,000,000 of the branch's funds.)

With Daniel Webster again arguing the right-wing side of the case (as chief counsel for the U.S. Bank over a long period of years, he never lost them a decision before the Supreme Court), Marshall and his colleagues backed the Bank, and branded the Maryland tax—and all other similar state taxes—unconstitutional. To do this, Marshall had to write into the Constitution two separate and reaching-beyond-the-horizon political principles that the Founding Fathers never saw fit, or dared, to put in the words of the document. Before calling the tax *un*constitutional, he had to make the Bank *constitutional*—for the list of Con-

gress' powers nowhere includes the power to set up banks.
What he did was to *infer* this unspecified power from Congress's specified control of U.S. currency, plus a couple of
other clauses of the Constitution. He thus gave to the
nation's charter of government a so-called "broad" interpretation and gave to the Congress a far-flung and flexible
judicial benediction to go ahead with whatever extras it
deemed necessary to supplement its narrowly listed
powers—a slant toward the Constitution and toward
Congress which men of Marshall's political stripe were
to bitterly denounce when the New Deal rolled around
more than a century later.

But granted the U.S. Bank was proper, what was improper about state taxes on its branches—inasmuch as the
Constitution, though forbidding some kinds of state taxes,
says nothing about these? Here Marshall pulled out of his
judicial hat a fat new rule of government which was not
even hung from some other rule written in the Constitution. He said, in effect, that since the Constitution creates
a dual sovereignty—federal and state—it *must* mean that
neither sovereign may destroy the legitimate activities of
the other; and since, in the tricky key phrase of the whole
decision, "the power to tax involves the power to destroy,"
therefore any state tax on any legitimate U.S. activity was
unconstitutional. It was this flat black-or-white logic
(instead of a sensible recognition that, whereas some taxes
may "destroy," others may not) that made all the federal
government's operations completely untouchable by state
taxes and vice versa—to the point where, until quite
recently, an oil company that leased oil lands from Indians
went scot-free from state taxes on its private profits, be-

cause Indians are "wards" of the United States; and state employees, from governors on down, paid no federal income taxes on their salaries. It is that same flat Marshallian logic that, even today, exempts the interest on state and city bonds from federal income taxes, and so makes those bonds a favorite investing refuge for the really rich. By saying far more than he had to say to decide the case, Marshall made of McCulloch *v.* Maryland the birthplace of two major principles of American law and government, both of them politically inspired and both of them full of political vitality ever since.

As in McCulloch *v.* Maryland, so too in Gibbons *v.* Ogden, five years later, Marshall expanded the powers of the federal government by reading what he wanted to read into the Constitution—and he did it again at the expense of the states. But whereas in the earlier case his talk of dual sovereignty had at least implied something resembling equality for the states, though the decision had of course gone against them, in Gibbons *v.* Ogden he denied any such equality and proclaimed clear and full supremacy for the federal government wherever it had the power to act at all. Since there were few realms where Marshall would have denied that power, the logic of his opinion here was perhaps the strongest blow he ever struck against the popularly run state governments with their soak-the-rich-and-help-the-poor political philosophies—although, paradoxically, the actual decision was one of the few he ever handed down that was greeted with popular cheers.

Gibbons *v.* Ogden is also called the steamboat case: Ogden had bought an interest in Robert Fulton's old steamboat company, which years before had been given by the New York legislature a monopoly to run steamboats in the state, and Gibbons was ignoring this state grant and running a rival service in and out of New York City. Ogden sued to have Gibbons's boats permanently beached. (The names of Supreme Court cases always list first the man who took the case to the Court, meaning the one who lost in the lower court, regardless of whether he started the case originally.) By the logic of the Dartmouth College decision, it might seem that Marshall would have called the state-granted monopoly a contract, like Dartmouth's charter, and upheld Ogden's plea. But among other factors here was the poor and quite inadequate service provided by the monopoly, so that the commercial growth of New York City was being hindered, and not only the general public but almost all business interests wanted more and competitive steamboat lines.

Marshall satisfied everyone save Ogden and his friends by turning to the clause of the Constitution that gives Congress power to "regulate commerce . . . among the several states" and endowing it with a meaning that is scarcely in its words. Since Gibbons's steamboat service hit several New Jersey ports, it clearly involved commerce among the several states or, as it has come to be called, interstate commerce. What Marshall held was that the Constitution's grant to Congress of power to regulate interstate commerce withdrew all such power, by implication, from the states—even when Congress was not doing any regulating. Therefore, the steamboat monopoly had been an attempt on New York's part to poach on the federal government's preserves and, as such, was unconstitutional. Gibbons could keep right on running his steamboat line and so could anyone else who wanted to start another one. But infinitely more significantly, it was written into the law of the land that wherever Congress has specific power, the states have none (or, as Courts since Marshall's have slightly modified it, practically none), despite the absence of any such exclusive rule from the words of the Constitution itself.

Before, during, and after this trio of memorable decisions, Marshall's Court indulged in some considerably less admirable judicial work, where the protection and fostering of property and business interests could hardly be linked in any way to the future development of the nation. There were, for instance, the Yazoo land claims, arising from the same crooked real estate deal that had kept James Wilson from the Chief Justiceship, and coming up to the Court for a direct decision a dozen years after Wilson's death. Despite the fact that the claims were based on the cheap "sale" of millions of acres of land by a Georgia legislature that was indubitably and confessedly bribed to sell it, despite the quick repudiation of this "sale" by a subsequent and honest legislature, despite the fact that the claims had been bought up by speculators, mostly from New England, who counted on political influence to bring them a fast profit—despite all this, Marshall's Court ruled that the claims, though concededly conceived in fraud, were still perfectly valid and that the state of Georgia had to honor them. The get-rich-quick gamblers eventually collected close to five million dollars. U.S. law collected a new principle: that judges were to take for granted the lily-white nature of government financial transactions even though thoroughly aware that the trans-

actions were fraudulent. As an obvious aftermath of this
decision by the great Chief Justice, unscrupulous operators
were encouraged for scores of years to take their chances
on the mild criminal penalties they might remotely incur
in acquiring state grants, state lands, state franchises, by
bribing or buying state legislators. There were no real
railroads in Marshall's day, but the railroad "robber
barons" of the second half of the century had him to thank
for the success of much of their political chicanery.

It was also under Marshall's aegis that the Court began
to uphold—in a series of cases that came to total more than
ninety—all sorts of patently phony claims to Florida or
Louisiana land, based on forged "copies" or copies of
"copies" of alleged grants from Spanish authorities just
before the U.S. acquired these territories. That the juiciest
of these claims were always, like the Yazoo claims, in the
hands of Northern speculators by the time they reached the
Court, and that the speculators were often well enough
fixed to hire the doughty Daniel Webster to represent
them, did not stop Marshall (indeed, *au contraire*) from
shrugging off as irrelevant their fraudulent character—
this time because of the sanctity not of government grants
but of foreign treaties. It was under Marshall's aegis, too,
after gold was discovered on Cherokee Indian land and
Georgia whites tried to grab it by fair means or, for the
most part, foul, that the Court in a trio of cases backed
and filled, ducked the biggest and toughest problem, and
ended up with the decision that led Andrew Jackson to
invite Marshall to enforce it himself. So raw was the
treatment of the Cherokees which Marshall blandly
countenanced that his almost *alter ego*, Justice Story, after

a rare dissent from a Marshall holding, blurted out in a letter to a friend: "Depend on it, there is a depth of degradation in our national conduct. . . . There will be, in God's Providence, a retribution for unholy deeds, first or last."

It was likewise under Marshall's aegis that the Court began its long and sorry history, only very recently corrected in some part, of winking at, if not actively blessing, the illegal and often inhuman treatment of Negroes in the South. A slave-owner himself, Marshall used all manner of technical, legalistic word-tricks to evade real enforcement of the Congressional outlawing of the slave trade; here, for once, he was not so anxious to uphold Congress's hand, presumably because he saw it as a threat, not a boon, to one well-propertied class. And when a couple of Southern states passed laws banning free Northern Negroes from crossing their borders, Marshall's passionate concern for exclusively federal control of interstate commerce did not carry over to this form of interstate movement. Justice Johnson, the one Court Republican who stood up against Marshall from the beginning, courageously branded one of these laws unconstitutional—as it clearly was—when it came before Johnson in a circuit court. Marshall not only declined to back up his colleague but wrote to Story in tremendously revealing vein: "Our brother Johnson, I perceive, has hung himself on a democratic snag in a hedge composed entirely of thorny State-Rights in South Carolina. . . . You have, it is said, some laws in Massachusetts, not very unlike in principles to that which our brother had declared unconstitutional. We have its twin brother in Virginia; a case has been brought before me in which I might have considered its constitutionality, had I chosen to do so; but it was not absolutely necessary, and as I am not fond of butting against a wall in sport, I escaped on the construction of the act." This, be it remembered, was the great "expounder of the Constitution," who was "escaping"—where human rights, not property rights, were at stake—from expounding it.

No such timidity—or disinterest—inhibited Marshall when state bankruptcy laws came within his ken. These were precisely the type of leveling laws (though of a rather mild variety, helping debtors at the probable expense of creditors) which all the Federalists, from the Founding Fathers on, had viewed with alarm. So Marshall did not try to "escape" from declaring a New York bankruptcy law unconstitutional in a decision (Sturges v. Crowninshield) that one historian has called "the principal cause of the Jacksonian Revolution"—even though, in order to get a unanimous Court behind him, he had to base his holding on a far narrower ground than was his wont, in one of the muddiest opinions he ever wrote. It was the compromised ambiguity of this opinion that opened the way for the only major defeat Marshall ever suffered as Chief Justice, when a bare four-to-three majority of his Court later ruled, over his dissenting protest, that state bankruptcy laws were not all automatically unconstitutional.

This defeat of Marshall on an issue dear to his heart and his politics took place in 1827, the year before Andrew Jackson was elected President in a popular uprising against not only John Quincy Adams's conservative regime but John Marshall's judicial attitude toward such things as

U.S. Banks and state bankruptcy laws. That a new and less
Federalist slant had begun to seep into Supreme Court
thinking, that the doom of the dominance of Marshall's
philosophy was presaged even eight years before his death,
was indicated not so much by the anti-Marshall decision
itself as by the tone of Justice Johnson's opinion for the
majority. "It is among the duties of society to enforce the
rights of humanity," wrote Johnson in strange-sounding
words to come from that citadel of conservatism, the
Court, "and both the debtor and the society have their
interests in the administration of justice, and in the general
good, interests which must not be swallowed up and lost
sight of while yielding attention to the claim of the creditor.
The debtor may plead the visitations of Providence,
and the society has an interest in preserving every member
of the community from despondency—in relieving him
from a hopeless state of prostration in which he would be
useless to himself, his family, and the community. When
that state of things has arrived, in which the community
has fairly and fully discharged its duties to the creditor,
and in which, pursuing the debtor any longer would destroy the one without benefiting the other, must always be a
question to be determined by the common guardian of the
rights of both; and in this originates the power exercised
by governments in favor of insolvents." It was from this
humanitarian view that Marshall dissented.

But the situation was far more frequently the other way
around during the twenty-nine years of Johnson's sometimes subtle, sometimes sharp heckling of his Chief. From
1805 through 1833—the period of Johnson's Justiceship—
only 74 dissenting opinions were written into the records

of the Court (there are usually more in a single term today); of these, 6 were Marshall's own whereas 34, or close to half, were the products of Justice Johnson's firm and unseducible anti-Federalism. Alone of the Republican-appointed Justices, the sturdy South Carolinian, who was one of the two youngest men ever named to the Court (he was barely thirty-two when nominated), stuck to his Jeffersonian political creed, with only a few lapses, in the face of Marshall's power and personal charm. Indeed, if past Supreme Court history had been written by men less partial to Marshall's views and hence less loadedly kind to the great Chief Justice, Johnson might well be currently rated much as Holmes, the great dissenter of a century later, is rated—as the voice of the nation's democratic conscience, even though it usually spoke ineffectively, because in dissent.

By contrast to Johnson, the only other man worth mention on Marshall's Court was the product and tool of conformity rather than conscience. Joseph Story, who came to the Court, like Johnson, at the ripe young age of thirty-two, was the epitome of the proper Bostonian—high-born and Harvard-educated, witty and well-to-do, a gentleman lawyer, banker, and dabbler in politics. Though formally a Republican, he was so socially surrounded by Federalists, from his forebears to his business associates, that ex-President Jefferson shrewdly but futilely warned his White House successor, James Madison, not to appoint Story; but Madison, impressed by the young man's brilliant legal record, fell back on him as a fourth choice after two other New Englanders had declined the job and a third had been turned down by the Senate. Like so many subsequent

Presidents who have misjudged beforehand their Supreme Court nominees, Madison soon regretted the appointment; Story was fast taken over, lock, stock, and basic conservatism, by Marshall, so that he became, for more than a score of years, the only Justice whom Marshall really trusted to write an occasional important opinion in his stead. (In none but the Negro cases, where Story's Northern anti-slavery sentiments stood fast against his Southern Chief, did the disciple disappoint his master.) For this reason, plus such scholarly activities as teaching law at Harvard and writing voluminous legal textbooks, Story is as celebrated in lawyers' conventional Supreme Court legend as the more imaginative, independent, and ahead-of-his-time Johnson is generally ignored.

Or perhaps it would be more accurate to say that Justice Johnson, like so few Supreme Court members before or since, was in step with his political time, whereas Marshall, Story and their carbon-copy colleagues lagged increasingly behind. Because of this lag and because of the steady accretion of top government power in the judiciary under Marshall's benevolent despotism, sporadic efforts were made from Jefferson's Administration through Jackson's to cut the Justices down to democratic size. Proposals included limiting the terms of the Justices (Jefferson once suggested six years as enough), packing the Court with new members, giving the last word on constitutional issues to the Senate instead of the Court, requiring a five-out-of-seven vote to call a law unconstitutional, and the outright repeal of Section 25 of the Federalists' old 1789 Judiciary Act under which the Court had first taken on, and under which, technically, it was still exercising, the right of judicial review. That all these Court-hobbling schemes came to naught, despite Presidential backing for several of them, was due in large measure to Marshall's masterly over-all long-range strategy.

For Marshall, after his initial announcement of the Court's supremacy over Congress in Marbury *v.* Madison —a decision which actually reduced in a minor way the Court's own power, not Congress's—never again called a Congressional act unconstitutional. On the contrary, thirty-odd years' worth of his subsequent significant rulings tended toward enlarging the powers of Congress at the expense of the powers of the states. Why, then, should Congress want to restrict, by either simple statute or constitutional amendment, the very Court that was always championing and expanding Congress's own powers? For all the political hostility of most Congressmen and Senators, individually, to what Marshall and his Court were really doing in the regular and often ruthless protection of property rights, they were lulled or flattered into inaction against the Court by the protection-of-Congress phrases in which he cloaked his more immediate and more specific purposes. By the time later Congresses finally caught on to what Marshall had so dexterously done in his politico-economic shell game (the pea of top government power was under the Supreme Court shell, not the Congressional shell, all the while), later Supreme Courts had built so solidly and sonorously on Marshall's words that all efforts to override or undercut judicial supremacy were considered akin to treason.

This judicial supremacy, this rule by judges, was Marshall's major and most fundamental contribution to the

American scheme of government—not that he created or
first invented it, for he did not, but that he established it,
emblazoned it into the unwritten Constitution, for the use
of generations of Justices to come. Even more than his
go-right-ahead encouragements to Congress and his
stop-right-there strictures to state legislatures, the assured audacity with which he lifted his own branch of the
federal government from neglect and contumely to respect
and power helped fashion a cohesive, consolidated nation.
But to say all this is neither to ignore nor to applaud
Marshall's own chief motive, his propulsive purpose; in a
sense, his achievements, however great, were fortunate
by-products of his immediate and constant concern for the
interests of private property. To be seen straight, the
famous decisions, the cases that wrote new chapters into
the law of the land, must be looked at as part of a larger
pattern, which covers the infamous decisions too, such as
the protection of unscrupulous speculators and slave-
traders and the denials of protection to Negroes and Indians as well as to bankrupts and debtors—and indeed to
whatever minorities, or majorities, seemed to stand in the
road of Marshall's dream of a nation run by and for men of
wealth, no matter how they acquired it. The average
citizen's concept of equal justice for rich and poor did not
rank high in Marshall's judicial guidebook.

But some such concept—of justice, of humanitarianism,
of democracy with a small "d"—was rampant in the land
by the time Marshall died. It had helped elect and re-elect
Andrew Jackson to the Presidency; now, in 1835, it was
to get its first chance at the helm of the Supreme Court.
For thirty-four long years, John Marshall, at political odds

with every Administration since his appointment save perhaps John Quincy Adams's, had braved and bested the growing forces of liberal democracy, had blended boldness and subtlety, force and charm, selective logic and a sort of home-baked law, to stand his ground for the brand of conservative and essentially autocratic government in which he so deeply believed. To replace him and to use for all of the people the power that mighty Marshall, last of the great Federalists, had won for the Supreme Court, President Jackson picked Roger Brooke Taney of Maryland—and of subsequent Dred Scott ill fame. No Chief Justice has ever had so bad a historical press as Taney, and, except for his one most egregious error, deserved it so little.

CHAPTER 4

Not States Against Nation but South Against North as the Court Leads on to War

JUST AS JOHN MARSHALL is known as the great judicial advocate of a strong central government, so Roger Brooke Taney is commonly catalogued as the Chief Justice who, above all others, championed against federal engulfment the rights of the separate states. Just as Marshall is praised for a benign and farsighted statesmanship that helped weld the union together, so Taney is damned for a cantankerous if not malevolent divisiveness that, except for Lincoln and the force of arms, might have rent the nation permanently asunder. The more Marshall

111

has been pictured as history's hero, the more Taney has become her convenient villain. History—and the explanation of events—is always so easy, so elementary, to those whose intellectual spectrums skip from black to white and back again, insensitive to factual shades of gray.

Yet it was no deep difference over theories of government, no disagreement about what might be abstractly best for the nation, that really distinguished Marshall from Taney in the context of their own times—no matter how hindsight may invent such a doctrinal dispute, for the satisfaction of those who like easy answers. Nor was it for any such conceptual reason—states' rights against national power—that Daniel Webster gloomily lamented, concerning Taney's appointment, "Judge Story thinks the Supreme Court is *gone,* and I think so too." What dismayed Webster and Story was precisely what dismayed people of their political ilk when Jefferson, or Jackson, or Franklin Roosevelt was elected President. It was the accession to top political power of a man whose slant, not toward so dull and recondite a matter as dual sovereignty but toward the bread-and-butter problems of day-to-day government —who gets favored and who gets hurt—was obviously at radical odds with their own.

True, Taney had recently said of judicial supremacy: "The opinion of the judges has no more authority over Congress than the opinion of Congress has over the judges, and on that point the President is independent of both. . . . Each public official who takes an oath to support the Constitution swears to support it as he understands it, and not as it is understood by others." And this might conceivably have been read by Webster and Story—on the

most unlikely assumption that they were so naïve as to
so read it—as presaging an abdication of the right of judicial review by a Court headed by Taney, so that *their* idea
of a Supreme Court would indeed be *"gone."* But Taney
had expressed this view as a high official in Jackson's Administration in the course of one of its quarrels with the
Marshall Court; to suppose that he was going to hold to
this position as Chief Justice and commit a sort of authoritarian hara-kiri would have been absurd; nor did he do so,
nor could Webster and Story have really expected that he
would.

On the contrary, they were afraid—and with considerable reason—that Taney would use the exact same powers
that their comrade-in-conservatism, Marshall, had used,
but toward quite different ends; for, in the words of the
Supreme Court's most orthodox historian, Charles Warren, it seemed "evident that Taney would approach a case
from the human . . . standpoint." Warren also opines,
after stressing and restressing all the abstract business of
Taney's preference for states' rights over federal dominance, that a "change of emphasis from vested, individual
property rights to the personal rights and welfare of
the general community . . . characterized Chief Justice
Taney's court"; and just such a "change of emphasis"—
not any forthcoming shift of supremacy from the nation
to the states or any possible self-demotion on the part of
the Court—was what Webster and Story and all the rest of
the commercial-creditor class along with their advocates
and sympathizers apprehensively deplored in advance
when Taney replaced Marshall. To put it plainly, they
feared that the new Court was going to look out for people,

as people, instead of continuing Marshall-wise to bend every effort and twist every law to look out for property, as property, and for the special interests of those who owned a lot of it.

Strangely, these prophets of impending doom and disaster for propertied folk were proved in the long run wrong, or at least half-wrong—just as Warren, though judging Taney's Court backward instead of forward through time, is essentially wrong in stressing states' rights and human rights as the keys to Taney's judicial philosophy. The error was and is an easy one to make. Because most of the big cases that hit Taney's Court for the first twenty years had to do with the special privileges of one type of property-owner, because Taney did not share Marshall's solicitude for the banker-investor-merchant group of the North and East, because Taney therefore overrode or modified some of Marshall's more extreme holdings in the realm of banking and bankruptcy and business monopolies, Taney seemed to be, and to a substantial degree actually was, a sort of defender of the people against flagrant financial exploitation backed by legal authority.

But there was another type of property than paper stocks and bonds and notes and credits in a ledger, and for this other type of property Taney had a far more protective feeling. This was the property of the agrarians, the planters, the farm bloc of Taney's time, whose wealth was almost exclusively in two things—land and the slaves who worked the land. When it eventually came to dealing with this kind of property in behalf of the landed aristocracy of the South and the growing West, Taney proved as staunch

a champion of vested rights as Marshall had been before
him. Indeed, whereas Marshall's economic and political
slant had been much like that of the twentieth century's
Eastern or Wall Street Republicans, Taney was far less a
precursor of today's up-the-little-man Democrats than of
Midwest Republicans and Southern Democrats rolled, as it
were, into one. The gloss of liberalism that shines from
Taney's first two decades as Chief Justice was the limited
if still useful liberalism of the big-time farmer who mis-
trusts city slickers—and even so limited a liberalism was
refreshing when first effectively expressed in Supreme
Court decisions. But the inevitable reversion to sectional
self-interest, to the protection of property rights at all
human cost once the ox that was threatened with goring
was agricultural, not commercial, could and should have
been foreseen long beforehand and ought to be far better
understood today. That Taney's judicial career culminated,
though it did not end, in the Dred Scott catastrophe was
his great misfortune; had he died eight years before he did
die, he might have gone down in history—half deservingly,
half by happenstance—as the most liberal Chief Justice of
them all.

If this seems a paradox, it is only so because "liberalism" and "conservatism" are rough and relative terms;
the statesman or the judge who is found "on the people's
side" against the economically strong and better favored
may be there on one issue out of ten or nine out of ten;
further, his liberal or conservative reputation is almost
bound to rest on the chancy business of how many instances
involving this basic issue, how many involving that, he
has to deal with in the course of his career. By contrast

to Marshall, who plumped for property rights in every instance and on every issue, no matter whether Northern businessmen or Southern slave-holders were pleading for judicial help (and so was that comparatively rare species, the complete economic conservative), Taney for years looked like a leftist because the problems he faced were all of a pattern to invite from him a popular instead of a property-protecting response. When the pattern and the problems and the kind of property that was asking for protection finally changed, Taney ran true to his slave-tended-plantations-and-mansions-and-magnolias form—and it is for this rather than his long previous record that he is chiefly and disparagingly remembered.

But there is even greater paradox—and greater poppy-cock too—in the stubborn and lasting legend that Taney, by contrast to the nationalist Marshall, was a dedicated devotee and defender of states' rights, *as such*. And this legend stems from a sweeping misconception of the whole supposed role of political theory in the very real and un-theoretical political battles of Marshall's and Taney's times—plus a flat misreading or twisting of history. As the story goes, the Federalists, including of course Marshall, had been strong for the central government, and the anti-Federalists or Republicans had been equally strong against it (and so much is superficially true); when the Federalist Party became, by and large, the Whig Party and the old Republicans changed their name to Democrats—which happened around Jackson's time—the same basic federal-power-against-state-power split continued to char-acterize the two; this deep doctrinal disagreement kept constantly on until it was bloodily resolved by the Civil

War (by which time the old Whigs were the new Republicans), with the Federalist-Whig-Republican group battling consistently through the years, and eventually
victoriously, for the principle of federal supremacy, and
the Republican-into-Democratic group fighting faithfully
and single-mindedly, on every level including the judicial
under Taney, for the principle of states' rights and state
autonomy. The story is nonsense.

It was not federal supremacy against states' rights but
the commercial interests of the North and East against the
agricultural interests of the South and West that sparked
and finally brought to flame the hostility between the two
political parties—their spokesmen on the Supreme Court
not excepted. When Marshall regularly upheld the national
government and extended its regulatory reach while
laying low state "leveling laws," particularly in the
South, his eye was not on the niceties of political theory
but on the practicalities of financial prosperity for business
—no matter in what grandiloquent and high-sounding
legalisms he may have formally justified what he did.
When the states, especially in the South, defied the federal
government, including sometimes Marshall's Court, on
banks or bankruptcies or tariffs (South Carolina tried to
"nullify" a Northerners' tariff act in 1833), their eyes
were not on states' rights *in principle*, regardless of their
state-proud protestations, but on the immediate and
sectional economic welfare of their citizens. And when
Taney's Court, for quite a time, turned the tenor of high
judicial rulings in favor of the states, under a novel extension of something called "state police power," it was
not because of any bookish notion about past federal

encroachment on states' rights; it was because of a complacent unconcern about state action that might hit or hurt Northern and Eastern merchants or investors, so long as such action did not threaten the pocketbook interests of Southern and Western agrarians, planters, farmers.

The tip-off on the fundamental foolishness of all the eloquence, judicial and otherwise, about states'-rights-against-national-power came in the decade before the Civil War, when national power was used, for a change, in behalf of the South, as the federal government sought to enforce the fugitive slave law. Now it was the former "states' righters" who touted the central authority to the skies while it worked to return to them their northward-fleeing slaves; now it was the sanctity of national supremacy, not the state police power, that Taney's judiciary preached and practiced; and now it was the Northern states, almost all of them, who flouted, both officially and surreptitiously, the government of the United States and claimed the rebel right to run themselves. The Wisconsin legislature, for instance, solemnly resolved "that the several states . . . being sovereign and independent, have the unquestionable right to judge of its [the Constitution's] infraction and that a positive defiance by those sovereignties of all unauthorized acts . . . is the rightful remedy." This reversal of roles, with the South for the union and the North for nullification—a reversal always glossed over by the easy-answer historians—came to a head in 1857 with the announcement of the pro-slavery Dred Scott decision by Taney's Court, since the Court was, of course, a branch of the federal government. Until that government, four years later, changed sides on the issue of slavery, the Democratic agrarian South was the union's lusty champion, while the Republican commercial North blazed with states' rights stuff. Then with Lincoln and war came a sudden reshifting of the mouthed political principles that camouflage, and have always camouflaged, what men really want and mean. Among the men who wanted and meant something other than what they nobly said, on the empty issue of states' rights, in the 1830's and '40's and '50's, were the honorable Justices of the Supreme Court, led by Roger Brooke Taney.

Except on the absurd if orthodox assumption that what Justices, or at least Chief Justices, think and do must be explained on some lofty level of government theory, of unearthly and infinite logic, involving such high-sounding matters as state sovereignty, national supremacy, and the proper postulates of federalism, the truth about Taney is, perhaps surprisingly, simple. He was a brilliant lawyer— which means, among other things, that he could weave a spell of impressive words about any argument toward any end that, as attorney or judge, he wanted to achieve. As counsel in one case, he orated: "A hard necessity, indeed, compels us to endure the evil of slavery for a time . . . while it continues it is a blot on our national character, and every real lover of freedom confidently hopes that it will be effectually, though it must be gradually, wiped away; . . . until the time shall come when we can point without a blush to the language held in the Declaration of Independence, every friend of humanity will seek to lighten the galling chain of slavery. . . ." But these inspiring sentiments, expressed in the course of litigation,

did not keep him, shortly after, from defending a noisome
character who had been charged, quite accurately, with the
crime of slave-trading. Nor did they keep him from insisting as attorney in another case: "The African race in
the United States, even when free, are everywhere a
degraded class. . . . The privileges they are allowed to
enjoy are accorded to them as a matter of kindness and
benevolence rather than of right."

Taney was also a shrewd politician whose shrewdness
was masked by the air of tremendous personal sincerity
that emanated from his ugly and unprepossessing person.
An ardent Federalist until he was well over forty, and a
leader of that party in Maryland who served it well in the
state legislature and out, he turned Democrat to support
Andrew Jackson, whose bitter opposition to the U.S. Bank
and whose sympathies for the South as against the North,
for the planters against the traders, Taney almost automatically shared. Both the lawyer and the politican in
Taney are apparent in his Court opinions.

But above all else—and explaining in obvious and
meaningful fashion his whole judicial philosophy—Taney
was a Southern gentleman, a straight political representative of what historian Charles Beard used to call "the
slavocracy." Though descended, generations back, from an
indentured servant who thus got to the New World, Taney
was born into a wealthy, slave-owning family of tobacco
planters. There is not one of his decisions as Chief Justice
—from his years of nipping at the Marshall-nurtured rights
of Northern capitalists to his ill-fated last-ditch effort to
hold the dike for slavery—but can be traced, directly or
indirectly, to his big-plantation birth and background. No

states'-rights nonsense distorted to fit a hypothetical pattern, no liberalism turned either suddenly or gradually to conservatism, makes the slightest sense about Taney. From first to last, he was simply the judicial spokesman of the old South.

When Taney took over the captaincy of the Supreme Court in 1836—after a slightly anti-Jackson Senate had rejected him as an Associate Justice a couple of years before, and after a somewhat pro-Jackson Senate debated his fitness for ten weeks before confirming him for the Chiefship—he found himself flanked on the high bench by four other Jackson appointees plus only two survivors from pre-Jackson days. With a Court thus loaded, five to two, for Democratic agrarianism, and with Marshall's old Federalist magic finally gone, Taney had no trouble making of the Court—and of the Constitution as read by the Court—the tool of a different political clique from the one that had run the judicial show for almost half a century. Those who persist in thinking of constitutional law and its top expounders as above politics might contemplate with profit, if with disillusion, a decision made by Taney's Court during his very first term as Chief. A few years earlier, Marshall's septet had blasted as utterly unconstitutional Missouri's issuance of paper money backed by the credit of the state, and had gone so far as to tell a debtor who had borrowed from the state in this paper money, and then spent it, that he need not repay it. Now Taney's tribunal gave constitutional benediction to a Kentucky law that achieved precisely the same practical purpose—that of putting easy money in the hands of the

hard-pressed, especially farmers—in a slightly different
formal manner; what Kentucky did was to set up and
completely run a state bank which made loans in the form
of bank notes, technically not issued on the credit of the
state but on the credit of the state bank; perfectly proper,
said Jackson's farmer-minded Justices. It did not matter
that Justice Story almost sobbed his disapproval in a dissent in which he presumed to talk for his old mentor,
Marshall, as well—probably the only time that a deceased
Justice has joined in a Supreme Court opinion. Nor
did it matter that the words of the Constitution, forbidding
states to "emit bills of credit," had not changed. What had
changed was the one all-important determinant of judicial
decisions about government matters: the personnel of the
Court and the politics of a majority of its members.

So too, during Taney's first term at the helm, one of
Marshall's great legal landmarks, the Dartmouth College
decision, was whittled down to size in the Charles River
Bridge case. A toll bridge across the Charles River,
operating under a charter granted by Massachusetts fifty
years before, had been making such fantastic profits out of
its monopoly on traffic between Boston and Charlestown,
the easiest route to the West, that shares of stock in the
bridge company had gone up from $100 to over $2,000,
when the state legislature authorized a rival bridge.
Against the claim of the profiteering monopolists that the
new charter was unconstitutional as an "impairment of the
obligation of contracts"—a claim thoroughly in line with
Marshall's Dartmouth College ruling—Taney and his four
fellow Jacksonians upheld the state and its new bridge,
on the ground that the old bridge's charter, while still

inviolable, nowhere forbade in so many words another bridge across the Charles at another place. Moreover Taney, though talking mostly legal language, gave away at the end of his opinion the fact that it was economics, not constitutional law, that dictated the decision: "If this Court should establish the principles now contended for, what is to become of the numerous railroads established on the same line of travel with turnpike companies? . . . The millions of property which have been invested in railroads and canals, upon lines of travel which had been before occupied by turnpike corporations, will be put in jeopardy. . . . This Court is not prepared to sanction principles which must lead to such results."

Neither Taney's legal principles nor his economics appealed to the more monopoly-minded relics on the Court from Marshall's day. Bemoaned Justice Story, in a long dissent that undoubtedly indicated how the case would have gone under Marshall, "I stand upon the old law, upon law established more than three centuries ago"—a slight overstatement, since the unprecedented Dartmouth College decision was only eighteen years old and the U.S. Constitution only fifty, and ancient Brisith law, to which Story referred, could scarcely control a case arising directly under the words of the American charter of government. But Story was quite accurate in his off-the-Court comment that "a great majority of our ablest lawyers are against the decision of the Court." He was not so accurate in predicting: "There will not, I fear, ever in our day, be any case in which a law of a State or of Congress will be declared unconstitutional." The "I fear" is immensely revealing of the politico-economic role that Story and the commercial-

creditor group wanted the Court to keep on playing—
under any legal principles that might come in handy.

For twenty years, Taney's Court continued to cut
down—little by little, now here, now there—the supposedly vested rights of investors. Corporations set up in
one state were denied the privilege of doing business as
they pleased in any other state, if the other state chose to
restrict them severely or even to keep them out entirely.
The unruly liquor industry was made subject to state
control by licensing laws, regulating the sale of liquor and
amounting to the first mild form of prohibition. These and
other similar rulings were said to be based on a fuzzy
concept called "state police power"—and Taney's frequent
use of the term is one reason why he is conventionally
classified as an anti-nationalist. But his efforts to explain
what he meant by it were so circular and question-begging
than any whole-hog nationalist might well have sub-
scribed to his words: "What are the police powers of the
state? They are nothing more or less than the powers of
government inherent in every sovereignty to the extent
of its dominions . . . its authority to make regulations of
commerce is as absolute as its power to pass health laws,
except in so far as it has been restricted by the Constitution of the United States." In view of the "except," how
could even Marshall have taken exception?

What "state police power" really meant in Taney's day
and has meant ever since is the use of state laws to do
things that a majority of the Justices, at any given time,
do not strongly disapprove of the state's doing—nothing
more, nothing less. For all Taney's comparative indifference to property rights of a commercial kind when they

came in conflict with state laws, it was something else
again when the kind of property or the kind of rights in
question were dearer to Taney's agrarian heart. And so he
upheld land grants, especially in California, as patently
forged and fraudulent as any Marshall had upheld before
him—and frequently had to do it over the shocked dissent
of two or three of his brother Jacksonians, who loved the
land-owning group as much as he but tolerated barefaced
dishonesty less. Here was the sort of case where the
essentially disparate judicial philosophies of Marshall and
Taney—one forever protecting the rich no matter what
their riches, the other forever protecting farmers and
land-owners, rich or poor—completely coincided.

Not so where banking was concerned. As Marshall,
most mightily in McCulloch *v.* Maryland, championed the
U.S. Bank with its policy of coddling the commercially
wealthy, so Taney was all for state banks with their more
liberal loans to local farmers, large or small—and his
violent hatred of the U.S. Bank was his most unwavering
political passion. This hatred stemmed originally, in
considerable part, from an experience that involved,
strangely, both Mr. McCulloch and Chief Justice Marshall:
the Bank's Baltimore branch had concealed McCulloch's
$3,000,000-plus defalcation to try to save itself some of
the loss by a subsequent insurance scheme, and Taney
argued the case against the Bank before Marshall's Court.
When Marshall ruled for the Bank on the bland—and
false—assumption that the Bank officials must be honorable men, he unwittingly chose his own successor as Chief
Justice. For Taney's resultant bitter hostility to the Bank
led in turn to his joining up with the Jackson Democrats,

to his appointment to Jackson's Cabinet, first as Attorney-General, then as Secretary of the Treasury (for the specific purpose of handling at each stage Jackson's battle with the Bank) and finally to Taney's reward in his elevation to the Court Chiefship. Of such little incidents is the supreme law of the land later born.

Along with his antipathy to the U.S. Bank, Taney retained an oversolicitous tenderness for state banks—so when a case came before his Court where Ohio had given its banks a boon, in the form of taxes lower than other corporations paid, and a later legislature had tried to take it back, Taney's reaction was all but automatic. Sounding exactly like Marshall, he berated the state for attempting to welch on its "contract," and declared the repeal of the tax boon unconstitutional; somehow, the vaunted "police power" here got lost in the shuffle when a state tried to use it in a way that offended the prejudices of its greatest exponent. But three of Taney's Democratic colleagues violently dissented against their Chief's apparently aberrational veto of a state law in order to protect vested rights of a non-agrarian kind—and in doing so, they gave "state police power," as they would have applied it here, a more trenchant meaning than Taney ever gave it. They asked: "What remedy have the people" against such "vicious legislation" as tax favors conferred by past legislatures on special groups, like state banks. "Under the doctrines of this court none is to be found . . . if the wrong has taken the form of a contract. The most deliberate and solemn acts of the people would not serve to redress the injustice, and the overreaching speculator upon the facility or corruption of their legislature would be protected by the powers of this court in the profits of his bargain."

The author of these strong words in dissenting defense of state governments against special privileges for property was Justice John Campbell of Alabama, a high-minded plantation-owner who had freed all his slaves when named to the Court but who later resigned his Justiceship to join the Confederacy, as a matter of principle, and survived the Civil War for almost a quarter of a century as one of the leading lawyers of the South. Campbell, along with Justices Daniel of Virginia and Catron of Tennessee, formed a rather radical and frequently dissenting trio on Taney's Court as Taney's Chiefship drew toward its Dred Scott climax. It was Daniel who—of course in dissent—questioned the whole doctrine of judicial supremacy as scathingly as it has ever been questioned, on the Court or off: "I ask upon what foundation the courts of the United States, limited and circumscribed as they are by the Constitution and by the laws which have created them and defined their jurisdiction, can, upon any speculation of public policy, assume to themselves the authority and functions of the legislative department of the government, alone clothed with those functions by the Constitution and laws. . . ." And Daniel added that the particular decision from which he was then dissenting was, on the part of the Court, "an act of usurpation."

But it was no judicial usurpation of the lawmakers' job to Daniel, nor to any of the other Southern Justices, when the big political question that was already rending the country in half—the question of Negro slavery, on which the South's whole economy was built—was finally thrown at the Court in a potentially farther-reaching fashion than had been involved in the sporadic upholding of fugitive-slave laws by the federal judiciary. This was in 1856; and the Court now had nine members, just as it has today, the extra two having been added to handle the new Western and Southwestern circuits shortly after Taney took over. Five of the nine were Southerners—Taney, Campbell, Catron, Daniel, and Justice Wayne of Georgia; the other four—McLean of Ohio, Curtis of Massachusetts, Nelson of New York, and Grier of Pennsylvania—represented (and the verb is accurate) the North. To these nine men fell the task of deciding *or of not deciding* the explosive political problems posed in the name of an illiterate and comparatively disinterested Negro by means of a cooked-up case— a case that made the Negro's name even more familiar in U.S. legal annals than those of Marbury and McCulloch, a case whose dramatic short-range impact made it the most famous, or infamous, in all Supreme Court history.

Dred Scott had been taken by his master, some twenty-odd years before, from the slave state of Missouri through the free state of Illinois into Wisconsin Territory, where slavery was outlawed by the Missouri Compromise. Later brought back to Missouri, he was induced to go to court to try to establish his status as a free man, since he had been free for years while living in the North. The Missouri courts ruled—in accordance with an almost forgotten Supreme Court decision of 1851 (where the slave's residence on free soil was, however, much shorter)—that Scott had gone back to bondage the second he crossed the Missouri border. To get the case into the federal courts and up to the Supreme Court, Scott was technically "sold" to a New Yorker named Sandford, who promised to free him and his family (and did so) no matter which way the decision went. As in so many momentous Supreme Court decisions, from Marbury *v.* Madison until last Monday's headlined ukase, the effect of the Court's action on the actual litigants was negligible; what the Justices were doing, for all their huffy denials that they ever do so, was not to settle a real and narrowed-to-its-facts dispute between two "parties" to a lawsuit, but to slap on, with broad strokes of the judicial brush, a major rule of government.

Nor need they have done so. To resolve the issue of Dred Scott's status, which was what they were supposed to be doing, the Justices need only have said—and could have said in a couple of sentences—that whether Scott, once back in Missouri, was a slave or a free man was Missouri's business, not the business of the federal government; and Scott *v.* Sandford (the case's technical name) would have dropped into oblivion. Indeed, this is precisely what the Justices planned to do after they first heard the case, with two of the Northerners prepared to join their Southern brethren in upholding Missouri—and re-enslaving Dred Scott—on this narrow and uninflammatory ground.

Then politics flooded into the case from every direction —just as politics has always flooded, seeped, or trickled into every really important Supreme Court case. Justice McLean, whose consuming ambition to become President was common knowledge, let it be known that he was going to tear the case wide open in a dissent which would amount

to a long, learned, but fiery tract against slavery—plus a
blast at his colleagues for supporting slavery, even by indirection. Georgia's Justice Wayne threatened a half-
dissenting pro-slavery treatise that would deplore the
Court's ducking of the big issues, and Justice Curtis of
abolitionist Massachusetts got ready to rip into Wayne
with another dissent that would supplement McLean's.
One of the main thrusts intended by both McLean and
Curtis was a fighting defense of the Missouri Compromise,
under which Wisconsin Territory had been designated as
free soil, and on which Dred Scott's claim to freedom was
therefore founded. And this despite, or more realistically,
because of, the fact that the Missouri Compromise had
been repealed by a pro-slavery Congress a couple of years
before. What McLean especially, and Wayne and Curtis to
a lesser degree, planned to deliver were political speeches
for or against slavery from the platform of the Supreme
Court.

Faced with this forensic free-for-all, the other Justices
decided to hear and discuss the case again. Meanwhile
James Buchanan, who, though a Pennsylvanian, was
mildly sympathetic to the South, had been elected President; and with the federal executive as well as the legislature thus safe for slavery, at least for a time, the Southern
Justices were encouraged to put their third branch of the
government in the same camp in a more substantial way
than they had at first intended. The result was the full-
blown Dred Scott decision, in which the Supreme Court,
for the first time since Marshall did it more than half a
century before, and so for the second time in its history,

branded an Act of Congress—the old and recently repealed Missouri Compromise—as unconstitutional.

The Court's pronunciamento that the Missouri Compromise had been invalid and void from the beginning was based on the broad, flat declaration that Congress had no power to ban slavery in any of the Western territories (as the Compromise had done, north of an agreed line)—and this in the face of the Constitution's grant to Congress of "power to . . . make all needful rules and regulations respecting the territory . . . belonging to the United States." What this meant was that not even any future anti-slavery Congress could re-establish something like the Missouri Compromise or designate any U.S. territory as free soil, that the institution of slavery was at liberty to spread wherever it could or it pleased, unless and until the Court's decision should be reversed by the Court itself, by constitutional amendment, or by force of arms. In effect, the Court told the fast-growing Republican Party to stop wasting its energy and its oratory on efforts to restrict slavery by federal law.

Not only the decision but the preparatory manipulation of its manner and its timing was pungent of politics. When President Buchanan, in his inaugural address, adjured the nation, North and South, to accept the Court's judgment in the by-then-well-publicized Dred Scott case, regardless of how it might go—and did it with a deliberate air of innocent impartiality—he had already been told exactly what the Court had decided, how the Justices were lined up, and when the decision would be announced (which date, by purposeful postponement, was two days after

Buchanan's inauguration). More than that, Buchanan, at
the request of Southern Justice Catron, had actually written some days earlier to his fellow Pennsylvanian, Justice
Grier, to urge him to vote with the five Southerners so
that the ruling would not be by a bare five-to-four majority along strictly sectional lines; and when the Court's
action was made public, it was indeed a six-to-three decision with Grier adding his weight to the advocates of
slavery.

   That the decision, including its substance, was the fruit
of a collusive and carefully conceived plot between the
President-elect and the Court majority, as many incensed
Republicans, led by Senator Seward, charged, is a considerable exaggeration; that there was shocking impropriety in
the prior revelation of the ruling to Buchanan, as lawyers
and other Court-worshippers have felt ever since the facts
came to light more than fifty years later, is a naïve notion,
stemming from the myth that Justices are, and ought to
behave like, high priests rather than political functionaries;
but that Buchanan's comment in his inaugural was loaded
with hypocrisy and deceit is beyond question, and that the
whole case was shot through, as are all big Supreme Court
cases, with plain partisan politics is as obvious as it should
be unsurprising.

   Like the meat of the Court's ruling and the contrived
circumstances surrounding its issuance, the opinions of the
Justices—and each of the nine said his separate say—were,
with one exception, political to the teeth. (The exception
was Nelson's; he alone stuck to the narrow point on which
the Court had first hoped to dispose of the case, and refused to take part in the bitter bigger debate.) And in all

the pseudo-judicial speechmaking, Chief Justice Taney, delivering the main opinion for the majority, stood out as the most patently political of the lot, as he more than matched the McLean dissent which had originally sparked the fireworks. Not content to label the Missouri Compromise unconstitutional and let the decision rest on that, he held that no Negro could be a U.S. citizen, so that Scott had no right to bring suit in a federal court in the first place—a holding which, by regular legal procedure, should have stopped the Court from so much as considering the constitutionality of the Compromise, since the case was over, there was no case left, once it was ruled that the plaintiff had no right to sue. But Taney, backed by five of his fellows, was not to be stopped.

With evident relish, he flayed the holier-than-thou attitude of the North, "where the labor of the Negro race was found to be unsuited to the climate and unprofitable to the master," and he jabbed and twitted New England for its pious protestations of concern for the Negro while its ship-owners grew rich "in the slave trade, procuring cargoes on the coast of Africa and transporting them for sale" to the South. No opinion could have revealed more clearly the economic and emotional roots of Taney's judicial credo; what had passed, for two decades, as a humanitarian concern for the poor against their commercial exploiters, and a consequent championing of regulatory state laws, was now illumined as, in large part, an almost envious competitive sectionalism, a loyalty to the South which encompassed a scorn for the North. Nor could any opinion have been better calculated to enrage the opponents of Negro slavery—and to wreck its author's judicial reputation, once his side lost the war that his opinion helped bring on.

Among those who were enraged by Taney's treatment of the Dred Scott case—although his was a slow boil—was Abraham Lincoln of Illinois. One of his earlier and milder statements, in which he counseled acceptance of the decision until it should be—as he thought it properly could be —reversed by Congress, went on to the trenchant and timeless comment that "our judges are as honest as other men and not more so. They have, with others, the same passions for party, for power, and the privilege of their corps. . . . Their power is the more dangerous as they are in office for life, and not responsible, as the other functionaries are, to the elective control." But eventually, Lincoln's seething indignation burst into belligerence: "Familiarize yourselves with the chains of bondage and you prepare your own limbs to wear them. Accustomed to trample on the rights of others, you have lost the genius of your own independence. . . . And let me tell you, that all these things are prepared for you by the teachings of history, if the elections shall promise that the next Dred Scott decision and all future decisions will be quietly acquiesced in by the people."

Despite Lincoln's dire forebodings, what might be classed as "the next Dred Scott decision" was conspicuously not "quietly acquiesced in by the people." In 1859, in a case arising out of the flagrant flouting of the federal fugitive-slave law by a Wisconsin abolitionist, the Court, now riding high, put its stamp of approval on the slave-catching statute—which clearly violated several sections of the constitutional Bill of Rights—and ordered it obeyed. Taney, in ringing words that would have stirred John

Marshall to pride in his successor, spoke out for national supremacy over the states and judicial supremacy over all; of the Supreme Court he said: "If such an arbiter had not been provided in our complicated system of government, internal tranquility could not have been preserved and if such controversies were left to the arbitrament of physical force, our Government, State and National, would cease to be a government of laws, and revolution by force of arms would take the place of courts of justice and judicial decisions." To all this sonorous self-defense the state of Wisconsin responded by calling Taney's decision itself unconstitutional, and encouraging—not that such encouragement was needed in any of the anti-slavery states—disobedience of the federal law. Now was the time when Southern support of the national government, including especially the Court, was at its crest, and state sovereignty was the watchword of the North. Little more than a year later, Lincoln was in the White House and Southern states were seceding from the Union that Northern soldiers were going to war to defend.

The Republicans went to Washington, war came to the nation, and the windy slogans that men use to lend a false dignity to their deep and human allegiances veered 180 degrees—but Taney and his Court stayed on; as so often, the Court became a mourners' bench for an old order that had passed. Inevitably, conflict between Lincoln and Taney soon boiled into an immediate and specific issue, but the odds against the Chief Justice—by contrast to those Marshall faced in his early challenge of Jefferson —were overwhelming in that Taney was now well over eighty years old, a war was on, and the issue was con-

siderably more vital than the commissioning of a justice of
the peace for the District of Columbia. Lincoln, especially
anxious to keep Maryland under control and out of the
Confederacy, had suspended the "writ of habeas corpus"
(under which men summarily arrested and imprisoned can
demand their temporary release for a fair trial); a Marylander named Merryman, suspected of rebellious activities,
had been whisked to jail by the local commanding general
and was being held for obvious conviction by a military
court; Taney, sitting as a circuit judge, heard Merryman's
plea for a habeas corpus writ and issued one; the general,
naturally obeying his commander-in-chief instead of
Taney, paid no attention to the writ; whereupon Taney
quixotically ordered the general arrested for contempt of
court.

In the course of declaring that only Congress, not the
President, could constitutionally suspend the writ, Taney
proclaimed that if judicial authority could thus be "usurped
by the military power at its discretion, the people of the
United States are no longer living under a government of
laws [*again, that ancient chestnut*] but every citizen holds
life, liberty, and property at the will and pleasure of the
army officer in whose military district he may happen to
be found." Both the general and Lincoln, to whom Taney
sent a copy of his opinion, shrugged and went on with the
war, Merryman stayed in prison, and the writ of habeas
corpus remained suspended—unused and useless—until
the war was over. Yet Taney, who was thoroughly prepared to be imprisoned himself for his brashness (Lincoln
was of course too intelligent and too gentle to make any
such move), had struck a brave blow for individual liberties

which, however futile, was a rare gesture for a Supreme
Court Justice. That Taney's motive may well have been
hostility toward Lincoln, the North, the war, and the new
order—rather than a passion for civil rights (would he
have ruled the same way against Jefferson Davis?)—does
not detract from the courage of what the old man did.

Around this time, and all within two years, Taney's
three ablest colleagues—Campbell, Daniel, and McLean—
either resigned or died. In replacing them, no more than
any other President did Lincoln look to merit alone; indeed, his first appointment was one of the worst ever made
to the Court, for Noah Swayne of Ohio—named as a barefaced sop to certain business interests who were supporting
the war for less than idealistic reasons—was a corporation
lawyer, as successful as he was callously unethical, who was
not to change his spots or his spottiness throughout his
long judicial career. Lincoln's other two selections were
happier; David Davis of Illinois, though chosen, like
Washington's Justice Blair, because he was an intimate
personal friend, soon demonstrated his high caliber (as
Blair did not); Samuel Miller of Iowa, humanitarian and
unlegalistic realist, became, despite the fact that history
has largely overlooked him, one of the Court's few top-
flight Justices. But bad or good, each of the three had
politics to thank, in part, for his appointment—and the
first big case that came before them italicized the importance, both to them and to the President, of the political
factor which underlay their choice.

In the normal course of the war, the North had been
blockading Southern ports and seizing ships and cargoes
headed not only for coastal trade but abroad; under inter-

national law, the legality of these seizures was highly questionable, since Congress had never formally declared war but merely authorized the President to suppress an insurrection; this technicality—somewhat suggestive of President Truman's twentieth-century "police action" in Korea—brought the problem before the Justices. That the blockade was given legal blessing by a bare five-to-four majority is less significant than that Lincoln's three brand-new nominees were among the prevailing five; without their presence, the decision would almost surely have gone the other way. Not that this would have affected Lincoln's conduct of the war or stopped the blockade, for a contrary ruling would doubtless have been treated as was Taney's . judicial demand that Merryman be released under a writ of habeas corpus, a couple of years before. In fact, what Lincoln's Justices achieved was less a substantial boost to the Union cause than a saving of face for the Court itself— which would otherwise have seen its solemn decree ignored, its last-word superiority brushed aside, and its very existence as a governmental force seriously threatened.

But to Taney, who was, of course, among the four dissenters, this was the end. Court prestige or no Court prestige, he could not stand to see the hated hordes of the North given the highest judicial sanction as they rampaged against his beloved South. At his venerable insistence, the Justices politely ducked, as only they, among top government servants have power to do, the two or three other major wartime issues thrust before them, and for the duration of the hostilities, the Court remained quiescent— and safe.

Embittered, impoverished, estranged from the new

people as well as the new policies that now surrounded him at the seat of the national government, Taney died just six months before the assassination of his arch-nemesis, Abraham Lincoln. Like so many heads of the Court, from John Marshall to Harlan Stone, he had, in his heyday, made his enduring imprint on the nation and its laws— and then had lived too long. The political beliefs he was born to and to which he dedicated his career were neither wholly bad nor wholly good, and although he saw them rudely crushed, many of their remnants and ramifications survived to grow again. The legal principles he planted or cultivated still crop up in Court opinions, although often as hybrids that he himself would disown. The culture he championed—the agrarian culture of the old slave-owning South—was on its deathbed when Taney died, although elements of it were to rise, phoenix-like, from its ashes decades later. He might have died a little happier had he known that in the era just ahead—the era of ruthless "reconstruction" and rampant capitalism and expansion high-wide-and-not-always-handsome—there would be no Chief Justice for almost fifty years who could hold a candle to Roger Brooke Taney.

CHAPTER 5

The Court Rides Back
to Power on the Nation's
Surge to the West

THE THREE DECADES following Appomattox and the
death of Lincoln are perhaps the most neglected and underrated in all U.S. history. There were no wars; there were
no great Presidents nor even, save only Cleveland, any
very good ones; there was none of the stuff of which conventionally name-and-date-conscious history is made. Yet
the nation grew more rapidly and rambunctiously during
the last third of the nineteenth century than at any other
time—riding westward with the railroads, spreading
across the continent with the shoulder-swinging confidence

141

of young manhood on the make. And in this coming of age
of American capitalism, the Supreme Court, like an ad-
miring and encouraging uncle, played—now unobtrusively,
now boldly—a major part.

Nor was this any mean accomplishment on the part of
the Justices. After the Dred Scott debacle, after the wartime caution which verged on cowardice and which was to
continue into the early Reconstruction years, the Court's
prestige and its consequent power were at a nadir unprecedented since Marshall had made of it a potent government force. There was no public outcry, such as greeted
years later Franklin Roosevelt's "Court-packing" plan,
when Congress calmly, within the short span of seven
years, first raised the number of Justices to ten, then
lowered it to seven (it never actually got below eight, since
a couple of Taneyan relics refused to resign or die), then
restored it to nine—although all three of these shifts were
barefaced political moves, each dependent on the current
occupant of the White House and dictated by a bland
before-the-fact taking for granted that any appointment
made by him would be acceptable (in the case of Lincoln
and Grant) or unacceptable (in the case of Andrew Johnson) to Congress.

Moreover, after the long and lusty incumbencies of
Marshall and Taney in the Chief Justiceship, the Court was
headed for the remainder of the century by a trio of poor-
to-middling jurists, none of whom had the personal or intellectual fire to lead, much less dominate, his own Court;
even lawyers asked to list the Court's past Chiefs are apt
to forget Salmon P. Chase, Morrison R. Waite, and
Melville W. Fuller. All three were outshone and over-

shadowed by a series of higher-calibered associates—from Samuel Miller, whom Chief Justice Chase himself had the grace to call "beyond question the dominant personality . . . upon the bench," to John Harlan, the brilliant precursor in liberalism and in dissent of Justice Holmes. All three were swept along—sometimes willing, sometimes protesting—as their crews kept the Supreme Court's craft pretty squarely in the current of the inexorably expansionist times.

Not that those crews kept smoothly in stroke; few of the telling Supreme Court decisions of the late nineteenth century were unanimous and many were five-to-four; as the Court's membership shifted, as new Presidents named new and politically sympathetic Justices, confessed or *sub rosa* reversals of recent rulings became the regular order of many a decision day. But neither the reversals nor the narrow margin by which they were often effected delayed for long the renaissance of a refreshed and refurbished Court prestige. Between the Civil War and the Spanish-American War, while the Court's personnel was in constant flux and no strong hand was ever at the helm, a majority of the Justices managed to ride the crest of the times back to power such as Marshall had never known.

This resurgence of the judiciary from impotence to dominance is best italicized by contrasting what the Court did not do in the late 1860's with what it did in the middle 1890's. Soon after the Civil War, in a series of dull cases dealing technically with state bonds and state debt-limits, dealing actually with the westward reach of the rampaging railroads, dealing legally with the right of state courts to change their minds and their decisions, the Justices spanked the state courts of Iowa; then saw their orders disobeyed and flouted; and eventually surrendered officially, if reluctantly. Nobody protested or even clucked at Iowa's successful defiance of the Supreme Court of the United States. At about the same time, Congress practically dared the Court majority, still sympathetic to the South, to declare the ruthless Reconstruction Acts, passed over President Johnson's veto, unconstitutional; the Court ducked this opportunity so obviously that a Cabinet member commented: "The Judges of the Supreme Court have caved in, fallen through, failed. . . ."

But a little less than thirty years later, the Court's self-confidence, indeed its cockiness, was such that in a single year, 1895, it made, and saw upheld, three of the most politically important decisions in its entire history, each of them in its separate way an almost insolent flaunting of judicial supremacy over Congress and over the government of the nation. One of these three was the Pollock decision, branding the Democratic-Populist income tax unconstitutional by a bare 5–4 vote, and so postponing until the Sixteenth Amendment was adopted, after a lag of eighteen years, what soon became the most fruitful (and, by different lights, the fairest or most unfair) source of federal revenue. One was the Knight decision, in which the high-riding Justices, instead of calling the new Sherman Anti-Trust Act invalid under the Constitution, so emasculated it, in the course of "interpreting" its meaning, that it has never since recovered its virility. The third was the Debs decision, where the Court took it upon itself, in the utter absence of any Congressional law calling for judicial action, to regulate interstate commerce on its own—though the

Constitution gives that power only to Congress—by blessing the order of a lower federal judge which sent the leader of a railroad strike to jail. Thus, through the veto of one Congressional statute in the name of the Constitution, through the near-veto of another in the guise of "interpretation," and through assumption of one of the powers of Congress where there was no statute at all, the Justices announced to all but the politically astigmatic that they were governmentally supreme in more than name.

Less than three decades earlier, a retired Justice, Curtis, had said: "Congress, with the acquiescence of the country, has subdued the Supreme Court. . . ." Six decades later, a sitting Justice, Douglas, was to say, specifically of the Debs decision but, by implication, of the Court's whole attitude, plus the nation's tolerance of that attitude, back in 1895: "No greater claim to judicial supremacy has ever been made. . . ." Here, in the words of two of its members, speaking almost a century apart, is highlighted the Court's quick rise from the subjugation of post-Civil War days to the proud government primacy that, once re-achieved, it has held for itself ever since. How was this rapid resurgence accomplished? There is at least a clue in the second half of Justice Douglas's comment on the Debs case: ". . . and significantly it [*the "claim to judicial supremacy"*] was made on behalf of vested interests that were callous to human rights."

It was indeed vested interests, property interests, the protection of accumulated and accumulating wealth, that dominated the philosophy and the decisions of most of the Justices during those years when the Court was regaining its power. Not that this was any judicial innovation; Mar-

shall's Court, and Taney's too, had read the law at a slant
to safeguard now this, now that, kind of property or wealth.
Nor was this new-era Court—at least at the start—out of
tune with the timbre of its own times; those were the days
of the robber barons, but more revealing is the fact that
they were not known as robber barons then; they were
rather the swashbuckling risk-taking leaders of America's
surge to the west—for all their financial finagling, more
adventurers than exploiters—and the railroads that were
their wealth and their life were the nation's life as well.
Hence, it is neither surprising nor necessarily sinister that
most of the men appointed to the Court in the late nineteenth century, including two Chief Justices, Waite and
Fuller, had made their names and their legal reputations
primarily as railroad lawyers.

But when many, though not all, of these former railroad
lawyers began to twist the law unduly in favor of the railroads and of other closely connected corporations, plain-
speaking Justice Miller was moved to blurt out, after a
Court conference in which his somewhat more objective
views had been voted down: "It is vain to contend with
judges who have been, at the bar, the advocates of railroad
companies, and all the forms of associated capital, when
they are called upon to decide cases where such interests
are in contest. All their training, all their feelings are from
the start in favor of those who need no such influence."
And when Justices who had leaned toward the railroads
when the railroads represented, in the true sense, free
enterprise, continued to lean toward them as they grew
fat and not so free, sentiments like Justice Miller's spread
far and wide beyond the confines of the Court and con-

tributed to the growing Populist movement: But by this time the Court, having unobtrusively regained its power, was ready to resist, in its own right, any would-be inroads on the course of capitalism flamboyant. As its chief weapon in judicial defense of an economy untrammeled by bothersome restrictive laws, it chose, and gradually fashioned to its purpose, one-third of one sentence of the long, new Fourteenth Amendment to the Constitution.

The Fourteenth was one of three amendments adopted soon after the Civil War and designed, according to all obvious intents and announced purposes, to guarantee the rights of the newly freed Negroes. As such, it was crammed down the reluctant craw of the defeated South by a law that banned any seceding state from re-admission to the Union until it had ratified the Amendment. In the middle of a sentence, in one of five sections of the Amendment, appears the phrase: "nor shall any state deprive any person of life, liberty, or property, without due process of law." The phrase was clearly copied from the Fifth Amendment, a bulwark of the Bill of Rights, which forbids the *federal* government to deprive any person of "life, liberty, or property, without due process of law." As originally written in the Fifth Amendment, it was no more than a roundabout and melodious way of saying that no one suspected or accused of crime could be hanged, jailed, or fined without fair and legal treatment, before and during trial.

But the Fourteenth Amendment's "due process clause" —as it is commonly called—(and even the Fifth Amendment's too) has come to mean something quite different today. Without so much as a close competitor it has become, to lawyers, the most familiar and useful phrase of

the entire Constitution; indeed, well over a thousand of
the Supreme Court's full-dress decisions have revolved
around the little due process clause. These decisions have
rarely dealt with Negroes, or with people of any color,
accused of crime. They have dealt instead with corporations
or, less often, with real (not corporate) "persons" who
claimed through their lawyers that some duly enacted and
fairly administered state law, taxing them or regulating
their business activities, "deprived" them of property
"without due process of law." In sum, the Fourteenth
Amendment's due process clause has become the last, and
quite often successful, resort of men or companies who
stand to lose money through the normal working of some
state law, properly passed by a properly elected legislature,
properly signed by a properly elected governor, and properly put into effect by properly chosen state officials, including judges—some law that perhaps clamps down on
sweatshops, or taxes big fortunes handed on at death, or
orders a monopoly like an electric company not to charge
so much. And this legal legerdemain, by which an old
Bill of Rights phrase has been inflated into a semantic
excuse for the judicial veto of state laws of any and all
varieties, was first perpetrated, toward the end of the
nineteenth century, by a Supreme Court hell-bent to guard
the business interests that had sparked the nation's westward growth, against what the Founding Fathers would
have called "leveling laws"—no matter that those laws
reflected the democratic will.

Although the pro-business perversion of the plain meaning of the due process clause (Justice Holmes once snorted
in disgust, and in dissent: "Of course, the words 'due

process of law' if taken in their literal meaning have no application to this case. . . .") came to effective life only after the Justices gave it their official benediction, the twist had been anticipated, ardently urged, and perhaps even plotted long before. At least, two members of the congressional committee that drafted the Fourteenth Amendment later insisted that they had planned it that way. John Bingham, a shrewd and successful railroad attorney, said so in a speech to Congress; and Roscoe Conkling, another prominent corporation lawyer, remarked before the Supreme Court, while trying to argue a railway client out of paying a state tax: "Those who devised the Fourteenth Amendment . . . planted in the Constitution a monumental truth to stand four square to whatever wind might blow. That truth is but the golden rule, so entrenched as to curb the many who would do to the few as they would not have the few do to them." In context, it was clear that Conkling's "many" were any democratic majority and his "few" any businesses or businessmen financially hit or hampered by a state law.

Regardless of whether Bingham and Conkling were indulging in accurate revelation or, perhaps, in clever and purposeful afterthought, it is a nice question whether the "intent" of the drafters of a constitutional phrase, or of a statute, should prevail if that "intent" has not been fully revealed to those who adopt, or enact, the words into law. Should a court say that a piece of legal language means what the man who wrote it wanted it to mean, or what other men understood it to mean when their votes gave it governmental sanction and force? The problem—characteristically legal in its potential convolutions and its essential irrelevance (judges use either answer as an excuse for reaching whatever decision they want)—is the basis of many an inconclusive court argument in many a case of constitutional or statutory "interpretation"; but it is a dead problem today so far as the due process clause is concerned. Despite the fact that practically every legislator, state or federal, who had a hand in putting the Fourteenth Amendment into the Constitution thought he was helping insure the civil rights of the Negroes—and had no notion that he was sheltering corporate and other businesses, way into the indefinite future, from vexatious state regulations and taxes—the legal clan eventually saw to it that the Bingham-Conkling "intent" held sway. As Charles Beard describes this lawyers' crusade: "In learned briefs and prolix arguments, counsel for these harassed concerns warned the Supreme Court with emphatic repetition against the oncoming hosts of communism and anarchy . . . and demanded that the Court stem the tide by assuming the function of passing upon the reasonableness of all menacing legislation."

The Court did not capitulate immediately. But as it regained its confidence after its near-hibernation of Civil War and early Reconstruction days, as Northern Republican railroad lawyers replaced Jacksonian agrarians on the high bench, the Bingham-Conkling vision of the due process clause, with its vast political potential, gained gradual acceptance among the Justices—first in dissenting opinions, then in half-concessions by a Court majority—until in 1890, a quarter-century after the war ended, it was first made the basis of a full-fledged and far-reaching Court decision. By that momentous decision, to quote Beard again, "every act of every state and local government which touched adversely the rights of persons and property was made subject to review and liable to annulment by the Supreme Court at Washington, appointed by the President and Senate for life and far removed from local feelings and prejudices." Five years later, in the income-tax and anti-trust and railway-strike decisions, the Court was spectacularly riding herd on Congress too. Within three decades, the Justices had climbed back from the depths to the heights of sheer political power.

The man who, at Taney's death, took over the Chief-ship of a Supreme Court deep in disrepute—and who, during his brief nine-year tenure, did little himself to repair the Court's prestige—is better known as Lincoln's brilliant but unruly Secretary of the Treasury and as an unabashed seeker after the Presidency, so persistent, if perennially unsuccessful, that he alternately wooed the Republicans, the Democrats, and the Liberal Republicans in his hunger for a nomination he never won. Salmon P. Chase of Ohio, so conventionally handsome that he was once called "a sculptor's ideal of a President," had been named to Lincoln's Cabinet from the U.S. Senate, largely as a reward for his legal and political record as an all-out abolitionist—a record which had earned him the sobriquet of "attorney-general for fugitive slaves." And it was for even more pointedly political reasons that Lincoln chose Chase to replace Taney at the head of the Court—however this fact may offend ingenuous idolators of the Court or of Lincoln. As the great President himself put it, in a blend of bluntness and shrewdness, "we wish for a Chief Justice who will sustain what has been done in regard to emancipation and the legal tenders [*the paper money of questionable validity, issued during Chase's Secretaryship of the Treasury to help pay for the Civil War*]. We cannot ask a man what he will do, and if we should, and he should answer us, we should despise him for it. Therefore we must take a man whose opinions are known." Had Lincoln lived he would have learned, as have other Presidents, that no amount of political shrewdness in naming a new Justice can keep that Justice—especially if he is ambitious—from changing his "known" opinions after he has donned the security of a robe.

While the legality of the Emancipation Proclamation never came before the Court, since slavery was abolished by the Thirteenth Amendment soon after Lincoln's death, the legality of the Civil War paper money was litigated to the teeth—and the most vocal and violent judicial contemnor of the paper-money laws he had helped to plan and put into effect was Chief Justice Chase, now out to swing for himself a Presidential nomination on some other ticket than the Republican. But before the Legal Tender Acts, as lawyers still call them, came up for constitutional review, Chase and his colleagues were faced with some other big government problems and managed to flub or flee them all—with one exception. The exception looms large only in the perspective of retrospect; it seemed singularly insignificant at the time and hence is paid little attention by most Court historians. What the Court did, and did admirably, though by a bare 5–4 vote, was to declare unconstitutional an Act of Congress requiring a loyalty oath from lawyers (and directed, just after the Civil War, against Confederates, not Communists); but the reason this decision stands out in the panorama of time is because it is one of three instances in the Court's entire history where the ultimate power of judicial review, in the veto of a Congressional law, has been clearly and significantly used in behalf of civil liberties. This case aside, the Chase Court did itself less than proud, and Chase's own record stands as a monument to the potential fallibility of even the best of Presidents in choosing Chief Justices wisely.

There was the Court's running battle with the state of Iowa over Iowa's financial magnanimity in trying to lure the railroads through its corn fields and into its cities—a battle notable on three scores. It was notable because—in stark contrast to what was shortly to come—the legislature of a farm state had sparked a legal tussle by taking official action for, not agin, the then-fledgling railroads. It was notable because of the vitriolic vigor of Justice Miller's dissent, in the first of several cases, not only against the Court's pro-railroad decision as rationalized by his fellow Justice, ex-railroad-lawyer Swayne (in reversing the Iowa Supreme Court's anti-railroad ruling) but also against "language as unsuited to the dispassionate dignity of this court as it is disrespectful to another court of at least concurrent jurisdiction over the matter. . . ." And it was notable because, in accord with Miller's dissenting doubt that the Justices could "induce the Supreme Court of Iowa to conform its rulings to suit our dictation," the Iowa court did indeed disregard the U.S. Supreme Court's orders in three consecutive cases until it forced the high tribunal, devoid at that time of the prestige that underlies its power, to ignominiously back down.

There was also the Chase Court's strategic retreat from battle with a revengeful Republican Congress, bent on beating down the defeated South with the misnamed Reconstruction Acts that in many ways defied all decent concepts of constitutional propriety. Paradoxically, this retreat came hard on the heels of a ringing declaration by the Justices in behalf of human rights, in a case called *ex parte* Milligan—a case much celebrated in legal annals but presumably celebrated rather for its language than for its beneficent impact on events, which was practically nil. Milligan, a Copperhead or pro-Southern Northerner, had been sentenced to be hanged by one of Lincoln's military courts, shortly before the war ended. In releasing him under a writ of habeas corpus—the same writ that old Taney had used in his gallant but futile gesture for Merryman, and that the Court as a whole had timorously backed away from using while the war was on—the unanimous Justices proclaimed through Justice Davis: "The Constitution of the United States is a law for rulers and people, equally in war and in peace. . . . No doctrine involving more pernicious consequences was ever invented by the wit of man than that any of its provisions can be suspended during any of the great exigencies of government." Noble words but scarcely brave ones, since the Court conspicuously failed to speak them—or, more importantly, to act on them—until the war was over.

Indeed, the real and immediate impact of the Milligan case was anything but beneficent. While the whole Court agreed that a *President* could not replace functioning civil courts with military courts, a five-man majority of the Justices went further and denied the same power to Con-

gress. But the Reconstruction Congress was at that moment gleefully setting up military courts below the Mason-
Dixon Line to help subjugate the beaten South. In no
mood to be cowed by a Court it held in contempt, Congress
forthwith reduced the Court's membership from ten to
seven as any sitting Justices should resign or die (lifetime
tenure prevented unseating them, but two of the five-man
majority were well over seventy)—and thus automatically
disposed, as well, of President Johnson's unconfirmed
nominee to fill the seat of Justice Catron, who had died
before the Milligan decision.

If the rampaging Republican Congress was not cowed
by an unsympathetic Court (nor by an unsympathetic
President), it was soon clear that the Court was now
cowed by Congress. In the first suit brought to test the
constitutionality of the Reconstruction Acts—technically,
a plea that the Court enjoin the President from administer-
ing them—the Justices bowed themselves out by denying
that they had any right, under the doctrine of separation of
powers, to give orders directly to a President. In the next
suit the President was not directly involved but two of his
highest subordinates, Secretary of War Stanton and General Grant, were; this time the Court's excuse for ducking
was one that has since acquired a familiar and tired ring;
the issue was not "legal," it was "political"—and as such
was none of the Justices' business. Then along came a suit,
by a Mississippi editor named McCardle, challenging
head-on the authority of the military tribunals set up by
Congress in the South; the membership of the Court had
not changed by one man since the proud pronouncement
of the Milligan case.

As the publicized McCardle case went up to the Court for argument, with the legal rightness-or-wrongness of the whole Reconstruction scheme potentially hanging on the decision, Congress—for all its self-assurance, not anxious to face the dilemma of either disobeying, flatly and arrogantly, a specific Supreme Court order or else submitting, meekly and weakly, to the order it anticipated—took fast action. Under its constitutional control of the Court's right to hear cases appealed from lower courts, it feverishly prepared a bill to prohibit the Court from going any further with the McCardle case (appealed from a federal circuit court) or from entertaining any others like it. Time was now, as lawyers say, of the essence. Before the bill could be perfected and pushed through, the Justices had finished hearing the McCardle pleadings—and they were well aware of what Congress was fashioning to handcuff them. But instead of announcing a quick and easily curt decision reaffirming—this time in cold fact, not just in warm oratory—the majestic Milligan manifesto of only two years before, they stayed their judicial hands until the Congressional handcuffs were welded into law. Then, in an opinion penned by Chief Justice Chase and redolent of sadly self-righteous abnegation in the face of the inevitable —which had not been inevitable—the Justices submitted to Congress's command and dropped the case. In popular esteem as in political power, the Court had hit rock bottom.

Comparative cowardice soon gave way to almost equally unimpressive confusion, as the Court finally tangled with the Legal Tender Acts that had led Lincoln to name their Cabinet sponsor to the Chiefship. Including Chase, the Court in 1869 numbered five Lincoln appointees out of eight members, the other four being Swayne, Davis, Miller, and Stephen J. Field of California—who had been chosen as a tenth Justice in 1863 to represent a new federal court circuit in the far West, who was an intimate and a protégé of Leland Stanford (better known in the nineteenth century for the political machinations of his Central Pacific Railroad than for the university he founded), and who devoted his considerable legal talents to the judicial support of ultra-conservative capitalism throughout a Court career destined to last for thirty-four years. It might have seemed that these five, at least, would vote to uphold the constitutionality of the close to half a billion dollars' worth of paper money issued, out of financial necessity, by the Lincoln-led U.S. government during its fight to preserve the Union—particularly since the railroads, by a strange quirk, were then on the side of the poor, the debtors, the easy-money class, because they were operating largely on bond-borrowed funds. But Chase, for all his close past connection with the issuance of the greenbacks, was more ambitious than consistent, and Field was more creditor-conscious than railroad-minded.

In the first of the Legal Tender cases, the Court, in conference, split four to four; but feeble seventy-six-year-old Justice Grier—the Northerner who had gone along with the pro-slavery Southerners in the Dred Scott decision after President-elect Buchanan so suggested—vacillated so vaguely in his views that his colleagues took the unprecedented step of unanimously asking him to resign from the Court. (By a sort of poetic justice, Field, who delivered the message to Grier, was himself the recipient of an identical request twenty-eight years later—at which date he was not too senile to mutter, when reminded of the Grier incident and his own part in it: "Yes—and a dirtier piece of work I never did in all my life.") Dirty work or no, Grier did resign, whereupon, early in 1870, the Court ruled, four to three, that the Legal Tender Acts were unconstitutional—with Chase, the Acts' chief sponsor, maintaining for the majority that Congress had no power to issue paper money and Miller, in blistering dissent, upholding the Acts as a "necessary and proper" (the Constitution's phrase) adjunct of Congress's unquestioned power to carry on a war. Had this decision stood until time encrusted it with sacredness—as has many a Court decision by a mere one-man majority—Congress's control of U.S. currency would still be limited, short of constitutional amendment, to the clumsy business of coining metallic money. But Congress, backed by its new ally in the White House, Ulysses S. Grant, was bound that the Court's hobbling decision should not stand long.

A month after Grant took office, and while the first of the Legal Tender cases was still on its way up to the Court, Congress, perhaps foreseeing trouble, had increased the number of Justices to nine (at which figure, despite Franklin Roosevelt's bid to raise the Justicial ante, it has remained ever since). Almost simultaneously with the announcement of the 4–3 decision, Grant named to the Court two more railroad lawyers—William Strong of Pennsylvania (Philadelphia and Reading R.R.) and Joseph P. Bradley of New Jersey (United Railway Companies of N.J.). Within a week after the quick confirmation of Strong and Bradley, the Administration started steps to bring the Legal Tender Acts before the Court—now a

slightly different Court—again. And the very next year—
with Strong and Bradley joining the former dissenters, and
Chief Justice Chase leading the former majority in futile
protest—the Supreme Court of the United States officially
and solemnly announced that the Constitution gives Congress the power to issue paper money, a power that Congress of course still exercises to this day. As when Justice
Roberts, in the New Deal era of the following century,
switched his views about the validity of minimum-wage
laws between one year and the next and, in so doing,
completely reversed the supreme law of the land as laid
down by the Court, so in 1871, the turnabout on the Legal
Tender Acts gave pause even to the most naïve of believers in the myth that Supreme Court Justices read the
law *out of* the Constitution instead of reading it *in*.

Made to look a little ridiculous by their own official flip-
flop (plus a push from Congress and the President) so soon
after Congress had made them look silly over Reconstruction, the Justices turned their primary attention, for more
than a score of years, away from the federal government
and toward the states. Now was the time when business
lawyers began to urge on the Court a free-wheeling version of the Fourteenth Amendment as a handy device to
keep unruly state legislatures in line. And as early as 1873,
the Court first listened, and almost succumbed, to this
functionally straightforward if legally tortuous argument.
The Louisiana legislature, probably bribed, had awarded
to one company a complete twenty-five-year monopoly of
all the slaughterhouse business in New Orleans—a move
made supposedly, and in part actually, as a health measure.
Competing slaughterhouse operators, faced with financial

ruin, hired former Supreme Court Justice Campbell to plead that they had been "deprived of property without due process of law" (and other things). Although the Court rejected this plea and resuscitated Taney's old concept of "state police power" to uphold Louisiana, it did so by a slim 5–4 margin. An entering wedge had been made and the wedge was wide.

But trenchant Justice Miller, speaking for the Court majority, produced perhaps the finest and certainly the most important opinion of his admirable twenty-eight-year career on the high bench. Like John Marshall, Miller had enjoyed very little formal legal training; indeed, he had been for years a practicing physician before he turned to the law. Like Marshall too, he had the practical capacity to cut through jungles of verbal legalism and hit a case or an issue in the jugular. Unlike Marshall, he did not consider the defense of private property rights as the prime duty of government or of the judiciary; one brief biographical sketch capsules him as "more concerned with the welfare of society as a whole than with the protection of vested property interests." Now, Miller, looking backward to the sources of the three post-Civil War Amendments, stated that "no one can fail to be impressed with the one pervading purpose found in them all, lying at the foundation of each, and without which none of them would have been even suggested; we mean the freedom of the slave race, the security and firm establishment of that freedom, and the protection of the newly-made freeman and citizen. . . ." Looking ahead, more prophetically than he knew, he warned that judicial acceptance of the newly proposed and far broader interpretation of the Fourteenth

Amendment "would constitute this Court a perpetual censor upon all legislation of the states. . . ." Despite Miller's historically accurate, humanitarian, and yet hard-
headed view of what the Amendment did and did not—or
should and should not—mean, four of Miller's fellows, including Chase, disagreed and dissented.

Within a matter of weeks after the slaughterhouse decision, death came to Chase, the most hapless Chief Justice
of them all—he who had been eclipsed on his own Court,
not only by Miller but by Davis and Field and Strong; he
he who had seen the one important majority ruling he ever
wrote, in the first Legal Tender case, overturned and con-
signed to operative oblivion the year after it was written;
he whose hunger for the higher office he coveted in vain
hamstrung and compromised his whole conduct of the high
office he held. Death may not have been unwelcome. But
the irony of events was to make Chase's minority slant in
the slaughterhouse matter the eventual law of the land,
while Justice Miller was to have his masterly majority
opinion, and all that it stood for, discarded by a differently
manned Court in the very year he died.

Even a Congress which, for the most part, coddled and
co-operated with President Grant could not quite stomach
the first two men he nominated to take the place of Chase;
each had little to account for his nomination save close
personal friendship with the President; one had recently
been publicly discredited as a Cabinet member and the
other was aged and also suspected to have been a Copperhead; both nominations, after widespread protest, were
withdrawn. Passing by a wealth of available legal talent,

including especially Justice Miller, who was generally
rated, even by his ideological enemies, as the nation's
finest judicial mind, Grant finally lit on a second-rate railroad lawyer from Ohio named Morrison R. Waite, con-
spicuous only for his inconspicuousness—and the Senate,
with a collective sigh of relief that the choice had not been
affirmatively worse, accepted him. It was under Waite's
Chief Justiceship, if not precisely under his leadership, that
the Court slid slowly away from Miller's humane and
restricted reading of the Fourteenth Amendment and
inched, under the insistent influence of railroad attorneys,
both off and on the bench, toward a broader and more
business-minded view. But before that view took precedence, there came, as a sort of death convulsion, a strong
re-affirmation by the Court of the states' police power to
regulate business, despite the due process clause, in a set
of decisions known as the Granger cases.

The railroads, in their rampant push to the West, had
been growing increasingly corrupt and contemptuous—
buying and bribing state officials, charging shippers uneven
and outrageous rates, counting for legal protection on the
kind of constitutional doctrine laid down by John Marshall
in the Dartmouth College case and others, whereby the
property and the privileges granted by a state to a private
concern were held sacred, as "obligation(s) of contracts,"
no matter by what malodorous means they were obtained.
As the Supreme Court, following the Marshall precedents,
began to uphold these claims to land and franchises, even
though based on proven bribery (which the Court was to
continue to do throughout the century), and as exploitation grew more arrogant and onerous, there had arisen in

the farm belt a political protest group, the forerunners of
the Populist Party. These Grangers had won control of the
governments of several midwestern states, and had passed
laws regulating railroad rates and reducing the charges of
grain warehouses and elevators as well. Immediately and
automatically, the owners of these businesses appealed to
the courts to save them from being deprived of their
property—meaning their considerable profits—without
due process of law. This time the Supreme Court failed
them—but not without planting the seeds of their future
success.

Speaking for an almost unanimous Court, with only
Field, that doughty defender of scot-free enterprise, dissenting, Chief Justice Waite announced that the businesses
in question were, by their essential nature, "clothed with a
public interest"—like ferries and stagecoaches and bakers
and millers under ancient English law—and that the prices
they charged could therefore be regulated as a proper
exercise of state police power. "For protection against
abuses by Legislatures, the people must resort to the
polls, not to the Courts." But by implication, might there
not be resort to the courts if a state tried to regulate a
business *not* "clothed with a public interest"? By implication, might not the due process clause then, and perhaps in
other instances, be used as a constitutional weapon to
strike down an offensive state law—since Waite had not,
as he might have, summarily dismissed the Granger cases
as based on a misconception of the meaning of the Fourteenth Amendment? Might not the hint of Waite be
coupled with the slant of Field—in contradistinction to
Miller's contemporaneously stated insistence that all "due

process of law" required was "a fair trial in a court of
justice"—to veto whatever regulations of business the
Court might choose to veto, especially if the Court's personnel should change?

Within five years of the 1877 Granger decisions, four
Justices, all of them members of the majority that upheld
the Granger laws, resigned or died. To replace them,
Presidents Hayes, Garfield, and Arthur appointed three
quite undistinguished but politically "right" legal per-
sonages named Woods (a carpetbag politician-turned-
judge from Georgia), Matthews (an Ohio railroad lawyer
whom the Senate finally confirmed by the margin of one
vote on his second try), and Blatchford (a reactionary
railroad-lawyer-turned-judge from New York)—plus one
conventionally deserving legal choice, Chief Justice Horace
Gray of the Massachusetts Supreme Court, as distinguished
for his personal wealth as for his precedent-bound judicial
orthodoxy and destined, in his twenty-year career on the
federal bench, to write but one memorable opinion (which
upheld, in the spirit of the eighteenth century's discredited
Alien Act and the twentieth century's controversial Mc-
Carran Act, the unlimited right of the U.S. government to
deport any aliens it pleased—and which even drew an acid
dissent from so firm an anti-liberal as Justice Field).

Thus reconstituted, the Court soon gutted the Granger
decisions by holding that a state could only regulate railroad rates for trips entirely within its own borders, since
the Constitution's interstate commerce clause (not, here,
the due process clause) gave control of all state-to-state
transportation exclusively to Congress. (Of course, no
such federal control was then being exercised; the Inter-

state Commerce Act had not yet been passed.) And an
astute cynic might well have commented that the Court's
switch on state regulation of railroad rates between 1877
and 1886 could be largely laid, no matter which constitutional clause was called in question, to the immediate
practical impact on the roads of each decision in its turn
and in its time. For in 1877, when the Justices sustained the
Grangers, rates had recently fallen so low, as an aftermath
of the panic of 1873, that the ruling did not, right then,
hurt the railroads at all; by 1886, rates were up again and
only the Granger laws were keeping them from going still
higher, so that the new ruling was a real financial boon.
Yet this explanation, however neat and plausible, inaccurately implies that the Court is a sort of continuing
unity, an integrated single force, instead of an ever changing group of men. They were a different group of men in
1886 than they were in 1877. And, although the interstate
commerce clause was their *technical* device for protecting
the railroads from regulation in 1886, the soon-to-come
perversion of the due process clause too to judicial defense
of *laissez faire*, in prosperity or depression, was telegraphed
by the politico-legal temper of the Court's new and business-minded members.

Meanwhile, the Justices had been busily perverting the
plain intent of the Fourteenth Amendment—and the
Fifteenth too—in another and even more indefensible
fashion. Through the 1860's and 1870's, Congress had
passed a series of laws designed to put teeth in the otherwise empty words of the post-War Amendments, by im-
posing criminal penalties on anybody who deprived the
Negroes of any personal or political rights, including "the

equal protection of the laws," which the Amendments were supposed to guarantee. Then, through the 1870's and 1880's, the Court imperiously and impatiently swept aside almost all of these so-called Civil Rights Acts, either by flatly branding them unconstitutional—no matter that the Constitution had been amended precisely to achieve what these laws were aimed to achieve—or by using legalistic chop-logic to "interpret" them out of effective existence. A federal statute that made it a crime for any state official to stop citizens from voting was vetoed by the Court as too far-reaching, and hence an improper invasion of states' rights—since the Fifteenth Amendment only forbids the states to stop people from voting "on account of race, color, or previous condition of servitude." (Actually, the statute did use the phrase, "on account of race and color," so the Court, by a weird contortion of words, had to hold that the statute meant more than it said in order to hold that, by meaning that much, by going that far, it was unconstitutional.) In another Negro voting case, the Court refused to let some Louisiana state officials be punished under federal law for their violent maltreatment of Negro would-be voters—simply because of a tiny technical slip in the wording of the indictment. Said the Court, quite straight-faced: "We may suspect that race was the cause of the hostility, but it is not so averred." On a broader and equally callous scale, the Justices gave a green light for the future to the brutality and terrorism of the Ku Klux Klan, by overthrowing a federal statute deliberately meant to curb the Klan—on the ground that the protections and guarantees of the Fourteenth Amendment could be enforced (if at all) only against official state acts, not against the acts of private persons. Amidst this judicial vandalism, one crumb was tossed to the Negroes in the form of a ruling that they could not be kept off juries just because they were Negroes—a ruling so obviously abstract and futile, in the light of Southern practices, that no effort was made by the Court to give it real effect for over fifty years.

Most important of all this group of cases, in its long-term effect on the Negroes' way of life in the South, was the decision that ditched, as unconstitutional, a congressional law that made it a crime for anyone to deny a Negro the same treatment accorded a white man in hotel or inn, restaurant or theater, or any public vehicle of transportation, whether horsecar, coach, ferry, or railroad—again on the ground that the Fourteenth Amendment had no force whatever to control the acts of non-official citizens. In eloquent, plain-spoken protest against the bland legalisms of his brethren, the Court's lone dissenter said: "I cannot resist the conclusion that the substance and spirit of the recent Amendments of the Constitution have been sacrificed by a subtle and ingenious verbal criticism. . . . Constitutional provisions adopted in the interest of liberty . . . have been so construed as to defeat the ends the people desired to accomplish, which they attempted to accomplish, and which they supposed they had accomplished by changes in their fundamental law." Broadening his protest to take in the whole fabric of judicial review, he went on: "The judiciary may not, with safety to our institutions, enter the domain of legislative discretion. . . . That would be sheer usurpation . . . which, if often repeated, and permanently acquiesced in, would work a radical change in our system of government."

The author of these wise but unhappily wasted words was a former slave-owner from Kentucky and grandfather of the present Justice who bears his name, John Marshall Harlan. Appointed by President Hayes—strictly out of political gratitude for his having swung the key Kentucky delegation from Blaine to Hayes at the 1876 Republican convention—Harlan had little in his past career to commend him, then aged forty-four, for so high a post. Like Marshall's and Miller's, his legal education had been meager; an unsuccessful office-seeker, he had run twice for the governorship of his state, and lost twice; his switch of allegiance from Democrats to Republicans, not long before, seemed to indicate an unstable political character. Yet what looked like instability was soon revealed to be a rugged independence of thought as Harlan proceeded to carve his name large on the small roster of really great Justices. For thirty-four years and under three Court Chiefs, consistent in his earth-rooted liberalism if not always in the airier niceties of legal logic, he waged a sniper's war that rolled up more than three hundred dissents against the monolithic drive of most of his colleagues to capture the Constitution for unbridled conservatism, for a political philosophy based—in the words of that illustrious contemporary attorney, Joseph H. Choate—on a belief that "the preservation of the rights of private property is the very keystone of the arch upon which all civilized government rests."

No dissenter from this philosophy, but rather one who rode it throughout his pre-Court and Court careers, was the second Chief Justice under whom Harlan served. At Waite's death in 1888, President Cleveland put in his place another man practically unknown to the country at

large at his appointment and, despite his twenty-two years
at the head of the nation's judiciary, practically unknown to
history, even legal history, today. Melville W. Fuller, a
Chicago corporation lawyer who had counted among his
clients Marshall Field, Philip Armour, and the Chicago,
Burlington, and Quincy Railroad, and who owed his elevation to the accidental fact that, despite having been born
in Maine, he was a Democrat, made no substantial contribution, except his predictably pro-business votes, to the
Court over which he presided, and wrote no memorable
opinions save two—his slipshod emasculation, in the
Knight case, of the Sherman Anti-Trust Act, and his
clumsy killing of the income tax in the Pollock case.

   Far more influential on the Fuller Court than its Chief
was David Brewer of Kansas—nephew and idolator of
Justice Field—who got his own Justiceship one year after
Fuller, who in effect gave Field two votes on the Court
while Field lived, and who faithfully followed his uncle's
Choate-like philosophy after Field died. Like Rufus Peckham of New York—who was soon to join him on the Court
and share with him its effective leadership, in Fuller's
default—Brewer, as a lower court judge, had presumptu-
ously refused to be guided in his own decisions by the
Supreme Court's ruling in the Granger cases which upheld
state regulation of railroads and other businesses. He had
barely taken his seat on the high bench—and Justice Miller, long-time guardian of the principle of no judicial interference with state regulation of business, had just died—
when the Supreme Court itself, quite differently manned
than thirteen years earlier, gave the *coup de grace* to the
Granger cases and opened the gate to unlimited judicial

supervision of state laws under the aegis of the Fourteenth Amendment.

It is unimportant that this crucial case arose in Minnesota, where a railroad protested to the courts against having its rates regulated by a state commission set up by the state legislature. It is important only that a majority of the Justices ordered that any such regulation must always be subject to court review to make sure that the required rates were "reasonable," because any rates that a court might deem "unreasonable" would *therefore* be unconstitutional as well, in depriving the railroad—or any other regulated business—of its property without due process of law. As Justice Bradley, certainly no Granger, no Populist, no business-baiter, exclaimed in his dour dissent, "the decision of the court in this case . . . practically overrules [the Granger decisions]. The governing principle of those cases was that the regulation and settlement of the fares of railroads and other public accommodations is a legislative prerogative and not a judicial one. This is a principle which I regard as of great importance. . . . All human institutions are imperfect—courts as well as commissions and legislatures." But the bars were down now; in the next thirty years almost one-third of the cases heard by the Court, or roughly seven hundred cases, stemmed, at the Justices' open invitation, from claims that this state law or that ran counter to the due process clause of the forgotten Negroes' Fourteenth Amendment.

Having tasted power such as even Marshall never knew, having regained the institutional self-assurance that soured at the end of Taney's tenure and was badly battered right after the Civil War, the Justices were not to be denied. The biggest single year in all Court history, seen in the light of governmental dominance, of putting into practice the undemocratic theory that judges know best, was 1895. Three disparate but deeply intertwined decisions made their mark on the nation and the pattern of its laws; and one of them dealt directly with the most dynamic force— now for good, now for evil—of the latter part of the century: the railroads.

This was the Debs case, in which the railroads—now more plagued by their newly unionized employees, out for higher wages, than by their farmer-customers, out for lower rates—got a compliant federal district judge in Chicago to issue a shotgun injunction which, in effect, ordered the head of the Railway Union, former locomotive fireman Eugene V. Debs, to call off the Pullman strike or go to jail. It was not the injunction but federal troops, unnecessarily (there had been no violence) ordered in over Illinois Governor Altgeld's protest, that broke the strike; Debs, summarily sentenced to prison for contempt of court, appealed to the Supreme Court to release him; the Chicago judge had not granted him a jury trial, such as the Constitution seemed to require, and had acted without authorization from any law passed by Congress. Neither of these latter details bothered Justice Brewer, who, speaking for the Court in a manner to make his uncle proud, proclaimed for the federal judiciary the right to send men to jail, however arbitrarily, without benefit of jury, and the right to protect interstate commerce from interference, however peaceful, without benefit of legislation. The immediate results of the Debs decision were to turn the political wrath of organized labor plus its sympathizers against judges in general and the Supreme Court in particular, and to turn Eugene V. Debs into a militant Socialist —which, as is rarely realized, he had never been before. The chief long-term result was to make of federal labor injunctions, here given the highest possible benediction, the favorite and most widely abused weapon, for thirty-odd years (until the Norris-La Guardia Anti-Injunction Act put a stop to their abuse), of employers dealing with recalcitrant labor unions.

If the nation's economic health could be protected by court order from strikes by workingmen, even in the absence of statute, it could nevertheless not be protected by court order from business monopolies, even in the presence of a pointed statute. Such, at least, was the purport of another of the Justices' Big Three 1895 decisions—in the Knight case, where Chief Justice Fuller wrote one of his two notable, though less than admirable, Court opinions. The Sherman Anti-Trust Act, only five years old, carried the high hopes of the people and their Congress that it would serve as a legal sword to cut down or cut apart the more arrogantly anti-social of the growing group of industrial monopolies and trusts that were ingesting, octopus-like, a large chunk of the American economy. Involved in the Knight case, first real test of the new law, was the sugar trust; there was no doubt about the fact, which Fuller conceded, that by buying up the stock of four other companies "the American Sugar Refining Company acquired nearly complete control of the manufacture of refined sugar within the United States." However, Fuller continued—in a classic legalism that was to echo significantly through the Supreme Court reports for almost fifty years—there is a vital distinction between manufacture and "commerce"; Congress, under the Constitution, may only regulate commerce, not manufacture; hence the sugar trust, a manufacturing monopoly, may continue on its merry and profitable way, untouched and untouchable by the Sherman Act. As effectively as if the Act had been declared unconstitutional, which it was not, judicial operation had rendered it at least temporarily impotent.

Yet, of the 1895 trio of judiciary-triumphant decisions, the most audacious in its disregard of democratic government, and the most arbitrary for its lack of any basis in law, in logic, or in constitutional history, was the Pollock decision, which throttled the federal income tax until the slow process of constitutional amendment brought it back to life eighteen years later. To detail the devious processes of legalistic argumentation by which, first, a small segment of the tax was said to be banned by the Founding Fathers' edict that "direct taxes" (a phrase so ambiguous that the Fathers, in Convention assembled, could not themselves define it) had to be "apportioned"—and then the whole dog followed its tail backward into the ashcan of unconstitutionality—would be as tedious as it would be wide of the mark. This was not law, in any scholarly sense of the word, that five of the Justices laid down; their judgment was purely, or rather impurely, political. Lawyer Choate put the whole business in honest perspective when, pleading against the tax, he warned his audience of nine that the "Communist march" must be stopped and that it must be stopped "now or never." Chief Justice Fuller, in his opinion for the Court, took up the same tune, if pianissimo, in a sneering reference to "the speculative views of political economists or revenue reformers." And Justice Field,

concurring a little louder, cautioned that "the present assault upon capital is but the beginning." Remarks like
these from the bar and the bench, regardless of whether or
not their ominousness was warranted, scarcely required or
rested on legal wisdom—and gave the pseudo-legal show
away.

Hence the four dissenting Justices, each one separately,
sharply denounced their colleagues' economic overlordship
for what it really was and called it utterly unjustified by
law. One described the decision, accurately, as "a judicial
amendment of the Constitution." Another protested that it
"dislocates—principally for reasons of an economic nature
—a sovereign power expressly granted to the general government." Said a third: "The decision involves nothing
less than a surrender of the taxing power to the moneyed
class. . . . Even the spectre of socialism is conjured up to
frighten Congress from laying taxes upon the people in
proportion to their ability to pay them." And the fourth—
Howell Jackson of Tennessee, who had just recently come
to the Court and who unfortunately died shortly after—
expostulated: "This decision is, in my judgment, the most
disastrous blow ever struck at the constitutional power of
Congress." But none of these bootless rebukes allayed the
jubilance of "the moneyed class" and their editorial
spokesmen of the press. "The wave of the socialist revolution had gone far," exulted the New York *Sun*, "but it
breaks at the foot of the ultimate bulwark set up for the
protection of our liberties." And then, with a whiff of un-
witting humor: "Five to four, the Court stands like a
rock."

Within the couple of years after their 1895 triple victory, the Justices added a few further flourishes to their now blatant dominance of the nation's dual (state and federal) scheme of government. In a case severely limiting the effective power of the Interstate Commerce Commission, they embarked on a slow suffocation-by-"interpretation" of the Interstate Commerce Act—the law passed, under political pressure from farmers and small businessmen, to control on a national level the money-making shenanigans of the railroads, right after the Court had taken such control away from the states. This left the control nowhere—or rather, left it in the hands of the railroads themselves. In a case that finally engraved on the law of the land for decades to come the full perversion of the Fourteenth Amendment to business use, as urged by Justice Field in lone dissent from the Granger decisions twenty years before, the Justices jettisoned a Louisiana statute regulating insurance companies, and did it on the ground that the due process clause protected businessmen's "freedom of contract"—their right to make any deals they pleased—from meddlesome state interference. (Despite a slight backtracking by the Justices the next year—when they let Utah limit miners' working hours to eight a day as a health measure, with that dauntless duo, Brewer and Peckham, dissenting—"freedom of contract" soon became, in a profusion of decisions, the one kind of "liberty" most jealously guarded by the Court under the Constitution.)

The Justices also turned their attention once more to the neglected Negroes, who were now protesting, under the Fourteenth Amendment's guarantee of "equal protection" for everybody, against the Jim Crow laws of the South.

There was no doubt that these laws were official state actions, not the actions of private persons. But in the case of Plessy *v.* Ferguson, the Justices dreamed up and declared their famous, or infamous, "separate but equal" doctrine in defense of segregation. That the South, as was plainly to be expected, latched onto the "separate" and laughed off the "equal" did not bother the Court into discarding its impractical principle until almost sixty years after. One small bright spot in the late 1890's—and one of the three meaningful times in its history when the Court has defied Congress in behalf of civil liberties—came when the Justices overruled a federal statute in order to grant the protections of part of the Bill of Rights, such as trial by jury, to aliens, who thus fared better judicially in this period than did Negroes or union members, albeit these latter groups were citizens.

The century was now drawing toward its close. For the Supreme Court, it had been a century of fabulous fluctuations in the Court's fortunes, its power, its prestige. Judicial supremacy, hard-won and hard-held under Marshall, had been used, then abused and lost under Taney. No man, no two or three or four men, had won it back, but rather a jumble of ever changing, often clashing Justices—some weak, some strong, some stupid, some wise—with never a captain capable of ordering his crew. As the years after the Civil War had been for the nation years of awkward, adolescent growth and of adventurous, uninhibited expansion, territorial and industrial, so too they had been anti-government, don't-hold-us-down years. And it was this anti-government, free-of-all-fetters political feeling (it was scarcely a philosophy) that the Court first learned to ride and then to direct.

As the nation slid into the twentieth century, its eyes were shifted for a time away from internal affairs and toward the Spanish-American War, the most blatant U.S. experiment in imperialism. During this interval, few cases of any import came before the Court (save a couple dealing —and dealing imperiously—with the legal and political status of newly won Puerto Rico and the Philippines). Lolling easily in the governmental driver's seat, ready to call and take the turns as need should arise, the Court idled along, waiting.

Then, shortly after the turn of the century, an event took place that was destined to shake the Court out of its comparative complacence and give it, whether it heeded or not, a vocal conscience more eloquent than any it had known before. Theodore Roosevelt named to the bench, to replace pedestrian Justice Gray, a wise and witty sixty-one-year-old Boston Brahmin who then headed the highest court of Massachusetts and was soon to become, in the popular mind, the perennial prototype of the genus Justice—Oliver Wendell Holmes. Holmes in no sense, except intellectually, ever effectively led the Court he graced; if he had, he could scarce have been dubbed "the great dissenter." Yet everything significant the Court did while Holmes was on it is better illumined and understood—as a dark object is reflected, even though backward, in a bright mirror—if seen in the light of the Holmes dissents over almost three decades.

CHAPTER 6

Associate Justice Holmes, Dissenting

ONLY A HANDFUL OF MEN in all U.S. history have made with their minds so manifest a mark on their own age and on ages still to come as did Justice Holmes. Benjamin Franklin probably, Thomas Jefferson surely, John Marshall possibly, and after him Abraham Lincoln—and the list is closed. Serving always as an Associate Justice, under four Court Chiefs—Fuller, White, Taft, and Hughes—he was commonly called, with a sort of astute inaccuracy, Chief Justice Holmes. But not till fastidiously fictionalized, after his death, as the Yankee from Olympus (that retreat of the gods, remote, as Holmes never was, from the earthy affairs of men) did he become, in memoriam and for popular consumption, a heavenly hero. In life, there was little heavenly about the irreverent agnostic, the twinkling skeptic, the down-to-the-ground judicial realist, of whom legal historian Walton Hamilton was later to say: "It has taken a decade to elevate Mr. Justice Holmes from deity to mortality." There was little heavenly, that is, save the almighty power of his mind to cut through legal humbug (his favorite sneer-word) to clean common sense—and the almost godlike tolerance of other men's ideas, however idiotic they might seem to him, that became the byword of his dissenting blasts at his more benighted brethren and gave to the Court and the nation a fresh, new breath of freedom and a deeper faith in democracy, aflaunt and un-afraid.

To label Holmes a "liberal," as he is universally labeled, is not to say that he was liberal in the current leftward-leaning connotation of the world. A stanch and solid Back Bay Republican from the time he fought for the Union and was wounded in the Civil War until, in the last five Presidential elections of his ninety-four-year life, he favored Hughes (over Wilson), Harding, Coolidge, Hoover, and Hoover again (over Franklin Roosevelt)—Holmes, in his personal politics, was a conservative. Almost by instinct (reinforced by environment) he tended to mistrust Democrats, and he brushed aside socialist talk and writing as "drool." Yet his passionate respect for the right of others to think differently than he did—that respect on which all of democracy is ultimately based—led him always to question even his fondest preferences and made him, in the truest sense, an *intellectual* liberal. His homage to human dignity (which he so effortlessly personified) made him, in defense of men's minds and persons, a *libertarian* liberal.

The two together, especially in contrast to the autocracy-grown-arrogant of most of his fellow Justices, made Holmes—for all his own political conservatism—the greatest *judicial* liberal the court had known.

This judicial liberalism found its chief targets, during Holmes's long span on the Supreme Court, in three different kinds of judicial illiberalism; indeed, the Court's record as a political power, throughout the first third of this century, can be written largely in terms of these three kinds of cases, where a majority of the Justices—not always but far too often—threw their we-have-the-last-word weight squarely against the brand of liberalism that Holmes believed in. One kind of case—and one that took up so much of the Justices' time that the Court's work fell as far as three years behind—was, of course, the complaint, coming in a flood, that some state law, using a new wrinkle to regulate business or tax wealth, was forbidden by the Fourteenth Amendment. A second and similar kind was the claim that some new *federal* tax or regulation, some law passed by Congress, was unconstitutional; and here there were two separate legal hooks on which the claim could be hung—either the due process clause of the *Fifth* Amendment, recently perverted like its younger brother to the protection of capital instead of the protection of criminals, or else a states'-rights sort of argument that something Congress had done went beyond what Congress had power to do by way of regulating interstate commerce. The third kind of case dealt with civil liberties, such as freedom of speech or freedom of the press, when some law, whether state or federal, threatened to cut them down.

To his colleagues' solicitude for property rights (in the first two kinds of case) and their indifference to more personal rights (in the third), Holmes, over the years, made multiple and always eloquent answer. Even when couched in legal terms to hit the precise point at issue, those answers weave tightly together into an all-of-a-piece philosophy of law. In the first kind of case, he once said, naturally in dissent: "There is nothing that I more deprecate than the use of the Fourteenth Amendment beyond the absolute compulsion of its words to prevent the making of social experiments that an important part of the community desires, in the insulated chambers afforded by the several States, even though the experiments may seem futile or even noxious to me and to those whose judgment I most respect."

Dissenting against the Court's veto of a Congressional law (on minimum wages) in the second kind of case, Holmes got more specific: "In the present instance the only objection that can be urged is found within the vague contours of the Fifth Amendment, prohibiting the depriving of any person of liberty or property without due process of law. . . . The earlier decisions upon the same words in the Fourteenth Amendment began within our memory and went no farther than an unpretentious assertion of the liberty to follow the ordinary callings. Later that innocuous generality was expanded into the dogma, Liberty of Contract. Contract is not specially mentioned in the text that we have to construe. It is merely an example of doing what you want to do, embodied in the word liberty. But pretty much all law consists in forbidding men to do some things that they want to do, and contract is no more exempt from law than other acts." (Holmes's last words here were more wishful than accurate since, by the decisions of his brethren, in this and other cases, contract *was*, in fact, "more exempt.")

And when the attack on a Congressional law (this one restricting child labor) was hung, not on the Fifth Amendment's due process clause, but on a claimed overextension of Congress's control of interstate commerce so as to butt into the field of states' rights, Holmes roared, again in dissent: "If an act is within the powers specifically conferred upon Congress, it seems to me that it is not made any less constitutional because of the indirect effects that it may have. . . . Congress is given power to regulate [interstate] commerce in unqualified terms. . . . This Act does not meddle with anything belonging to the States. They may regulate their internal affairs and their domestic commerce as they like. But when they seek to send their products across the state line, they are no longer within their rights. . . . It seems to me entirely constitutional for Congress to enforce its understanding [of 'the national welfare'] by all the means at its command."

In situations like these, where ambiguous constitutional language was being stretched by his fellow Justices into a legal excuse to lord it over legislatures, out of a coddling concern for unfettered freedom-of-enterprise, Holmes's liberalism led him to defend the legislative will —even though, as a legislator himself, he might have voted against the very law that, as a judge, he fought to have upheld. Not so in the third kind of case, where civil liberties were involved and constitutional language was usually less obscure—as in the First Amendment's flat: "Congress shall make no law . . . abridging the freedom of speech or of the press. . . ." Here, Holmes would not have hesitated, as did his colleagues, to wield judicial supremacy in behalf of the personal rights of the unpopular and the persecuted. Perhaps the most famous of all his singing sentences were among those penned in protest against that part of the first World War's Espionage Act which made almost any kind of critical or nonconformist political expression a federal crime:

"But when men have realized that time has upset many fighting faiths, they may come to believe even more than they believe the very foundations of their own conduct that the ultimate good desired is better reached by free trade in ideas—that the best test of truth is the power of the thought to get itself accepted in the competition of the market, and that truth is the only ground upon which their wishes safely can be carried out. That at any rate is the theory of our Constitution. It is an experiment, as all life is an experiment. Every year if not every day we have to wager our salvation upon some prophecy based upon imperfect knowledge." Yet the moral courage and the intellectual humility of Holmes, emblazoned brilliant in these words, were rarely sufficient—and were not enough in this instance—to win a majority of the Justices to his cause. Only after his death were some, not all, of his dissenting essays and epigrams gradually turned, by judicial acceptance, into constitutional doctrine. It was rather as a critic than an actor, as a prophet than a present leader, that he made an indelible mark on the political law of his own time.

For the political law of Holmes's time was, with a few brief lapses and interludes, merely a more concentrated continuation of the let-business-alone-and-let-it-run-the-country jurisprudence that had come to full flower late in the preceding century. Theodore Roosevelt with his trust-busting crusade against the "malefactors of great wealth," and Woodrow Wilson with his New Freedom reforms might occupy the White House in between McKinley and Taft and Harding and Coolidge; they might get their progressive programs enacted into law; they might even name a few Justices less property-minded and business-dedicated to the Supreme Court. But there were never enough such Justices on the Court at any one time to change significantly its spots or its decisions. As state and federal governments stepped up their legislative efforts to control snowballing wealth and financial power for the welfare of all their constituents, the Court stepped up its use of the stop-sign, "Unconstitutional"; more federal statutes were branded void during Holmes's Justiceship—most of the important ones over his dissent—than during the 112 preceding years of the Court's existence; state laws went down the judicial drain by the hundreds. And this quantitative quickening of pace in their urge to exercise their government supremacy revealed how far the Justices were lagging once more behind the political temper of most of the nation.

Holmes saw quite clearly how his intransigent associates were steering the country toward a sort of anarchy by judicial decree. Let a state try to curb the self-serving excesses of big-and-growing-bigger business in the interest of workers or customers—and hence at the expense of investors and entrepreneurs—and the Fourteenth Amendment's due process clause would likely be flashed as a red light to regulation, a green light to business. But let the central government at Washington try the same sort of curb on a nationwide scale, and the bulk of business, judicially divorced from interstate commerce and hence from all Congressional control, would suddenly become the private and exclusive stamping-ground of *state* regulation, although such regulation was largely imaginary, being forbidden by the Justices under the Fourteenth Amendment. In this Court-created vacuum from almost all government restriction, this open invitation to a money-making mazurka, the kings and captains of industry and finance moved with loose-limbed abandon all the way from McKinley's "full dinner-pail" to Hoover's "two cars in every garage." And should any skeptical spokesman for those whose dinner-pails or garages somehow remained empty raise his voice too high in protest, he might be slapped in jail—for all his supposed civil liberties—with the passive, or sometimes active, approval of the Justices. Holmes, as politically conservative, as economically upper-class, as any of his fellows, could coin out of his wisdom-lighted-by-wit such *bon mots* as: "The Fourteenth Amendment does not enact Mr. Herbert Spencer's Social Statics." He could make such subversive statements as: "I do not think the United States would come to an end if we lost our power to declare an Act of Congress void." Yet, a constant majority of his colleagues continued to vote him down.

Those colleagues, when Holmes first came to the Court, were feckless Chief Justice Fuller; hard-hitting John

Harlan, growing a little less liberal with age; Brewer and
Peckham, the tough-minded twins of ultra-conservatism;
verbose but able Edward D. White of Louisiana, former
sugar-planter and U.S. Senator, who was later to be
elevated to the Court Chiefship; and three onetime railroad lawyers (along with Fuller)—Henry Brown of
Michigan, George Shiras of Pennsylvania, and Joseph
McKenna of California—of whom Shiras remained undistinguished and still a railroad lawyer throughout his term
on the bench, McKenna was to become a sporadic spokesman against vested property interests under Holmes's
tutelage, and only Brown ever flashed with any judicial
fire, as in his searing dissent against the income tax decision. When Holmes quit the bench in 1932, at the age of
ninety-one, his teammates were Chief Justice Hughes and
Hughes's fellow switch-hitter, Owen Roberts; the close-
playing conservative infield of Van Devanter, McReynolds,
Sutherland and Butler; and Holmes's two cronies in
dissent, Brandeis and Stone. During his not quite thirty-
year tenure, Holmes outlasted seven other Justices—including a Chief Justice, Taft—who were appointed after
him. Thus twenty-three men shared at different times—on
the bench, around the conference table, in chambers, or at
home—the searching sweep and the clean thrust of his
mind. Yet rarely did more than three of them at once, and
usually only one or two, go along with Holmes on the big
issues. For no more than any government group do most
Justices bow to reason when politics points the other way.

The chronological story of the Court from 1902 to 1932
—while his colleagues were too regularly ignoring the

sweet reason of Justice Holmes—can be quickly told. During the last eight years of Fuller's technical Chiefship, the Court remained a citadel of economic conservatism— so much so that one unusual liberal ruling, allowing a state to limit women's working time on factory jobs to ten hours a day despite the dear old due process clause, came as a shocking surprise. Then, after Fuller was succeeded in 1910 by White, the Louisianan with the "rodomontade writing style," and the first man ever promoted from Associate Justice to Chief, the Court relaxed for six or seven years its *laissez faire* rigidity (a paradox of phrase but not of fact) until America entered the first World War. That this comparatively liberal inter- lude almost precisely coincided with the first of Charles Evans Hughes's two terms of service on the high bench was not entirely coincidental; Hughes was then fresh from the New York governorship that he had won from William Randolph Hearst, largely as an electoral reward for his exposure of insurance frauds and rackets in his state; until he resigned his Justiceship in 1916 to seek—and almost win—the Presidency, the better balance of the Court was witnessed by the temporary wane in Holmes's significant dissents.

Back to reactionary regularity went the Court even before the war was over and the typical postwar period of do-nothing (except sit on civil liberties) normality had set in. At White's death in 1921, President Harding played it straight and safe by appointing William Howard Taft of Ohio and, more recently, Connecticut—who thus became unique in U.S. history as the only person who ever served the nation in its two top posts, President and Chief Justice.

Physically the biggest man who ever held either job, easy-going Taft could at least compete, on his dual record, for the smallest accomplishment in both. Presumably he preferred the Chief Justiceship; as President he had once burbled: "I love judges and I love courts. They are my ideals on earth of what we shall meet afterward in Heaven under a just God." But regardless of this beatific personal feeling on the part of its Chief, the Taft Court was so anachronistic in its attitude toward law and government that Holmes was again led to step up the tempo of his bubble-bursting dissents until Taft died in 1930. Then an older, less legally limber Hughes came back to the Court, this time as Chief Justice—after a long interval of lucrative corporation law practice and over the anti-confirmation protest of twenty-six Senators, led by Borah, La Follette, and Norris. Holmes gave vent to a couple of dissenting swan-songs (including his "hardly any limit but the sky" crack against judicial veto of state laws under the Fourteenth Amendment) and soon resigned.

The only Justices other than Taft and Hughes (on his first run) worth passing mention, who both came and went while Holmes was dignifying the Court he never headed, were four in number. William Rufus Day of Ohio, appointed right after Holmes, had been—in triply classic mold—a successful railroad lawyer, a personal friend of a President, and a lower court judge. The friendly President, McKinley, made Day his Secretary of State during the Spanish-American War, and it was Day who decently insisted that the Philippines be bought (for $20,000,000) instead of claimed by conquest; McKinley then put him on the federal bench and Theodore Roosevelt soon raised him to the highest Court; for twenty years as a Justice, Day unspectacularly displayed his business-grown-imperalist background, tempered, in occasional dissent, by personal decency. By contrast to Day and his *noblesse oblige mais reste noblesse* philosophy, there was Mahlon Pitney of New Jersey, who sat with Holmes for ten years and actually dissented, in his unpredictably discordant fashion, more often than Holmes. Earlier known as a stiffly logical anti-labor judge in his home state (the unions bitterly fought his confirmation), he carried to the Court a near-compulsion to have his old decisions in the field of labor law approved by his new and nationally powerful brethren. His success was such, despite a few deviational pro-labor votes (most of his dissents were on rather trivial matters), that he set, for years to come, a hold-them-down Court attitude toward unions—and so raised the issue whether past judicial experience is always an asset in a Justice if that Justice is mainly out to justify his own judicial past. There was also, during Holmes's long tenure, gentle Edward Sanford of Tennessee, so in tune with his genial Chief that Taft could practically cast two votes and that the two men died almost simultaneously. And there was John Clarke of Ohio, whose slight and more than slightly liberal Court service was self-terminated so that he could devote himself to what he deemed the more important cause of world peace—and who, fifteen years after his resignation, as the only ex-Justice then living, emerged briefly from obscurity to publicly support (to the hush-hushing horror of most of the press) Franklin Roosevelt's plan to "pack" the Supreme Court.

But the thirty-year story of the Court under Holmes's
chidance can best be told neither in strict chronological
sequence nor in the specific records of specific Justices
(other than Holmes)—most of whom managed most of the
time to read their business-minded bents into the Constitution whenever the chips were really down. The story can
be more meaningfully told in terms of the three different
kinds of cases where the Justices used constitutional words
to have their own political way. And of the three kinds,
first billing properly goes to the cases where the Court
pushed judicial review to its farthest limit by killing—as
always, more in sorrow than in anger—Acts of Congress.

Most momentous of these judge-made murders of
national laws were five decisions, each of them centered on
some effort by Congress to better the not too happy lot of
workingmen— or of working women or children. A typical
legal mouthful entitled the Federal Employers' Liability
Act would have made a railroad pay for death or injury to a
worker if caused by the railroad's carelessness. There was
no socialistic innovation here, since many states had this
sort of law on their books; but because the Act failed to
specify that only *interstate* railroad workers were to be
protected (Congress can only regulate interstate, not
within-one-state, commerce) five Justices—with Holmes,
of course, captaining the four dissenters—cut down the
entire Act as an unconstitutional trespass by Congress on
states' rights. That Congress soon passed another law,
properly limited in its scope, which the Court upheld four
years later, did not stop the railroads from saving millions
of dollars in the meantime (that being the obvious purpose

of their winning legal gamble)—nor did it do much good for the workers, or their families, who were wounded or killed in the interval between.

In the same year, 1908, when the Court overruled Congress on making the railroads pay for avoidable accidents to their employees, it also forbade Congress to help the railroad workers help themselves. Congress had made it a crime for a railroad to fire a worker for belonging to a union—or to hold a worker to a so-called "yellow-dog contract," in which the worker, anxious for a job, had promised not to join a union. Unconstitutional, said seven Justices—under *both* the interstate commerce clause (Congress was again treading on states'-rights toes) and the Fifth Amendment's due process clause (Congress was interfering with freedom of contract). Strangely, the Court's opinion was penned by that old human-welfare war-horse, Justice Harlan, then nearing the end of a life that began when Andrew Jackson was President, and perhaps unable to fit his old-fashioned agrarian brand of liberalism to the facts of a far more mechanized nation. But Harlan's only-eight-years-younger colleague, Holmes, wryly remonstrated in dissent that he thought labor unions for railway workers had as much to do with interstate commerce as did safety-couplers on trains (about which the Court had recently let Congress legislate). Said Holmes, with his devastating directness: "I quite agree that the question what and how much good labor unions do is one on which intelligent people may differ . . . but I could not pronounce it unwarranted if Congress should decide that to foster a strong union was for the best interest, not only of the men, but of the railroads and the country at large."

It was again in defense of that will-o'-the-wisp, freedom of contract, that the Court struck down, some years later, a Congressional statute setting minimum wages for women workers in the District of Columbia. This law had been supported, in Congress and before the Court, as protective not merely of female health but also of female morals. But five elderly Justices thought, with something less than gallantry, that "the ancient inequality of the sexes . . . has continued 'with diminishing intensity.' In view of the great—not to say revolutionary—changes which have taken place . . . in the contractual, political, and civil status of women, culminating in the Nineteenth Amend- ment, it is not unreasonable to say that these differences have now come almost, if not quite, to the vanishing point." Where a Frenchman might have remarked:— *"Vive les différences,"* the Court's majority continued with unwonted worldliness: "The relation between earnings and morals is not capable of standardization. It cannot be shown that well paid women safeguard their morals more carefully than those who are poorly paid." To which Holmes, less concerned here with the unwisdom of women than with the constitutional unwisdom of his colleagues, tartly replied: "The end, to remove conditions leading to ill health, immorality and the deterioration of the race, no one would deny to be within the scope of constitutional legislation. . . . When so many intelligent persons, who have studied the matter more than any of us can, have thought that the means are effective and are worth the price, it seems to me impossible to deny that the belief *reasonably* may be held by *reasonable* men."

Considerably farther-reaching than its Court-killed attempts to protect railroad workers and Washington women were Congress's two tries at getting rid of child labor throughout the United States. On its first try, Congress simply and flatly forbade the shipment from one state to another of any goods made in a shop or factory where children worked; whereupon the Court—as so often, by a bare five-to-four vote—simply and flatly upheld the exploitation of youth for the sake of fatter profits, on the old excuse that Congress had no right, even under its control of interstate commerce, to interfere obliquely with the right of the states to control (or, more accurately, *not* control) the way goods were manufactured within their borders. A shocked Holmes expostulated in doubly grounded dissent: "But if there is any matter upon which civilized countries have agreed . . . it is the evil of premature and excessive child labor. I should have thought that if we were to introduce our own moral conceptions where in my opinion they do not belong, this was pre-eminently a case for upholding the exercise of all its powers by the United States. But I had thought that . . . this Court always had disavowed the right to intrude its judgment upon questions of policy or morals. It is not for this Court to pronounce when prohibition is necessary to regulation . . . as against the product of ruined lives."

Balked in its first effort to do away with child labor through its control of interstate commerce, Congress tried again—this time by using its power to tax. What it did was to impose on all goods made by the exploited youngsters a federal tax at so high a rate that it would no longer be profitable to employ children, even at the low wages they were usually paid. The gimmick of using the taxing power for something other than raising revenue had been resorted to by Congress before—as in clamping down on the dope racket with a stiff tax on narcotics, and in protecting easily gulled housewives (as well as dairy farmers) with a prohibitive tax on yellow oleomargarine. Moreover, the Court had given these tax tricks official benediction, though the Justices were thoroughly aware that Congress's intent had not been to pour money into the Treasury. Came the child-labor tax and the Court decided, all of a sudden, that taxes could be levied only for revenue, not for regulation in disguise—though a realist might reasonably charge the Justices with somewhat greater concern for the economic welfare of dairy farmers (who far outnumbered the oleomargarine men) than with the physical welfare of children. Not until a New Deal Court, almost twenty years later, upheld the New Deal's Fair Labor Standards Act did the all-powerful Justices permit the nation to move as a nation, toward eliminating the curse of child labor.

In other, less spectacular ways, the Court cut down Congress's taxing power where it was really being used for revenue—and always over Holmes's dissent. A series of 5–4 and 6–3 decisions shortened the reach of the federal estate and gift taxes, in cases where well-advised wealthy men had used lawyers' stratagems, fully foreseen and planned against by Congress, to hand on their fortunes tax-free. Another 5–4 decision—which still plagues the U.S. Treasury today and still determines the dividend policy of thousands of corporations—opened the door to immense, and now legal, avoidance of income taxes, when a company's profits are paid out to stockholders in new stock instead of in cash. (Grumbled Holmes: "I cannot doubt that most people not lawyers would suppose when they voted for [the Sixteenth Amendment] that they put a question like the present to rest.") And in practically all these tax-cutting cases, the Court's slim but stubborn majority could find no more substantial justification for saying "Thou shalt not" to Congress than the Fifth Amendment's now grotesquely bloated due process clause.

But the most flimsily founded of all the Court's anti-tax decisions—and also the one that most clearly revealed how human, and humanly greedy, Supreme Court Justices can be—was the ruling by seven members of the Court that Congress could not, under the Constitution, tax the sala- ries of federal judges, including of course their own. To reach this remarkable result (reversed by a less selfish set of Justices many years later) the Court had to hold that, by making a judge pay an income tax along with everyone else, Congress would be lowering the judge's salary— which the Constitution does forbid. Here Holmes, with Brandeis alone joining in his dissent, could see "no reason for exonerating him from the ordinary duties of a citizen, which he shares with all others. To require a man to pay the taxes that all other men have to pay cannot possibly be made an instrument to attack his independence as a judge. I see nothing in the purpose of this clause of the Constitu- tion to indicate that the judges were to be a privileged class, free from bearing their share of the cost of the institutions upon which their well-being if not their life depends." And Holmes, as did Brandeis, voluntarily paid

as long as he lived the income taxes that his colleagues had
ruled he did not have to pay.

Not only by branding Congressional laws unconstitutional, but also by "interpreting" others into comparative
innocuousness, did the Court, during Holmes's tenure,
serve as bodyguard for wealth undisturbed and business
unbridled. Thus the Sherman Anti-Trust Act, whose teeth
had been mostly pulled in the previous century, was fitted,
for show, with false teeth that turned out to have no bite.
With great fanfare, the Justices stopped the merger of the
Northern Pacific and Great Northern Railroads, and later
broke up—in name though not in effective fact—the
American Tobacco and Standard Oil monopolies. But by
balking at the use of the Act's criminal penalties and by
reading into the statute Justice White's pet "rule of
reason"—whereby only such "restraints of trade" as the
Court thought "unreasonable" were to be forbidden—the
Justices actually invited the big industrial combinations to
continue, just a touch more politely, on their lucrative way.
Labor unions alone, when they tried to use group pressure
on behalf of their members, were really restrained from
"restraining trade," with the Court's hearty approval.

When Congress, in Woodrow Wilson's time, added the
Clayton Act to the government's legal armory against
business abuses—and set up the Federal Trade Commission to stop such shameless shenanigans as secret price-
fixing by supposed competitors, price-cutting to drive
small rivals bankrupt, and the deliberate misleading of the
public with false branding or false advertising—the
Justices gaily began to "interpret" the new Clayton Act
down to the defanged feebleness of the old Sherman Act.

Said the Court in one important case, overturning an F.T.C. ruling and telling the Commission bluntly who was boss: "The words 'unfair methods of competition' are not defined by the statute, and their exact meaning is in dispute. It is for the courts, not the commission, ultimately to determine as a matter of law what they include. . . . The Act was certainly not intended to fetter free and fair competition as commonly understood and practiced by honorable opponents in trade." (In fact, the Act had been precisely "intended to fetter" many of the dog-eat-dog practices considered both "fair" and "honorable" by business in its free-for-all fight for profits.)

But when the Commission turned from trying to protect little dogs from big dogs, and tried instead to protect the sheep-like buying public from all the pack—as Congress also clearly intended—the Justices suddenly saw the Clayton Act as meant only to keep competing businesses from unduly hurting each other, no matter how the public might be fleeced. Thus, in the classic Raladam case, where the Federal Trade Commission had ordered a patent medicine concern to quit fooling the fat with faked-up claims in its get-thin-quick advertising, the Court threw out the Commission's order—and actually did it on the ground that *all* "obesity remedies" were plugged with phony advertising, and hence none of the firm's competitors could be unfairly hurt. (Presumably, the Act was "not intended to fetter free and fair competition" between *dis*honorable "opponents in trade," either.) Just as under the Sherman Act, the only real losers under the Clayton Act as the Court read it (except, of course, the whole consuming public) were the labor unions, who saw an

entire section of the new law—put in for the sole purpose
of protecting peaceful union activities from the over-
eagerly antipathetic orders of federal judges—"interpreted" to nothingness, with Taft, in sorry-but-this-
won't-hurt-too-much manner, performing in person the
major judicial operation.

As with the new Federal Trade Commission, so with the
old Interstate Commerce Commission, especially when
regulation of railroad rates was in the wind; Holmes's
colleagues, determined to have their own economic and
political views prevail, insisted on overseeing and often
overruling the judgments of the technical experts to whom
Congress had entrusted jobs requiring specialized knowledge; marketing or mechanical engineering, statistics or
cost-accounting, whatever the field, the Justices thought
they knew most and best. From the fruit of this assumed
omniscience, Holmes frequently dissented; but his heart
was less with these "interpretation" questions, for all
their sometimes great significance, than with the constitutional cases where power of Court met power of legislature
head-on. No less than when judicial autocracy was aimed at
Congress did Holmes's voice ring in resonant protest when
the solemn acts of state legislatures were treated cavalierly
by his Court. And here it had the chance to ring more
often.

To list in full the scores of instances when Holmes, with
the patient persistence of water dripping on rock, repeated
and rephrased and repeated his steady dissent, against his
colleagues' misuse of the Fourteenth Amendment to veto
state laws that they happened to disapprove, would be to

elaborate—as Holmes was forced to—the obvious. Those
laws ranged from a Nebraska statute fixing a standard
weight for loaves of bread (to protect both buyers and
honest bakers) to a Kansas statute setting up an "Industrial Court" to deal peacefully with wage and price disputes in vital industries, from a New Jersey regulation of
the scandalous fees charged by employment agencies to a
Wisconsin tax to stop the wealthy from giving their
fortunes away tax-free just before they died. And the
regular ritual for overriding some legislature's will was
the magisterial mouthing of those magic words: ". . . deprived of property—or of liberty of contract—without
due process of law."

   Not that every state tax or regulation brought before
the Court was ushered to "unconstitutional" oblivion; the
due process plea was not quite an automatic ticket to
freedom from any tax and from all restraint. During the
Court's comparatively tolerant interlude—which ran from
around the end of Fuller's Chiefship up to the nation's en-
trance into World War I—two important Oregon statutes
limiting hours of labor, first for women, then for men,
were upheld, albeit over strenuous conservative dissent.
In a later case, which significantly did not involve business
interests, Holmes himself spoke for the Court in permitting a state to sterilize congenital idiots—and remarked
with some relish: "Three generations of imbeciles are
enough." But the bulk of the state laws that ran the
Fourteenth Amendment's gauntlet dealt with trivial
matters or else forbade such obviously evil business
practices as cheating coal miners by underweighing the
coal they mined in a day.

Moreover, it is worth recalling here that the Court's power in constitutional cases is basically only the power to say No; when the Court says Yes—in Fourteenth Amendment cases or elsewhere—that fact is noteworthy only because it *might* have said No; for, beyond this, its saying Yes amounts to no more than letting the affirmative branches of government govern. Hence the many instances when Holmes's colleagues did *not* strike down state laws deserve little mention—except as the Justices might have been expected to say No, or came close to saying it. They came close in a couple of cases challenging the due-process propriety of laws passed by two Western states, Washington and Arizona, which set up slightly *avant-garde* schemes to make employers help pay for injuries to their employees; both schemes were upheld by five to four.

And the Arizona case is also notable because one of the due-process dissenters here gave expression, far more frank than discreet, to the kind of sentiments that so often swung a Court majority to their support—and so often elicited dissent, in somewhat less emotional vein, from Holmes. Said Justice McReynolds: "In the last analysis it is for us to determine what is arbitrary or oppressive upon consideration of the natural and inherent principles of practical justice which lie at the base of our traditional jurisprudence and inspirit our Constitution. . . . Until now I had supposed that a man's liberty and property—with their essential incidents—were under the protection of our charter and not subordinate to whims or caprices or fanciful ideas of those who happen for the day to constitute the legislative majority. The contrary doctrine is revolu-

tionary and leads straight toward destruction of our well-
tried and successful system of government." It was about
nothing more than a rather routine but better-than-most
"employers' liability act"—be it remembered—that Mc-
Reynolds waxed so emotional.

By contrast to this sort of near-psychopathic concern for
profits at any cost, including the cost of human limbs or
lives (McReynolds and the rest never thought or suggested
that "legislative majorities," however transient, should
shut up their lawmaking shops entirely), came the cool and
conservative clarity of Holmes. And four of his dissents
against the due process doings of the Peckham-Pitney-
McReynolds clan cry for special mention, and for quota-
tion beyond what has earlier been quoted. Each appeared
in a key case of considerable moment.

Holmes had been on the Court less than three years
when a New York statute, limiting bakers' work-days to
ten hours, came up for review in the Lochner case as the
first real test of maximum-hour laws. For the Court's
majority, Peckham, straight-faced, defended the constitutional right of bakery *employees* to work as many hours as
they might choose—and listed, among the imaginary
horrors that might ensue from upholding the statute, some
future law "prohibiting lawyers' . . . clerks . . . to
labor for their employers more than eight hours a day."
Retorted Holmes: "This case is decided upon an economic
theory which a large part of the country does not entertain. . . . It is settled by various decisions of this court
that state constitutions and state laws may regulate life in
many ways. . . . Some of these laws embody convictions
or prejudices which judges are likely to share. Some may

not. But a constitution . . . is made for people of fundamentally differing views, and the accident of our finding
certain opinions natural and familiar or novel and even
shocking ought not to conclude our judgment upon the
question whether statutes embodying them conflict with
the Constitution of the United States."

In another test case, ten years later, Holmes tore into
his colleagues' veto of a state law, which protected the
right of all workers to join unions in much the same manner
as had the previously Court-vetoed federal statute for
railroad workers: "In present conditions a workman may
not unnaturally believe that only by belonging to a union
can he secure a contract that shall be fair to him. . . . If
that belief, whether right or wrong, may be held by a
reasonable man, it seems to me that it may be enforced by
law in order to establish the equality of position . . . in
which liberty of contract begins. Whether in the long run
it is wise for the working men to enact legislation of this
sort is not my concern, but I am strongly of opinion that
there is nothing in the Constitution of the United States to
prevent it. . . ."

As unions flourished despite the Court's efforts to help
business hamper their growth, business began to appeal
to local judges to prohibit such union activities as strikes
and picketing. Local judges, largely business-minded, com-
plied by issuing those peremptory court orders, called injunctions, which in effect commanded, as some parents do
their children: "Whatever you're doing, don't"—and the
price of disobedience was jail. The unions, in turn, went to
state legislatures to get laws passed which curbed the anti-
labor use of injunctions; and business, in its turn, went of

course to the Supreme Court to get these laws declared
unconstitutional. In the first and definitive case, Holmes
cut, as customary, to the heart of the matter: "The dangers
of a delusive exactness in the application of the Fourteenth
Amendment have been adverted to before now. . . . By
calling a business 'property' you make it seem like land
and lead up to the conclusion that a statute cannot substantially cut down the advantages of ownership existing
before the statute was passed. . . . But you cannot give
[a business] definiteness of contour by calling it a thing.
It is a course of conduct. . . ." And then: "Legislation
may begin where an evil begins. If, as many intelligent
people believe, there is more danger that the injunction
will be abused in labor cases than elsewhere, I can feel no
doubt of the power of the legislature to deny it. . . ." It
goes without saying that Holmes was speaking in dissent.

Though the major Fourteenth Amendment dissents, like
the most important protests against judicial veto of federal
laws, came in cases dealing with workers' rights, Holmes
could be just as trenchant when other types of state statutes
were struck down. Toward the end of his career on the
Court, his brethren, still worrying the word-stuff of
"state police power" and of businesses marked by "public
interest" or "public use," rejected a New York statute
aimed at Broadway ticket-scalpers. It seemed to Holmes
that "theatres are as much devoted to public use as anything well can be." And this despite his regret that: "We
have not that respect for art that is one of the glories of
France." Beyond this personal touch, however, Holmes
keelhauled his colleagues for their niggling manner of
decision, even regardless of result: "We fear to grant

power and are unwilling to recognize it when it exists . . . and when legislatures are held to be authorized to do anything considerably affecting public welfare it is covered by apologetic phrases like the police power, or the statement that the business concerned has been dedicated to a public use. . . . I do not believe in such apologies. I think the proper course is to recognize that a state legislature can do whatever it sees fit to do unless it is restrained by some express prohibition in the Constitution of the United States or of the State, and that Courts should be careful not to extend such prohibitions beyond their obvious meaning by reading into them conceptions of public policy that the particular Court may happen to entertain."

So strong was Holmes's belief in leaving legislatures alone that he once took a stand in their defense which many people consider his most illiberal view and vote. The problem was a tough one, for it pitted state-freedom-to-legislate-without-judicial-veto against a civil liberty of a sort—and hence was not only a due-process question but also one of the third major kind of case that the Court dealt with while Holmes was a Justice. In the anti-German hysteria during and after the first World War (which spawned such absurdities as calling German measles "liberty measles"), a few Midwestern states—where many recently emigrated German families lived—had banned the teaching of German in their grade-schools. When the Court declared these Philistine statutes unconstitutional, as offending the Fourteenth Amendment, Holmes—who would have thundered, as lawmaker, against these inroads on common culture—registered troubled dissent. His dissent was doubtless the more troubled by reason of the fact that McReynolds, scarcely a champion of human rights, was this time the Court's chief spokesman.

But where more important infringements of more clear-cut civil liberties were attempted by governments—national, state, or local—Holmes was almost always found on the side of the angels. He dissented against the Court's refusal to save, by a habeas corpus writ, a radical Northern Jew who had obviously been framed for a murder rap and then convicted by an anti-Semitic lynch jury in the South. (Novels have since been written about the case of Leo Frank.) In defense of a free press, he dissented against the Court's pat-on-the-head for a lower federal judge, who had held a Toledo newspaper in contempt of court because it dared to criticize that judge's own decisions; here, Chief Justice White, with his usual grave longiloquence, saw the "safeguarding and fructification of free and constitutional institutions" as "the very basis and mainstay on which the freedom of the press rests" and so declined to grant the defendant newspaper "the right virtually to destroy such institutions"; to which Holmes replied: "A judge of the United States is expected to be a man of ordinary firmness of character. . . . I confess I cannot find . . . in the evidence in the case anything that would have affected a mind of reasonable fortitude."

Holmes also dissented when a bare majority of his brethren, in three of the silliest rulings the Court ever handed down, barred from U.S. citizenship a well-known woman pacifist (Rosika Schwimmer), a minister who had

been a chaplain in World War I, and a religiously conscientious woman who had served as a nurse in World
War I—because none of the three would take an unqualified
oath to bear arms in any future war. Said Holmes, in one
of these cases: "I would suggest that the Quakers have
done their share to make the country what it is, that many
citizens agree with the applicant's belief, and that I had
not supposed hitherto that we regretted our inability to
expel them because they believe more than some of us do
in the teachings of the Sermon on the Mount."

Again, Holmes dissented on a point even more important today than it was then—the question whether a man
can be convicted of federal crime on evidence obtained by
wire-tapping, despite the Constitution's guarantee of "the
right of the people to be secure in their persons, houses,
papers, and effects [*there were no such things as telephones
when those words were written*], against unreasonable
searches and seizures." In 1928, it was big-time boot-
leggers, not Communist stooges or sympathizers, that the
wire-tapping feds were after—and a five-man Court
majority gave the wire-tappers the nod, with Taft doing
the talking as he read into the Fourth Amendment an
eighteenth-century literalness. ("There was no scarching.
There was no seizure. The evidence was secured by the
sense of hearing. . . .") Holmes felt otherwise: "It is
desirable that criminals should be detected, and to that
end all available evidence should be used. It also is
desirable that the Government should not itself foster and
pay for other crimes. . . . We have to choose, and for my
part I think it a less evil that some criminals should escape

than that the Government should play an ignoble part."
Wire-tapping, said Holmes, was "dirty business"—but
he said it in dissent.

Yet, most crucial of all the civil liberties, in Holmes's
time and long before and since, is freedom of speech—or,
more pointedly, the right of every man to speak his mind
on political matters without being punished by some
government that dislikes what he has to say. Along with
majority rule, and here restricting majority rule, the
government ban against *government* action to shut men's
mouths or minds is one of the cornerstones, the *sine qua
nons*, of the system of government commonly called
"democracy." Outside such totalitarian states as the
Fascist and Communist countries, freedom of speech today
is taken for granted—up to a point; no U.S. Republican
seriously tries to stop or censor Democratic criticism, nor
vice versa; only against the extremists, labeled "dangerous," "destructive," "subversive"—against the Jacobins of 1798 or the Copperheads of 1863 or the anarchists
of 1918 or the Communists of today—do American laws
get passed, on any level of government, that do, in fact,
limit freedom of speech. Yet it is precisely in protecting
the expression of all views, however extreme or unpopular
and no matter how much it may hurt to protect them, that
freedom of speech has a more than mushy meaning. This
nation would not have become a nation had laws against
"dangerous" or "subversive" talk been enforced by the
local henchmen of a British king.

Hence, the eighteenth-century revolutionaries who
wrote the Constitution flatly banned, without one iota of
qualification, any Congressional law "abridging freedom

of speech." But, strange as it may seem, there is not one word in the U.S. Constitution, as written then or as since amended, which says that state or local governments may not abridge freedom of speech. Between these two constitutional extremes, the Court has taken, all on its own, a middle way—allowing Congress, despite the ban, to restrict some freedom of speech, and often forbidding the states to restrict it, despite the absence of any ban. Both these anti-constitutional trends, these clear examples of lawmaking by judges, came to a head during Holmes's tenure—and in both of them Holmes himself played a major part.

Judicial protection of freedom of speech against state laws actually had its source in a decision dealing with freedom of the press (though the two freedoms are political Siamese twins) and *not* protecting it. A New York Communist named Gitlow had published a pamphlet, full of the customary canned exhortations that the "proletariat" throw off their "bonds"—and had been convicted, during the Red scare that followed World War I, of violating New York's "Criminal Anarchy Act." The Supreme Court upheld the conviction despite Holmes's daring riposte in dissent: "If in the long run the beliefs expressed in proletarian dictatorship are destined to be accepted by the dominant forces of the community, the only meaning of free speech is that they should be given their chance and have their way." But the majority Justices, while not here agreeing with Holmes's vote, did express general agreement with his constitutional view when they said: "We may and do assume that freedom of speech and of the press . . . are among the fundamental personal rights

and 'liberties' protected by the due process clause of the
Fourteenth Amendment from impairment by the States."
Approve or disapprove, this judicial use of the due process
clause to protect *human* rights (and it has since been so
used many times) was just as unwarranted by the words of
the Constitution as was its earlier and far more abundant
use to protect *property* rights. To read "liberty of speech"
into the Fourteenth Amendment's "liberty" is quite as
far-fetched a play on words as to read in "liberty of
contract." And it is a mark of Holmes's humanity that,
even at the expense of constitutional consistency, he
encouraged the one after long deploring the other.

It was not humanity, however, that caused Holmes to
join—and even to lead—his fellow Justices in diluting the
strong, straight stuff of the First Amendment, with its
absolute ban on Congressional meddling with freedom of
speech. Holmes's motive here was presumably a com-
promising realism, which the test of time has revealed as a
touch misguided. Indeed, Holmes's famous formula—allowing free speech to be abridged in the face of a "clear and
present danger"—was perhaps his greatest, and only major, judicial error. The pat phrase was first used in a case
where an anti-war extremist, who had urged that young
men dodge the draft, was jailed for thus committing a federal crime. Holmes went along with the whole Court in upholding the conviction, despite the First Amendment—and
may well have done so in order to write the opinion himself and make its grounds as narrow as possible. What
Holmes said was: "The question in every case is whether
the words used are used in such circumstances and are of
such a nature as to create a clear and present danger that

they will bring about the substantive evils that Congress has a right to prevent. It is a question of proximity and degree." (It was no such question to the authors of the First Amendment.) "When a nation is at war," Holmes continued—ignoring an earlier Court's words in the Milligan case, after an earlier war where Holmes was fighting, not judging—"many things that might be said in times of peace are such a hindrance to its effort that their utterance will not be endured so long as men fight and that no court could regard them as protected by any constitutional right."

Little more than a year later, Holmes himself had cause to regret the "clear and present danger"excuse for letting Congress curb freedom of speech, which he had handed his colleagues on the platter of his eloquence. Five ignorant Russian-born pacifists had tossed, off a New York City roof, a few leaflets reprinting the hackneyed phrases of Communist propaganda; the war, at that time, was not quite over; all five, including a girl, were convicted under the federal Espionage Act; three got the maximum sentence. Said Holmes, in deeply disturbed dissent (which also included his "best test of truth" creed): "In this case sentences of twenty years imprisonment have been imposed for the publishing of two leaflets that I believe the defendants had as much right to publish as the Government has to publish the Constitution of the United States now vainly invoked by them. . . . I think that we should be eternally vigilant against attempts to check the expression of opinions that we loathe and believe to be fraught with death, unless they so imminently threaten immediate interference with the lawful and pressing purposes of the

law that an immediate check is required to save the
country." But the "unless" was too much and the warning
came too late. Future Courts would continue to widen the
clear-and-present-danger breach in the wall of the First
Amendment—and to give their free-speech-sapping operations the protective cover of the words of Holmes.

For Holmes was a legend—and his words were like
scripture—long before he died. When he quit the Court
in 1932, the nation was at the economic ebb of boom-
turned-to-bust-turned-to-depression—and for the breadlines and the apple salesmen, Holmes's brethren, with
their business-blinkered faith in enterprise kept free from
government control, were not entirely unresponsible.
They had heard Holmes and—except when he sometimes
talked to their taste—had politely or rudely overridden
him. But a rising generation of lawyers, judges, plain
politicians, had heard Holmes too—and had listened. This
new generation took over the executive and legislative
branches of the national government when Franklin Roosevelt went to the White House, the year after Holmes
resigned. It required several more years, and a constitutional crisis, before the ever-lagging Supreme Court adjusted its judicial sights to the realities around it and to
the prophetic views of Holmes.

Twenty years before the New Deal came in, Holmes
had written of the Court: "We are very quiet there, but
it is the quiet of a storm center. . . ." It was still the
quiet of a storm center in 1933. But the time when the
storm was to move off-center and hit the Court in the
fullness of its fury was not far away.

CHAPTER 7

The Court Collides with the New Deal and Wins the Battle by Defaulting the War

IF MARBURY v. MADISON was the most important decision in Supreme Court history and the Dred Scott case the most famous or infamous, if 1895 with its trio of triumphs over Congress was the Court's biggest year from the standpoint of blatant judicial supremacy, still the most important and famous and exciting short-span period in the annals of the high tribunal, to date, was the three-year stretch from early 1935 through 1937 when the Justices clashed, head-on and eyes wide open, with Franklin Roosevelt's New Deal. Strong Presidents—Jefferson,

Jackson, Lincoln—had fought the Court or been fought by the Court long before FDR was born; Jefferson in a major way and Jackson in a minor way had been licked by mighty John Marshall; Lincoln had been forced to resort to war to undo what Taney's Court had done in time of peace. But it was a single and immediately insignificant decision that marked Marshall's major victory over Jefferson; it was a few rulings on the faraway periphery of federal politics that let Jackson know the judiciary was boss; it was an edict issued before he ever took over the reins of government that led to Lincoln's battle with the men in black robes. Never before Franklin Roosevelt's time had the Court taken almost the entire governmental program of a contemporary President plus his (the pronoun is accurate) Congress and vetoed it law by law—as the Justices did with the first New Deal. Never before had a President taken up the challenge of a judiciary determined to dominate the other two branches of national government and countered it by peaceful political means—as did FDR with his "Court-packing" plan. Never before had the proper place of the Court in the constitutional scheme been so hotly and ubiquitously debated, from tabloid headlines to subway strap-hangers, as it became, first in the election campaign of 1936, later and even more intensely after the President sprang his plan on a taken-by-surprise nation. And it is a tribute to the toughness and resiliency of American democracy that, in different senses, both the Court and the President won.

To catch in retrospect the full significance of the most acute constitutional crisis in the life of the nation as a nation—the crisis that led an airplane-age President to accuse the Court of a "horse-and-buggy" view of the Constitution and led one Justice, speaking for four, to exclaim, extemporaneously yet *ex cathedra*, "The Constitution is gone"—it is necessary first to recapture a touch of the mood of immediate urgency, of desperation barely buoyed by hope, that pervaded the U.S. people between Roosevelt's election and the first frantic Hundred Days of his incumbency, when the most pressing measures of the New Deal were hurried into law. History has already begun to record Franklin Roosevelt as primarily a war President. Recollection of what he did on the home front during his almost nine non-war years in the White House has already begun to fade into an oversimplified black-or-white, for-or-agin formula—into the adulatory poor folk of Harold Rome's song, "Franklin D. Roosevelt Jones," against the bitterly angry rich folk of Peter Arno's cartoon, "Let's all go down to the Trans-Lux and hiss Roosevelt." Largely forgotten is the well-nigh unanimous national sense of supplication for relief by a strong savior that greeted and cheered FDR in the otherwise dark days of early 1933; largely forgotten too is the frightened confusion that gripped the nation—as it never did on that December Sunday when the Japanese attacked Pearl Harbor—during the months before Roosevelt took the oath of office.

Those were the months of mounting unemployment, made visible on every street corner, for all of Herbert Hoover's whistling-in-the-wind assurances that prosperity lay just around it; those were the months of bank failures and business collapses, of barbers and brokers alike losing their life savings invested in Wall Street on margin, of farmers losing their farms although farm mortgages were

selling at less than ten cents on the dollar; those were the
months when the American bubble-dream of every-man-a-
millionaire turned into nightmare, and even businessmen,
their infallibility lying in fragments at their feet, were
begging, like a dying man who turns to God, for the
government intervention in industry and finance which
they had hated and successfully resisted for over fifty years.
They got it, close to the instant FDR was inaugurated;
starting with the immediate executive declaration of a bank
holiday to stop runs on banks, emergency regulations and
far-reaching laws dealing with every phase of the U.S.
economy were rushed through the Administration hopper;
and from the National Industrial Recovery Act, or NIRA,
on down, the onetime wizards of free enterprise applauded
and co-operated with the profusion of new federal agencies
to regulate and plan and direct—which less than a year
later, with catastrophe averted, would be damned by the
same free enterprisers as "alphabet soup." Aloof and remote from all this hoopla and hurly-burly, the Justices of
the Supreme Court read their newspapers and waited.

They knew, did the Justices, that soon or late these new-
fangled government innovations, these NIRA's and AAA's
and TVA's, these products of the pooled brains of bright-
eyed young lawyers and economists and college professors,
would come before the Court for final judgment. They
knew that the spate of non-political unanimity in support
of the President, bred as it was of sudden deliverance from
confusion and fear, could scarcely be so unanimous or ever-
lasting that nobody would take to the law and toss the
Constitution at the New Deal. They knew the continuing
truth of what Tocqueville had said almost a century be-

fore: "Hardly any political question arises in the United States that is not resolved sooner or later into a judicial question." And the oncoming conflict between Supreme Court and New Deal makes little sense on any but a flat, two-dimensional legal level without some picture of each of these eight survivors and one successor of Justice Holmes, who came to be christened the Nine Old Men.

Reading roughly and perhaps a bit perversely from right to left, just as their decisions were to read, first billing naturally goes to Van Devanter, McReynolds, Sutherland, and Butler (though not necessarily in that order, which was the order of their appointment), whom New Dealers were soon to dub the Four Horsemen of Reaction, and who followed the narrow-gauge, anti-government *constitutional* slant of Thomas Jefferson, whose *political* purposes they would have loathed, instead of the broad-interpretation slant of Alexander Hamilton, whose politics they would have embraced. The paradox, be it remembered, is a paradox of words alone; the constitutional theories of all politicians, including Supreme Court Justices, are no more than high-faluting ways of arguing for the political ends they are really after; in Hamilton's and Jefferson's time, the new federal government—whose "powers" under the Constitution can be argued to be broad or narrow—was pretty largely run by the same kind of "economic royalist" against whom much of the Roosevelt New Deal was aimed. It was their basic and bone-deep Hamiltonian empathy with the well-to-do that dictated the Jeffersonian constitutional talk of the Court's Four Horsemen.

Willis Van Devanter of Wyoming, dean of the Nine Old Men in length of service, had been an astute attorney for the Union Pacific Railroad, a chairman of his Republican State Committee, an Assistant U.S. Attorney-General (where he handled matters involving the Union Pacific— and always gently) and a federal circuit judge (where he decided cases involving the Union Pacific—and in the railroad's favor) when Taft named him to the Court in 1910. For all his frontier roots, a rather reserved and timid aristocrat with the technical-fine-point mind of a lawyer's lawyer, his contribution to the Court's work was largely oral, for a rare neurosis made the physical act of writing so difficult for him that he managed to turn out only three or four opinions a year during his twenty-seven years as a Justice. But his vote could almost always be counted beforehand on the conservative or corporation side, especially when a railroad or other public utility was a litigant, and he even remained active, behind the scenes, in Wyoming Republican politics for many years after he joined the Court.

Unlike the urbane Van Devanter, James McReynolds —whom Woodrow Wilson had side-doored onto the Court after a cantankerous year as Attorney-General—was a rough-cut Democrat from a small Tennessee town. His career had alternated, almost schizophrenically, between a lucrative law practice, both in Tennessee and in lower Manhattan, and some stints of trust-busting for the federal government. Although as an anti-trust attorney he had once called the American Tobacco Company a gang of "commercial wolves and highwaymen" (an outburst laid by some to the personal abhorrence of tobacco which led him to forbid all smoking in his presence), the anti-government part of his personality took full control soon after

he reached the Court; for some years a lazy judicial workman whose opinions were largely copied from lawyers'
briefs, he became the New Deal's most vocal and violent
Court opponent, and it was he who expostulated from the
bench, after an early pro-New Deal holding (in the "gold
clause" case) that the Constitution was gone. A crusty
lifelong bachelor, whose intense and narrow prejudices led
him to snub first Brandeis, then Cardozo, because they
were Jews, he carried his bluster and bluntness over from
personal to official matters so that his impatience with the
polite legalisms of his three comrades-in-ultra-conserva-
tism unwittingly gave a substance and a reality to the
Court majority's stubborn resistance to Rooseveltian reforms.

Ablest and hardest-working of the Four Horsemen was
George Sutherland of Utah, a master at the lawyerly use
of precedent and logic to paint a smooth-surfaced veri-
similitude of unanswerable argument in defense of deci
sions actually arrived at for less lofty and more mortal
reasons. Like Van Devanter, Sutherland, though born in
England, had grown up with his Western territory-turned-
state and had mingled politics with corporation law to
become one of the top bosses of the new state's Republican
machine. Repudiated at the polls after two terms as U.S.
Senator—in which post his party regularity plus his soft-
spoken scholarly manner had immeasurably impressed
his heartier colleague, Warren Harding—the trim-bearded
ex-Senator moved from a major brain-trusting job in
Harding's 1920 "front-porch campaign" to become "the
Colonel House of the Harding Administration," and thence
to a Supreme Court Justiceship, courtesy of Harding, in

1922. Any doubts about how he would some day react to the New Deal could have been set at rest by reference to a typically mild-tempered sentence from one of his Senate speeches: "It is not strange that, in the universal fever of haste, government itself should be swept by this mad spirit of impatience which has given rise to this . . . demand that we shall abandon the methodical habits of the past and go careering after novel and untried things."

Fourth of the Horsemen, and least intellectually gifted of the Nine Old Men, was Pierce Butler of Minnesota, the farm boy become millionaire by his monolithic legal services to the Great Northern, Northern Pacific, and Chicago, Burlington & Quincy Railroads—whom Harding appointed as a second-rate successor, of sorts, to far abler Justice White, when he was pressed to put another Catholic on the Court after he had named Protestant Taft to White's place. Like so many risers from rags to riches, big, bull-headed Butler had an almost religious devotion to the status quo, and especially to the railroads; he was an expert at only one thing—the complicated accounting involved in figuring out railroad values and railroad rates—and his expertness was single-mindedly onesided. Confirmed by the Senate only after he had solemnly pledged that he would not sit in railroad rate cases, he got around his pledge by actually writing the Court's opinions in two major rate cases (dealing with water companies) which he knew would set a clear precedent for railroad cases to come; nor did he disqualify himself when railroad taxes, not rates, came before the Court—even though, in one big tax case, the railroad was his old client, the Great Northern (and Butler, of course, voted to cut the tax).

His attitude toward scholarship and civil liberties had been presaged when, as ruling regent of the University of Minnesota, he had engineered the firing of three professors because of their liberal views. The whole New Deal could not but prove anathema to his Philistine philosophy of politics and law.

These, then, were the four men, haphazardly appointed by three different Presidents for politically or personally opportune reasons, who were destined to dominate, anywhere from twelve to twenty-five years after their separate appointments, the government of the United States. These were the men, all products of earlier political ages, three of them over seventy years old (and the fourth, Butler, sixty-seven) when Franklin Roosevelt was inaugurated, who held the power to say No to the President, the Congress, and the overwhelming majority of the nation at a time of crucial crisis. To do so, they needed only one more judicial recruit to the cause of reaction-in-the-name-of-the-Constitution—and they found him, until he turned coat on them two long years after he joined them, in Owen Roberts of Pennsylvania.

Roberts is the perfect personification of the chanciness of government by judges. It was he who, during a Court career from 1930 to 1945, changed his mind and his major votes three separate times—from liberal to conservative to liberal to conservative—on the bed-rock issue of government power to regulate business; it was he who, by holding the decisive Court vote in the first three stages of his switch act, was for years the most powerful person in the United States; (and it was he who, with unintended irony, in the light of his own record, damned the law-changing decisions of his New Deal brethren as comparable to "a restricted railroad ticket good for this day and train only," shortly before he resigned). More than this, it was chance that made Roberts a Justice and gave him the extraordinary power he held over 150 million fellow citizens. President Hoover had named federal Judge John Parker to replace Justice Sanford; the Senate's liberals had succeeded in defeating Parker's confirmation—the only such Senate action this century—because of a Negro-slurring speech he had once made and a routine labor injunction he had once issued; that they were misguided in blocking Parker was subsequently proved by Parker's outstandingly liberal judicial record for more than a quarter of a century after. The same Senators had then nodded Roberts onto the Court, looking mainly at his doggedly able prosecution, for the government, of the Teapot Dome oil scandal cases that had wrecked the reputation of Warren Harding. What they had overlooked about the ambitious plugger, who was right-wing-Republican Senator George Wharton Pepper's protégé, was the rest of his respectably eye-on-the-main-chance career as a conventional corporation lawyer with clients ranging from the Pennsylvania Railroad to the Philadelphia affiliate of J. P. Morgan & Co. Also overlooked was a speech of a few years before in which Roberts had said: "The business man in America today feels that he is doing business with a minion of government looking over his shoulder with an upraised arm and a threatening scowl. . . . Are we to go into a state of socialism, or are you men, and men like you, prepared to get out, take off your coats, and root for good old-fashioned Anglo-Saxon individualism?"

Along with Roberts, whose basically pro-business bent
of mind was cannily camouflaged by two tentative stretches
of flirtation with his less old-fashioned-Anglo-Saxon-in-
dividualist fellows, the Chief of the Nine Old Men, Charles
Evans Hughes, is regularly catalogued by legal historians
as having shared the balance of power between the liberal
and conservative wings of the Court that sat intact through
the first four years of the New Deal. What the Court
records prove is that Hughes held no such power at all.
True, his votes did veer, as did Roberts's, from one side
to the other; but never once in a major case did he cast
the deciding vote; for never once in a major case was
Hughes to the right of Roberts. Thus, with five brethren
to right of him and three clearly to left, Hughes could only
choose whether a conservative decision should be scored
5–4 or 6–3; he could never determine that a decision be
liberal unless Roberts, the Court's swinging keystone,
came along. Proof of this lies in the simple fact that Hughes
dissented several times—and always on the liberal side—
in the big cases that came up during that drastic age,
whereas Roberts never dissented once. It was Roberts
who, for practical purposes, steered the Court that Hughes
headed, whenever the Justices called them close.

This so-near-yet-so-far futility in just failing to capture
power was, of course, no new experience to Hughes. The
slight, shy bookworm of a boy with a rigid Baptist background, who had lifted himself, by the strength of his
mind, to the governorship of New York and thence
through six stunningly liberal years at Holmes's side on
the Supreme Court, had missed the Presidency of the
U.S. in 1916 by the bare margin of 4,000 votes in one

state, California. Obviously embittered, he had left public service to make a fortune in the practice of corporation law, then gone back to government as able Secretary of State under Harding and Coolidge, and again returned to the arguing of cases for a wealth of wealthy business clients, before the bench he had once sat on, at the remarkable rate of more than ten a year. Re-appointed to the Court as Chief Justice by Hoover in 1930, just twenty years after his appointment by Taft, he was now an austere, white-bearded figure, seeming taller than his medium height because of his stately carriage—and he was again somewhat embittered, this time by the slurs on his probable future judicial integrity cast by the twenty-six insurgent Senators who opposed his confirmation because of the character of his recent clients. In between his two Justiceships, Hughes had written a book on the Supreme Court, in which he had deplored his predecessors' lack of statesmanlike sagacity in the Dred Scott case, in the legal tender cases, and in the income tax decision of 1895; he was soon to be faced himself with an opportunity and an obligation of judicial statesmanship such as had never confronted the Court in all its long past history.

To join in judicial statesmanship at a time of national crisis, Hughes could scarcely look to any of the colleagues on his ideological right; the quixotically turn-back-the-clock quartet would give no inch in their creeds or convictions, come depression, panic, or possible constitutional revolution; vacillating Roberts might be persuaded or pressured if things got uncomfortably hot, but he lacked the fortitude to help lead. For assistance of this sort, for vision and wisdom, Hughes would have to look to his left, to the three great Justices who were carrying on, as immediate heirs, the Holmes tradition—Brandeis, Stone, and Cardozo.

Newcomer to the Court, though no newcomer to the job of judging, was Benjamin Cardozo, fresh from almost a score of years on New York's highest bench, the Court of Appeals, where, as Chief Judge, he had built that Court's prestige in legal circles well above the prestige of the Supreme Court of the United States under Taft. The saintly white-locked ascetic, whose private tutors (he was always bright beyond his years) had included Horatio Alger of rise-to-the-top-the-hard-way fame, had devoted his whole adult life trying to live down, for the Cardozo name, the political peccadilloes of his less idealistic father, a Tammany judge whose flagrant malfeasance in office had led him to resign rather than face impending impeachment. With a rare unanimity, practically the entire legal profession pushed Cardozo for the post left vacant when the legendary Holmes quit the Court in 1932; but President Hoover, unenchanted by the shy scholar's apolitical liberalism, dragged his feet on the excuse that there were already two New Yorkers on the Court— until one of those two (the other was Hughes) offered Hoover his resignation, if necessary to let Cardozo be named a Justice. The man who made the gallant offer was Harlan Stone.

Stone had been put on the Court by his fellow Amherst alumnus, Calvin Coolidge, in 1925, after serving one year as U.S. Attorney-General—during which year he had restored the Daugherty-depleted prestige of the Department of Justice, appointed J. Edgar Hoover as head of the FBI, and set in motion an anti-trust suit against the

Aluminum Company of America, to the considerable con-
sternation of Coolidge, who forthwith jumped his too
conscientious Attorney-General to a Justiceship. The
husky, heavy-set New Hampshire farm boy, whose penchant for slow-fused hell-raising had got him kicked out
of one college before he graduated from Amherst (Phi
Beta Kappa, president of his class, and, paradoxically, right
guard on a famous football team), had been causing con-
sternation in a conscientious way all his adult life. As a
Wall Street lawyer, a director of large corporations, an
intimate of Morgan partners, he had simultaneously been
a liberal law professor at Columbia, unreluctant to casti-
gate the financial skulduggery sometimes indulged in by
his clients and friends. A shambling, easy-going character
—nicknamed "Slug" and later "Doc"—he could still get
so indignant at the dictatorial tactics of Columbia's President Nicholas Murray Butler as to resign the law school's
deanship, only to be recalled by popular demand plus
presidential promises not to interfere. Once on the Court,
his open-minded honesty soon made him, despite his
dogged Yankee Republicanism, a disciple and co-dissenter
of fellow-Yankee Holmes and of a different breed of New
Englander, Louis Brandeis.

Brandeis was a New Englander only in the sense that
Stone was a New Yorker—that is, by choice, not by birth
—for Holmes's militant partner-in-protest through the
sixteen years they served on the Court together had been
Kentucky born. Attracted to the cultured intellectualism of
Boston during his Harvard Law School days, Brandeis had
settled there, made a fortune in the practice of corporation
law, and then—unlike his future colleagues who had

started the same way in Wyoming and Utah and Minnesota and Tennessee—had switched, as though suddenly pricked by a somewhat self-righteous conscience, to become a sort of counsel for the people, often without fee. Like Hughes in New York, he had fought the insurance overlords in Massachusetts—and had set up a model system of cheap state-run insurance which he ever after rated his greatest achievement; he had argued before the Supreme Court for such progressive state laws as Oregon's novel maximum-hour statutes, stressing economic facts instead of conventional legal abstractions in a manner that came to be commonly called by lawyers "the Brandeis brief." Named to the high Court by Wilson in 1916, his confirmation had been bitterly opposed by all the forces of legal conformity, from the unanimous past presidents of the American Bar Association to then-President Lowell of Harvard and future Chief Justice Taft—and the Senate debate had raged from January to June. As a Justice, the thin, stooped, deep-eyed aristocrat, though regularly teamed with Holmes in his votes, reached the same results by a quite different route; where Holmes was human and tolerant, Brandeis was austere and ruthless; where Holmes was the philosopher, Brandeis was the crusader. No less than McReynolds, on the far side of the fence, did Brandeis seek to write his own economic ideas into law. Chief of those ideas was a credo of economic democracy to supplement political democracy—a credo which would not tolerate the concentrated power of bigness (one of his books was titled "The Curse of Bigness"), whether it cropped up as big business, big labor unions, or big government; it can have been no surprise to those who

knew Brandeis any less vaguely than as "that other liberal
Justice" that he was to join with enthusiasm in the decision
that declared the New Deal's NIRA, with its overtones of
a corporate state, unconstitutional. But governmental experiment on a smaller scale fitted neatly into Brandeis's
somewhat nineteenth-century scheme of things; perhaps
his most famous opinion was his protest against the Court's
veto (under the Fourteenth Amendment's due process
clause, of course) of an Oklahoma law mildly regulating the
ice business. Said Brandeis: "It is one of the happy incidents of the federal system that a single courageous state
may, if its citizens choose, serve as a laboratory, and try
novel social and economic experiments without risk to the
rest of the country." Anti-bigness Brandeis might have
rated the same regulation less "happy" had it come from
the far-reaching federal government.

Yet the same opinion held words not limited to the
progressive pyrotechnics of the test-tube states: "To stay
experimentation in things social and economic is a grave
responsibility. Denial of the right to experiment may be
fraught with serious consequences to the Nation. . . .
This Court has the power to prevent an experiment. . . .
But in the exercise of this high power, we must ever be
on our guard, lest we erect our prejudices into legal principles. If we would guide by the light of reason, we must
let our minds be bold."

That these words were spoken in dissent and that they
were spoken in the very year when Franklin Roosevelt
was first elected President might have presaged to the
prophetic what the Nine Old Men—Van Devanter, Mc-
Reynolds, Sutherland, Butler, Roberts, Hughes, Cardozo,

Stone, and Brandeis—held in store, by their majority vote, for the conglomeration of new and experimental national laws that were to be known as the New Deal. Secure in their judicial supremacy, armed with their arsenal of constitutional word-weapons to achieve political ends, the Justices, *en masse*, made their customary courtesy call on the new President shortly after his inauguration. In the same month—March, 1933—the new President, polio braces and all, made a call that was considerably more than conventionally courteous at a little old house on I Street, where lived ninety-two-year-old retired Justice Holmes. This extraordinary gesture of homage hinted what was in the political wind.

The wind did not so much as touch the Supreme Court for well over a year; whether by design or happenstance, none of the test cases challenging the constitutionality of the congeries of laws that were lick-and-a-promised into shape to deal with the nation's economic crisis, in long-term or short-term ways, hit the high tribunal during its 1933–34 term. But a couple of key cases, involving state laws passed to relieve depression-bred hardships, did come before the Justices, whose duo of decisions were widely read as showing which way the *judicial* wind would soon be blowing on *national* legislation. That the predicters predicted in both directions was not so strange, considering what the Court did and said in the two cases.

A Minnesota statute, delaying the foreclosure of mortgages and obviously aimed to help the hard-pressed farmers hang onto their farms for the duration of the depression, was argued (by a modern version of a movie-

villain mortgagee) to be in violation of Founding Father
James Wilson's old constitutional ban against state laws
"impairing the obligation of contracts." Five to four, the
Court upheld the Minnesota law—with the four (who
scarcely need specification) having far the better of the
argument by logic and by legal precedent, if not by the
facts of life. Roberts, then in his early liberal phase, cast
the decisive vote but the Chief Justice wrote the majority
opinion. "Emergency," said Hughes, "does not create
power. Emergency does not increase granted power or
remove or diminish the restrictions imposed upon power
granted or reserved . . ."—and anti-New Dealers could
read this to their taste. "While emergency does not create
power," Hughes continued, "emergency may furnish the
occasion for the exercise of power . . ."—and pro-New
Dealers beamed. That the two statements in fact completely contradicted each other, as the dissenters bitterly
remarked, did not bother the predicters on either side; the
one certain thing, however, was that the law had been
upheld—barely.

By an identical 5–4 division, the Justices allowed New
York to help its dairy farmers by fixing minimum prices
for milk. This time it was the due process clause that was
hurled against the statute, and this time it was swing-man
Roberts who wrote the opinion, the most liberal of his
whole judicial career. Sounding almost like Holmes or
Brandeis, Roberts remarked: "The due process clause
makes no mention of sales or of prices any more than it
speaks of business or contracts or buildings or other incidents of property. The thought seems nevertheless to have
persisted that there is something peculiarly sacrosanct

about the price one may charge for what he makes or
sells. . . . This view was negatived many years ago." At
which point, Roberts cited as authority the old post-Civil-
War Granger decisions, practically ignoring the multitude
of contrary due-process rulings in between—and also misleading most of the country, including possibly his colleagues, as to what his stand would be in major cases soon
to come.

They came in a rush, beginning in the winter of 1934–
35. First of the New Deal's doings to be judged by the
Justices was not in itself a matter of major import, but it
carried the seed of a far more momentous decision, now
only four months away; one small section of the "code"
set up under the NIRA to police the oil industry—by letting the President stop state-to-state shipments of "hot,"
or illegally produced, oil—was thumbed to unconstitutional oblivion by the Court, with only Cardozo dissenting.
It was the novel reason given for the decision that made
astute lawyers prick up their ears; what the Court said
was that Congress had improperly turned over part of its
lawmaking power to the President, and so violated (though
the Constitution nowhere forbids this in so many words)
the ancient three-way separation of government powers.
New Deal attorneys found hope in the fact that the ruling
was so narrow, for the Court, had it wished, could have
broadened its ukase to toss out the whole NIRA. Business
attorneys—no longer so enamored of the NIRA, now that
the nadir of business helplessness was almost two years
in the past—wondered if this slap at the New Deal might
not telegraph tougher punches in the near future.

In the very next month, the eagerly anti-Administration

wonderers were taken somewhat aback as the New Deal won—albeit by a cheerless five-to-four vote—its first major Court victory. This was in the "gold clause" case; the President and his Congress had followed the lead of England and France in taking the U.S. off the gold standard; hence the promise to pay old debts in gold (if the creditor asked for gold) which had commonly been written into private and public bonds (and commonly ignored) would be worthless—unless the Court should call the Administration scheme unconstitutional. The practical issue was simple; since depression had made gold more valuable, as measured in ordinary paper dollars, than it was when the bonds were issued, bond-holders hoped for the windfall that would come to them if their debtors had to pay them in gold, as promised. The legal issue was less simple; five Justices said that, for all bonds except U.S. government bonds, this action by the U.S. government was proper; the same five Justices then said that it was improper for the U.S. government to welch on its *own* promises, *but* that the machinery of the law provided no method by which the holders of U.S. bonds could collect on these broken promises to pay in gold. It was this last typically tortuous legal ruling that led McReynolds, heading his quartet in dissent, to exclaim extemporaneously from the bench: "The Constitution is gone." And it may well have been in order to hold Roberts's vote that Hughes, for the Court majority, gave the New Deal a verbal—but only verbal—spanking. If so, Hughes held Roberts for this case alone; by the next big decision, the Four Horsemen had won him away.

Where Roberts left the liberals and reverted to type as an old railroad lawyer, more comfortable among other old railroad lawyers than among bolder bedfellows, was in the rejection of the Railroad Retirement Act—to the dismay of the railroad workers, who thus lost their pensions, and to the pecuniary profit of the roads. As if to make a far-flung formal announcement of his reconversion to "old-fashioned Anglo-Saxon individualism," Roberts wrote the opinion that blasted the Act as beyond Congress's power to regulate interstate commerce and as a violation of the Fifth Amendment's due process clause too. The grave timbre of Hughes's potent dissent—in which Brandeis, Stone, and Cardozo joined—backed a tenor of warning to the country and the Court with a bass of mourning for a comrade apparently lost to the cause of judicial open-mindedness.

Yet when the most sweeping anti-New Deal decision of them all was handed down in the same month, May of 1935, it was Hughes who wrote the opinion that scuttled the NIRA, under which the nation's whole economy had been operating for almost two years—and wrote it for a surprisingly unanimous nine. The case that put an abrupt end to Administrator Hugh Johnson's government guided co-operative empire—"codes of industry," Blue Eagle symbol, and all—was known officially as the Schechter case and popularly as the case of the sick chickens. Four brothers named Schechter who ran a small-time poultry business in Brooklyn had sold diseased fowl in brazen violation of the poultry code of the NRA (or National Recovery Administration, created by the National Industrial Recovery Act) and had been sentenced to brief terms in jail. Somewhere along the ladder of appeal, the large and legendary Wall Street law firm of Cravath, de Gersdorff, Swaine, &

Wood had taken a sudden interest in the Schechters' plight and had found the funds to carry their case to the Supreme Court. Chief contention of the lawyers was that Congress had no power, under the interstate commerce clause, to regulate, even with industry co-operation, such little local businesses as poultry markets—and this despite the widely overlooked fact that, just four years before, the Court had held that poultry markets were enmeshed enough in interstate commerce to bring them under the federal anti-trust laws. Not only did the whole Court accept this argument, brushing its own recent anti-trust decision aside; it went infinitely farther and, taking its cue from the "hot oil" case, branded the entire NIRA, even as applied to interstate businesses, an unconstitutional "delegation of legislative power to the executive." A few sick chickens had murdered the mighty Blue Eagle.

That the Justices, almost simultaneously and again unanimously, threw out—this time on a due-process excuse —the New Deal's effort to lighten the load of farmers with mortgaged farms (much as Minnesota had done, with five Justices approving) came as utter anti-climax. It was the Schechter decision that made headlines around the world. On the stock market, prices shot skyward in a sheerly emotional reaction, quite out of character for financial folk, to the prospect of government-free enterprise mercifully restored by the nine wise men of Washington. But conventionally sober second thought—of the myriad problems suddenly dumped for solution in business's lap—sent the soaring stock prices down the next day in a wave of heavy selling. And an unsmiling President, at his weekly press conference, spoke in solemnly ominous tones of the Court's anachronistic attitude in trying to turn a mechanized and economically all-of-a-piece nation back to the "horse-and-buggy days" of here-a-little-there-a-little government. As for the Justices, they read their predominantly praise-laden press notices and went separately and serenely home to rest up over the summer for whatever further political problems, couched in constitutional clichés, might confront them the following fall.

This was the term of Court—from the fall of 1935 through the spring of 1936—that set off the fireworks. Most of the nation, while not joining in the jubilance of financial leaders (including publishers of large newspapers) over the NIRA decision, had been more surprised than dismayed; with the economy clearly on the upgrade, with employment rising and breadlines shrinking, Hugh Johnson and his Blue Eagle had become to many rather a minor nuisance than a boon; their demise had occasioned very little sorrow or anger throughout the country—just as the wind-sniffing Justices must have foreseen. But comparative popular indifference to the fate of the NIRA did not mean indifference to the New Deal as a whole; by the time of the 1936 nominating conventions, the Court had made itself a major issue for the coming Presidential campaign.

First and most manifoldly meaningful of the big decisions of that historic term of Court was the plowing under of the Agricultural Adjustment Act, or AAA. The Act was intended to raise the prices farmers got for their crops and other products by reducing the number of farm products for sale; to do this, farmers were, in effect, bribed by the government to produce less food, so that there would be no more of the surpluses that were keeping farm prices low; the money to pay these "subsidies" came from "processing taxes," not on the farmers but on those who handled the first step of turning farmstuff into food, as when wheat was milled into flour. It was, of course, a food processor, hit by the new tax, who challenged the constitutionality of the AAA. But it was no country lawyer— it was Justice Roberts's suave city-bred sponsor, George Wharton Pepper—who argued the case before the Supreme Court for a six-figure fee, and who wept like a Thespian trooper before the high bench as he perorated: "I pray almighty God that not in my time may the land of the regimented be accepted as a worthy substitute for the land of the free."

To the slight offense of those who were fastidious about the emulation of Caesar's wife by Supreme Court Justices, Pepper's protégé wrote the Court opinion that answered Pepper's—and the food processors'—prayer. The AAA was unconstitutional, said Roberts, in seven thousand words, because, despite Congress's uncontroverted power to raise taxes and spend money for the "general welfare," Congress could not use this taxing-and-spending power in ways that interfered with the states' right-of-regulation— and control of agriculture was the states', not the federal government's, domain. As if to try to ward off, beforehand, criticism of his quite unprecedented reading of the Constitution, based on a circular argument (for only those powers *not* granted to the federal government are "reserved to the States" and one of the powers *granted* is taxing-and-spending for the "general welfare"), Roberts wrote into his anti-New Deal tract one of the most ingenuous disclaimers of rule by judges ever penned: "When

an act of Congress is appropriately challenged in the courts
as not conforming to the constitutional mandate the judicial
branch of the Government has only one duty—to lay the
article of the Constitution which is invoked beside the
statute which is challenged and to decide whether the
latter squares with the former." By Roberts's metaphor,
a draftsman with a T-square—or perhaps a chemist with
his litmus paper or, at best, a philologist with a dictionary
—would be adequately equipped to lay down constitutional
law.

It was here that an outraged Stone—speaking for a
three-man minority that embraced Brandeis and Cardozo
—was moved to say, in one of the most magnificent opinions ever written: "Courts are not the only agency of
government that must be assumed to have capacity to
govern"—and "the only check upon our own exercise of
power is our own sense of self-restraint." Stone also said,
after wickedly ridiculing Roberts's parade of imaginary
future horribles if the AAA were upheld: "The suggestion
that it [*the governmental power of the purse*] must now be
curtailed by judicial fiat because it may be abused by unwise use hardly rises to the dignity of argument. So may
judicial power be abused. . . : Interpretation of our great
charter of government which proceeds on any assumption
that the responsibility for the preservation of our institutions is the exclusive concern of any one of the three
branches of government, or that it alone can save them
from destruction is far more likely, in the long run, 'to
obliterate the constituent members' of 'an indestructible
union of indestructible states' than the frank recognition
that language, even of a constitution, may mean what it

says. . . ." Not even Holmes ever flayed the-divine-right-of-judges-to-rule more tellingly or more truly.

And what of Hughes? The unhappy Chief Justice, completely aware that Stone's stark common-sense was infinitely righter and wiser than Roberts's nonsense, was torn between his twin duties as Justice and as Chief. As Justice, his intelligence-plus-integrity bade him join the dissenters; as Chief, his responsibility to the Court as an institution bade him beware what a 5–4 decision on so major a matter (the AAA had been second only to the NIRA in the Administration's alphabetical assortment) might do to the Court's prestige across the nation. There is no longer any doubt, despite the secrecy of Supreme Court conferences (the story has been told scores of times and never denied), that Hughes both talked and voted for the AAA's validity until, unable to win Roberts back to reason, he let himself be counted with the majority to make the score 6–3; his concession to personal conscience was in assigning the opinion to Roberts instead of writing it himself, as he had done in the unanimous NIRA case. Thus it was Roberts who bore the main brunt of Stone's cold-angry blast (indeed, Hughes practically never, during his eleven years as Chief, took on a majority opinion that would lay him open to the devastating dissents of his liberal colleagues) in the case that, more than any one other, sparked what Hughes had hoped to avoid—a direct attack on the Court by the President.

Not that the Court was yet through with the New Deal for the term. As if to apologize slightly for the AAA blow. the Justices upheld, on the narrowest and flimsiest ground possible, a part of the vast Tennessee Valley Authority, or

TVA, program—with only the immutable McReynolds dissenting. But this grudging concession by the Court was soon followed by another judicial veto of a vital New Deal statute—the Bituminous Coal Act (or "Guffey Coal Act") which regulated production, prices, and wages in that sick industry in such a manner that it was called "the little NIRA." Unlike the big NIRA, which was perforce loosely worded because it dealt with hundreds of industries, the Coal Act, dealing with one, was so specific that it could scarcely be thrown out of Court as an improper "delegation of legislative power"; unlike the little local poultry dealers of the Schechter case, the Carter Coal Co. (of the Coal Act case) was, like almost every coal company in the country, doing—and affecting—interstate business in an obvious and large-scale way; unlike the public apathy that had settled like a fog around the NIRA by the time of the Schechter decision, a continuing enthusiasm for the order-out-of-chaos results of the Coal Act persisted among most of the coal operators as well as the miners. None of these facts sufficed to save the law from a Court with the bit in its teeth.

Sutherland, for the other three Horsemen and Roberts, gave the rather personal slant of the anti-New Deal ruling away by the use of such adjectives as "obnoxious" and "intolerable," while resting the decision technically on the interstate commerce clause, with a due-process assist. It did not matter that the Court had catalogued the coal industry as deep enough in interstate commerce to let federal judges give orders, and jail sentences, to striking miners; it did not matter that every major coal-producing state filed a brief in favor of the Act, begging that the national government keep control rather than toss the ball back to them; with legal words winging and plain facts flouted, the majority Justices proclaimed that coal mining was a "local" business and hence federal regulation was an invasion of states' rights. Harried Chief Justice Hughes this time managed to split his vote between his colleagues to right and to left, going with the conservatives on wage control and with the liberals on price control (though the very next week, he completely capitulated to the liberals in a case that killed the New Deal's Municipal Bankruptcy Act by a clear-cut 5–4 vote). John L. Lewis, looking ahead undaunted, began to line up a contribution of almost half a million dollars from the United Mine Workers to Roosevelt's 1936 campaign.

It was at this point that the five dominant Justices, perhaps heady with power, made a grave strategic error. As matters stood, it was clear that one of the Republicans' rousing rallying-cries in the coming election would be Rooseveltian contempt for the Constitution, as conclusively proved by the Court's veto of most of the New Deal. To exploit this angle and to exalt the Court for saving the Republic, an organization of wealthy people and their lawyers, cleverly called the Liberty League, had sprouted fast and made many a headline. With nominating conventions only a few weeks away, one Justice was by no means unaware of popular interest in the Court and its members, nor unmindful of the fact that Hughes had been "drafted" from the Court to run for President twenty years before. This Justice, moreover, had for two years held the Court's close, tough decisions as much in the hollow of his raised or lowered hand as if he had sat on the Court alone. But it was not in a case involving the New Deal—except as the New Deal symbolized progressive help-the-people-who-need-help laws—that Roberts killed his chance for the nomination; it was in a challenge, under the Fourteenth Amendment's due process clause of course, of New York's minimum-wage statute for women.

Back in the 1920's, during prosperity, during Holmes's dissenting heyday, a Court ruling that no American government could require that workers, even women workers, be paid a living wage—since to do so would frustrate "freedom of contract"—would have caused little stir; those few lapses where the Justices had let legislatures limit business's right to bargain had dealt with prices or with hours of work, not with wages. But this was 1936; memories of poverty and hunger were still fresh in the minds of millions; more than one-third of the forty-eight states, plus twenty-one foreign countries, including England, had put laws like New York's on their books. As though thumbing their noses at a starving woman while self-righteously wrapping themselves in the flag, the Four Horsemen and Roberts held the law bad. Hughes, unable to stomach, even for his Court's prestige, such let-'em-eat-cake smugness, spoke in grim dissent of "the seriousness of the social problem." Said a Holmesian Stone in separate and stronger protest, with Brandeis and Cardozo agreeing: "The Fourteenth Amendment has no more embedded in the Constitution our preference for some particular set of economic beliefs than it had adopted, in the name of liberty, the system of theology which we may happen to approve." This pointed suggestion of something like religious fanaticism in the unbudgeable economic obstinacy of the majority was not unintentional.

Nor could the Court's final flourish after two years of knocking down laws like tenpins be laughed off as one last proof that the New Deal cared nothing about the Constitution. Here was no visionary product of professors and other brain-trusters who swarmed around that "traitor to his class" in the White House; here was a carefully drafted, badly needed law that had been backed by Republicans as well as Democrats in the nation's most heavily peopled state. Newspapers that had been chortling over the score —reported in sport-page fashion—of judicial "knock-outs" inflicted on the New Deal were plainly perturbed and troubled; the New York *Times*, no admirer of Administration experiments, called the decision "unfortunate in more than one respect." Among the "unfortunate" respects were the facts that the vetoed law had such wide approval, that the ruling was so close, and that the almost reverently respected Chief Justice rated the decision as radically wrong. Most significantly, if the majority Justices could perhaps misread the Constitution in a non-New Deal case, might they not have misread it in some of the New Deal cases too? The fervor of a save-the-Constitution crusade to stop Roosevelt's re-election simmered down; the Liberty League lost some of its luster; the Republican nomination went, not to Roberts, but to unjudging and almost unknown Alf Landon of Kansas.

Still, the Court and the Constitution by no means dropped out of the campaign. Senator Barkley, keynoting the convention that renominated FDR by acclamation, spoke of the New Deal as having been "cast aside by the rigors of technicality and the application of antiquated economic predilections"; of nine Justices who "could not agree on what the Constitution means"; of four dissenters "equally eminent, learned, and sincere, and equally alive to the compulsions of modern life," so that citizens were "relieved of any obligation to underwrite the infallibility of the five whose views prevail." On the other side, the anti-New Dealers, now a touch less aggressive and more apprehensive, made a slogan of Roosevelt's horse-and-buggy slur on the Justices and warned of sinister plans afoot to hobble the Court, to intrude on the vaunted independence of the judiciary, to debauch the Constitution, should Roosevelt win.

As always, a flock of factors—including especially the contrasting personalities of the two candidates—influenced the election; but the question of the Court's proper, or improper, place in the American scheme of government stayed a top-flight issue from start to finish. And when the voters gave their aggregate answer in November, Landon and the Liberty League lost every state save only Vermont and Maine. What effect this avalanche may have had in the marble temple, where the Court had convened for its new term a month before, must remain a matter of informed conjecture—at least until intimate memoirs are possibly published at a decent interval after the death of Roberts, last survivor of the Nine Old Men. What Franklin Roosevelt said, with bland and confident ambiguity, in his second inaugural on a rainy January day in 1937, was: "The Constitution of 1787 did not make our democracy impotent." Just what Franklin Roosevelt had in mind, not even his personal friends, much less his political enemies, knew.

As the government crisis approached its climax, a spate of literature about the Court and the Constitution kept increasing—not just in scholarly journals but in popular magazines and in books by professors and politicians, by lawyers and newspapermen, books that often hit the best-seller lists, so aware were literate citizens of the urgency and explosiveness of a problem long left to the learned discourse of academicians. As had happened sporadically throughout its history, though seldom since the nineteenth century, the Court was the target of all sorts of schemes, some new, some old, some mild, some tough, to break the impasse that had temporarily made "democracy impotent." Give Congress broad and specific power to pass laws promoting the "general welfare," regardless of old interstate-commerce or due-process limitations; let Congress overrule the Court's veto of federal statutes (as it can the President's veto) by a two-thirds, or perhaps three-fourths, majority; take away, partly or completely, the Court's *appellate* power (controlled by Congress) to rule on the rightness-or-wrongness of national legislation; require a 6–3, or maybe a 7–2, vote by the Justices to declare an Act of Congress void; on down to the pious plea: Educate the people to elect better Presidents who will appoint better Supreme Court Justices. But all the suggested schemes that held any real possibility of working needed an amendment to the Constitution—and that slow and, despite FDR's electoral avalanche, always uncertain procedure, however attractive for the long pull, seemed a less than practical answer to problems of the moment. By contrast, the big virtue of President Roosevelt's surprise package was the immediacy of its impact.

It was just two weeks and two days after he took the Presidential oath of office for the second time that FDR bombshelled the nation, including the bulk of his own most intimate advisors, with the proposal which the predominantly anti-Roosevelt press quickly branded, with semantic shrewdness, "the Court-packing plan"—and which might have been called, with equal accuracy and opposite overtones, "the Court-unpacking plan." Though obviously aimed at the intransigent Nine, or Five-out-of-Nine, the plan, on its literal terms, dealt with the entire federal judiciary. What the President asked was that, whenever a federal judge reached the age of seventy and failed to retire, another judge be appointed to supplement, not to replace, the old fellow— with the total number of new judges who could be so named not to exceed fifty, and with the Supreme Court held to a top membership of fifteen Justices. Since six sitting Justices, including all Four Horsemen, had reached the last side of noventy by 1937, enactment of the Court plan would have given Roosevelt the privilege and the pleasure of forthwith appointing six new Justices— enough to outvote with the liberal trio the Four Horsemen plus Roberts plus, if need be, Hughes. The beauty of the plan was its simplicity; the size of the Court had been varied several times before and the three post-Civil War shifts had been for strictly political purposes; nor was there any slightest doubt of the plan's constitutionality, since the Constitution left the size of the Court entirely up to Congress. Indeed the simplicity of the plan

was part of its eventual undoing; it was so simple that it
seemed to many diabolically clever—no amending of the
Constitution, no curbing of the Court's power, merely (as
FDR put it) the "infusion of new blood" into the otherwise
untouched federal judiciary.

It has since become a commonplace to blame the bitter
battle that led to the plan's ultimate defeat on the "de-
viousness" or "indirectness" with which it was presented
—as simply a routine move to improve the whole federal
court system. True, the President did stress in his message
the need for more judges, to help the federal courts catch
up with their calendars of pending cases and to cut down
the frequent delays in handling litigation; and this argument, while quite warranted with respect to many lower
federal courts, let Chief Justice Hughes enter the fray a
little later by allowing publication of a letter in which he
rather indignantly stated that the Supreme Court was
"fully abreast of its work." But those who insist that the
plan might have passed, had FDR come out flatly with his
wish to get more liberal Court decisions by adding a few
liberal Justices, overlook such remarks in his message as:
"New facts become blurred through old glasses fitted, as it
were, for the needs of another generation; older men, assuming that the scene is the same as it was in the past,
cease to explore or inquire into the present or the future."
Considering eighty-year-old Brandeis on the one hand and
sixty-one-year-old Roberts on the other, Roosevelt erred
in equating chronological age with conservatism. Yet it is
scarcely accurate to say that he did not indicate his purpose
to change, with the Court plan, the course of constitutional
law.

What eventually defeated the plan, despite the so recently proved and overwhelming popularity of the Court-killed New Deal, was a host of little political factors—plus two big ones. One was the reverential awe-bred-of-ignorance, with which most Americans regarded the Court, however they might disapprove some of its decisions; this awe blinded both Republicans and Democrats to the blasphemous fact that the Court was a rather random collection of nine men exercising a political function atop one of the three branches of the federal government; and this awe was exploited to the hilt by more practical and purposeful folk whose motives were as mundane as the President's in that they wanted to keep the Court conservative as much as he wanted to make it liberal. Even granting a degree of obliqueness in FDR's tactical approach to the problem, there was no monopoly of masked motives on either side of the fight over the Court plan. The other big factor in the plan's defeat was the sudden and self-saving about-face by the Court itself in its constitutional decisions—an about-face which none could be so naïve as to call coincidental, and which made a cliché of "A switch in time saves nine."

Of these two major means of effective attack on the Court plan, the don't-touch-the-Court-it's-sacred stuff, while spread across the country by press, radio, and club-car conversation, was all focused on the Senate committee-room where heated hearings were under way. All the old saws about an inviolate, independent judiciary were dragged out and dusted off by the political descendants of those who had damned and ignored the Court after the Dred Scott case and had violated its independence to get the decision they wanted on Legal Tender. But strict party lines meant little as Democratic Senator Glass rushed to blast the plan on a national broadcast, Vice-President Garner took off for Texas "on vacation" until the shooting was over, and Democratic Senator Wheeler—La Follette's running-mate in 1924, whose long liberal record was unimpeachable—assumed, to the joy of Republican hearts, the leadership of the opposition. Many, like Wheeler, who attacked the plan did not defend the Court or its recent decisions; they thought the Court should be curbed but in a different, more dignified way, as by constitutional amendment; here was where the simple ease and essential directness of the President's proposal helped defeat it.

Yet, for all the forensics and falderol, political pressure would have pushed the plan through had not Hughes proved the most astute statesman of them all. Quite unnoticed—in January, 1937—was a Court decision upholding a minor New Deal tax, of a kind (it applied retroactively for a period before it was passed) that the Court had called unconstitutional a few years earlier; the Court plan had not yet been proposed. Noticed by the whole nation, however, and spread on every front page, the month *after* the plan was proposed, was a decision giving the Justices' bare 5–4 blessing to a Washington state minimum-wage law almost identical to the New York statute that the Court had scuttled, 5–4, the preceding June; and despite Hughes's gallant effort to save his re-won colleague's face by finding a technical difference, where none existed, between the two cases, it was plain to lawyers and laymen alike that Roberts had simply switched sides. But again unnoticed was the most intriguing, and revealing, fact of all; the Washington minimum-wage case, though the decision came down in March, had been argued in Court and decided in conference in January—*before* the President proposed his plan. Thus the circumstantial evidence is strong (Justices can, but very rarely do, change their votes after conference on a case is over) that Hughes had begun to counter the plan and save his nine-man Court a little ahead of when the plan was launched; for there can be no doubt that it was Hughes, as Chief, whose personal appeal, in the name of the Court's prestige, won Roberts away from the camp of the Four Horsemen. Whether there was a leak to Hughes from the Department of Justice where the plan was drafted, or whether, alerted by the election, he shrewdly foresaw what was coming, he got the jump, as few ever did, on Roosevelt.

Still, this one Court concession to the trend of the times, whatever it might portend, dealt only with a state statute, not a national New Deal law. The turning-point in the fight over the Court plan, and hence perhaps the biggest day in the Court's whole history, came a fortnight later, on April 12. In a series of five cases, headed by the Jones & Laughlin Steel Corp. case, the Court upheld the National Labor Relations Act—or "Wagner Act"—designed to protect labor unions and promote collective bargaining in industries throughout the nation. Factories and mills and mines and stores, whose activities had long been legally classified as "local," subject only to state regulation, and so immune, under the Constitution, from federal meddling, were suddenly found—in flat contradiction of the barely dry Schechter and Carter Coal Co. decisions— to "affect" interstate commerce "directly" enough to warrant Con-

gressional control under the commerce clause. In vain did
the Four Horsemen pull out all the free-enterprise stops
and invoke all the old precedents; Hughes, who read the
magisterial majority opinion himself, had held Roberts to
the twin causes of Court-saving and constitutional liberalism. Franklin Roosevelt's remark, when told of the
decision, was a smiling "It's been a pretty good day for
all of us"—but Wheeler and his Senate kill-the-Court-plan
cohorts were jubilant too. As one conservative Democratic
Senator put it, with I'm-off-the-hook relief: "Why run for
a train after you've caught it?"

Inevitably, all that followed was anti-climactic. Even the
Court's 5–4 decision, later in the term, sustaining the
Social Security Act—although its reasoning ran directly
counter to Roberts's unfortunate opinion in the AAA case
(and Roberts now was, naturally, with the majority)—occasioned no surprise. Like the child of the fairy tale, who
saw that the king's alleged fancy raiment was non-existent
and the king naked, the U.S. citizen was quite unfooled by
the fancy legal language in which the Justices dressed up
what they had done; with childlike clarity, the citizen saw
that the Court had nakedly succumbed to political pressure
—maybe wisely, maybe unwisely—and had beat a hasty
strategic retreat. The wisdom of the retreat was soon apparent. In June, the Senate Judiciary Committee, by an
appropriately Court-like margin of one vote, reported
against the President's plan as an "utterly dangerous abandonment of constitutional principle" which would "destroy
the independence of the judiciary" and which "violates
every sacred tradition of American democracy"—with
seven Democrats joining in this violent denunciation of

their party's chieftain. As the plan's supporters in the Senate went to work on a compromise proposal to let FDR add two, not six, new Justices, their leader, Senator Robinson—who had been Al Smith's running-mate in 1928 and whose loyalty had him marked for Roosevelt's first Court appointment—suddenly died. Back from his long Texas "vacation" rushed less loyal Vice-President Garner to help put the finishing touches to the burial of the whole scheme. The Court-plan battle was over.

But the war for a more up-to-date judicial reading of the loose-jointed (as was now plain to all) Constitution—the war that the President, while losing the battle, had begun to win—was to go gradually and steadily on. With emergency past, with the Court unviolated, might not Roberts, his job done, go home again to the conservatives; were the Court's decisions not still entirely dependent on its personnel? The first break in the five-year monopoly of the Court by the same Nine Old Men—and FDR's first chance to name a Justice (Taft had named six in four years, and Harding four in two)—came when seventy-eight-year-old Van Devanter, after the historic term was ended, took advantage of a new law that let Justices retire at full pay. This opened the way for Roosevelt to achieve as much in rebalancing the Court as enactment of the two-extra-Justices compromise would have done—for the subtraction of one conservative and the addition of one liberal is exactly equal, balance-wise, to the simple addition of two liberals. The President did not muff his opportunity.

Indeed, FDR took a double delight in dramatically appointing, during the summer, the militantly liberal Senator Hugo Black of Alabama. No possible appointment could

more have enraged the conservatives, in and out of the
Senate, who had done the Court plan to death; but the
silly rule of "Senatorial courtesy," whereby members of
the club never question very deeply the qualifications of a
fellow member named to a new post, made Black's confirmation—just as Roosevelt knew it would—almost automatic. Later in the summer, the President's master-move
almost backfired; a reporter on a reactionary Pittsburgh
newspaper found, in the easily available files of an Alabama paper, proof of what all Alabama had long known—
that Black, as a young Southern politician, had briefly been
a member of the Ku Klux Klan; the reporter's syndicated
stories, though wholly based on other men's work, won
him a Pulitzer prize and set the nation agog. But thoughtful
folk were well aware that the trumped-up furor over Black
in no sense stemmed from his old Klan membership (for
instance, McReynolds's openly Klannish race prejudice
had never stirred a whisper) but from a seething conservative sentiment of any-stick-to-beat-a-New-Deal-dog.
Black rode out the storm with the help of a radio talk, in
which he accurately assured the country that there was no
iota of intolerance in his record or in his bones, and his new
brethren greeted him to the Court in the fall.

Next of the Nine Old Men to go was Sutherland; at his
retirement, Roosevelt rewarded Stanley Reed of Kentucky
who, as Solicitor-General, had argued most of the big
New Deal cases before the Court with a patient passion
that had caused him once to faint in the course of argument.
Meanwhile, the slightly re-slanted nine were quietly re-
writing constitutional law; the Federal Power Commission, the New Deal's Labor Relations Board, and the New

Deal's finance-policing Securities and Exchange Commission were all upheld in anti-business actions that might have been slapped down two years before. A vital tax decision or two went for the government instead of against; soon to topple were some tax-law landmarks hoary with age—like the one that let federal judges out of paying an income tax and the series of cases, dating basically back to John Marshall's McCulloch *v.* Maryland, that exempted state employees from federal taxes and vice versa. Step by slow step, Roosevelt's war was being won.

Between 1938 and early 1939, the Court lost two of its all-time greats as Cardozo died and Brandeis resigned; to replace them, Roosevelt named two law school professors, selecting—with Ivy League impartiality—one from Harvard and one from Yale. The "scholar's seat" on the bench, previously warmed by Gray and Holmes and Cardozo, went to Felix Frankfurter, old friend and advisor of FDR, who had been sending his bright, young disciples to Washington to work in government (the Corcoran-and-Cohen team was among them) since long before the New Deal. To forty-year-old William O. Douglas, of the far West and, more recently, Connecticut youngest appointee since Story, over a century before—went, appropriately enough, the seat of the financial expert and crusader; for Douglas had quit his academic job at Yale, first to help, then to head, the SEC, and had done it so well that Brandeis remarked to his less-than-half-as-old successor: "I wanted you to be here in my place."

When Butler died late in 1939, leaving McReynolds as the Four Horsemen's sole survivor on the Court, the politically sagacious President chose another Catholic—U.S.

Attorney-General Frank Murphy, who had formerly been a pro-labor mayor of Detroit and governor of Michigan. Thus, in a span of little more than two years, the inexorable processes of time had enabled Roosevelt to accomplish more, by way of reconstituting the Court's membership, than would have been achieved by his battered and beaten plan. With five Justices, a majority of the Court, now his hand-picked personal selections, and with old liberal war-horse Stone still going strong, it seemed as though the Court were set in a harmoniously leftward-looking pattern for years to come. But ever since the Civil War, the Court had tended to split, amoeba-like, along one or another political or constitutional line. Moreover, men who are granted great government power, to be wielded for the rest of their lives, with no real responsibility save to their own prejudice-propelled consciences, sometimes begin to mistake their separate selves—however liberal or conservative they may be—for God. And Supreme Court Justices are men.

CHAPTER 8

A Court Attuned to a
Liberal Key Develops
Its Own Discordance

THE TEN YEARS stretching from Butler's death and
Murphy's appointment as the fifth Roosevelt Justice up
to the summer of 1949—when those consecrated co-
champions of civil liberties, Murphy and Wiley Rutledge,
suddenly and almost simultaneously died (and their close
associate, Douglas, was almost killed in a mountain accident)—were the years of the New Deal Court. Not
merely that a majority of the Justices, throughout that
decade, had been Roosevelt-chosen; that fact remained
true of the Court for five subsequent years, until Justice

Jackson's death in 1954. Rather that the Court's political and constitutional slant remained, for just that long—and despite incessant and increasing internecine warfare—a New Deal slant. New laws were upheld even at the cost of overruling old decisions; old laws were given, by new "interpretation," a wider sweep; protection of personal freedoms, at least against the states, took precedence over protection of property rights; it was characteristic that, when Holmes's 1918 dissent against the first child-labor decision became, in 1941, the new law of the land, a unanimous Supreme Court so proclaimed. Indeed, inasmuch as FDR and the Congress began, in 1939, to neglect and even negate the domestic New Deal as they set their sights for war, it could be said that the Court—in remaining the most liberal branch of the federal government—was once more, though on the opposite swing, behind the political times.

Yet the outstanding fact about the New Deal Court was not its over-all liberalism; it was what occurred within the Court when liberalism, at long last and for the first time in Court history, was promoted from a vehicle of eloquent dissent to an instrument of actual judicial power—when views that had been fine and brave and outvoted five or fifty years before became taken-for-granted truths, and the battle moved beyond them. Liberalism—or at least, last year's liberalism—did not take to power smoothly; where the Court, from the time of Taney on, had split along fairly predictable political lines, it now began to splinter; relieved of a common cause in resisting reaction, the Roosevelt Justices were soon infighting among themselves. Nor did they keep their quarrels within the close confines of the conference room. As early as the 1940–41 term, scarcely a year after the New Dealers attained numerical court supremacy, close-reading lawyers could catch in occasional intramural dissents a note of annoyance and personal bitterness; not long after, Washington gossip columns began to "leak" word of a feud between Douglas and Frankfurter; by 1946, when Justice Jackson—from far-off Nuremberg where he was prosecuting Nazi war criminals—released to the press, despite President Truman's plea that he desist, an unprecedented attack on Black's character and integrity (which Black never dignified with an answer), the hostility of some of the Justices toward some of their colleagues was already common knowledge. If the New Deal Court had done nothing more—and it did a great deal more—it should have shown to even the most saint-seeking citizen that Supreme Court Justices are extremely human beings.

Still, the crossfire clash of personalities that once or twice went so far as to erupt into front-page headlines did not stem, at bottom, from simple man-to-man antipathies; It was not that Justice A could not stand Justice B's religion (shades of McReynolds) or mannerisms or morals—nor that Justice X was envious or contemptuous, on a purely personal level, of Justice Y. All the emotional aftermaths were marks of an originally and essentially intellectual disharmony; they came from the sudden catapulting of the liberals, long accustomed to the comparative irresponsibility of we're-so-few-we've-got-to-stick-together dissent, into the saddle of judicial leadership. The bickering and backbiting were symptoms; the basic fact was the splintering of the Justices in five or six or seven legal directions, once the liberals took control. And why did they splinter? The manifold answer can be rough-cut, for convenience, into two categories of explanation: They splintered because "liberalism" is so fuzzy-meaning a political concept, and "liberal" so inexact a political definition of a man, that neither prediction nor unanimity is possible when a group of liberals get together to decide a mass of many-faceted and mostly new political problems; in short, one reason why the liberal New Deal Court splintered was that different men thought differently on different *issues*. The other, and overlapping, reason for the splintering was more complex; it was the accept-or-fight-or-compromise reaction of each separate liberal Justice to the views of his fellow liberal Justices when *their* ideas of legal liberalism differed from *his*. In short, it was the different response of different *personalities* to intra-liberal differences on the issues. And both the *issues* and the *personalities* of the men who met—or failed to meet—those issues ranged (as those who would put "liberalism" or "Supreme Court" into a neatly patterned pigeonhole are so loath to recognize) over the whole of a colorful spectrum in which only black and white, the colorless colors, were missing.

In the time of Holmes and of the Four Horsemen, the political issues that hit the Court had seemed, if they had not always actually been, almost black-or-white simple— with a clear-cut conservative side, and with the liberals, although even then for dissimilar reasons (as was often true of Holmes and Brandeis) protesting, and thus being better classified as anti-conservative. Congress would pass a law to regulate business or tax wealth and the Court conservatives would talk states' rights or due process to veto it, over liberal dissent; a federal regulation or tax would come to the Court for "interpretation" and the majority Justices would read it—whether an anti-trust act or a new income tax wrinkle—with business-bound eyes, over liberal dissent; a state statute that regulated or taxed business or wealth would run afoul of the Fourteenth Amendment, courtesy of the Court, over liberal dissent; some federal or state or local law (or official) would trample on somebody's non-financial rights or freedoms, with judicial benediction, over liberal dissent. That was about all there was to it; to be liberal meant merely to disapprove, for whichever of dozens of reasons, the consistent conservatism, state and national, economic and civil-liberties-wise, of the Court's ruling clique.

After the New Deal Court took over, half of these major black-or-white areas of judicial disagreement disappeared. On the economic level, on the power of governments to regulate business, no further federal laws were vetoed outright on *any* constitutional pretext, and the Fourteenth Amendment's due process clause, that old sword of Damocles over the head of every new state control of finance or industry, passed into near desuetude. Yet a plethora of practical problems in government-by-judges continued to plague the Court. There was still the "interpretation" of federal laws, old and new, and there were still the delicate and democratically crucial questions of civil liberties, exacerbated first by hot, then by cold, war. Even in the economic field, where the Roosevelt Justices seemed, at surface glance, to have set government-regulation-of-business free, old political wine was often poured into new legal bottles; federal laws might not be flatly branded uncon-

stitutional but they could, on occasion, be so cautiously
Court-"interpreted" as to achieve almost the same conservative end; state statutes, rid of the threat of the
Fourteenth Amendment, might be, and often were, cut
down by another and newly-sharpened constitutional sword
—none other than the interstate commerce clause, once
used so recklessly against federal laws in alleged defense of
dormant and unexercised states' rights, now used with
equal abandon against state laws in alleged defense of
dormant and unexercised Congressional power. Indeed,
one or two of the Justices, apparently unaware that liberalism can never be static while the world moves, seemed
to feel they had done their liberal duty, and could call it a
day, once they had helped make majority doctrine of the
Holmes-Brandeis dissents that had thundered out the
judicial liberalism of a quarter of a century before.

It was over the complications and cross-currents of
newly raised or newly phrased issues of this kind that the
New Deal Court began to splinter. Might not a Justice be
an economic liberal and a civil-liberties conservative, or
vice versa?—the New Deal Court included both. Did
economic liberalism mean upholding all business-regulating and wealth-taxing, state or national, or did it mean
giving a clear priority to national laws and so rejecting
state laws that might, some time in the future, interfere?
—both views were represented on the New Deal Court.
Was economic liberalism always pro-labor and anti-
business when the two clashed, or was it always for the
underdog, the little fellow, as when a small company came
up against a big and powerful union?—there were New
Deal Justices on both sides. Where should an economic

liberal take his stand when a conservative Congress or Administration or a conservative state government passed a law or used a law to help the economic upperdogs at the expense of the economic underdogs (workers, farmers, consumers) and the underdogs came to a liberal Court for relief?—the New Deal Justices had half a dozen answers. Ought a liberal Justice defer to the legislative will, state or national, as readily on civil-liberties restrictions as on economic regulations?—both answers, plus a half-way-between answer, had adherents on the New Deal Court. Should civil-liberties liberalism give greater protection against national restrictions or against state restrictions, or equal protection against both?—each of the three views was held by at least one New Deal Justice. Did civil-liberties liberalism envisage a different degree of protection for one kind of civil liberty than for another, for freedom of speech than for fair treatment of suspected criminals?—some New Deal Justices thought Yes, some No. Should a liberal be a bit more tolerant of intrusions on civil liberties at home, during a real war against international illiberalism or a cold war against a powerful and illiberal enemy? —the New Deal Court was torn, and divided, both ways. Nor are questions like these a complex index—they are rather a set of illustrations —of the issues whose countless combinations-and-permutations of answers intellectually splintered the nine men whose job, as Justices, was to answer them. And strangely, the one complex of attitudes and answers that was paralleled by no member of the New Deal Court was that of its so-to-speak patron saint, Holmes, the civil-liberties liberal who, with rare exceptions, defended the legislative will on every level against the economic conservatism of judges as zealously as he defended civil liberties on every level against the legislative will—*and was himself an economic conservative.*

No less than the interlacing issues they faced, the separate and sometimes prima-donna-like personalities (Supreme Court Justices are human) of the members of the New Deal Court helped splinter them six ways to Sunday. There were two Justices, each of whom patently felt that he and his views were entitled to special deference on a Court at last controlled by liberals; one was Stone, sole survivor of the Holmes-Brandeis-Stone team and, from 1941 on, the Court's senior member as well as its Chief; the other was ex-professor Frankfurter, nationally known as an expert in Supreme Court lore, to which he had dedicated most of an academic lifetime; when such comparative upstarts as Black and Douglas declined to follow either of their leads and began to push ahead of them along new liberal trails, first Frankfurter, later Stone, seemed to sulk into a sort of we-won't-play conservatism. There were two Roosevelt Justices who lost, each for a different reason, the first fine careless rapture of the New Deal crusade soon after settling into the security of the Court; one was Reed who, despite his intense and workmanlike advocacy of New Deal laws when that was his job as Solicitor-General, had always been more a Kentucky Democrat than an ardent New Dealer; the other was Reed's successor as Solicitor-General, Robert Jackson, whose chief intellectual attribute was a forceful eloquence in support of whatever cause he espoused (a not unlawyerly characteristic), and whose command of language was increasingly dedicated on the Court to a conservatism that better fitted both his personality and his economic status. Each of the rest of the Roosevelt Justices had his idiosyncrasies too—as do all men: Black, the self-made scholar from a dirt-poor part of the South, deeply offended at the uproar over his youthfully thoughtless joining of the Klan and at slurring references to him as a police-court judge (which he once briefly was), overdid his efforts to give an aura of legal respectability, through history and precedent, to his own constitutional views, which neither needed nor gained much from such excuse and semi-apology; by contrast, Douglas, temperamentally direct, forthright, and executive, was sometimes too impatient with the roundabout reasoning of the law to give his ideas their due in his opinions; Frank Murphy tended to think more with his heart than with his head, so that his unabashed humanitarianism (though Presidents are not belittled for their humanity) was often equated with legal incompetence; Wiley Rutledge, a scholar of a different ilk than the cocksure Frankfurter, regularly weakened his influence on the Court through a sense of super-fairness that made him worry interminably every angle and approach to a problem which might lead to a different conclusion than his. Small wonder that so kaleidoscopic a collection of men, each with his own Achilles' heel, splintered apart when confronted with politico-legal issues that were tough and many-sided and mostly new.

These were the eight Roosevelt Justices—with Stone, of the Nine Old Men, included because FDR raised him to the Chiefship, and with James Byrnes of South Carolina omitted because his one year on the bench, in between high administrative chores for the President, produced nothing worth noting. During the ten years of the Roosevelt Court, from 1939 to 1949, there were three different Chiefs (which fact also contributed to confusion)—since Hughes remained head man until he resigned in 1941, and Fred Vinson took charge, by Truman's appointment, at Stone's death in 1946. Along with Hughes and Stone, McReynolds for two years and Roberts for six lapped over from the old Court into the New Deal decade. Along with Vinson, Harold Burton of Ohio presaged the dawn of a different and duller span in the life of the Court when he replaced Roberts in what might well have been called "the Republican seat"—the only one to which Roosevelt never made an appointment. But the essence of the New Deal Court consisted of Stone, its five-year Chief, and those seven stars with their separate orbits—Black, Reed, Frankfurter, Douglas, Murphy, Jackson, and Rutledge. More pointedly than for any other period in its whole history, the Court's record, while these men wrote it, is quite incomprehensible except in the light of what they were like and how they got that way.

Hugo Black—first FDR appointee, more-or-less acknowledged (or else resented) intellectual leader of the New Deal Court, and dean of today's Court—was born in a crossroads cabin in the small-farm cotton country of Alabama, eighth child of a onetime volunteer in the Confederate Army, and, despite some slight formal schooling including less than two years of copy-book law, has been rigorously educating himself throughout most of the sixty-nine years since his birth. Like at least two great Justices of the past, John Marshall and Samuel Miller (and Black has already earned a place, in the minds of many, among the great Justices), Black turned his meagerness of conventional training into a see-things-straight boon rather than a confusion-ridden curse; unlike some of his recent predecessors who also rose from the bottom to the top under their own steam, Black continued to care about, and identify himself with, those less lucky or less gifted than he. As Alabama's ablest trial lawyer, he made a modest fortune selling his services, not to the big corporations, but for use against them; as a U.S. Senator, he was a New Dealer before there was a New Deal, and his tenacious yet trenchant investigations, notably of the shipping industry and of large-scale lobbying, led to new laws and also to a hatred and fear of Black on the part of the business world. By contrast, Black, a mellow and gentle-mannered man whose slight Southern drawl belies his tempered-steel mind, has the rare capacity of not transmitting his militant ideas and ideals into personal enmity toward those who disagree.

On the Court, his captaincy of the liberals was achieved from the start by the sheer power of his mind—to the sometimes quite unconcealed exasperation of Frankfurter and Jackson, who were less bold, and thought they were brighter, than he. His mental boldness was illustrated in an early dissent where he argued, brilliantly and alone, that, despite mountains of precedents running the other way, corporations should not be, and should never have been, judicially rated as "persons" entitled to the protections of the Fourteenth Amendment. It was shown again in a later dissent, which missed by only one vote carrying a Court majority with him, where he contended that the

Bill of Rights, with all its protections of civil liberties against *federal* encroachment, was meant to be carried over and used against *state* encroachment by the adoption of the Fourteenth Amendment. These two dissents also illustrate Black's general slant toward the whole Constitution: let judges use it to protect personal freedoms, not property rights, against the acts of lawmakers. Thus intellectual boldness supports human compassion in the judicial philosophy of the man who has been aptly dubbed "an evangelical progressive," and who once wrote, in overturning the murder conviction of four Negroes on torture-wrung confessions: "Under our constitutional system, courts stand against any winds that blow as havens of refuge for those who might otherwise suffer because they are helpless, weak, outnumbered. . . ." Black has also said—but this time in super-Holmesian dissent: "Freedom to speak and write about public questions is as important to the life of our government as is the heart to the human body. . . . If that heart be weakened, the result is debilitation; if it be stilled, the result is death." Except that Black is, as Holmes was not, an economic liberal, so that some of his votes come easier, Black approximates more than any other present Justice (though Douglas runs him a close second) a sort of Holmes-brought-up-to-date—and also most nearly approaches Holmes's stature.

Contrasting with Black, big, kindly, disconcerting Stanley Reed—least controversial, least intellectually gifted (save one-term Byrnes) and most conventionally law-minded of the Roosevelt Justices—never was poor and never had to be self-taught. From the rich tobacco land of Kentucky, where his father was a first-rate doctor and where Reed later owned a sizable farm himself, he was sent to Kentucky Wesleyan and Yale, to the University of Virginia and Columbia for law, and then abroad for a year at the Sorbonne in Paris. Characteristic of his middle-of-the-road political unmilitance (though he served briefly and capably in his state legislature) is the fact that the Hoover Administration, not the New Deal, first took Reed, who was naturally born a Democrat, from a successful law practice to a government post in Washington. As counsel for a couple of pre-Roosevelt alphabetical agencies, including the RFC, Reed did a workmanly lawyerlike job; staying on with the Democrats, he won the next-to-top spot in the Department of Justice (the Attorney-General heads the Department, while the Solicitor-General argues the big cases) just as the crucial two-years'-worth of tests of New Deal laws was about to hit the Supreme Court; his thanks for his work before the high bench was a seat be hind it.

It has become common to assess Reed's record on the Court in terms of his allegedly inconsistent voting position and his consequent shifts between left, right, and center during his seventeen years as a Justice. Thus, it can be said that he started on the left, as a liberal dissenter with his first New Deal colleagues; that he moved to the center or swing-man position when the Roosevelt Justices achieved a bare Court majority; that at the height of the New Deal Court—roughly from Rutledge's appointment in 1943 to Stone's death in 1946—Reed was to right of center; and that he has since moved back through center to slightly left as death has reduced the Roosevelt Justices to four. All this is relatively, numerically, and superficially true. Yet, better than any other Justice, Reed illustrates why the New Deal Court splintered; for most of his votes have been neither inconsistent nor even unpredictable if read in terms of the different kinds of *issues* he has faced. From the beginning, he has been a strong federal-government man, upholding its laws and the orders of its administrative agencies, whether directed against wealth or against personal freedom of citizens; correlatively, he has been against state regulations and taxes where they might butt into national control. If he has sometimes seemed liberal on labor problems and conservative, or anti-tax, on taxes, it was partly because the labor cases dealt more often with pro-labor *federal* action and the new taxes came mostly from the *states;* beyond this, Reed retains proud memories of having sponsored two liberal labor laws in the Kentucky legislature, so that his anti-states'-rights slant is softer in this field; further, a well-to-do farming and professional background might tend a man to look more kindly on the restriction of industry, than on the collection of taxes, by government. In the civil liberties cases, where Reed, despite his personal good-will-toward-men, built up the most reactionary record of any Roosevelt Justice, he was simply deferring as usual to any federal government action, and also deferring here to state action where it did *not* interfere with the supremacy of the nation. Only in the Negro cases has Reed been regularly on the side of the angels (as in outlawing all-white primary elections in the South)—which might be due to the desire of a Southern gentleman not to seem guilty, as a judge, of racial prejudice. Finally, where Reed's votes fall outside this rather complicated yet consistent pattern, a look at the comparative technical competence of the lawyers who argued the cases might provide the answer—for Reed unduly but naturally appreciates precision of craftsmanship in the practice of the attorney's trade.

Viewed as the not abnormal product of the Justice's past life—born a well-to-do Southerner, reared in rich farm country, professional family, expensive but conventional education, respectable law practice, no real contact with industry or big-city finance, high federal administrative officer under both political parties, chief advocate and court defender of all the laws of the United States—viewed thus, Reed's judicial record loses most of its surface contradictions and begins to be consistent with the *man* who is Justice Reed. So too, the past lives of the next pair of Roosevelt appointees, named to the Court less than three months apart, help reveal why—despite the coincidence that both had been liberal law professors—Frankfurter and Douglas have differed so vastly and sometimes violently in their legal attitudes, their judicial temperaments, and the answers they give to the big issues of constitutional law.

Felix Frankfurter, technical successor to the magnificent Holmes and the great Cardozo, stands out as the New Deal Court's most controversial and unhappy figure, its most tragically wasted brilliant mind. Brought to New York at the age of twelve from Vienna, where he was born in middle-class comfort, he plunged precociously through public school, C.C.N.Y., and the Harvard Law School— which latter was to be forever after his intellectual home. Shunning private practice in Wall Street after a two-month try, he devoted his quick-witted capabilities to govern-

ment service, with trust-busting stressed, until called back
to Harvard in 1914 to teach. Except for a short stint in
Washington during the first World War—worth noting
only because he sat on the War Labor Policies Board beside
an Assistant Secretary of the Navy named Franklin Roosevelt—Frankfurter spent the next quarter-century instruct-
ing, inspiring, befriending, and finding jobs for the cream
of the crop who attended Harvard Law School. Fascinated
by, and idolatrous of, that uniquely U.S. institution, the
Supreme Court, intimate with both Holmes and Brandeis,
whose law clerks he chose for years, he became a nationally
acknowledged authority on the Court's works and ways;
that he sometimes exalted form over substance ("Jurisdiction and Procedure of the Federal Courts" was his pet
subject) seemed not out of line for an academician. His
courageous and compendious defense of the murder-
convicted anarchists, Sacco and Vanzetti, as victims of
gross judicial injustice, made him a liberal hero, but did not
prevent his being offered, a few years later, a seat on the
stodgy Supreme Court of Massachusetts—which he declined. When the jaunty little scholar with the electric
charm, the darting mind, and the hosts of high-and-low
friends was named by one of those friends to a Justiceship,
his appointment was applauded as a natural by both
liberals and conservatives across the nation.

As a freshman Justice in the New Deal camp, Frankfurter helped turn old Holmes and Brandeis dissents into
majority doctrine, while revealing in his one-man "separate opinions"—which were soon to flow in unprecedented
flood—an insistence on doing and saying things his way.
What happened next is best, if bluntly, described in the

words of Professor Walton Hamilton, writing in 1947 of
Frankfurter's first eight judicial years: "Mr. Justice
Frankfurter has no feel for the dominant issues; he operates
best when weaving crochet patches of legalism on the
fingers of the case . . . it is a calamity that his skills
happen to be petty skills." For not only did the ex-
professor remain notoriously a professor, lecturing and
heckling attorneys and Court colleagues alike; he also
remained a rather narrow academician, engrossed in the
trivia of formal legal propriety (he has been called "the
Supreme Court's Emily Post") to the disregard of the
tough stuff of judicial statesmanship. This reluctance to
face the real issues (he once announced that he was
"reserving judgment"—or refusing to vote at all—in a
case on which he sat) may have had its source, long before
the professorial years, in his earliest environment, for
Continental education and scholarship are commonly more
concerned with abstract ideas and patterns of logic than
with down-to-the-dirty-earth problems of living people
and working governments. Along with the sliding away
from solid issues went an equally academic and Continental
teacher-knows-best authoritarianism when Frankfurter
was forced to face solid issues. Thus, an extraordinary
outburst by mild-mannered Justice Black (in a patent-law
case), written solely "in order that silence may not be
understood as acquiescence in the views expressed in the
dissenting opinion of Mr. Justice Frankfurter," exploded,
with Holmesian indignation: "The dissent in question
. . . mentions no statute at all. Instead the chief reliance
appears to be upon . . . the writer's personal views on
'morals' and 'ethics.' . . . And for judges to rest their

interpretation of statutes on nothing but their own conceptions of 'morals' and 'ethics' is, to say the least,
dangerous business."

Despite this sort of "dangerous" authoritarianism,
Frankfurter kept proclaiming that he was strong for
"judicial self-denial"; hence he was usually against up-
setting state infringements on civil liberties (most blatantly in the flag-salute cases, where school-kids had
been locally ordered to violate, with a physical gesture,
their salute-only-God religious training—and where
Stone got a Court majority to back the children on the
second time around). Yet it was Frankfurter who spear-
headed the Court in using its judicial power, over multiple
dissent, to veto a series of state taxes that vaguely im-
pinged on business activities in interstate commerce.
Insistence on procedural propriety, self-assured authoritarianism, selective "judicial self-denial"—whatever the
excuse, Frankfurter was soon nestled, in most closely
contested cases, with the far-right wing of the New Deal
Court. Only where Holmes or Brandeis had voted liberally,
years before, on the identical issue, or where a liberal
answer fitted his private blueprint of how "the federal
system," as an abstract concept, ought to work—*and* where
strict adherence to impeccable legal etiquette left open no
side-door escape—might Frankfurter be found on the
liberal side. It was thus he, not Reed, who was the most
unpredictable of the Roosevelt Justices on major issues—
simply because those issues so often did not determine his
stand. And though the mediocre caliber of most recently-
appointed Justices has let Frankfurter lately shine brighter

by contrast, it was he—unable to wield among equals the preceptor-like personal influence he had long been accustomed to wield as a professor—who became, in the light of his great potential, the New Deal Court's outstanding disappointment.

Frankfurter's opposite on the Roosevelt Court, in so many different ways that their oppositeness soon flared into personal antagonism, was the other ex-professor of law who was named almost simultaneously, William O. Douglas. Where Frankfurter was the cautious and self-conscious scholar, Douglas was get-it-over-and-done-with decisive; (Douglas wrote two or three times as many opinions *for the Court*, per year, as did Frankfurter, whose anxiety to express his own views precisely led him, in one term, to talk for the Court in only seven cases while talking for himself, in dissent or "separate concurrence," on thirty-three occasions). Where Frankfurter was the circumspect backer-away from issues, Douglas, like Brandeis, his predecessor in crusade, wanted always to hit them head-on. Where Frankfurter was the whisperer, Douglas was the shouter. Where Frankfurter was ingratiating, Douglas was blunt. Where Frankfurter was the oldest man Roosevelt put on the Court, Douglas was by far the youngest in temperament as well as years. And perhaps most significantly of all (whether causally or only symbolically), whereas all the rest of their colleagues came from the comparatively small geographic area of the Eastern United States, between the Atlantic Ocean and the Mississippi River, Frankfurter's roots were thousands of miles to the East in a civilization long past its prime; Douglas, despite his Minnesota birth (he was still an infant when his family left the state), was a product of the Pacific Northwest, the last American frontier.

The forty pre-Court years of Douglas's life are straight in the Horatio Alger tradition—except that the riches he both sought and won carried no dollar mark in front of them. In the state of Washington, where the family happened to be when his itinerant-preacher father died, Douglas put himself through school and Whitman College with a ragtag succession of jobs ranging from newsboy to berry-picker to window-washer to sheepherder; (he also licked the after-effects of polio by mountain climbing, which strenuous pastime he has ever since indulged in all around the world). Riding east on a freight car, he arrived at Columbia Law School with less than a dollar to his name; earned while he learned with the help of a kindly dean named Harlan Stone; graduated number-two-man in a class that included, considerably farther down, one Thomas E. Dewey. Initiated into the intricacies of fancy corporate finance by a couple of years with a Wall Street law firm, the dour and rough-cut dynamo, who looks like a cross between a cowboy and a wary hayseed, took a law-teaching job at Columbia, quit it when President Butler flouted academic democracy in naming a new dean, was snapped up by Yale, and became a full professor just five years after he got his own LL.B. A less popular but far less orthodox teacher than was Frankfurter at Harvard, he worked with ideas more than with students and revolutionized the old-style approach to business law. When the New Deal's fledgling Securities and Exchange Commission asked him to investigate the mysteries and skuldug-

geries of "corporate reorganization," his report packed
such a solid punch that Roosevelt made him a member of
the SEC; the same sort of tough-minded expertness soon
won him the SEC chairmanship. His executive skill,
backed by knowledge and courage, as in bringing that
holy-of-business-holies, the New York Stock Exchange,
to heel, led many to rate him as the New Deal's finest
administrator and to regret the submerging of this talent
in the contemplative work of the Supreme Court—less
than three years after the meteoric man-in-a-hurry hit
Washington—even though the Court badly needed, at
Brandeis's retirement, a member who knew all the ins and
outs and underneaths of big-time business and finance.

From the start, Douglas teamed with the Court's other
ex-poor-boy, Black, and for three terms the two never
voted apart in a single case; some divergence began during
the war and increased shortly after, but today, though differences still crop up, the phrase, "Black and Douglas dis
senting," now that Murphy and Rutledge are gone, has
become as common—and means the same thing—as
"Holmes and Brandeis dissenting," thirty-odd years ago.
Recognized, even by colleagues who disagreed with his
conclusions, as the Court's wizard in matters financial, he
was soon, except when outvoted, writing the bulk of the
tough opinions in this field; for instance, in upholding the
Interstate Commerce Commission in a major freight-rate
case, he produced an essay to delight an economist, complete with seventeen tables and a graph. His Brandeis-like
mistrust of bigness was best expressed in a pile-driving
dissent against letting the U.S. Steel Corp. expand its huge
empire into his beloved Far West: "Power that controls

the economy should be in the hands of elected representatives of the people, not in the hands of an industrial oligarchy. Industrial power should be decentralized. It should
be scattered into many hands so that the fortunes of the
people will not be dependent on the whim or caprice, the
political prejudices, the emotional instability of a few self-
appointed men. The fact that they are not vicious men but
respectable and social minded in irrelevant. That is the
philosophy and command of the Sherman Act. It is founded
on a theory of hostility to the concentration in private
hands of power so great that only a government of the
people should have it." "Government of the people" got
his steady support, whether state or nation was doing the
governing—except where civil liberties were stepped on,
and sometimes even then. Through the New Deal Court
days, Douglas ranked only fourth in defense of personal
freedoms, behind Murphy, Rutledge, and Black; indeed, in
the wartime cases—dealing with spying, with treason, and
with the pushing around of Japanese-Americans on the
Pacific coast—Douglas voted one hundred per cent with
the government, regardless of claimed violations of the
Bill of Rights. More recently, Douglas has become, both
on the Court and off, the most vigorous and eloquent
judicial champion of civil liberties. In cumulative dissents
that vitalize cold facts with fire, he has damned all the
"loyalty" programs and oaths and laws—like the Smith
Act, under which the top native Communists have been
jailed—as directed, in disregard of "the first article of our
faith," against a tiny band of "miserable merchants of
unwanted ideas. . . . Only those held by fear and panic
could think otherwise." Blasting the New York "Feinberg

Law" that lets schoolteachers be fired "on a principle repugnant to our society—guilt by association," Douglas blended Brandeis and Holmes into his own mature credo: "We need be bold and adventuresome in our thinking to survive. . . . The Framers knew . . . the strength that comes when the mind is free. . . ."

As though time ran backward, the first four Roosevelt appointees—Black, Reed, Frankfurter, and Douglas—are today, and again in minority, the last four judicial survivors, each with more than sixteen years of service behind him. If joint survivorship, in the face of their five less luminous (Warren perhaps excepted) Truman-or-Eisenhower-appointed colleagues, has maybe brought them a little closer together, still Frankfurter misses the one intimate friend he found on the Court—his long-time ally in action, Robert Jackson; and Black and Douglas sorely miss their two stanch comrades against conservatism, mid-twentieth-century style—Wiley Rutledge and especially Frank Murphy.

Murphy—the New Deal Court's most underrated member, whose alleged lack of judicial skill or temperament led to such cracks, and not only by conservatives, as "Justice tempered with Murphy"—was a Michigan Irishman with a sense of mission, who might well have been a priest instead of a public servant. A onetime assistant U.S. district attorney, law teacher, local judge, mayor of Detroit, high commissioner of the Philippine Islands, he burst into national prominence when he refused, as newly elected governor of Michigan in 1937, to call out the state troopers to break up the sit-down strikes in the depression-hit automobile factories. Although his characteristically patient and unviolent handling of the explosive situation brought him thanks, not just from the unions, but from Ford and General Motors as well, he was defeated for re-election as an enemy of the rights of property. Roosevelt immediately named the non-drinking, non-smoking, bushy-browed bachelor, who looked a little like a saint with a red halo, to the U.S. Attorney-Generalship, where he spent a militantly liberal year—which included the setting up of a civil-rights section in the Department of Justice—before being elevated to the Court.

No Justice in all Court history—not Holmes, not Stone, not Black, not Douglas—was so consistent and passionate a judicial crusader for civil liberties for everyone, for Nazi spies and for Japanese generals, in peacetime and in wartime, as was Murphy. Not even his ardent Catholic faith kept him from defending the rights of the Catholic-hating sect called Jehovah's Witnesses ("To them . . . befalls the burden of testing our devotion to the ideals and constitutional guarantees of religious freedom")—nor from flaying official efforts to deport, as a former Communist, labor leader Harry Bridges ("The record in this case will stand forever as a monument to man's intolerance of man"). Despite his past as a federal law-enforcer, he insisted—as Reed so conspicuously did not—on giving criminals every constitutional break; dissenting in a search-and-seizure case, he pilloried his brethren for permitting a "shabby business: Lawlessness by officers of the law." His chief other legal-emotional slant was pro-labor—and his very first major opinion for the Court, upholding the right to picket peacefully as a form of freedom of speech, neatly combined the two. That Murphy was so predictable on civil liberties and labor, always finding some lawyer's-reason to reach the end he sought, was why lawyers belittled his ability as a judge; and yet John Marshall, for one, used exactly the same technique—though he used it to reach entirely different ends. "The law," Murphy said, "knows no finer hour than when it cuts through formal concepts . . . to protect unpopular citizens against discrimination and persecution." Marshall was never so forthright—nor so human.

As forthright as Murphy, but again not so human—in the sense of concern for others—was the New Deal Court's most obvious turncoat-to-conservatism and most gifted wielder of words, Robert Jackson. Maybe Jackson wrote so unlegally well—with the force of plain and pointed talk replacing lawyers' jargon—because he never went through law school nor won a law degree; indeed, though born on the proper side of the social and economic tracks, he never even went through college, and one ungraduating year of law study (shades of Marshall, Miller, and Black) was his only formal education after high school. Something of an adolescent prodigy, he learned law fast as an office apprentice and soon had a practice of his own in Jamestown, N. Y., sufficiently lucrative to let him be a gentleman farmer, with a stable of trotting horses, on the side. As that *rara avis*, a well-to-do upstate New York Democrat (his forte was lawyering for little companies against big ones), he did a chore or two for another gentleman farmer, Governor F. D. Roosevelt—and in 1934 a third New York gentleman farmer, Treasury Secretary Morgenthau, summoned Jackson to Washington "for six to eight months" to get the legal affairs of the Internal Revenue (or income-tax)

Bureau in shape. The solid and frog-mouthed man with the leisurely manner and mercurial mind never went back to Jamestown, except to vacation or visit. Jackson moved from tax work to anti-trust work (in both, he tackled and tamed the mighty Mellon financial interests), to the Solicitor-Generalship (he lost only one of twenty-four cases before the subdued Supreme Court in the 1938–39 term), to the Attorney-Generalship (with war in the wind), to a Justiceship shortly before war came. The most brilliant and vigorous verbal advocate the New Deal had known, he was counted on to continue his down-the-line New Dealing on the Court. Forgotten were three little facts: Jackson was ambitious—and a bit embittered that FDR had taken a third term when Jackson had high hopes and high chances to succeed him; Jackson was wealthy—the richest of the Roosevelt appointees; Jackson was independent, with far more than the turn-the-switch-either-way lawyerly independence of the counsel accustomed to fit his cause to his client—and the lifetime tenure of Justices invites the turning of legal and political switches.

For a term or two, Jackson used his freshness and pungency of phrase largely on the liberal side; he warned that, if California's keep-the-Okies-out law should be upheld (which it was not), "then our heritage . . . is only a promise to the ear to be broken to the hope, a teasing illusion like a munificent bequest in a pauper's will"; speaking for the Court, and for the schoolkids, in the second flag-salute case, he remarked that "compulsory unification of opinion achieves only the unanimity of the graveyard." But on economic issues, and soon on most civil liberties too, the gentleman of property early began to talk like a gentleman of property; as he edged right, to vote more and more often with his friend, Frankfurter, his virtue—as against the little scholar's pose of utter impartiality—was his plain-spoken approach to the job of judging. Dissenting against a liberal anti-trust decision, on policy grounds, he said: "To use my office at a time like this . . . to catapult Congress into . . . supervision of the nation's insurance business is more than I can reconcile with my view of the functions of this Court in our society." Dissenting against a liberal patent-law decision, he lampooned the majority view as based on "a legal concept which either is very profound or almost unintelligible, I cannot be quite sure which." Dissenting against a pro-labor decision, he protested: "This Court now . . . permits to employees the same arbitrary dominance, over the economic sphere which they control, that labor so long, so bitterly and so rightly asserted should belong to no man." And dissenting against a decision upholding religious freedom, his final metaphor must have made friend Frankfurter wince: "Religious symbolism is even used by some with the same mental reservations one has in teaching of Santa Claus or Uncle Sam or Easter bunnies or dispassionate judges." Jackson's frank disclaimer of judicial dispassion was made more pointed in his own case when, at President Truman's plea, he took a year off from the Court to prosecute war criminals in Germany—a diversion which bothered naïve believers in an independent and apolitical judiciary (as Justice Roberts's more judge-like investigation of Pearl Harbor, for President Roosevelt, had not) and also bothered Jackson's colleagues, mainly because a lot of 4-to-4 cases had to be held over for decision

until the following term. It was from his voluntary exile
that Jackson, uninformed or misinformed, bitter that he
did not get the hoped-for Chief Justiceship at Stone's
death, loosed his intemperate attack on Black, on whom he
blamed his disappointment; the attack put a finish to
Jackson's effective influence on his fellows. For the eight
years until he died, a frustrated man, in 1954, Jackson
followed an increasingly conservative line with only
occasional aberrations—though the quartet of Truman
appointees made him, like Frankfurter, look a little less
illiberal toward the end. But he never lost his mastery of
language; indeed, his Court career could well be capsuled
in the fact that an anti-labor, anti-civil-liberties "concurring opinion" which he wrote in 1950 was published—
and it read as though intended to be published—intact,
in the magazine section of the New York *Times*.

Where Jackson remained, as a judge, the aggressive
and hell-for-leather advocate, Wiley Rutledge—FDR's
last appointee and the only one with important past judicial
experience—precisely fitted the popular picture of a
Justice as a patient explore-every-angle-and-then-quietly-
make-up-your-mind sort of man. Roosevelt is said to have
named Rutledge partly because he "had geography"—in
that he could be designated "of Iowa," his last pre-D.C.
home, as Douglas had been designated "of Connecticut."
Rutledge did indeed have geography—in more than the
silly sense of scattering Justiceships East, South, West,
and North, according to George Washington's first-
Court precedent. Born in Kentucky—and, like Douglas, a
wandering minister's son—he had lived as a youth in
North Carolina and Tennessee, graduated from the

University of Wisconsin, taught high school in Indiana and New Mexico, taught law in Colorado and Missouri, and ended his peripatetic academic career as dean of the Iowa Law School. First plucked from his professorial swivel-chair to sit for four years on the federal court of appeals in Washington, the genial and slightly jowly scholar with the modest and slow-spoken mien was made a Justice to replace Byrnes (who had replaced McReynolds, and who now went back to more obvious politics, where he belonged).

Rutledge immediately joined the Black-Douglas-Murphy team and turned it, for six years and on most major matters, into a solid four-man core of living legal liberalism. Close to Murphy on civil liberties, more hesitant to go whole-hog on economic issues, as by blanket benediction of state taxes or of labor unions, he often gave to the Court's left wing, with his wordy, thinking-out-loud and respectful-of-precedent opinions, a more solid if stodgier support in lawyers' law than did the other three. If his touch was sometimes heavy, his rectitude was impeccable and could rise, on occasion, to heights of indignation. When the Court, with even Black and Douglas going along halfway, pretzel-twisted past law and plain common-sense in upholding—to most of the nation's emotional delight—an unprecedently tremendous fine for contempt of court, slapped on John L. Lewis and his striking United Mine Workers, Rutledge (and Murphy) refused to join in the lynching bee. In a magnificent dissent, running to forty-four pages and reminiscent in tone of Stone's dissent in the AAA case, Rutledge tore every majority argument to shreds, commented that one of several strange things the Court approved (the combining of a civil suit and a criminal suit in a single case) should be "shocking to every American lawyer and to most citizens," and hit a climax of superb and subtly double-edged disgust with: "No man or group is above the law. All are subject to its valid commands. So are the Government and the courts." Soon after, explaining his unpopular stand without apology, he said: "I could not see the law in any other guise than as I wrote. Accordingly there was nothing else for me to do than what I did." These words might well have served as Rutledge's epitaph.

Here then were the seven men, none a Chief Justice, whose separate, varied, and sometimes veering views of life-translated-into-law accounted, in main, for the Court's zig-zag-to-leftward course during its New Deal decade. For the two years from 1943 to 1945, when Stone and Roberts (until his retirement) made up the rest of the nine, the Court was—without even a close competitor—the most brilliant and able collection of Justices who ever graced the high bench together; the least of them would have stood out on many Courts of the past. Indeed, that very fact was one reason why they differed and fought and splintered. Another reason was the executive incapacity of Stone as Chief—for his tolerance of endless debate, New England town meeting style, in conference, made the early Roosevelt appointees, despite their respect for Stone as a Justice, look back longingly to the crisp but fair efficiency of headman Hughes. Still, the New Deal Court, for all its internal differences and its leaderlessness, laid down a lot of law, much of it new. And that part of its political, or government-guiding, array of decisions which has not already

gone with the conservative wind calls for summary even
in an effort to picture the Court's work with the focus set
for distance—as though what is still close were far away.

In the long perspective of time, probably no more than
a handful of the multitude of cases of great contemporary
importance decided during the New Deal decade will still
stand above the horizon as enduring landmarks of government law. Such a perhaps brash prediction stems from a
clutter of ill-assorted causes, chief among which is a hunch
that the Roosevelt Court's over-all slant and the more
compelling separate statements of its oh-so-individual
members are more likely than a ruling here and a ruling
there to affect the law's future course and to catch the attention of political and legal historians. The major break
with the past had been made by the Nine Old Men before
the appointment of a single Justice by FDR; what the New
Deal nine did, in main—and usually in otherwise unusual
unanimity—was to follow the lead that had been laid out
for them; it was of no special moment, except maybe statistically, that the Court, in a single year, 1941, overruled
no less than ten of their predecessors' decisions—decisions
ranging in age from five to thirty-three years back, and
ranging in importance from one that forbade a state to tax
a man on sales he made to the U.S. government, to the
one, made famous by Holmes's dissent, that vetoed the
outlawing of child labor. None of these overrulings
sparked more than casual comment, among laymen or even
lawyers—so accustomed was the country, in four short
years, to a radically new trend in constitutional law.

Moreover, many decisions that did hit the headlines,

because of their news value at the time, will soon fade to footnotes in Court annals; that the Justices upheld the National Labor Relations Board in letting the unions get away with a few selfish and generally resented tactics, under the terms of the Wagner Act, lost all long-term interest once those tactics were banned by Congress in the Taft-Hartley Act; whether granting children "released time" from public-school attendance for brief religious instruction menaces the "separation of church and state," or violates the constitutional guarantee of religious freedom (for whom?), is scarcely calculated to shake the law in proportion to the attention the public—and the Justices—paid it. Specific matters of immediate moment, or seeming moment—judicial or otherwise—rarely retain much significance unless they carry the seed, not merely the verbal symbol, of something larger and lasting.

Yet another reason why few of the New Deal Court's *decisions*—as opposed to some of the *opinions* of its brilliantly motley-minded members—are apt to achieve permanent stature is because, once the clean-up job on constitutional errors of past Courts was out of the way, those decisions lost the force of a united front. In "interpreting" federal statutes, in supervising federal agencies like the NLRB and the FTC and the FPC and the FCC and the old ICC, in reviewing state (and sometimes federal) taxes, and especially in dealing with claimed kicks-in-the-pants to civil liberties—by national, state, or local governments—not only did decisions go 5–4, or sometimes 4–4 or 4–3 (as one or both of the ex-Attorneys-General, Jackson and Murphy, disqualified themselves on cases started in the Department of Justice while they were there); decisions that went 5–4 or 6–3 or even 9–0, on many occasions, found the majority voting together for different reasons, so that no one could tell what the law was—or would be in the next case. And a decision made by five or six or eight or nine Justices, on two or three or four divergent grounds, is not the kind of decision that endures. In the John L. Lewis contempt-of-court case (where Rutledge superbly dissented), Vinson, who spoke "for the Court," based his ruling on two wholly separate grounds; Reed and Burton agreed with both; Frankfurter and Jackson agreed only with one; Black and Douglas agreed only with the other (and also, quite unrelatedly, protested against the penalty); Murphy dissented with Rutledge. What is the law and how likely is it to last?

One way to chronicle the New Deal Court's doings— and an easy and popular way with current commentators, lay or legal—is strictly chronological, so that "trends" to right or left can be stressed and spotted as the Court's personnel gradually shifted (for only the Black-Reed-Frankfurter-Douglas-Murphy five covered the whole ten years). Thus, it can be written that, during the 1940–41 session, which was Murphy's first *full* term, the nine (or enough of them) upheld the federal Wages and Hours Act; gave the federal government, for the first time, some control of state primaries where national officials, like Congressmen, are up for election; let the NLRB ban an employer from *not* hiring a job-seeker just because the man was a union member; broadened the control of Congress over "navigable" rivers in a way to give a legal boost to such public power programs as TVA; put labor unions almost all the way out of reach of the anti-trust acts; refused

to let a judge, on his own and without a jury sitting, punish
a newspaper editor for publishing criticism, however intemperate, of the judge's conduct of a case; gave its
blessing to peaceful picketing, even by a union that had
no members at work (or formerly at work) in the place
being picketed—and made almost all these decisions by a
divided Court. Or it can be written that, during the 1948–
49 session, the last of the New Deal decade, the Court did
almost nothing of note save uphold a Nebraska anti-union
statute and a Missouri anti-union court order (labor by
now, with the swing of the pendulum, had become, in
many minds, too big and strong for its boots); restrict,
though more in words than with any practical punch, over-
eager "searches and seizures" by state policemen; and
barely defend the right of even a filthy-mouthed native
fascist to freedom of speech. Again, three of these four
decisions were by a variously divided nine. Perhaps more
meaningful and a little less boring than any such year-
by-year catalogue of cases would be a quick over-all
survey of the New Deal Court's work in different fields
of government law, with special mention of some of the
big decisions not already noted.

In the economic field, in the regulation and taxing of
business, the old meat-axe of this-whole-law-is-uncon-
stitutional rusted on the wall—except where a series of
state taxes (as on state-to-state sales) and a few minor
state regulations struck a slim majority of the Justices as
interfering with national control of national commerce.
Into judicial vogue came the stiletto of "interpretation,"
of deciding whether a legislature, almost always Congress,
"intended" this particular use of a law when it acted—*or*

when it did *not* act, to override, as it can, some old "inter-pretation" of that law by the Court. Thus, the bitterly argued case that made the insurance business subject to the anti-trust laws, by a 4–3 vote, revolved around what Congress meant or did not mean when it failed to specify insurance as coming under those laws—especially in the light of a seventy-five-year-old Court decision, here over-ruled, that held insurance was a *local* business and so subject to *state* control. Likewise, a strangely split trio of rulings, that left some corporation dividends, when paid in stock instead of cash, free of the income tax, centered on what Congress meant when it *did* amend (a further twist) the income tax law to deal with an old decision (Holmes and Brandeis dissenting) on just this point. Most of the Congressional acts the New Deal Court undertook to "interpret" concerned the anti-trust laws, the patent laws, and laws regulating the rates charged by railroads and other "public utilities," when some administrative agency (FTC, FPC, ICC) or the Department of Justice tried to give them a new or different reach. Sometimes the government won—notably in the insurance case, in a case blessing the more-often-damned Interstate Commerce Commission for lowering railroad freight-rates for South-ern and Western shippers while raising them for the here-tofore favored East, and in two cases letting the Federal Power Commission set gas company rates by a broader and far more consumer-conscious formula than an older Court had ordered, years and years before. Sometimes the government lost, as in most of the important patent and anti-trust cases, notably the one allowing U.S. Steel to expand its vast operations to the West Coast—which

Douglas's strong protest (for four dissenters) called "the most important anti-trust case . . . before the Court in years." Not one of these decisions was unanimous and most were not nearly so.

On civil liberties—on the protection of people's personal and political freedoms against some government's efforts to take them away—a tremendous fuss has been made of the New Deal Court's allegedly liberal record. It is true that that record is brighter than the record of any court in the past; it is true that in two overlapping ways—in speaking out against such barbaric police techniques as the third degree, especially as practiced by state and local officers, and in making a start toward granting Negroes the same living and voting and not-being-lynched-by-law rights as white people—the New Deal Court did make big strides toward giving life to the marble motto on the building where they work, "Equal Justice Under Law"; it is even true that, had there been one more Justice to regularly join the Black-Douglas-Murphy-Rutledge quartet, those strides might have been considerably longer. But the bulk of the New Deal Court's record, as a Court, on civil liberties consisted in deciding now this way, now that—with the Justices split in a dozen directions— a score of disparate little issues, some of them as petty as whether Jehovah's Witnesses (apparently the Court's pet religious sect, though none belonged to it) could peddle their literature on the streets without buying a cheap local permit. Chief basis of much of this backing and filling was the philosophic poser that not even Holmes had quite solved to his own satisfaction: If judges ought to respect the majority will when faced with *economic* laws (whether of nation, state, or village), if these laws were entitled to a "presumption of constitutionality," why were not laws that cut down or hemmed in civil liberties entitled to the same presumption? If the Court should not stop a state from regulating milk prices as the state saw fit, should it stop a state from letting its police officers tap telephone wires to get evidence of crime? It was Stone, not Holmes, who—in a famous footnote to an otherwise unimportant opinion (U.S. *v.* Carolene Products Co.)—first faced the issue squarely and maintained that, despite the loss of logical consistency, civil liberties deserved the greater judicial protection against lawmakers. But some of the Roosevelt Justices could not bring themselves to accept Stone's view; indeed Frankfurter once flatly, and at length, disowned it. Still another basic issue that bothered and divided the New Deal Court in civil liberties cases was how far the Fourteenth Amendment carried over, against state or local government action, the guarantees of the Bill of Rights against *federal* action. No Justice took the position—most sensible, if not necessarily most appealing, to any non-lawyer who reads the Amendment's words—that *none* of it was carried over, four Justices, headed by Black, argued and voted that the *whole* Bill of Rights was carried over; the rest thought some of it was and some was not—free speech, for instance, yes, but no-hint-of-self-incrimination in a criminal-case defendant's refusal to testify, no. Small wonder, then, that the New Deal Court's civil-liberties rulings were, for the most part, spotty and uncertain, and that a few of them have already been overturned.

As the slicing up of the Bill of Rights, where it hits the

states, suggests (with parts of it used, parts of it not used, by the Court majority's choice), there are many types of civil liberties and of civil-liberties cases. And the story of the New Deal nine's decisions in the field can best be told by dividing the cases, roughly and arbitrarily, into three different kinds: those stemming from the First Amendment's guarantees of freedom of religion, of speech, of press, and of the right of assembly; those dealing with the fair treatment of suspected criminals, before and during trial, to which most of the rest of the Bill of Rights is devoted; and those involving discrimination, political or personal, against minority groups (meaning, during this decade, for practical purposes, Negroes). Of the First Amendment's freedoms—which the whole Court thought carried over, though by no means in every instance, to the states—religious freedom got the greatest attention and protection; from the flag-salute cases to the released-school-time cases to the peddling-of-religious-propaganda cases to the question whether a state may pay to transport children to parochial schools by bus, the Court interminably worried comparative trivia in personalized opinions, and usually came out, by a close vote, on the side of free (unpaying and unpaid-for) religion. Far more important was the decision that upset, but only by 5–4, the rulings of the Nine Old Men that conscientious objectors against bearing arms could not become citizens—and there was something sadly symbolic in the fact that Stone, who had dissented with Holmes and Brandeis and Hughes in the old cases, here dissented in the opposite direction on the very day he died. Freedom of speech—which today practically embodies freedom of assembly—got some minor and divided support from the New Deal Court until the Communist cases and "loyalty" cases began to come in; neither then nor, especially, later were a majority of the Justices as alert to defend the right of radicals, including Communists, to speak their minds as the old Hughes Court had been, in a trio of anti-state-suppression-of-speech decisions during the 1930's. As for the freedom-of-press cases, they dealt chiefly with the right of newspapers to blast judges without being hauled into court for contempt; and with the protection of the courts from undue outside pressure weighing against press liberty, sometimes seen as license, the Justices—and the decisions—went both ways. The First Amendment got no great lift, no new breath of life, during the New Deal decade.

In the second big category of civil-liberties cases, where fair treatment and fair trial of suspected criminals was at stake, the New Deal Court's decisions defy all description. Not only did the Justices differ as to whether and which Bill-of-Rights guarantees here carried over to the states; not only were 5–4 decisions, on most points, the rule rather than the exception in cases going either way; not only did individual Justices switch back and forth on the same point (in one case, involving high-handed and highly questionable search procedures by the FBI, Black and Douglas voted to uphold the federal police while Frankfurter wrote a brilliant libertarian dissent, in which Jackson was one of three who joined); more than this, the very points at issue varied from protection against "unreasonable searches and seizures" (to get evidence of crime), to protection from third-degree confessions (here the Court was its best), to the right of indictment by a grand jury, to the right to be represented by counsel, to the right of a "speedy and public trial by an impartial jury," to the protections against self-incrimination and "double jeopardy" (for the same crime) and "cruel and unusual punishment" (shadows of the Georgia chain-gangs). It is enough to say that the Court's decisions ran about fifty-fifty where federal criminals and federal officials were concerned, and that civil liberties got less than an even break in the state-originated cases. This last fact led Black, in dissent against the 5–4 upholding of an Illinois burglary conviction, where the defendants had had no lawyers to represent them, to blister his colleagues' decision as "another example of the consequences which can be produced by substitution of this Court's day-to-day opinion of what kind of trial is fair and decent for the kind of trial which the Bill of Rights guarantees." Black's statement might stand as a summary of all the Justices' joint and separate treatment of this whole hodgepodge of issues—including on occasion his own.

It was in defense of the Negro race against discrimination that the New Deal Court struck its strongest blows for civil liberties—and may indeed have made its most enduring contributions to public law. Far fewer issues and far fewer cases came before the Justices in this field of personal freedoms (though many of the fair-trial decisions, as in banning use of the third degree to get confessions, were given double meaning and heavier Court support because the defendants were Negroes in the South). Yet what little, speaking quantitatively, the Court accomplished here was done with the force of unanimity or near-unanimity; most of it broke new ground; and its sheer momentum has already carried the post-New Deal Court farther and farther along this humanitarian line. What the Roosevelt Court did first was to toss out, as offending the Fifteenth Amendment (which forbids states to keep people from voting because of their race or color), the device then widely used in the South whereby states would turn over control of primary elections—the only elections that mattered—to the political parties, and the state Democratic Party would not let Negroes vote; in so doing, the new Justices overruled a less-than-ten-years-old *unanimous* decision by the Nine Old Men (who included Holmes, Brandeis, and Stone); further, when South Carolina tried to get around this by the gag of turning its Democratic Party into an un-state-authorized all-white "private club," the Court would not even listen to South Carolina's case after a lower federal court outlawed the gag. Next, the Justices, under the questionable cloak of the commerce clause, forbade Jim Crow arrangements on interstate buses, and upheld a state law forbidding similar segregation, even when applied to boats making excursion trips to Canada. Finally, "restrictive covenants"—whereby property-owners in "white sections" of Northern cities contracted never to sell or rent to people "not of the Caucasian race"—were dealt a long-range death-blow in a set of rulings which said that state courts could not enforce such contracts, even in private lawsuits, without violating the Fourteenth Amendment.

One supplementary and special group of civil-liberties issues arose directly from the war. Considerably more concerned for fairness than any of its predecessors who sat during previous wars, the New Deal Court overturned a

few treason and espionage convictions. But the most illiberal decision it ever handed down was in giving judicial
blessing, by a 6–3 vote, to the cruel, wholesale evacuation
from the West Coast, under Army orders, of all Japanese
and Japanese-Americans, regardless of their citizenship or
their later-proved loyalty and solely because of their race.
On the opposite or credit side of the Court's ledger—
though otherwise entirely unrelated—was a unique decision that branded a part of a federal law unconstitutional;
when Congress attached a rider to an appropriations bill,
specifically removing from the federal payroll three liberal
(though not Communist), high-placed employees, named
Lovett, Watson, and Dodd, the Justices struck down the
rider as a "bill of attainder"; this was the only time, in
the New Deal decade, that judicial supremacy was exercised to veto a Congressional act—and one of the three
times in the Court's history that it has been so used in
significant protection of civil liberties.

   Civil liberties and economic, or bread-and-butter, matters meet and overlap in a third major area of government
law—that concerned with the rights of, or the restrictions
on, labor and labor unions. The overlapping is most apparent where the right to picket peacefully, obviously for
economic purposes, is judicially upheld as an exercise of
good old freedom of speech—as the New Deal Court, at
first, upheld it, only to repent and restrict its original
generosity in later cases. The overlapping was perhaps
most meaningful, during the New Deal decade, when the
unanimous Justices refused—though for different reasons
—to "interpret" the anti-union Taft-Hartley Act's ban on
the spending of union money for political purposes as for-

bidding political propaganda or palaver in union newspapers—a suggested curtailment of press freedom that
might some day have led, had it been honored, to a government ban on political editorials in the supported-by-
business-through-advertising New York *Times*. For all
that the New Deal Court's labor decisions—from portal-
to-portal pay to the legislative protection or, later, outlawing of the closed shop—were as publicized as they
were numerous, they are perhaps the most ephemeral of
all. What a majority of the Justices did (for unanimity was
as rare in this field as in others) was, by and large, to
follow the legislative lead—and thus the election returns
—in consistently upholding statutes and administrative
rulings made under them, on national and state levels, regardless of the about-face of both statutes and rulings from
pro-union to anti-union during the decade. Although the
aberrational and quite incomprehensible Lewis contempt
case (where Rutledge's dissent is most likely to influence
future Justices) and the first peaceful-picketing-is-free-
speech decision (where Murphy's doubly self-expressive
coup has already won consideration in literally hundreds of
subsequent cases, largely in disagreement or qualification)
can neither be completely ignored, little if anything that
the New Deal Court did on the labor front—save bow, in
general, to the shifting popular and legislative-or-admin-
istrative will—is likely to endure.

Yet it was a rather routine, and routinely divided, decision in the labor-law field that set off—or served as an
excuse for—the most dramatic and symbolic single episode
in the New Deal Court's ten-year tenure; this was, of
course, Jackson's poisonous, public, long-distance attack

on Black in the late spring of 1946. The excuse for the
attack was that Black had sat and voted in a case where
one litigant, the United Mine Workers, had been represented by a former law-partner of Black's, named Harris.
Ignored in Jackson's intemperate and unprecedented yelp,
and generally unknown even to lawyers, were several facts:
Other Justices—Butler regularly, Roberts regularly, Stone
once (though he preferred not to)—had sat in cases argued
by former law-partners; Black's short partnership with
Harris had ended nineteen years before, and the two men
had scarcely seen each other since; Black's meticulous sense
of propriety had led him to disqualify himself (disqualifi-
cation, as even Jackson conceded, had always been left to
the conscience of each individual Justice) in all cases involving the FCC, of which his brother-in-law was a member; the decision in the U.M.W. case would have gone the
same way had Black declined to sit. But it was clearly not
the case that caused the outburst; it was Jackson's deep
disappointment that he had not been named Chief Justice
when Stone died—plus stories that reached him abroad to
the effect that Black was mainly responsible. Frustrated
once, during his pre-Court New Deal days, in an abortive
attempt to win the New York governorship, frustrated by
Roosevelt's third term in his hope to become President,
Jackson's last ambition was to head the Court—an honor
allegedly promised him, long back, by FDR and left still
unbestowed at FDR's death.

If Black blocked Jackson's elevation to the Chiefship
(and there is some evidence that he indirectly helped do
so), Frankfurter similarly stymied the naming of *his* arch-
enemy, Douglas. President Truman compromised by ap-

pointing that long-time laborer in the Democratic vine-
yard and top utility-man for the New Deal, Fred Vinson
of Kentucky—with the hope that Vinson's conciliatory
talents and slow patience might settle or smother the
feuds within the Court. Vinson was Truman's second
Justice, Harold Burton of Ohio having been named to the
"Republican seat" a year earlier, at Roberts's why-bother-
to-stay-on retirement. Three years later—when Murphy
and Rutledge died, and Truman chose Tom Clark of Texas
and Sherman Minton of Indiana—the New Deal Court,
as a Court, with all its conflicts, its contradictions, its
personal spats, and its splintered brilliance, passed into
history. An era was ended.

CHAPTER 9

Yesterday's Court, the Court Today, and a Court That Could Be Tomorrow

FIVE YEARS AFTER the New Deal Court shut up shop in 1949, and adjourned for that sorry summer when Murphy and Rutledge died, the Justices were back in headlines and politics up to their robe-rimmed necks as they ordered the Southern states to let Negro children attend the same public schools as did white children. This is not to say they had not been front-page political news in the interim between; they had. In the May-or-June late spring of each of the four intervening terms, some matter of immediate moment—and of potential long-range reach—had been decided: In 1950, it was the 1954 ruling's feebler forerunner, which ordered the South to let Negroes into the classrooms of white universities and to let them eat in the same sections of the same dining-cars on railroads; in 1951, it was the blessing bestowed on Judge Harold Medina's prosecution (*sic*) of the eleven so-called "top native Communists," which blessing meant giving the Smith Act the judicial nod of constitutionality; in 1952, it was the refusal to bless President Truman's technical "seizure" of the steel plants to keep steel production going, despite a threatened strike, during the Korean War; in 1953, it was the back-and-forth legal and judicial moves —ending in an extraordinary special Court session after the Justices had adjourned—to decide whether the Rosenbergs should be executed as spies, which they were, within hours after the Court announced its final order.

Yet, if the Rosenberg business, because it was so dramatically personalized, made a bigger two-or-three-day public splash; if the you-mayn't-do-it-unless-Congress-lets-you spanking of Presidential steel-seizure had a more drastic short-term impact, in that it sparked the wartime strike that Truman had tried to avoid; if the Dennis decision that sent the unconcealed U.S. Communist leaders to jail—to be followed by lesser pip-squeaks of the party— was far more significant, seen in the light of U.S. constitutional history, since it all but obliterated the free-speech guarantee of the First Amendment by letting Congress ignore that guarantee at will—still, the anti-segregation-in-public-school decisions were clearly destined to affect more deeply, over a snowballing period of time, the day-to-day lives of the greatest number of citizens. A bit overenthusiastically described in parts of the press as the most important Supreme Court action since the diametrically opposed Dred Scott decision, this set of unanimous rulings led to silly talk of secession-again by a few Southern hotheads, and to plans for subtle disobedience of the Court's orders by millions in the South—including a former member of the Court, Governor Byrnes of South Carolina. Little mentioned or noticed was the fact that the post-New Deal Court was here moving, in a sense, on the momentum of the Roosevelt Justices in the one area where they had teamed *together* to blaze a new trail toward more liberal government law.

Little noticed, too, was the fact that all the Vinson-into-Warren (or Truman-into-Eisenhower) Court's big decisions, and a disproportionately large part of all its decisions, dealt with, stemmed from, or were mainly motivated by the cold war (or the Korean hot war) with Communist Russia. The relation of the steel seizure case, of the Smith Act convictions of home-grown Communists, and of the Rosenberg spy rulings is apparent; nor is there any doubt that the pro-Negro pronouncements—as many Southerners have accurately, if angrily, charged—although following the New Deal Court's direction, were pushed to such unprecedented lengths to help counter Communist propaganda in Asia and Africa about American maltreatment of people whose skins are not white; and in free-speech cases, in "loyalty" cases, in cases on admitting or deporting aliens (or alien-born citizens), in Fifth Amendment self-incrimination cases, in such labor cases as that dealing with the non-Communist affidavit (for union officers) demanded by the Taft-Hartley Act—in all these and others, the dark shadow of the U.S.S.R. lay over the U.S.S.C. If there was ever any question that the Justices were primarily political figures, the past five or six years should have dispelled it; and never in the long history of this political group of men—not even when, acting separately on circuit, they were ruthlessly enforcing the Sedition Act at the end of the eighteenth century—did international politics, on a world scale, so overweigh and dominate their work and their decisions.

The tragedy—as history is sure, some day, to record it —is that the Supreme Court's majority, with the most magnificent opportunity ever granted so small a group to show the world the profound difference between the humanity of a democracy and the brutality of a dictatorship, so miserably failed; that the Court—except in the Negro cases—while purporting to fight a foreign tyranny, actually aped it. From the Dennis decision that makes a mockery of the First Amendment—in a way that would have shocked Holmes and Brandeis, and did shock Black and Douglas—on down to such seemingly little things as letting government servants be fired as "disloyal" on the random charges of unrevealed and so unanswerable informers, or letting an alien be torn from his U.S. wife and child, and deported, because he was once a Communist, though he quit them twenty-three years before (and eleven years before the law under which he was deported was passed)—the Truman-Vinson Court was more often the nation's shame than its pride at giving life to democracy's high ideals. Nor has the bare beginning of an Eisenhower-Warren Court significantly changed the picture yet, despite a few signs hinting to the hopeful that it may.

Although Vinson became Chief in name in 1946, the Court did not become his, in fact, until Clark and Minton joined him and Burton in 1949 to form a quartet of Truman-appointed Justices. In the three years between, two things about the Court's new captain had been made abundantly clear: One was that, despite his vast administrative skill as a compromiser of conflicting issues or men, and despite Truman's hope that this skill would suffice to suffocate or soften the Black-and-Douglas against Jackson-and-Frankfurter row, it did not suffice—because the real basis of that row was intellectual, not personal, and all four of the participants were Vinson's intellectual superiors. The other soon-apparent thing was that Vinson could not begin to fill the shoes of Stone, not even the slightly soured Stone of the last years, as a judicial liberal; perhaps by coincidence, perhaps not, Vinson's slant toward civil liberties was at least as ungenerous as that of his fellow-Kentuckian, Reed, and made the same exception for the rights of Negroes. Indeed, Vinson's views were so close to Reed's on most other matters, not just on civil liberties, that when Vinson at last became king of his Court, Reed, more often than not voting with the Truman chosen four, became their chief spokesman as well as their ablest—though he had rated about at the bottom of the New Deal Justices.

For the four Truman Justices, judged by either ability or industry, in qualitative or quantitative estimate of their work, were the least happy choice of a Court quartet since President Harding picked Taft, Sutherland, Butler, and Sanford, about a quarter of a century before. Where the Hughes Court used to give complete treatment, meaning

a hearing and a full-dress Court opinion, to about two
hundred cases a year, the Vinson Court in only one of its
four terms handled as many as a hundred—and its more
industrious holdovers from the Hughes days chafed at
their inactivity. Where the New Deal Court had pushed
public law toward a greater respect for human dignity, the
Fair Deal Court in a dozen ways pushed it back; prophetic
and symbolic were the overrulings, less than a year after
Murphy died, of a pair of paint-fresh Bill-of-Rights decisions he had penned. Fifty years hence, none of the
Truman Justices, appraised by what they have shown up to
now, will be any better remembered—or deserves to be
better remembered—than the nameless Justices (save
Johnson and Story) who sat with Marshall are remembered
today. But since three of the Truman group are still on the
Court, and the other ran it, his way, for the four unfortunate terms that preceded his death in 1953, a contemporary
account demands that they be described as the men they
were and are.

It would be neat, if less than profound, to lay Fred
Vinson's judicial disregard of most personal freedoms to
the fact that he was born, in a small Kentucky town, the
son of the county jailer. Equally far-fetched would be the
blaming of his bland and blighted hope to get the Court
to work together, like a team, on the fact that he once
played shortstop, in the semi-pro Blue Grass League, on
a somewhat more coordinated nine. More likely, both
attitudes stemmed from his more mature career. For over
a score of pre-Court years, the mathematically-minded law-
trained man with the ponderous split-personality face (one
side looked like a strong statesman, the other like a weak,

sly politician) worked for the federal government in all three of its branches in a shifting succession of top-flight jobs. As a Democratic Congressman, he was the Capitol's acknowledged-by-both-parties expert and chief spokesman on taxes; as a federal court of appeals judge (one rung below the Supreme Court), he was efficient enough to have Roosevelt choose him to head simultaneously an emergency court to hear OPA cases; drafted from his judgeship by FDR to be Economic Stabilizer, then Federal Loan Administrator, then "assistant President" as head of the Office of War Mobilization and Reconversion, Vinson next spent a year as Truman's Secretary of the Treasury before being named Chief Justice. It was the one-man power he held in his high administrative posts that perhaps led him to erroneously suppose that he could boss the Supreme Court in the same firm-if-gentle way. And if ever a Court member's past life clearly tended him toward upholding whatever the federal government did or wanted to do, it was Vinson's.

To Vinson—as to Reed alone of the Roosevelt Justices —Uncle Sam could almost do no wrong. Only against the states would Vinson use judicial power in important ways; of his six or eight major opinions for the Court, during seven years as Chief, the two indubitably liberal ones, on "restrictive covenants" in the North and on law-school segregation in the South, spanked the states for unconstitutional action against Negroes. When he voted against state taxes, his concern was for national control of commerce; when he cut down a couple of state limitations on labor's right to strike, it was not out of love for labor but because he thought they contradicted federal law. Let the

U.S. move against labor and Vinson would back any action to the hilt; it was he who spoke first and strongest in the splintered-four-ways decision that upheld the huge federal fine on Lewis and the miners; and it was he again who talked for the majority in letting Congress require non-Communist oaths from union officers. The outstanding instance of a pro-labor stand, however indirect, and perhaps his most forceful opinion, was his dissent—and Vinson dissented reluctantly and rarely—against the ruling that forbade pro-labor President Truman to seize the steel plants in the name of the federal government. When that government kicked civil liberties around, Vinson regularly wrote and voted in its behalf; "loyalty" programs or "loyalty" oaths, reviews of rough draft-boards or military courts, brutal treatment of aliens or of citizen-criminals— he could always be counted on the anti-libertarian side. Freedom of speech meant nothing to him, except as a pretty phrase; indeed, it was a state, not a federal, police action that let him write into the law of the land (with the backing of five of his fellows) the extraordinary rule that, when a political speaker is threatened with violence by some of his audience, the speaker, not the threateners, may be arrested. (Said Black, in dissent: "I will have no part or parcel in this holding which I view as a long step toward totalitarian authority.") But it was the Dennis decision, upholding the twentieth-century version of the Federalists' aged-in-disrepute Sedition Act—by letting native Communists be jailed simply for trying to spread their psychotic gospel—for which Vinson will be longest, and least admiringly, remembered. And it was fitting that the last official act of the thirteenth Chief Justice was to reconvene his Court and rush through a reversal of the stay of execution which Douglas had granted the spy-convicted Rosenbergs—in a manner that led even Frankfurter, no devotee of spies or of Douglas, to protest, but that let the Department of Justice do its electrocuting on schedule. For all his undoubted patriotism, chauvinist style, Vinson, less than any other man who ever headed the Court—less than Ellsworth, less than Waite, less than Taft—understood the real meaning of American democracy.

Chiming in with almost everything of any import that their Chief said or did were the three other Truman Justices—whose names have been linked and intoned by legal wags in imitation of Franklin Roosevelt's sneering campaign references to three right-wing Republicans, Martin-Barton-and-Fish. Certainly, Minton, Burton, and Clark, to date, have displayed nothing remotely resembling judicial statesmanship; and unless their new Chief, Warren, can (and wants to) win them away, as Black and Douglas could not, from their tame and timorous conception of their job—scared by legal precedents, scared by native Communists, scared to say No to the other branches of the federal government in the name of liberty—these three will continue to sog down the Court's work in a way that both the conservative Marshall and the liberal Holmes would have scorned. Rarely has there been such triple and simultaneous proof of the folly of letting even a pretty-good President carelessly pack the Court with his personal friends.

Harold Burton, the Court's senior non-New Deal member—who was once publicly designated as the least able Justice in a hundred years—is the product of a comfortable background, an upper-class education, a conventional career in corporation law, and a New England conscience (he was Massachusetts-born) that led him first to dabble, then to dive, into respectably conservative, and hence Republican, public service. Three terms as an upright mayor of Cleveland led to a U.S. Senatorship; a conscientious and not too partisan or reactionary Senate record led then-Senator Truman to ask for him as an opposition member of the famous "Truman Committee" to investigate defense contracts; the friendship that was cemented there—plus nationwide demands for a Republican replacement when the Court's lone Republican, Roberts, retired—led President Truman to pick the godly yet amiable white-thatched Ohioan, who looks like a small, neat version of a village storekeeper, as his first appointment to the high bench. At the start, Burton was clearly out of his depth on the Court; plodding along in pursuit of old cases to use as precedent like a lady shopper trying to match colors, exploring irrelevant trivia for page after dull page in near-parody of the job of judging, he managed, despite hard work, to turn out only five or six majority opinions a year (the figure was precisely six in one term when Black wrote twenty-nine and Douglas twenty-seven). But Burton has grown some in stature as the Court has shrunk; his nine or ten cases a term are today standard for a light and lazy docket; further, the New England conscience has pricked him, on occasion, into gingerly shucking off the anti-libertarian strait jacket which still binds the two other surviving Truman Justices. Indeed, the least-able-in-a-century label, once hung on Burton, would far better fit either Clark or Minton.

Tom Clark—who characteristically changed the Thomas to Tom, perhaps in fealty to his first sponsor, old-time U.S. Senator Tom Connally—has been a Texan Democrat all his life and a politician-prosecutor for most of it, his six years on the Court not excluded. From district attorney for Dallas County, when only five years out of law school, he moved in the mid-New Deal days to the Department of Justice, where he worked on anti-trust cases and later on war frauds, supervised without wincing the evacuation of Japanese from the West Coast, and was—by reliable report—about to be relieved of his assistant Attorney-Generalship by Roosevelt for comparative incompetence when FDR died. Instead of removing him, Truman—for whose political friends Clark had done a few Departmental favors—raised him to the Attorney-Generalship, where his running of the loyalty program took scant heed of civil liberties. That the smooth and smiling glad-hander, whose perpetual bowtie (worn today even under his robe) adds to the appearance of an over-aged college boy, would next be named to the Court was widely taken for granted; Vinson, who backed the appointment, was apocryphally said to have done so because he wanted someone on his Court who knew less law than he did; whether or not that was what Vinson wanted, it is what he—and the country—got. As a Justice, Clark has been uninteresting, unintelligent, and—in line with his own career and his late boss Vinson's lead—illiberal; left-wingers, aliens, suspected criminals, all who do not conform to the conformist picture of a one hundred per cent Amurrican, get from him short shrift. Given a chance to pen an exciting opinion when he joined a unanimous Court in long-delayed overruling of a

1915 decision that movies (then in their infancy) were not entitled to freedom of the press, he turned out a dull and muddy technical treatise. Or perhaps it was his law clerk who turned it out—for Clark's chief virtue is a rather appealing awareness of his own limitations as lawyer and as judge. More than any other present Justice, he votes with the pack and is rarely in dissent; more than any of his brethren, he depends on his young fresh-from-law-school assistants to outline and even write his opinions for him.

By contrast, Sherman Minton, fourth of the Truman appointees—whom freedom-defending Elmer Davis would doubtless like to disown as a fellow Hoosier—is conspicuously unaware of his judicial shortcomings. The very air of militant self-assurance that moved the lower-middle-class Midwesterner ahead, first in law, then in partisan Democratic politics, became a handicap and a vice once the goals to be reached were no longer chosen, the orders no longer given, by others. As New Deal whip during his one term in the U.S. Senate, the square-faced man with the quick anger, the quick tongue, and the build of a heavyweight boxer, forcefully backed—and followed —the whole Administration program. It was there, of course, and for that reason, that he became Harry Truman's friend. Licked for re-election in 1940, he served briefly as an administrative assistant to FDR before being hoisted to one of the federal courts of appeals where, for eight years—with nobody to give him the orders or tell him the answers (save the uncertain precedent of prior judges' opinions)—Minton turned out pedestrian, often off-the-point, but always flatly stated, law. None of this stopped Truman—who knew him as a regular Democrat, a personal friend, and a man with that overrated qualification for the highest Court, judicial experience—from naming Minton, over scores of other and abler federal judges, to a Justiceship. With Minton still wanting and needing to be led, and with Vinson—after three frustrating years as Chief in name only—wanting to lead, it was inevitable that the freshman Justice would immediately join the Court captain's anti-libertarian camp. During his very first term, he wrote one of the opinions (Reed wrote the other) that discarded Murphy-penned Bill-of-Rights decisions only two years old. Soon, as so often happens, the disciple's ardor was greater than the master's; through the four years they sat together, Minton's votes against civil liberties exceeded by a few even Vinson's—and Reed's and Clark's. Indeed, during Vinson's final term, when the Court struck down one further device to deprive Negroes of their voting rights (the Texas "Jaybirds," an all white club, held their private election *before* the state primary and then joined together to vote officially for *their* winner), Minton dissented alone. Highly out of line was Minton's joining with Black and Douglas to protest the arrest of the political speaker who was threatened by hostile members of his audience. But it was characteristic that Minton wrote the ruling which gave constitutional sanction to the disgraceful guilt-by-association doctrine, in the firing of New York schoolteachers—and that he blithely blurted, in its defense: "One's associates, past and present . . . may properly be considered in determining fitness and loyalty. . . . In the employment of officials and teachers of the school system, the state may very properly inquire into

the company they keep. . . ." To which Black retorted:
"Basically these laws rest on the belief that government
should supervise and limit the flow of ideas into the minds
of men. . . . Because of this policy, public officials . . :
vested with powers to select the ideas people can think
about . . . or choose the people or groups people can
associate with . . . are not public servants; they are
public masters." And Douglas recoiled from the whole
idea as "repugnant," "alien to our system," and "a real
threat to our way of life." But Black and Douglas were
dissenting from what is now the law of the land, courtesy
of the Vinson Court—with Minton here, as so often, its
spokesman against freedom.

The mass attack on civil liberties by the 1949–53
Truman-Vinson Court—except that some semblance of
legal decency for Negroes was carried a little way along
from the start made by the New Deal Court, toward the
big step since taken by the Warren Court—was one of two
major contributions of those four years to Supreme Court
history. The other—equally unadmirable if less portentous,
though often employed to achieve the same end—was the
new spendthrift use of "denial of certiorari," to refuse even
to hear a lot of important cases and thus to cut the Justices'
work-load down to a twentieth-century low. Just as Reed
became the Truman quartet's elder statesman on anti-
civil-liberties stuff, so Frankfurter, the stickler for propriety and reluctant facer of solid issues, became their
leader and guide in the sparse use of their usable judicial
power. Where Murphy and Rutledge had teamed with
Black and Douglas to force Court consideration ("certi-

orari" is granted if four Justices vote for it) of many touchy problems, especially in the fair-trial field, the Court, at Frankfurter's open urging, now turned dozens of such cases down. More than that, Frankfurter went so far as to refuse to sit in several cases where, over his objection, Black and Douglas had managed to corral two more votes for a hearing; when this form of prima-donna pouting resulted only in his tossing away his chance to vote on the case itself, Frankfurter switched to a new tack; he began insisting, *after* a case was heard, that it be summarily dismissed because "certiorari" had been "improvidently granted"—a twist which it takes *five* Justices, not four, to prevent; this in turn provoked Douglas to protest, on the public records, against his colleague's persistence at having his own way. But Frankfurter usually did have his own way, thanks to the co-operation of the four Truman Justices—and the double result was to slice the number of cases the Court heard to less than half the number it used to hear ten years before, and to let the Justices duck making any decision at all on many a tough and vital constitutional problem, with Bill-of-Rights problems, of course, at the head of the docket list.

Among the comparatively few public-law cases per year that Vinson's slowed-down nine did deign to handle, some —though a smaller proportion than ever in the past—dealt with economic matters, with the old question of regulation of business, or labor, by government. Topping these in contemporary and probable future importance was the steel-seizure decision, in which the legal issues were so tangled that each of the six majority Justices wrote his own separate opinion (though Black spoke "for the Court") and these, plus the three-man dissent, fill 133 pages of the official Court reports. The political problem was simpler: The steelworkers' demands for higher wages, refused by the steel companies, pointed toward a nationwide strike; the nation needed steel for the undeclared war in Korea; a pro-labor President, rather than use the Taft-Hartley Act of an anti-labor Congress to stop the strike, "seized" the steel plants in the name of the United States (which meant signing a legal paper and hoisting a few symbolic flags) without any clear authorization from Congress—just as Roosevelt had seized plants to stop strikes even before the U.S. entered World War II. With its three strongest let-the-federal-government-do-anything members, Vinson, Minton, and Reed, violently dissenting (and Clark joining the majority only on a comparative technicality), the Court forbade the President to poach on the preserves of Congress—and also precipitated the steel strike that Truman wanted, but in his own way, to avoid. Whether the ruling be rated good or bad, right or wrong, the outstanding fact—little noted at the time or since—was that the Court, while purporting to protect Congress under the old separation-of-powers theory, actually appropriated the top power and the last word, as usual, for itself. Few other economic decisions of the four Fair-Deal-Court years deserve so much as minor mention. State "fair trade laws," forbidding price-cutting on nationally sold products, were knocked out—to the delight of cut-rate drug stores, big low-price department stores like Macy's in New York, and consumers everywhere. The technical expertness of the Federal Communications Commission was honored by the Court in backing the Commission's choice between two competing types of color television. A federal-minded bench naturally upheld national claims over state claims to tidelands oil (until overridden by a more oil-company-minded Administration three years later). Tax laws, labor laws, anti-trust laws, patent laws were applied and "interpreted" pretty much as during the preceding decade; only in the civil liberties field was there significant progress—backward.

The most important and appalling of the Vinson Court's assaults on human dignity and democratic decency, other than those already touched on, concerned the treatment of aliens in a manner to make the Statue of Liberty blush for shame, and the treatment of citizens—especially those subjected to "loyalty" checks or oaths by nation, state, or city—in a manner to do a dictatorship proud. While President Truman was bravely branding the McCarran Act of 1952, before it was passed over his veto, as "worse than the infamous Alien Act of 1798," his Justices were making the new law almost superfluous by their blessing of official outrages committed by his Department of Justice under the not-quite-so-nauseous McCarran Act of 1940. Illustrative of the Vinson Court majority's sorry-but-what-can-we-do attitude was the case of the twenty-three-years-ago ex-Communist who was shipped back to Italy, his American family left behind—with Jackson seeming to say for the Court that the issue was political and so none of the Court's business, with Frankfurter explaining, in characteristic concurrence, that "the place to resist unwise or cruel legislation touching aliens is the Congress, not this Court," and with Black and Douglas of course dissenting. But Jackson and Frankfurter joined Black and Douglas in futile protest when the four Trumanites plus Reed let Truman's Attorney-General arrest, on unproved "charges" of Communism, and then hold indefinitely *without bail* a whole batch of aliens—including a waiter, thirty-nine years in this country, with sons in the U.S. Army, who had donated blood seven times during World War II. And the same five Justices outvoted the same four in apparently condemning to Ellis Island for life a man named Mezei who had lived in the U.S. for twenty-five years, who had gone to Rumania to see his dying mother, who had been refused re-admission to the U.S. on his return, who had been shipped back to Europe where no country on either side of the Iron Curtain would have him (he applied to more than twenty and the Western nations barred him simply because the U.S. had barred him), who had therefore been forced to come back to the prison of Ellis Island —and who never was granted a hearing nor given the slightest notion what the "confidential" charges against him were that kept him from going home to Buffalo. Said Jackson, with the eloquence he could use so strongly on either side: "This man, who seems to have led a life of unrelieved insignificance, must have been astonished to find himself suddenly putting the Government of the United States in such fear that it was afraid to tell him why it was afraid of him. . . . No one can make me believe we are that far gone." But five of his colleagues clinched it that we were.

In some of those cases, too, where fear—which is the only word for it—had spawned official infringements on the rights of U.S. *citizens*, Frankfurter, sometimes Jackson, and occasionally Burton (all three at the Court's far right

during most of the New Deal decade) looked liberal, by
contrast to the Vinson crew, as they now and then backed
Black's and Douglas's steady crusade. When the loose and
look-backward-Angelino "loyalty" oath that Los Angeles
demanded of all city employees was upheld, 5–4, with
Jackson casting the key vote, Frankfurter and Burton
agreed with the two stalwarts of dissent that the oath
requirement was an unconstitutional "bill of attainder"—
in that it punished people for their past doings, as Douglas
put it, "by legislative act, not by judicial process." When
the whole federal "loyalty" program, with its paid, secret
informers and its star-chamber methods, came up for review in the renowned Bailey case, it was Frankfurter and
jumping Jackson who teamed with Black and Douglas to
disown such totalitarian tactics. Part of the Bailey case's
renown stemmed from the fact that the Court, though it
heard the case at length, delivered no opinion—as it never
does when it splits 4–4; with Clark not sitting because, as
Attorney-General, he had played a major and partisan
part in the program, the official announcement merely said,
as is customary, that the lower court's decision (upholding
the program, 2–1) was "affirmed by an equally divided
Court"—and no names given. But the way the Court
divided was made clear, later in the same term, when one
small segment of the program—the listing of "subversive
organizations" by the Attorney-General without giving
them a hearing—was forbidden, by a 5–3 vote, with Burton
crossing to the liberal side on the narrow ground that this
particular procedure was a bit too arbitrary and high-
handed. Here, six of the eight Justices who sat wrote
separate opinions that revealed their views of the program

as a whole; Douglas, for one, openly discussed the Bailey
case in damning the entire supposedly anti-subversion
system as "subverion from within" and "abhorrent to
fundamental justice"; the adamant-against-liberty trio of
Vinson, Minton, and Reed were forced, for a change, into
dissent. But the trio won Burton and Jackson back in the
Dennis (jail-for-the-top-native-Communists) decision's
aftermath, where Judge Medina had sentenced the Communists' *lawyers* to one-to-six months in prison for contempt of court, meaning contempt of him. This time, only
Frankfurter stuck with Black and Douglas, and his long
separate dissent with its forty-seven-page appendix is
perhaps his finest judicial job; the bench and bar should
have blushed with Medina to read in detail of "incontinent
wrangles between court and counsel," as though in "an
undisciplined debating society," which served to "weaken
the restraints of respect" for a judge whose "self-concern
pervades the record"; nor is it any derogation of his
opinion here to point out that—as in the "loyalty" cases
and as when he spoke up, way back, for Sacco and Vanzetti
—it was procedural (or judicial) impropriety that stirred
the scholar-Justice to liberal protest.

For Frankfurter—and Jackson and Burton—had been
right up there with the pack in the Dennis decision itself,
the biggest blot on the Vinson Court's blot-marked ledger.
The importance of the Dennis case did not lie in the front-
paged fact that a few leaders of Russia's feeble fifth column
in the U.S. were jailed, to the undoubted delight of their
propaganda-conscious party and their martyred selves; it
lay in the fact that the Supreme Court of the United States,
without renouncing its self-proclaimed power and duty to

uphold the Constitution even against Acts of Congress, gave its ultimate benediction (as even the old Federalist Chase-Ellsworth Court had never done *in the name of the Supreme Court*) to a law that flatly violated the free-speech guarantee of the First Amendment. Dennis and the others were not convicted for, nor accused of, treason, spying, sabotage or any such *act* of any kind; they were put in prison for talking and writing—for "teaching and advocating" Communism. Although Vinson—for himself and Minton and Reed and Burton (with Clark again not sitting)—purported, by a strange sort of legal legerdemain, to be sticking to Holmes's old and unfortunate "clear and present danger" exception to the Amendment's clear command, he admitted that any danger to the nation *created by these defendants' known and nonsensical Communist activities* was not very clear and was certainly not present. This ignorant, or else intellectually dishonest, distortion of ideas by the wayward use of words was too much for Jackson or Frankfurter to stomach; yet each of these abler Justices, in his own characteristic fashion, went farther than Vinson had gone toward undermining the First Amendment. Jackson boldly urged judicial abandonment of the Amendment, "clear and present danger" rule and all, wherever a "conspiracy" was at large—despite the fact that the Amendment makes no mention of conspiracies and that Holmes originated his rule in a conspiracy case; Frankfurter, judicial-restrainedly timid and voluminously academic, deplored Congress's cavalier treatment of freedom of speech while simultaneously deploring his own obviously self-imposed inability to do anything about it. Equally characteristic of the men who wrote them were the

Black and Douglas separate dissents. Douglas hewed straight, in the Holmes-Brandeis tradition, to the clear-and-present-danger line: "Free speech—the glory of our system of government—should not be sacrificed on anything less than plain and objective proof of danger that . . . is imminent," not out of "prejudice nor hate nor senseless fear." Black, as bold as Jackson, but in the opposite direction, suggested scrapping the Holmes restriction "as to speech in the realm of public matters" and taking the First Amendment at its face; he also hoped, with a wistful note of near-despair which put the whole case in its proper light, that "in calmer times, when present pressures, passions and fears subside, this or some later Court will restore the First Amendment liberties to the high preferred place where they belong in a free society."

While Black's words might well stand as an epitaph for the Vinson Court, a couple of final and comparatively minor matters further italicize the tragic trend of that four-year span. One was the Court's backward stride in the fair-treatment-of-criminals field, where the New Deal nine had most steadfastly held the states to the Bill of Rights; during Vinson's final term, his Court did hear—as it rarely deigned to—a protest against barbaric police techniques; and with only Black, Douglas, and Frankfurter dissenting, it upheld the conviction of two New York thugs who had been kept incommunicado until confessions were literally wrung from them. But far more revealing of the whole temper of the four Fair Deal years was the hesitant, half-hearted way the Vinson-men handled the one issue that won them a semblance of liberal repute—the issue of segregation in the South. Back in 1896, when Fuller's Court gave segregation the judicial nod and invented the separate-but-equal excuse for it, the first Justice Harlan, in strong dissent, exclaimed: "Our Constitution is color-blind." Over half a century later, Negroes hoped that a Court majority might have caught up with Harlan; in the cases urging admission of Negroes to a white Texas law school, a white Oklahoma graduate course, and the white section of Southern dining-cars, the main plea was that the entire separate-but-equal doctrine be discarded; what the Vinson Court did was to sidestep the big point and order all the Negroes admitted on the old, narrow ground that the separate facilities offered them were *not* equal. But no such avenue of escape was handy when cases began to come up to the Court where the separate public grade-schools of the South—with the Negro schools sometimes newer and better equipped than the white schools—were attacked on the simple theory that "separate," *per se*, could never be "equal." Little appreciated is the fact that cases of this kind were duly before Vinson's Court for two full terms before he died; but by sending them back to lower courts for the flimsiest of reasons, by asking for later re-arguments after they were fully argued, by delays and postponements, Vinson managed to evade till his death the touchy political problem at their core. That Vinson himself was mainly responsible for ducking the high, hard one was made clear when the same eight Associate Justices faced it head-on during the first season of their new captain, Earl Warren of California.

If Vinson was a better and smarter real-life ballplayer than his successor—who never got beyond a symbolic center-field on a sandlot team—Warren already bids fair to eclipse the late semi-pro shortstop in the slightly more important job of Chief Justice of the United States. The handsome, blond hulk of a man, who looks like a kindly Viking (the family name was once a Norwegian "Varran"), grew up in the healthy and healthily unsegregated San Joaquin Valley of south central California. Son of a former railroad mechanic, Warren seems to have inherited the practical bent of mind that goes with use of the hands (a political opponent once said, intending it as an insult, that he "never had an abstract thought in his life"); Warren himself is ambidextrous; he writes right and throws left— which may again be symbolic. And he has the easy, outgoing manner with people, of whatever political persuasion, that marks the Westerner tinged with the politician. For Warren has been in politics—and, unlike any of his new brethren, in *state* politics—practically the whole of his adult life. Beginning a few years out of law school, he climbed a prosecuting ladder from deputy city attorney through several ranks in the county district attorney's office up to the state attorney-generalship; if the conviction of criminals seems a strange career for so inherently and almost indiscriminately friendly a man, he has said, despite his steamroller success as a prosecutor, that it used to make him sick to win a murder case. He was happier in the California governorship, to which he was elected for an unprecedented trio of consecutive terms with unprecedented bipartisan support. There, his budget-balancing Republicanism did not stop him from raising old-age pensions, nor from urging unsuccessfully a state plan for compulsory medical insurance; his prosecuting past did not stop him from taking a moderate stand against unbridled "loyalty" oaths for teachers; his scorn for race prejudice led him to name a Negro, for the first time in state history, to California's Superior Court, and also to write a gratuitous and indignant letter of sympathy to a Chinese family whom an all-white section of San Francisco had voted not to let live there. Though Warren's lone personal excursion into national politics was his run for the Vice-Presidency with Dewey in 1948, he was long a power in the party (and a recurrent dark-horse Presidential possibility) because he controlled the big California delegation. And it was partly as thanks for his state's support at the 1952 convention that Eisenhower named him Chief Justice; but the main reason for the President's choice was his view of Warren as a universally respected, reliable middle-of-the-roader—which is precisely what the ambidextrous ex-center-fielder had always been.

It is of course too early to make a substantial *judicial* assessment of the healthy sixty-four-year-old, who may have another ten, or even twenty, years to go. Yet his first term on the bench did begin to bear out Eisenhower's, and the nation's, confidence that Warren the judge, like Warren the governor, would be neither reactionary fish nor radical fowl. In the close civil-liberties cases, he occasionally forced Reed and Minton, instead of Black and Douglas, into dissent—as Vinson had rarely if ever done; indeed, where the Court split in this kind of case, Warren was on the Black-Douglas side almost half the time. In economic areas of dispute, a states'-rights tendency on the part of the new Chief began to crop up—as might have been expected; for whereas every one of the twelve Justices who immediately preceded him to the Court had been picked from federal government posts (save only Frank-furter, who had once worked in Washington and whose unofficial influence and activity in the New Deal had been greater than those of most of its employees), Warren came straight from a lifetime in state office. That he was thus probably destined to be less federal-government-minded than any of his colleagues was hinted, not only in his vote to uphold the Eisenhower Congress's Submerged Lands Act (giving tidelands oil back to the states), but more pointedly in his dissent, with Black and Douglas, against banning a *state* tax on sales to a company working for the *U.S.* Navy—where the Court majority followed the old dual-sovereignty line that Marshall started way back in McCulloch *v.* Maryland. But Warren's pull toward real and unseparate racial equality was considerably stronger than his pro-state slant. And—despite the sport-paged ruling that professional baseball was still as far out of reach of the anti-trust acts as when Holmes had put it there, long before the days of television (a ruling that was anti-federal in both essence and origin)—the one major, and clearly historic, move of the Warren Court in its first term was its head-on handling of the Segregation Cases.

That the flat outlawing of separate public schools for black and white children, as a violation of the Fourteenth Amendment's "equal protection" clause, was done by a unanimous Court and that the new Chief spoke for his Court—without so much as a "separate concurrence" to sap the strength of his words—are tributes to Warren's executive skill and force. More impressive still was the way he spoke; with no skirting around old cases or tight-roping between them, with no pseudo-scholarly array of legal or historical arguments, he simply said with refreshing straightforwardness that the separate-but-equal rule was out of date. Politely dismissing as "inconclusive" the exhaustive and, of course, conflicting efforts of both sides to "prove" what those who wrote and adopted the Fourteenth Amendment "intended," he added that, in any event, "we cannot turn the clock back to 1868." Hitting straight to the core of the issue, he said: "To separate them [*school children*] from others of similar age and qualifications solely because of their race generates a feeling of inferiority as to their status in the community that may affect their hearts and minds in a way unlikely ever to be undone. . . . We conclude that in the field of public education the doctrine of 'separate but equal' has no place."

Had this masterly performance, on every level, with its vast political repercussions, national and international, made up the Court's entire work for the term, the term would not have been wasted—and indeed, it very nearly did so; only sixty-five cases, the record low for over a century, got full treatment from the Justices. Presumably, a tremendous amount of backstage time was spent on the segregation matter; presumably also, it took some months for the man who had never been a judge, much less a Chief Justice, to adjust to the mechanics and the formalities of his brand-new job. If the Warren Court's slow gait continued into its second year, it was partly because the Justices were worrying throughout the term the complicated business, officially held over, of how and when to put their blanket anti-segregation order into effective operation, in different parts of the rumblingly rebellious South. But an-

other reason for the snail's pace involved politics in an
even more obvious way; for the Court kept putting off the
hearing of many major and possibly 4–4 cases while a
Senate Judiciary Committee run by maverick Senator
Langer (who was demanding a top federal judgeship for
some fellow-North-Dakotan), and then a new Committee
run by Democrats, deliberately dawdled at confirming
Eisenhower's choice for Jackson's seat—the second Justice
John Marshall Harlan, this one from New York.

Prediction in print is a preoccupation for the foolhardy.
And yet, if the prior lives of Justices help shape, and so
help foretell, what their slants and bents on the Court will
be, a rough guess—to be checked ten years hence—can be
made about Harlan. Too conventional in background, too
conformist in career, ever to match the fiery independent
thinker and liberal dissenter who was his grandfather,
Harlan may yet prove not so orthodox a Justice as many
suppose; indeed, he is a new breed of cat on the Court.
Though born in Chicago, he is a Princeton-to-Oxford-to-
Wall-Street-law-practice product—the Court's first Ivy
League "white-shoe boy," its first Rhodes Scholar, its first
full-fledged Eastern Dewey Republican. That he has always been well-to-do and upper-crust does not necessarily
betoken automatic conservatism; so was Holmes. Politically closer to Warren than to any other present Justice,
despite major differences in their pre-Court work and
lives, Harlan is also apt to be *judicially* closer, but without
the Westerner's strength and simplicity. Like his Chief, he
has never held federal office—except for a brief apprentice-
ship on a federal court of appeals—and his stints of public

service (odd jobs of investigating or prosecuting) have
been for the state; the national government will get from
him no special preference. Again like Warren, his prosecuting was tempered with humanity, and the few criminal
cases he heard as a court of appeals judge display concern
for the fair treatment of defendants; he will be no Vinson
at kicking the Bill of Rights around.

In all likelihood, the general slant of the new Justice
will be just about the opposite of Reed's—except for a
similarly super-lawyerlike over-attention to detail. On
economic issues, where the country-bred boy tended anti-
business, the big-city boy will tend pro-business; where
the rural small-town lawyer tended pro-labor, the Wall
Street financial lawyer will tend anti-labor; where the federal government servant tended strongly pro-national and
somewhat anti-state on taxes and regulation, the private
practitioner and occasional state servant will tend strongly
anti-national and somewhat pro-state. It is on civil liberties
that Harlan may turn the tables the other way; for where
Reed, ex-Solicitor-General of the U.S., came close to
thinking that government, especially the federal government, could not be wrong—no matter how it treated the
Bill of Rights—Harlan may have that sense of *noblesse
oblige* on such matters which so often goes with born-and-
bred economic conservatism. True, Harlan, during the
court-of-appeals prelude to his Justiceship, did deliver the
decision that sent a dozen second-string Communist leaders to jail under the Smith Act; but it was not his job to
question the Smith Act's constitutionality, so recently upheld by the Vinson Court in the Dennis case; and his
patient, painstaking, sixty-page opinion reads almost as

though he were seeking some way to set the poor fools free. It is far more meaningful that, in 1940, Harlan served as special counsel to New York City's Board of Higher Education in its futile effort, blocked by local judicial Philistines, to bring to the City College faculty the famous if unconforming philosopher, Bertrand Russell. Just possibly, if hopefully, the appointment of Harlan may give the Court one more and badly-needed vote for freedom of the mind.

There are other harbingers of hope. One is the sharp drop in the proportionate number of Douglas's dissents between Vinson's last term as Chief and Warren's first; in 1952–53, Douglas set an all-time record by protesting 49 per cent, or just one less than half, of the Court's decisions, the biggest batch of them in the civil-liberties field—and by being concerned enough to write 33 dissenting opinions (while still carrying more than his share of majority "opinions for the Court"); in 1953–54, the proportion had gone down to 38 per cent—and he bothered to elaborate only 15 of his minority votes; Black's dissents fell off too, but less sharply. Statistics also point up another hopeful sign; Clark, so unsure of himself that he always prefers to follow the pack and its current leader, has dissented from less than 5 per cent of the Court's decisions, or a total of less than 25 times, since he came to the bench six years ago; whenever Warren goes with Black and Douglas, and takes Harlan or Frankfurter or maybe Burton with him, Clark is sure to desert Reed and Minton, and trot along. Moreover, the present Court's two most determined defenders of the judicial bridge against any influx of civil liberties may soon be cut to a single Horatius, named Minton; for recurrent rumors of Reed's imminent retirement have recently grown louder. On a more tangible level, it is heartening that the Warren Court has "granted certiorari" in a new challenge (the Peters case) to the whole crux of the federal "loyalty" program, which was handled so inconclusively and unsatisfactorily by the Vinson Court in the Bailey case; what this implies—since Jackson was dead, and Clark probably disqualified himself again, and the Reed-Minton-Burton trio presumably stuck to their pro-"loyalty"-program stand of the Bailey case—is that Warren cast the fourth vote for "certiorari."

Indeed, the most hopeful and happy omen of them all is the apparent judicial character of the new Chief Justice. Unblinded by the tweedledum-tweedledee twaddle of much that passes for learned legal argument, unblinkered into the narrow vision so often so typical of those with past judicial experience, he seems essentially a direct, plain-spoken politician who knows that his is primarily a political job. Of such, when they combine humanity with honesty, are judicial statesmen made. Not so wise as Holmes, not so intellectually daring as Black, not so dedicated as Brandeis or Douglas, not so independent as the nineteenth century's Johnson or Miller or Harlan, and clearly not so liberal as any of these, he comes closer to resembling a might-be twentieth-century Marshall. The same easy strength is there, and the same earthy approach to the esoterics of law. But where Marshall's achievement was to protect a weak nation, as a nation, from its people, Warren's opportunity is the precise opposite; it is to protect the people, as people, from their strong nation. Given the will and the good-will to do it, he can succeed.

O'Shaughnessy, the Irish poet, once sang: "For each age is a dream that is dying, or one that is coming to birth." Over eight score years and five, through age after different age, the men who are the Supreme Court of the United States have attended the birth and the death of different dreams. Today it would be a tragedy if the Black and Douglas dissents—which are rather affirmations of a faith—should prove a dirge for the bravest dream of all. For under the inspiration of those two great Justices and the aegis of a potentially great Chief Justice, the American dream of freedom may be reborn.

INDEX

A

Adams, John, 10, 62, 66, 68, 69, 71, 80, 91
Adams, John Quincy, 93, 104, 110
Alger, Horatio, 225, 274
Altgeld, John Peter, 171
Armour, Philip, 169
Arno, Peter, 215
Arthur, Chester A., 164

B

Bailey case, 319, 331
Barkley, Alben W., 242
Barton, Bruce, 309
Beard, Charles, 95, 120, 150
Beveridge, Albert J., 96
Bingham, John, 149, 150
Black, Hugo L., 16, 251–252, 257, 262, 263, 264–266, 271, 275, 276, 277, 278, 279, 282, 283, 287, 290, 291, 293, 294, 298, 304, 305, 308, 309, 310, 313, 314, 315, 317, 319, 320, 322, 325, 326, 330, 331, 332

Blaine, James G., 168
Blair, John, 49, 61, 137
Blatchford, Samuel, 164
Borah, William E., 189
Bradley, Joseph P., 158, 159, 170
Brandeis, Louis D., 31, 187, 196, 219, 225, 226–229, 230, 233, 237, 241, 246, 253, 258, 260, 262, 270, 272, 273, 275, 277, 292, 295, 304, 322, 331
Brewer, David J., 169, 171, 187
Bridges, Harry, 278
Brown, Henry, 187
Buchanan, James, 130, 131, 132, 157
Burr, Aaron, 92–93
Burton, Harold H., 264, 287, 299, 305, 309–310, 318, 319, 320, 321, 330, 331
Butler, Nicholas Murray, 226, 274
Butler, Pierce, 30, 187, 217, 220–221, 228, 253, 255, 298, 305
Byrnes, James F., 263, 266, 283, 303

OUT IN SPORT

Research has shown that since the turn of the millennium, matters have rapidly improved for gays and lesbians in sport. Where gay and lesbian athletes were merely tolerated a decade ago, today they are celebrated.

This book represents the most comprehensive examination of the experiences of gays and lesbians in sport ever produced. Drawing on interviews with openly gay and lesbian athletes in the US and the UK, as well as media accounts, the book examines the experiences of "out" men and women, at recreational, high school, university and professional levels, in addition to those competing in gay sports leagues.

Offering a new approach to understanding this important topic, *Out in Sport* is essential reading for students and scholars of sport studies, LGBT studies and sociology, as well as sports practitioners and trainers.

Eric Anderson is Professor of Sport, Masculinities and Sexualities at the University of Winchester, UK.

Rory Magrath is Lecturer in the School of Sport, Health and Social Sciences at Southampton Solent University, UK.

Rachael Bullingham is Lecturer in Physical Education at the University of Worcester, UK.

OUT IN SPORT

The experiences of openly
gay and lesbian athletes
in competitive sport

*Eric Anderson, Rory Magrath and
Rachael Bullingham*

Routledge
Taylor & Francis Group

LONDON AND NEW YORK

First published 2016
by Routledge
2 Park Square, Milton Park, Abingdon, Oxon OX14 4RN

and by Routledge
711 Third Avenue, New York, NY 10017

Routledge is an imprint of the Taylor & Francis Group, an informa business

British Library Cataloguing in Publication Data
A catalogue record for this book is available from the British Library

Library of Congress Cataloging in Publication Data
Names: Anderson, Eric, 1968-
Title: Out in sport : the experiences of openly gay and lesbian athletes in
    competitive sport / Eric Anderson, Rory Magrath and Rachael Bullingham.
Description: Milton Park, Abingdon, Oxon ; New York, NY : Routledge, 2016. |
    Includes bibliographical references.
Identifiers: LCCN 2015036386| ISBN 9781138182219 (hardback) |
    ISBN 9781138182240 (pbk.) | ISBN 9781315646572 (e-book)
Subjects: LCSH: Gay athletes. | Gay athletes—United States. | Gay
    athletes—Great Britain. | Sports—Social aspects. | Homophobia in sports.
Classification: LCC GV708.8 .A63 2016 | DDC 306.4/83—dc23
LC record available at http://lccn.loc.gov/2015036386

ISBN: 978-1-138-18221-9 (hbk)
ISBN: 978-1-138-18224-0 (pbk)
ISBN: 978-1-315-64657-2 (ebk)

Typeset in Bembo
by Swales & Willis Ltd, Exeter, Devon, UK

CONTENTS

DEDICATION

We dedicate this book to two of the most influential leaders of the movement to make sport more inclusive to sexual minorities, Cyd Ziegler and Jim Buzinski.

Jim Buzinski came out of the closet as America's first openly gay sports editor in 1987; although he received much hostility, he featured articles on the topic of gays in sports long before it was fashionable. Years later, he met Cyd, an openly gay sprinter and sports journalist with an aptitude for public speaking and advocacy. Together, they decided to do something to reduce homophobia in sport, which at the time was rampant.

They began by first giving interviews to the gay press, and helping closeted gay athletes out of the closet. Over the next few years Jim and Cyd began to lobby sport organizations and connect gay athletes to support networks. Most significantly, however, in 1999 they launched Outsports.com.

Buzinski and Zeigler have written hundreds of profile and other pieces about gay athletes for the website, and Jim and Cyd have expanded the site to cover virtually every aspect of the topic for international presses. Over the next decade, Jim and Cyd became two of the few key movers and shakers in the world. They are regular commentators for all four major US television and the leading Canadian television networks, have appeared on the BBC and provided radio and print interviews for hundreds of other outlets around the world.

Whenever a major athlete comes out of the closet—from Esera Tuaolo in the NFL in 2003 to Jason Collins in the NBA in 2013, or more recently Michael Sam in the NFL—Outsports is the go-to source for journalists worldwide. Cyd and Jim have been active in dealing with policy makers on the issue as well: consulting for professional teams and sporting bodies.

Outsports.com has also become the vessel for academics wanting to research the topic. Cyd and Jim have helped connect at least a dozen researchers with gay and lesbian athletes for their work, and they freely disseminate the results of that research on their website.

Together with a growing chorus of advocates and athletes who look to Cyd and Jim for guidance, they have helped turn the tide from what Buzinski once described as "the last closet" to what we find in our research: despite what the media sometimes says about sport, it is actually a place where gay and lesbian athletes most often find inclusion and celebration. While the public perception is that a gay male athlete would be silenced or harassed on a team, in reality teammates are more likely to go to a gay club with them. This is the message that Outsports spreads; this is a message that the research in this book supports.

Today, Cyd and Jim's Outsports has gone so mainstream that it has been bought by the largest sports website network in the US, reinforcing Outsports and its founders' position within the movement for years to come.

It is for their decades of service toward making sport, and its ancillary institutions, more inclusive that we dedicate this book to them.

FIGURES

1
STUDYING GAYS AND LESBIANS IN SPORT

This book represents the most comprehensive examination of the experiences of gays and lesbians in sport ever produced. Unlike previous works that have focused on only men (i.e. Anderson 2005a) or women (i.e. Griffin 1998), and unlike research that has only examined recreational athletes (i.e. Hekma 1998) or closeted athletes (i.e. Pronger 1990; Denison and Kitchen 2015), this research examines both men and women, at the recreational, high school, university and professional levels of play who are out of the closet, as well as those competing in gay sports leagues. It is a scientific endeavor based in empirical research conducted in both the United States and the United Kingdom.

Throughout this book, we highlight that social matters for lesbian athletes, and particularly for gay male athletes, have dramatically changed for the better over recent decades (Anderson 2015a). This is not to suggest that gay and lesbian athletes play without any difficulties, nor is it to suggest that homophobia has decreased to a level that permits inclusivity within all geographical sporting spaces within these two countries—declining homophobia is an uneven social process—but it is to suggest that the older research on the topic of gay men and lesbians in sport is now not only dated, but irrelevant. Accordingly, while the cultural change we examine in this book is steady, if at times gradual, we argue that research on the topic should be divided between that which occurred prior to and after the turn of the twenty-first century.

Illustrating this shift, researchers who examined the issue of gay men in sports in the waning decades of the twentieth century largely agreed that organized sports were a highly homophobic institution (Bryant 2001; Clarke 1998; Hekma 1998; Pronger 1990; Wolf-Wendel, Toma, and Morphew 2001). Hekma (1998: 2) wrote that "Gay men who are seen as queer and effeminate are granted no space whatsoever in what is generally considered to be a masculine preserve and a macho enterprise." And Pronger (1990: 26) agreed: "Many of the (gay) men I interviewed said they were uncomfortable with teamsports . . . orthodox masculinity is usually an important subtext if not *the* leitmotif in teamsports."

Although women have traditionally maintained more progressive attitudes toward sexual minorities (Loftus 2001), matters were not much better for lesbian athletes. Krane (2001: 118) wrote that "Although there is greater acceptance of females engaging in sport behaviors, there still are limits as to how much athletic prowess and muscularity are socially acceptable." Griffin wrote (1992: 252), "Because lesbians were assumed to be masculine creatures who rejected their female identity and roles as wives and mothers, athletic women became highly suspect."

We argue that the research prior to the twenty-first century also varies on another important dimension of homophobia in men's and women's sport. Namely, female athletes are suspect of being lesbian simply for their participation, regardless of their gendered performance. Conversely, male athletes are assumed to be heterosexual unless they violate gendered norms. Burton-Nelson (1994: 1) nicely captured this twentieth-century prescription on women playing sport: "If you grew up female in America, you heard this: Sports are unfeminine. And this: Girls who play sports are tomboys or lesbians."

Accordingly, female athletes who challenge the norms of femininity by playing competitive team sport often use homophobia in order to distance themselves from being thought lesbian (Lenskyj 2003). In order to distance themselves from being socially perceived as lesbian, female athletes wear feminine clothing and jewelry, and use makeup, despite its sporting impracticality (Krane 2001). Griffin (1998) gave the example of a female basketball coach pacing the paraffin courtside lines wearing high heels and a miniskirt, suggesting that coaches do this because sporting women who do not hyperfeminize themselves face increased suspicion regarding their sexuality (Cox and Thompson 2001). This gendered phenomenon is described as apologetic (Felshin 1974), and exists as a tool of marginalization to police orthodox gender roles (Anderson 2009a).

Once a lesbian athlete came out of the closet, they faced both overt and covert forms of discrimination (Griffin, 1998). However, it was impossible to study openly gay men's twentieth-century experiences, as too few came out at any level of sport (recreational, educationally based or professional). This is why in Pronger's (1990) treatment of the subject he wrote only of closeted athletes' fears of what coming out would be like—he could find no gay men who were out in sport.

Although scholars did not identify or recognize it this way, studying gay and lesbian athletes prior to the new millennium was not only done in an era of high homophobia, but also an era of high homohysteria. This is a concept that we flesh out in Chapter 4, but the general idea is that a homohysteric culture is a homosexually panicked culture in which suspicion of homosexuality permeates. In other words, because heterosexuals cannot socially prove that they are not gay, in a culture of high homophobia, they attempt to prove their heterosexuality by aligning their gender and sexual behaviors in opposition to whatever is deemed homosexual.

We show that cultural homohysteria in America escalated rapidly in the mid-1980s, partially as a result of heightened cultural homophobia that combined with the HIV/AIDS epidemic and a revival of fundamentalist Christianity. This means that there was cultural awareness that homosexuality existed as a stable orientation within a sizeable percent of the American population, which was 'morally' opposed to it; heterosexuals thus feared being thought a sexual minority.

However, unlike the male scholars who studied homophobia in sport at the time (i.e. Pronger 1990), in 1998 Pat Griffin suggested that if gay male athletes, who are stigmatized as being feminine can be as strong and competitive as heterosexual male athletes, they may threaten the perceived distinctions between gay men and straight men, and thus the perceived differences between men and women as a whole. While this contention did not receive much attention in the world of sport scholars, French theorist Pierre Bourdieu (2001) agreed.

Bourdieu maintained that the gay male was uniquely situated to undermine masculine orthodoxy because of his ability to invisibly gain access to masculine privilege before coming out as gay. Because of this, Bourdieu theorized that the gay male may be positioned to align with feminists in a terrain of progressive coalition politics to symbolically attack male and heterosexual dominance. Thus, gay male athletes—who are seen as a paradox because they comply with the gendered script of being a man through the physicality involved in sports, but violate another masculine script through the existence of same-sex desires—may threaten sport as a prime site of orthodox masculinity and masculine privilege. It is perhaps for this reason that Clarke (1998: 145) wrote that gay males are perceived, "largely as deviant and dangerous participants on the sporting turf . . . in that they defy culturally defined structures of hegemonic masculinity."

Examining gay and lesbian athletes in contemporary sport

Since Griffin in the 1980s and 1990s surmised that gay athletes could be key in reducing the binary ways of thinking about sexuality and gender, she has been proved correct. Anglo-American culture has changed its disposition toward homosexuality rapidly, and progressively, in the intervening years. If there is one thing that we are certain of, this shift is happening so fast it is hard to keep up with.

This argument might seem oxymoronic to most readers. Public perception that sport is a highly homophobic institution remains high. This is fueled, largely, by the near-total absence of openly gay male players in sport (less so for lesbians). Here, there are contradictory messages: on the one hand, broadcast media and popular opinion (Denison and Kitchen 2015) are often quick to decry homophobia due to this absence. On the other hand, the absence of gay male players in sport is not evidence of homophobia.

Gay men, as we are readily aware, are over-represented in art, dance, music, theatre and multiple individual and aesthetic sports. This over-representation must be met with an under-representation elsewhere: in other words, gay men are a finite resource. To be more specific, although we do not have precise data to support our claim apart from some data on cheerleading (Anderson 2005b) and ice-dancing (Adams M.L. 2011), it is not something many would contest if we stated that gay men are also over-represented (i.e. more than 2.8 percent of the population) in gymnastics, diving, swimming, twirling and perhaps some individual sports like weight-lifting and distance running. This suggests that, whether a product of biology or social construction, sporting taste is related to sexuality.

Further evidence supporting our hypothesis of diminished homophobia in sport comes from the experiences of professional gay and lesbian athletes who come out of the closet in recent years has been overwhelmingly positive. Rather than being drummed out of sport after coming out, professional soccer player Robbie Rogers received a standing ovation when he took the field for his first match as an out player, while out NBA player Jason Collins was invited to meet the President.

In July 2015, the United States Women's Soccer Team won the Women's World Cup. The US team had three openly lesbian players, and it was also led by an openly lesbian coach: Jill Ellis. In fact, after winning, one of the players, Abby Wambach, ran over to kiss her wife Sarah Huffman, in a photo that set social media networks ablaze with grandeur and the Twitter trending of #lovewins. The event came only a week on the heels of the US Supreme Court's decision to legalize gay marriage across the United States.

How then do we make sense of perceptions versus reality?

Adding to this complex situation, Denison and Kitchen (2015) released a non-academic study on the perceptions of homophobia across multiple Western countries and according to multiple age categories. Their findings are rather complex, and this is partially due to the complex design of their study. The study, available online as "Out on the Fields," claims to represent the "First International Study on Homophobia in Sport." However, we highlight a number of problems: first, the study permits people to retrospectively account for their experiences in sport (closeted or out). To this we argue: if you ask 60-year-old men if sport is homophobic, they will undoubtedly say "yes." For example, one question asks if you have ever "Witnessed or experienced homophobia in a sporting environment." This is an entirely misleading question, for it does not reflect contemporary experiences. With more than 80 percent of their respondents (9,500) being older than 21, people can reflect upon experiences from even decades ago and these show as current results. Seeing an act of homophobia three decades ago does not mean that sport is homophobic today. Sociologically speaking, seeing an act of homophobia even today does not make sport a homophobic enterprise.

Second, the study conflates the experiences of heterosexuals, bisexuals and transgendered people with gays and lesbians. Yet considerable research has shown that the experiences of bisexuals and, particularly, transgendered individuals are *far worse* than gays and lesbians in Anglo-American and Western European countries (Robinson and Espelage 2011). But the experience of boxing promoter Frank Maloney, whose gender reassignment now sees her go by the name Kellie Maloney, as well as that of retired American athlete Bruce Jenner, now known as Caitlyn Jenner, suggests that this inclusivity could also now extend to transgendered individuals.

Third, the inclusion of heterosexuals in this questionnaire also generates bias. In all likelihood, the only heterosexuals that would be interested enough to complete a survey about the experiences of gay and lesbian athletes would be ones that are so politically aligned to supporting LGBT rights that they would over-report the negative and under-report the positive. The victimization framework (declaring how awful society is for gays and lesbians) is one way leftist individuals, and particularly left-leaning heterosexuals, prove their left-wing credentials. It sounds conservative to say that homophobia is not a problem. Taking this framework thus biases one's perceptions.

Fourth, the study also conflates witnessing an act of homophobia in sport with experiencing one—an egregious error that fails any standard of academic accountability. Worse, the same question—"Have you witnessed or experienced homophobia in a sporting environment as a player or spectator?"—conflates one's recreational participation with professional sporting environments: so someone who plays sport without incidence for 30 years, but once, 31 years ago, saw one homophobic act in professional sport counts.

Fifth, the study had no controls or measures on who took the survey. Anyone, including a jokester, can take the study and distort its results. Equally, just as you are much more likely to fill out a customer feedback form if you've had bad service than good, one is much more likely to take this survey if they feel victimized by sport than if they have not been. Thus, the study had no controls to approximate a general survey of the population.

Thus, Denison and Kitchen's 2015 report was very much a "hearts and minds" study of perceptions and fears, not necessarily reflecting empirical realities. It was a piece of advocacy work, more than one of academic rigor. For example, it takes homophobia as granted, asking participants to answer, "Thinking of all sporting environments where homophobia could occur, where do you think it occurs most often?" Yet none of the answers permit a respondent to say that it does not occur at all, or that it is highly unlikely. Furthermore, the question does not separate out the sport that one actually plays versus professional sport.

Perhaps the best example of the study's measuring of fears, and not realities, comes from the question about whether people perceived that openly gay or lesbian people would be safe at a spectator sporting event. Here, 83 percent of American participants said that they would not be very safe. Interestingly, at the same time the survey was released, the LA Dodgers "kiss cam" (available on YouTube) showed two gay men in the audience kissing. In response, the crowd audibly cheered two or three times louder than they did for any of the heterosexual couples kissing, in an overt display of support.

Highlighting the broader perception of fear over reality even among those central to the issues of gays in sport is the story of baseball's first openly gay umpire, Dale Scott, compared to gays-in-sport activist, Dave Pallone. Pallone was pressured to resign from baseball in 1988 after he was outed in a *New York Post* article. He has fought for equality in sport since. However, when Scott came out as an openly gay baseball umpire in 2014, there was no pressure to retire. At the time,

Pallone said that "He's going to find out how much hate there really is out there." Yet, in a June 11, 2015 article on Outsports.com, Scott reports that after both spring training, and completing the first third of the baseball season, he has had no difficulties whatsoever—that he has not even heard a single gay slur. These cases thus highlight the perception of the lingering fear of homophobia, versus its reality. As we argue in this book, this is a generational phenomenon: in general, older men expect homophobia and younger men do not.

This book therefore takes a different approach than fear-mongering, or seeing the world through the lens of victimization. We are less concerned with individuals' fears, and instead interested in the empirical *realities* of what happens when a gay or lesbian athlete does come out to his or her ostensibly heterosexual team. It documents four mechanisms for the changing relationship between sexual minorities and sport:

1. Primarily, we rely on our own comprehensive empirical studies—including over a hundred openly gay male athletes and 43 openly lesbian athletes across multiple sports teams in the UK and the US;
2. We use academic data on the attitudes of over a thousand heterosexual athletes to show that they maintain positive attitudes toward sexual minorities;
3. We show how contemporary media is more closely aligned with positive narratives of gays and lesbians in sport, documenting a shift towards inclusivity for openly gay athletes, and
4. We draw on data from a range of secondary sources evidencing how homophobia outside of sport has dramatically decreased in contemporary Western cultures.

We are not the only ones to notice this shift. Outsports.com has also touted the cultural change for gay and lesbian athletes in sport. They argue, for example, that no sport-related story dominated the 2014 year like that concerning LGBT issues in sports. For them, 2014 was the year of the gay athlete.

Indeed, 2014 was a year of many firsts for gay and lesbian athletes. Within American sport, there were some big name outings. The US received its first openly gay NBA player with Jason Collins, and its first gay male NFL player with Michael Sam. The English Premier League saw its first openly gay (albeit now retired) footballer, Thomas Hitzlsperger. The leading medal scorer of the 2014 Winter Olympics was Dutch lesbian speed skater, Ireen Wüst—who won five medals (two gold and three silver).

There were other firsts, a first openly gay collegiate football player and the first openly gay male Division 1 basketball player, too. It is not just 2014 that has been important of course. There has been a steady and increasing flow of gay and lesbian athletes coming out in all sorts of sports, in both of the countries we study. There are world and Olympic champion athletes too: Eric Radford in pair skating, Matthew Mitcham and Tom Daley in diving, Chris Morgan in powerlifting. The world's most revered rugby union referee, Nigel Owens (who refereed the 2015 rugby union

World Cup final), is openly gay, and more coaches are also coming out, such as Evan Risk, a high school track and cross-country coach based in Iowa, US. Readers can see more about openly gay coaches on the Facebook page, *Equality Coaching Alliance*.

We are also seeing an increasing number of young people coming out of the closet. Although his parents will not let us identify his name in this book, there is an openly gay 8th-grade (14-year-old) tennis player who has received tremendous support from his teammates and classmates. Outsports.com even profiles the story of an openly gay 12-year-old lacrosse player. Yet there is no systematic research on the experience of open or closeted gay or lesbian schoolchildren in sport. We regret that this book does not address this population.

Equally as important, the list of professional sportsmen and women who are heterosexual, but nonetheless publicly advocate for the acceptance and inclusion of sexual minorities in sport is, simply, too large to compile. They come from those who have dedicated their lives to helping support sexual minorities in sport, such as former wrestler Hudson Taylor, along with Olympic Team GB diver Chris Mears, judo athlete Ashley McKenzie, and gold medalist boxer Luke Campbell, who all posed nude for *Gay Times* magazine. Coaches, team owners and heads of all sorts of sporting organizations are also coming out in support of sexual diversity in sport. Many sports stadiums host a LGBT day; many British soccer teams have worn rainbow laces to help kick homophobia out of sport and a few university-based sports teams have stripped down to help raise money for support of sexual minority causes—the Warwick Rowers being the best example. A simple Google search for their, almost entirely nude, images will help illustrate just how far some straight people are willing to go in order promote sporting inclusivity.

Decreasing homophobia

The increasing numbers of sexual minorities coming out in sport is directly related to the changing cultural attitudes toward homosexuality and bisexuality in Western cultures. While people of all ages are changing their attitudes from antipathy toward support of sexual minorities, nowhere is this more visible than it is with young people.

If millennials (those born 1990 or later) will be known for anything, it will likely be that they are the first generation to grow up with the Internet and smartphones, and—of importance to this book—that they have rejected the homophobia of the previous generation. As we thoroughly demonstrate in Chapter 3, there are numerous reasons why cultural homophobia has declined so fast in the West: politics, religion, media, the Internet and openly gay celebrities are just some.

The US, which has always maintained higher degrees of cultural homophobia than Britain, has particularly changed. The political party of homophobia—the Republican Party—alongside the Christian right are in the last stages of despotism concerning homosexuality. Whereas they have staked a cultural war against sexual minorities for decades, and continue to fight some battles, the war is largely won.

As evidence of this, in 2003, the United States Supreme Court eliminated the remaining sodomy laws that still made homosexual sex illegal in 13 states; in 2011, the United States finally permitted sexual minorities to serve openly in the US military and, most recently, in 2015, the Supreme Court determined that people in all 50 US states had the right to marry someone of the same sex. In passing these laws, the United States caught up to the laws that have been passed to promote equality for sexual minorities in the United Kingdom—which brought marriage equality into play in 2013 (with the first same-sex marriages taking place the following year). While there remain some legal and institutional roadblocks to full equality in the US today, the change toward legal equality in the previous decade has been phenomenal.

This change is matched by the cultural shift in acceptance toward sexual minorities, particularly among young people (McCormack, Anderson and Adams 2014). We therefore suggest that those born in Generation X (those born between 1960 and 1980) were steeped in heterosexual notions of masculinity and highly restrictive notions of human sexuality. Men of this generation desired to be like Sylvester Stallone's 1982 movie character, Rambo. This is to say that they wanted to be physically buff, emotionally stoic and prepared to fight. More importantly, the research shows that they were "soldiers" in a war of masculinity over femininity, and of heterosexuality over homosexuality.

In this book, we use empirical sociological evidence from the lives of young sporting men—those we would expect to maintain conservative notions of sexuality and gender—to show that the millennial generation looks nothing like their fathers' did. Instead of representing Rambo, they much prefer the feminized charms and homosocial tactility of the members of the boy band, One Direction. In Britain, the most popular young male YouTube celebrities are highly feminized, emotionally expressive and strong advocates of sexual minority equality (Morris and Anderson 2015). Essentially, those born after 1990 are what Anderson (2014: 6) calls, "better dressed, digital hippies," in that they are young men who have grown up with less interest in conservative religion (or any religion at all) and with gay friends. They express a feminine notion of masculinity and have greatly expanded upon the gendered and sexual behaviors that are not only permissible, but expected of their friends. By the standards of masculinity that those of the previous generation grew up with, these are highly feminized men. They express emotional love for each other, kiss each other and cuddle in bed together (see Chapter 8). Furthermore, these behaviors do not only occur in private spaces, but are displayed publicly.

The form of masculinity that we describe existing among straight men is that of "inclusive masculinity" (Anderson 2009a) and its chief characteristic is that young men today are inclusive of what was once chiefly exclusive to them: homosexuality. It is their inclusivity of homosexuality that allows them to engage in behaviors that were once coded as being the domain of women and gay men only. This inclusion, as we show in this book, necessarily extends to websites such as Outsports.com and organizations such as "Stand up Foundation" (founded by retired rugby union player Ben Cohen), which provide support for the LGBT community and help to raise the profile of athletes. However, this is where women's and men's sport differ dramatically. While there are numerous heterosexual male athletes who actively campaign for the LGBT community, for women things are more complex. Melton (2013: 18) notes:

> The absence of women in the campaign for LGBT equality is striking. This may be because of the difference in coverage that men's and women's sport receive. Men become household names and role models whereas the limited coverage of women's sport coupled with a potential image problem may prevent women from speaking out. In many respects it highlights the immense fear associated with being labeled a lesbian and illustrates how sexual prejudice serves to maintain women's status in sport.

There are perhaps several reasons why issues of lesbians in sport are not as represented in the media as gay men are. One of these is because homophobia has always been worse among men than woman (Loftus 2001). It might also be because the way that homophobia has policed/limited the lives of young straight men is not as severe for women.

While Worthen (2014) shows that homohysteria also applies to women, they have been less policed by the strictures of homophobia than men have. Hence, women have been able to display a far wider range of gendered behaviors than men (Sprecher and Sedikides 1993, Kring and Gordon 1998). For example, not only could women dress in a wider variety of ways, but unlike men who maintained friendship through shared activities, women have maintained friendships through sharing emotions and disclosing secrets (Caldwell and Peplau 1982). Williams (1985) showed that men were not permitted to be emotionally vulnerable, whilst women were free to express themselves in intimate friendships. This is not to say that certain hypermasculine behaviors did not associate women with lesbianism (Griffin 1998; Worthen 2014), but that women were given more leeway for emotional expression and other behaviors than men. Simply put, women can do more without being thought lesbian than men could before being thought gay.

Lesbian women in sport also receive less attention than gay men in sport because men's sport is vastly more popular than women's. Even when not discussing issues of sexuality and sport, men's sport receives virtually all of the mainstream media's press coverage, while women receive hardly any at all (Bruce 2015).

Finally, the issue of lesbians in sport receives less attention than gay men in sport because people, correctly, assume that lesbians are already over-represented in sport. Thus, being labeled as a lesbian does not necessarily pose a problem in the same way that being labeled gay has in men's sports. Still, as we will show in Chapter 5, matters are not necessarily that straightforward. For example, one lesbian within a team can cast suspicion on the rest of the players in a way that having one gay teammate does not cast homosexual suspicion onto the other males of the team.

Whom we do not address with this work

In charting the trend of decreasing cultural stigma against gay and lesbian athletes, it is also crucial to highlight where our work is lacking. Namely, while societal attitudes toward bisexuality have been tightly linked with society's disposition toward homosexuality (Hubbard and deVisser 2014)—and thus we should expect the experiences of bisexual men and women in sport to mirror that of lesbian and gay men—we do not have the systematic data to make such claims. While bisexual men and women are certainly part of our research—and while there are no cases of biphobia within our findings—we do not have enough bisexuals to draw conclusions from. Furthermore, most of the social research that we draw from concerns homosexuality, not bisexuality. So even though bisexuals outnumber homosexuals, we recognize that they have been squeezed out of much academic research. Bisexuality has frequently been erased both culturally and from academic investigation. We hope to investigate the experiences of bisexuals in the near future, and recommend Anderson and McCormack's forthcoming book on men's bisexuality, *He's Hot, She's Hot.*

We also recognize that our research is limited by its focus on sexual minorities, and not gender minorities. That is, we have not studied the lives of transgendered athletes. However, we believe that, even more so than with bisexual athletes, it is scientifically unjustifiable to simply lump transgendered athletes in with lesbian and gay athletes. The lives of transgendered people outside of sport are found to be much more difficult than are the lives of sexual minorities (see Sykes 2006). Put simply, people are far more transphobic than they are homophobic.

Second, transgender athletes challenge sport, and the gender binary upon which it is built, in a way that cisgender gay and lesbian athletes do not. This challenge is met with backlash. For those interested in better understanding the unique social positioning of transgendered athletes we recommend reading section VI of the *Routledge Handbook of Sport, Gender and Sexuality* (2014).

Finally, we recognize that most—though not all—of the athletes that we have studied in this book are white. We provide a brief investigation of the complexities of intersecting racial and sexual orientation identities in the final chapter by highlighting complexities of being both black and gay, but highlight that the lack of openly gay athletes of color have made more definitive analysis of their experiences harder to make. There is very little research conducted on, for example, Asian, Hispanic or Arabic ethnicities, and with few exceptions (i.e. Hamdi and Anderson forthcoming) no research concerning the experiences of gay and lesbian athletes living outside of the West.

Our writing style

The theories we use, along with our writing style, are designed to be inclusive of most readers. We maintain that if a sociologist can't explain his or her ideas in a relatively straightforward manner, with language that any undergraduate can understand, then that academic probably is not worth listening to.

Also, while recognizing the philosophical relevance of post-structural or post-modern thinking, we are committed empiricists. We find that categorical thinking helps to make sense of otherwise complex matters, and reflects the reality of people's lived experiences. So while we understand that what it means to be gay or straight is highly contentious, we rely on people's self-reported identity labels for this research without complication.

We are also largely opposed to the way that most post-structuralist authors write. We agree with Oakley (2002: 190) who says that post-structural writing is "dense, imprecise, long-winded, grammatically complex, hugely inaccessible and hence intrinsically undemocratic." We shorten this to say that it represents a shameful act of academic exclusion.

You will therefore not be reading the unintelligible writings of gender theorists like Judith Butler in this book. We have taken the *opposite* approach and write in a straightforward and accessible way.

If readers have questions about what is meant by something, they are encouraged to email any of the three authors:

ProfessorEricAnderson@gmail.com
RoryMagrathPhD@gmail.com
R.Bullingham@Worc.ac.uk

Meet the researchers

The authors of this book are three disparate and devoted researchers, whose life stories lead them to desire to help make sport a more inclusive place. Collectively we are a gay male (Eric Anderson), a straight male (Rory Magrath), and a lesbian (Rachael Bullingham). We represent different age cohorts (47, 26, and 33 respectively), and Rory and Rachael are British, while Eric is an American who lives in England.

We each have a unique story to tell about how we became involved in studying the field of sexualities in sport. Yet because both Rory and Rachael earned their PhDs on the topic under the supervision of Professor Eric Anderson, we bring a united voice, and theoretical writing style, to this book.

Professor Eric Anderson

Eric came to study the relationship between sport and society through a circuitous route. Although he was never talented at sports that required coordination or body mass, nor sports that necessitated that one commit violence against an opponent, he found joy in the sport of distance running. As a high school runner, Eric found sport to be a place where he developed friendships, and maintained contact with a valuable role model, his coach. However, he also used cross-country running as a way to escape the mandatory participation in sports through Physical Education, where, as a closeted gay adolescent, he was intimidated by the level of masculinity imbued in invasion sports.

Eric always knew he was gay. Yet he is definitively able to trace it back to 1977, aged eight, when he sat in the movie theater on the opening day of *Star Wars*. Before the curtain rose, he spotted an attractive boy a few aisles down and a couple of seats over. With his eyes fixed upon him, he realized that he was staring at him for an unacceptable period of time. Aware that his actions could alert others to his secret desires, he looked for an excuse for his staring and said, "Mom, I want my hair cut like his." In other words, he knew that he both had to hide and how to hide his true sexual identity: he was already "passing" at age eight.

Eric didn't particularly like sport as a child, either. He was something of a motor-moron. Making matters worse, he never learned the rules and practices of formal sport. By the time he was old enough to realize that he didn't know how to play baseball, football or basketball, he was too embarrassed to ask his friends or father to show him. Thus, sports that involved balls, or contact, intimidated him.

The paranoid fear of being thought gay (which of course he was) and feeling inferior to other boys were hallmarks of his adolescence too. He was frustrated, scared, intimidated and felt alone in his attraction to boys. Complicating matters, he was in high school during the extreme AIDS phobia and homophobia that characterized the years 1982–87. To be gay in the mid-1980s was detestable: there could be nothing worse.

Ironically, despite sport being highly homophobic, it was perhaps one of the only things that saved him from the intense cultural, and his own internalized, homophobia. He grew more competitive as a runner, and his self-esteem improved. Because of his leadership role in sport, he began to feel confident that he could speak to, lead and influence others. Thus, when he graduated high school in Southern California, he returned to his old high school to coach. The better his athletes performed, the more his self-esteem he grew. He learned to love the acquisition of knowledge that helped him win. Thus, he began to read books related to running, health, psychology and the hard sciences—all topics that would make him a better coach. He occupied his days with studying, writing and coaching. All of these diversions were good for him; they not only gave him confidence and knowledge, but they also provided him an excuse for not dating.

By the age of 25, Eric had earned an MA in Sport Psychology, written two distance running books and coached some of the best runners in the state of California. However, his body (psychosomatically) began to spite him. He began to develop migraine headaches, stomach pains and the symptoms of an ulcer. He knew that in order to regain his physical health, he had to come out of the closet. So, in the summer of 1993, Eric came out of the closet as America's first publicly recognized, openly gay high school coach (Anderson 2000).

Over the following years, the knowledge of his sexuality spread through the school. Homophobia was instantly utilized, not only against Eric, but also his athletes, who were assumed to be gay simply because their coach was. Eric's life, and those of his athletes, became a daily battle with homophobia. It was directed at them from students and athletes at their own school, runners from other schools, parents and even his own school's administration. The culture of harassment of the beleaguered coach and his runners reached an apex in 1995, when a football player brutally assaulted one of his heterosexual athletes. The football player knocked the runner to the ground, then sat atop him and began pounding at his face. The assailant even tried to gouge out the runner's eyes. When a bystander begged the football player to stop the beating, he did not. Instead, he proclaimed, "It ain't over until the faggot's dead."

Although his vision was obscured by blood, the runner managed to squirm from beneath the football player's legs and run away. He climbed a fence that the pursuing football player was too large to scale, and got away. The runner was left with four broken facial bones, and for the rest of his life has two screws through his pallet. The police department reported the incident as "mutual combat"—*not* a hate crime or aggravated assault—and the assailant received no time behind bars. Essentially, he got away with it.

It was clear to Eric that the incident did not "just happen": the beating was influenced by factors, people, perhaps even institutions (Anderson 2000). He immediately suspected that the assailant's actions were covertly encouraged by what seemed a lack of administrative action against those who previously displayed hostility toward his team. In their inaction, the high school administration sent an institutional message of support for the continuation of violence against the team.

Such homophobia was not surprising at the time, especially when one considers that the assailant had been socialized into the homophobic language of masculinity embedded in the combative teamsports, like American football, of the time. Perhaps his training served as a powerful socialization into the norm of violent masculinity

In addition to a predictable anger that lingered for years, Eric was left with an intellectual angst over not fully understanding how such intense homophobia could develop within an individual, and how educated people (like the school principal) could dismiss such violence as "simply a fight." He was not satisfied with the "boys will be boys" or "people hate what they don't understand" rationalizations. He sensed the matter was much more complicated. He sensed that the beating was attributable to the manner in which the assailant was socialized into masculinity, the value of physical brutality he learned in sport, and the culmination of many years of growing aggression and hostility that largely went uncontested by the school administration. Essentially, Eric was more clear in understanding why the football player assaulted his runner—what he was less clear about was why the school's administration had been so unwilling to stop the harassment before it got to the point of serious bodily injury.

His master's degree in Sport Psychology had equipped him to understand how to help athletes negotiate psychological problems in society, but it failed to explain the origins of social problems in the first place. He had been trained to help athletes negotiate the pressures of competition, but not to examine our cultural addiction to competition. Realizing that his training was insufficient to fully understand the social dynamics that culminated in this beating, he returned to school to earn a doctorate in sociology at the University of California, Irvine.

Today, Eric is a professor of sport, masculinity and sexuality at the University of Winchester. He holds four degrees, has published 13 books, over 50 peer-reviewed journal articles, and is regularly featured in international television, print and digital media on the topic of gays in sport.

Professor Anderson is recognized for research excellence by the British Academy of Social Sciences and is a Fellow of the International Academy of Sex Research. His work maps a decline in cultural homohysteria leading to a softening of heterosexual masculinities. This permits heterosexual men to kiss, cuddle and love one another, and promotes inclusive attitudes toward openly gay athletes and the recognition of bisexuality. His sexuality work finds positive aspects of non-monogamous relationships and explores the function and benefits of cheating as well (Anderson 2012b). Professor Anderson also writes about sport psychology, distance running and the social problems of organized teamsports (Anderson 2010).

Dr. Rory Magrath

Rory came to the study of gays in sport not because he was directly affected by homophobia—he is heterosexual—but because he is an avid British football (soccer) fan who was deeply affected by witnessing a famous incident in the world of sport and British homophobia. The incident centered on heterosexual Premier League player Graeme Le Saux, who was ridiculed throughout his career for failing to convey an acceptable masculine image. His perceived femininity was also associated with his perceived intellectualism: he was known as the "*Guardian*-reading footballer" because the *Guardian* is the UK's most progressive mainstream newspaper.

This lack of masculinity was, at the time, associated with homosexuality. It was the year 1999; society was still relatively homophobic, and sport was even more so. Illustrating this, Justin Fashanu, famous for winning *BBC Match of the Day*'s "Goal of the Season" competition in 1980 whilst playing for Norwich City, was vilified for coming out in 1990. He was harassed by his teammates, the press and sport fans. Ultimately, he committed suicide in 1998.

In that same decade, Le Saux's perceived femininity made him seem to be homosexual to a vehemently homophobic fan base. They chanted, "Le Saux takes it up the arse" on a regular basis while opposing players consistently labeled him "queer" and a "faggot" (Le Saux 2007: xiii). This infamously culminated in an impassioned exchange with Liverpool striker Robbie Fowler in February 1999 who, during a match in front of 35,000 people at Stamford Bridge, provocatively bent over in front of him suggesting that Le Saux wanted anal sex with him.

Rory was in the stands that day as a young Chelsea supporter; he remembers the event vividly, for his father had taken him to the stadium that day. Though only nine years old, and too young to completely comprehend what had happened, he still remembers the exchange between the two players, the discomfort of the assistant referee who was standing close by and the angry response of the Chelsea supporters sat nearby. Over a decade later, this moment would continue to weigh heavily on his conscience. He was a football fan, but a football fan who wanted to make a difference in the social acceptability of sexual variance.

However, Rory's desire to change cultural perceptions of homosexuality is also personal. As we illustrate in Chapter 3, cultural homophobia also negatively impacts upon the lives of heterosexual males, who are unable to—in a homophobic culture—prove that they are straight. Accordingly, during Rory's adolescence, he attended an all-boys state school which was notorious for bullying. From his first day, it was clear to him that he needed to quickly learn how to look after himself – physically and mentally. In this environment, behaviors associated with femininity were stigmatized and Rory is a heterosexual male whose level of femininity commonly associated him with homosexuality. Because Rory feared being labeled gay, like closeted gay men who also fear being socially perceived as gay, he learned to raise his heterosexual and masculine social capital by engaging in the ridicule of others. In Chapter 3, we describe this as homohysteria.

This ridicule normally came in the form of challenging one's sexuality through employing certain forms of homophobic discourse (see Chapter 8). He felt that he had to engage in homophobic taunts and epithets in order to avoid having them levied at him. Rory, however, did not necessarily believe that these discourses were employed with homophobic intent. Compared to the culture that Eric Anderson grew up in, Rory's peer group was much more gay friendly. Still, the language from the earlier decades of homophobia remained in cultural currency enough for him to feel victimized and to act as a perpetrator of stigma by it.

It was only in studying for his PhD that he learned that his educational experience was one that reflected a culture in transition. A plethora of older research has shown high levels of homophobia residing in educational institutions (Epstein and Johnson 1998; Mac an Ghaill 1994; Thurlow 2001), while newer research sometimes shows a complete absence of homophobia among youth (McCormack 2012a, 2012b). Rory's schooling experience was thus situated between traditional and evolving masculinity research (Anderson 2012a).

Rory carried his experiences of being a somewhat feminine straight male into his master's studies. He was aware that, although football had long been viewed as a masculine domain (Giulianotti 1999; Russell 1997), very little empirical research had been conducted on the extent of homophobia within the game. Instead, football has merely been culturally perceived as homophobic. For example, British journalist Owen Jones (2014) claims that "football remains one of the greatest fortresses of homophobia." It is for this reason that there exists great cultural fascination with uncovering which professional footballers in Britain are gay (Willis 2014). Such conversations are usually borne out of fan speculation, fuelled by media discourses. Highlighting this, Lilleaas (2007) describes how, in 2004, a professional player kissed a teammate on the lips in celebration; the following day, the kiss was spread in a national newspaper, and the player's family was bombarded with questions about if the player had "turned gay." Today, however, heterosexual men kissing each other on the lips is not only common, it's almost a social obligation (see Chapter 9).

The decreasing homohysteria (see Chapter 3) that we find in British culture today is abundantly evident by looking at straight male athletes (Anderson 2014). One can see it in their wearing feminine clothing, sharing beds together, kissing, cuddling and loving one another (Chapter 9). These behaviors are not unfamiliar to Rory, either. He engaged in similar activities on nights out as an undergraduate student. Thus, Rory comes to this research from a standpoint of being interested in how cultural homophobia negatively impacts not only on gay and bisexual men in sport, but also on straight men. This was the topic of his doctoral work (2015a).

Dr. Rachael Bullingham

From a very early age Rachael was conscious of her own sexuality, that she was different to other girls. She was fortunate enough to attend one of the top public schools in the UK, where regular participation was an expectation and sporting excellence was the norm. However, she was acutely aware that outside this school setting excellence and participation in teamsports called a woman's heterosexuality into question. She vividly remember comments by fellow students concerning the topic of individuals' sexuality, which were always negative, so she actively sought to maintain a heterosexual identity by ensuring that she was always too engaged in work or training to be fully involved in the social scene of school life.

Choosing a London university, she thought that this would allow her to express her sexuality. She assumed that there would be an open and inclusive atmosphere on campus-designated sports teams. However, she found the opposite; the hockey club, for example, was exceptionally hostile to lesbian athletes.

What little support existed quickly deteriorated when two female players were caught kissing while intoxicated at the Christmas social. As a consequence, the two players were socially excluded from all of the team's social events. However, more lesbians joined the team in the second year of her university career. This addition helped the team move from a hostile environment to one of greater tolerance, even if some remained silent. Still afraid of social repercussions, Rachael remained closeted throughout this transition. However, when the team captain came out, the attitude toward homosexuality dramatically and rapidly shifted to one of acceptance.

Rachael later joined a rugby team. Here she found an open and inclusive environment. It was the first time she had seen and met lesbians who were effortlessly open about their identity within a sport, and the first time she saw heterosexual teammates who were so accepting that sexuality became non-consequential.

Rachael continued to play sport throughout her twenties, and despite the sport she played or the team she played on, she never again saw the hostility of her youth. Instead, she found women's sports teams in the UK to be highly inclusive. However, when she was studying for her master's degree in sport sociology, she noticed that there was no literature reflecting the change she had seen in the previous decade.

After completing her master's degree, Rachael settled in Gloucestershire, where she started her career as a physical education teacher in a large comprehensive school. Here, she started to see pupils coming out of the closet without homophobia. She noted that the staff's attitudes were also more liberal toward homosexuality than staff attitudes were when she was in school. Furthermore, just as Anderson (2014) shows, she noticed that male students were becoming more tactile: boys regularly hugged and leaned on each other, and sometimes even kissed one another publicly. She longed to study this changing culture, particularly in regard to how lesbian athletes navigate sport.

It was then that she met Eric Anderson, who talked to her about his findings on masculinity in sport and the changes he has researched in openly gay male athletes (Anderson 2002, 2005a, 2009a, 2011a). However, the dearth of research on lesbian athletes was evident, with only a few articles published since the turn of the century; these have been predominantly written about American athletes, or from a post-structuralist standpoint that is often written in such complex language that it is nonsensical (see Caudwell 2002). The desire to produce research to reflect lesbian athletes' experiences in a meaningful way, and with accessible prose, culminated in her studying for her PhD with Professor Anderson.

Rachael's doctoral work consists of 31 interviews of openly lesbian athletes who participate in sports from the grass-roots to international level. Three participants were still competing at international level at the time of interview and one had recently retired but still playing a different sport at a lower level.

During this research, Rachael also worked as a secondary school teacher. Throughout this time, she remained closeted to students at her school. She did so out of fear of false allegations of sexual impropriety while supervising the girls' locker room. However, in the last few months of this job, before she took a post at the University of Worcester, Rachael spoke to students more openly about her sexuality—and there was no backlash whatsoever. She found her students overwhelmingly supportive. The experiences helped Rachael realize that just because one fears homophobia might happen, it does not mean that it will.

Rachael's research therefore captures a cultural moment in which lesbian athletes, too, are coming out more publicly—also without repercussions. Since starting her doctoral work in 2011, numerous positive changes have occurred in women's sport. Casey Stoney, then captain of the England football team, has come out; and in hockey, two Great Britain players, Kate Walsh (captain of the team) and Helen Richardson, have married. However, in her research, Rachael has also come across many lesbian athletes on national sports teams that have yet to come out. Thus, more cultural and organizational change is needed.

Outline of subsequent chapters

Chapter 2

Outlining the value placed on competitive teamsports in Western cultures, this chapter focuses specifically on the codification of many of these sports during the late nineteenth century. Significantly, this coincided with the growth of industrialization in the Western world, and the development of a modern homosexual identity.

We outline how, from the outset, these sports were solely a male domain. Thus, we tie these together by discussing how sport was responsible for the promotion of athletic masculinity, excluding all others—including gay men and women.

Chapter 3

This chapter draws upon Anderson's (2009a) concept of homohysteria—the fear of being culturally homosexualized—to discuss how masculinities are historically situated. We outline a stage model of homohysteria to conceptualize the decrease of cultural homophobia in Western culture and its subsequent effect on both men's and women's sports.

Chapters 4 and 5

Using over a decade's worth of academic research with participants in both the UK and the US, these chapters document the experiences of gay men and lesbians in high school and university sport. We highlight the influence of "don't ask, don't tell" from older research and decreased heterosexism in recent research. We discuss the effect coaches and administration have in altering these climates toward inclusivity and show the overwhelming inclusivity and support that heterosexual teammates offer to their openly gay and lesbian counterparts today.

Chapter 6

Because academic research on gay and lesbian athletes in sport is predominantly limited to high school and university sports, limited research examines recreational sport. Accordingly, this chapter predominantly relies upon research focusing on gay sports clubs and leagues, documenting overwhelmingly positive experiences for athletes. We then use this research to hypothesize how findings can be applied to recreational sport, too.

Chapter 7

This chapter addresses the presence of openly gay and lesbian athletes in professional sport, providing an explanation for the proportionally low number of out athletes at this level of play. Due to issues of access, we rely on published media accounts of these athletes—including two openly gay athletes (John Amaechi and Thomas Hitzlsperger) and two openly lesbian athletes (Amelie Mauresmo and Sheryl Swoopes). Here, we show that despite relatively low numbers, the media positively represents gay and lesbian athletes.

Chapter 8

Using Pat Griffin's taxonomy of climates that lesbians can move through—*hostile, tolerant* and *inclusive*—underpinned with Anderson's (2009a) concept of homohysteria, this chapter outlines the varying experiences of gay and lesbian athletes. It then progresses to discuss the complex terrain surrounding homosexually themed language, outlining various different conceptualizations, before including McCormack's (2011a) model to explain the complexity of homosexually themed language in sport.

Chapter 9

In this chapter, we show that decreased homophobia does not just impact gay men and women: it affects heterosexuals, too. Accordingly, this chapter focuses on the softening of masculinity exhibited by young, heterosexual men. Situated within a framework of decreased homohysteria, we show young straight male athletes kissing, cuddling and loving each other. We highlight that young, straight men develop "bromances" in accord with the types of relationships that females have had traditionally.

Chapter 10

This concluding chapter summarizes the research discussed throughout this text, highlighting the continuing decline in cultural homophobia and the effect this has on openly gay men and lesbians in sport. We conclude by outlining significant factors not discussed within this book—such as athletes of color—and then discuss directions for future research projects.

Underpinning research projects

To illustrate the changing relationship between sport and homosexuality, we draw almost entirely on peer-reviewed research projects. While we understand that peer-reviewed research can be faulty (Anderson 2013a), it is the best form of knowledge production we know of. To this effect, we utilize multiple, innovative methods (McCormack, Anderson and Adams 2014) including ethnographies, qualitative investigations and quantitative research on teamsport athletes, conducted in both the US and England. We have interviewed gay and lesbian athletes a decade ago, and more recently, as well. We have interviewed or otherwise researched them from both low- and high-quality teams, and studied athletes both in and out of the closet.

In order to highlight the positive impact of declining homophobia, we also include research on the experiences of straight male and female athletes. This helps us understand more thoroughly how the experiences of gay and lesbian athletes are changing, and better theorize how homophobia serves to regulate gender, for people of all sexualities.

Finally, all ethical procedures of both the British Sociological Association and the American Sociological Association have been followed in these various projects. Research approval was first obtained prior to conducting all of these research projects, informed consent was given by all participants and their names and institutional affiliations have been changed in order to protect anonymity unless we are given specific permission to do otherwise, or they are already a famous athlete.

Specifically, we rely on data collected by all three authors with the following set of sports teams across the world:

United States interviews

- 26 openly gay male high school and college athletes from a variety of sports (2000–02)
- 22 openly gay male high school and college athletes from a variety of sports (2002–05)
- 20 closeted gay male high school and college athletes from a variety of sports (2002–05)
- 26 openly gay male high school and college athletes (2008 and 2010)
- 68 heterosexual male high school collegiate cheerleaders from various teams (2001–02)
- 32 fraternity members from one fraternity in California (2002–04)
- 20 collegiate soccer players from the American South (2009)
- 20 collegiate soccer players from the American Midwest (2009)
- 20 collegiate soccer players from the American Northeast (2009)
- 75 undergraduate men from 11 universities across the United States (2011).

United States ethnographies

- 1 team of co-ed collegiate cheerleaders from the American South (2001–02)
- 1 team of co-ed collegiate cheerleaders from the American Midwest (2001–02)
- 1 team of co-ed collegiate cheerleaders from the American Northeast (2001–02)
- 1 team of co-ed collegiate cheerleaders from the American West (2001–02)
- 1 fraternity in Southern California (2002–04)
- 1 team of men's collegiate soccer players from the American South (2009)
- 1 team of men's collegiate soccer players from the American Midwest (2009)
- 1 team of men's collegiate soccer players from the American Northeast (2009)
- 1 high school boys cross country running team in California (2012–13).

United States surveys

- 698 male athletes from four universities in the Southeastern United States (2004)
- 442 short interviews with undergraduate men at 11 universities across the US (2011).

England interviews

- 19 university men's hockey team members in the South West of England (2003–09)
- 19 university men's rugby team members in the South West of England (2003–09)
- 16 university men's soccer players in the Midlands of England (2009)
- 22 male sixth-form students (some athletes) in the South West of England (2009)
- 24 university rugby players in the South West of England (2009)
- 39 teamsport athletes in the South West of England (2009)
- 40 heterosexual university athletes in the South West of England (2008–09)
- 20 gay university students in the South East of England (2009)
- 22 academy-level soccer players in the South East of England (2013)
- 18 academy-level soccer players in the East of England (2014)
- 20 university men's soccer players in the South East of England (2014).

England ethnographies

- 1 university men's hockey team in the South West of England (2003–09)
- 1 university men's rugby team in the South West of England (2003–09)
- 1 university soccer team in the South West of England (2007)
- 1 university British rugby team in the South West of England (2009)
- 1 university soccer team in the Midlands of England (2010)
- 1 sixth-form college in the South West of England (2010)
- 1 group of sixth-form students from the South East of England (2013).

England surveys

- 107 heterosexual male university students in the South West of England (2009)
- 120 heterosexual male university students in the South East of England (2013).

Australia interviews

- 90 short interviews with undergraduate heterosexual men from one university (2012).

2

THE LINK BETWEEN SPORT AND HOMOPHOBIA

The purpose of this chapter is to explain why we once valued organized, competitive and combative team sport in Western cultures (i.e., American football, rugby, soccer, etc.) and how that value has changed in relation to Western economies. We particularly focus on the relationship between sport and homosexuality and its meanings at the dawn of the twentieth century.

We begin by highlighting that organized sport emerged at a particular historical moment in the West. It was a time in which culture was rapidly changing as a result of industrialization. Simultaneously, society was gradually recognizing that homosexuality existed as an immutable, unchangeable characteristic. This led to a turn-of-the-twentieth-century moral panic, in that society feared that young men were becoming weak, soft, feminine and thus homosexual. Sports were, at this time, culturally promoted because they were perceived as being able to build positive attributes in young men's lives, attributes perceived to be useful in an industrial economy. Sport was thought to teach notions of sacrificing for the family, being complicit to authority, as well as training young men to be prepared for war. Crucially, sport was also thought vital in turning young men away from softness, weakness, and homosexuality.

In this chapter we discuss how, during the last decades of the nineteenth century and the early decades of the twentieth, the role of women also changed: in this case to one of increasing domesticity and hyperfemininity. Women were largely prohibited from playing sport under the social mythos that it would lead to sterility. Women were instead structured into housework and motherhood (Worthen 2014). We also track the increasing participation of women in sport as the twentieth century progresses, to show how they fought to gain access to the sporting arena. We show how women were kept from sport not only by the erroneous medicalization of their bodies, but through their homosexualization, too. Finally, we show how, even today, women are prevented from participating on an equal playing field.

In discussing how the homophobia engrained within sport is reproduced, we highlight the impact of intersecting structural variables. First, we examine the premise that sport can be defined as a near-total institution (Anderson 2005a). By this, we mean that sport draws on similarities with the military. We show how the total control of athletes is exacerbated by a culture which promotes sports so thoroughly that athletes negate their agency and subscribe to the team ethos, culture and ethics even if the culture is abusive, in order that they might excel in a decreasing opportunity structure. Finally, we highlight that the sporting institution, even today, is gender segregated. While this may be beneficial for women, on some level, it has shown to enhance the reproduction of orthodox masculinity and leads to the reproduction of patriarchy (Joseph and Anderson 2015).

These variables are intensified because sport is also a closed-loop institution. Sport coaching is not monitored by outside agencies; it is athletes who benefited from sport that go on to become coaches, and they thus seek to reinforce the same practices that they learned as an athlete—even if those practices are biased, exclusive or abusive. It is in this light that the negative practices become engrained in a cycle that is reinforced with each generation.

The birth of the heterosexual jock

Although the invention of the machinery and transportation necessary for industrialization began early in the 1700s, the antecedents of most of today's sporting culture can be traced to the years of the second Industrial Revolution—the mid-1800s through early 1900s. During this time, farmers replaced their farm's rent for that of a city apartment instead. The allure of industry, and the better life it promised, influenced such a migration that the percentage of people living in cities rose from just 25 percent in 1800 to around 75 percent in 1900 (Cancian 1986).

However, just as cities attracted people, the increasing difficulty of rural life also compelled them to leave their agrarian ways. This is because the same industrial technologies that brought capitalism also meant that fewer farmers were required to produce the necessary crops to feed a growing population. With production capacity rising, and crop prices falling, families were not only drawn to the cities by the allure of a stable wage and the possibility of class mobility, but were equally repelled by an increasingly difficult agrarian labor market and the inability to own land (Cancian 1986).

For all the manifestations of physical horror that was factory life before labor laws, there were many advantages, too. Families were no longer dependent on the fortune of good weather for sustenance, and industry provided predictable, if long, working hours. Having a reliable wage meant that a family could count on how much money they would have at the end of the week, and some could use this financial stability to secure loans and purchase property. Also, the regularity of work meant that between the soundings of the factory whistle, there was time for men to play. The concept of leisure, once reserved for the wealthy, spread to the working class during this period (Rigauer 1981). It is the impact of this great migration that is central to the production of men's sport in Western cultures. It is also around this time that the majority of dominant sport forms were codified and regulated into how we know them today (Guttman 1978).

However, sport held little cultural value prior to the Industrial Revolution. Social historian Donald Mrozek (1983) wrote: "To Americans at the beginning of the nineteenth century, there was no obvious merit in sport . . . certainly no clear social value to it and no sense that it contributed to the improvement of the individual's character or the society's moral or even physical health."

However, by the second decade of the next century, these sentiments had been reversed (Miracle and Rees 1994). Sport gave boys something to do after school. It helped socialize them into the values thought necessary in this new economy, and to instill the qualities of discipline and obedience of labor that was necessary in the dangerous occupations of mining and factory work (Rigauer 1981). Accordingly, workers needed to sacrifice both their time and their health for the sake of making the wage they needed to support their dependent families.

In sport, young boys were socialized into this value of self-sacrifice; they were asked to do so for the sake of team victory. As adults, this socialization taught them to sacrifice their health and well-being in the workplace for the sake of family. Most important to the factory owners, however, workers needed to be obedient to authority. This would help prevent them from rebelling or unionizing. Sports taught boys this docility to leadership and authority. Accordingly, organized competitive teamsports were funded by those who maintained control of the reproduction of material goods.

Spontaneous street-playing activities were banned, and children's play was forced off the streets and into parks and playgrounds where children were supervised and their play structured. In the words of one playground advocate, "We want a play factory; we want it to run at top speed on schedule time, with the best machinery and skilled operatives. We want to turn out the maximum product of happiness" (Bancroft 1909: 21). Just as they are today, organized youth sports were financially backed by business in the form of "sponsors." Today, as part of a compulsory state-run education system, they are also backed by the state. This is an economical way of assuring a docile and productive labor force. Sport teaches us to keep to a schedule, under production-conscious supervisors (Eitzen 2001).

This shift to industry had other gendered effects, too. Although there was a gendered division of labor in agrarian work, there was less gendering of jobs and tasks compared to industrial life. On the farm, both men and women toiled in demanding labor. Accordingly, in some aspects, heterosexual relationships were more egalitarian before industrialization. Factory work, however, shifted revenue generation from inside the home to outside. Mom's physical labor no longer directly benefited the family as it once did, and much of women's labor therefore became unpaid and unseen. Conversely, men's working spaces were cold, dangerous and hard. Men moved rocks, welded iron, swung pick axes and operated steam giants (Anderson 2009a).

These environments necessitated that men be tough and unemotional. Men grew more instrumental not only in their labor and purpose, but in their personalities, too. As a result of industrialization, men learned that the way they showed their love was through their labor. Being a breadwinner—regardless of the working conditions in which one toiled—was deemed a condition of manhood (Cancian 1986).

Furthermore, because women were mostly (but not entirely) relegated to a domestic sphere, they were reliant upon their husband's ability to generate income. Thus, mostly robbed of economic agency, women learned to show their contribution through emotional expressiveness and domestic efficiency. Cancian (1986) describes these changes as a separation of gendered spheres, saying that expectations of what it meant to be a man or a woman bifurcated as a result of industrialization. Accordingly, the antecedents of men's stoicism and women's expressionism were born during this period. She suggests that one way to examine this is looking at how men and women are socialized to love during this epoch. Men were taught that they expressed love in sacrificing their health by working in a factory or coal mine in order to provide for the family. Conversely, women were taught to express their feelings of love through words and tactility.

Much of our cultural obsession for competitive teamsport came during this time. It was a result of a cultural hysteria that men were going soft (Anderson 2009a). This was an unintended consequence of the absence of men in the lives of their male offspring, thus leaving women to care for them (Hartmann 1976). The fear of softness was not just about men acting feminine; however, it was directly related to the fear that boys could be socialized to become homosexual.

Anderson (2009a, 2010) argues that the value of competitive (particularly combative) teamsports was bolstered during this time not only because sport was a way to indoctrinate people into the complicity to authority that the military or factory work required, but also because of the growing cultural awareness that men's homosexuality existed. He argues that because heterosexuals cannot socially prove their heterosexuality, men had to socially prove and re-prove their heterosexuality by aligning their gendered identities with an extreme (orthodox) form of masculinity, while simultaneously denouncing homosexuality. Kimmel (1994) argued that men, desiring to be perceived as straight, had to prove and re-prove their heterosexuality through hypermasculinity, so much so that masculinity essentially became synonymous with homophobia.

Anderson (2009a) illustrates the emergence of the modern gay identity through the British trials and conviction of famed poet, playwright and author Oscar Wilde. His 1895 conviction for "gross indecency" established what a sodomite/pervert/homosexual "looked like." But it would take the works of Sigmund Freud a decade later to implicate sport with a heterosexualizing project.

Freud noticed that city dwelling resulted in elevated rates of same-sex sexual activity. Rather than attributing this to the increased chances of men with similar desires being able to meet under the cloak of anonymity, however (the sociological explanation), he instead attributed the increased visibility of homosexuality to the separation of children from male role models. Although Freud (1905) was sympathetic to those we now call gay men, he wanted to figure out how homosexuality was caused so that he could encourage its prevention.

Freud also thought that homosexuality was the product of "inversion," what he recognized as a form of gendered wrong-doing. In *Three Essays on the Theory of Sexuality*, Freud wrote, "the presence of both parents plays an important part. The absence of a strong father in childhood not infrequently favours the occurrence of inversion" (1905: 146). While Freud's theories have been categorically disproved as the etiology of same-sex sexual desires (LeVay 2010), they carried cultural weight at the time, sending a largely homophobic population into moral panic.

Freud, however, highlighted a social problem: namely, that boys did not have enough male influence/role models in their lives because their fathers were absent, working long hours in the factories before labor laws took effect. Sport provided the answer: it gave young boys time in the company of a coach—a male role model who could provide the requisite male (and moral) vapors.

Anderson (2009a) argues that this was part of the project of "muscular Christianity," and that it was at this point that sport (which was not needed for physical fitness) became organized, culturally valued and nearly or fully made compulsory for young boys to "play." Accordingly, sports like rugby and football were culturally valued, as this provided sufficient masculinity for the prevention of feminized or homosexual boys (Anderson and McCormack 2010; Chandler and Nauright 1996).

There were of course other reasons that teamsports were valued for boys. For example, sport helped teach the values of self-sacrifice and obedience to authority needed in both factory work and the military. However, the key factor was that sport accentuated the extreme version of masculinity that Western culture demanded. This is why women were excluded from sport for so long: women who competed equally alongside men would disrupt the myth of men's athleticism and women's frailty (Burton-Nelson 1994).

Women's participation in sport

As discussed in the previous section, the Industrial Revolution forged a stronger image of the acceptable woman as being a subservient, domesticated housewife, who was obliged to raise the children (White and Vagi 1990; Brailsford 1991). Women were expected to display characteristics of being "emotional, passive, dependent, maternal, compassionate and gentle" (Krane 2001: 117). Sports served as a method of enforcing the domestic role of women by first preventing their participation, and by also keeping boys and men away from the home after school or work (Lowerson 1993). Women were mostly excluded from sport and recreational life (Brailsford 1991).

However, not all middle-class women were relegated indoors. Some nineteenth-century middle-class women served as trailblazers in the sporting arena by participating in croquet and tennis, particularly in the UK; but it was not until the early twentieth century that working-class women began to participate in sport. Unlike men, however, for whom sports was argued to physically benefit, participation for women was fraught with medical backlash. It was feared that women taking part in sport would become "de-sexed" (Hargreaves 2000). Additionally, women were discouraged from sport through means of cultural stigma for their perceived lack of femininity. For example, the facial expressions of women competing were considered to be offensive to the feminine image (Ferez 2012). Sport was also said to cause undesirable personality changes of women (Lenskyj 1990).

The frailty of women has long been used as an excuse for limiting their participation; coupled with suspect Victorian medical advice, women's participation in sports was thus hindered from the outset. Only certain physical activities were seen as acceptable, those that maintained aesthetic principles or required little strenuous movement.

Throughout the twentieth century, as women quite slowly made inroads into playing competitive sport, they continued to be hampered by both social stigma and medical dogma. "Women would never achieve high standards in the game [of hockey]," one physician wrote, "because they lacked discipline and were temperamentally unsuited to the real restrictions of team activities" (Lowerson 1993: 213). Perhaps in an attempt to compromise on women's physicality, in 1921, English doctors approved numerous activities including team games (with the exception of football), as long as women met the following conditions: "medical examination before participating and the avoidance of excessive exertion" (Lenskyj 1990: 58). However, participating in football at this time would have been challenging enough, because, in 1921, the Football Association (FA)—the governing body of football in England—banned women's football from taking place under its jurisdiction. Not all forms of exercise were ruled out for women, however. In the nineteenth century, light exercise, like walking, was welcomed to improve health and help bear children (Hargreaves 1994). Gymnastics was a form of exercise also encouraged as appropriate and necessary for women to prepare for motherhood (Park 2007). Indeed, gymnastics programs for women in the US and England can be traced back to the 1850s (Hargreaves 1994; Bandy 2005).

Thus, from a young age in twentieth-century Western cultures, just as boys are encouraged into sport to develop masculinity, girls were steered away from competitive teamsports because their participation was thought to cause them to behave in an unfeminine and therefore socially unacceptable way. While boys' participation in sport was thought to affirm their masculinity and heterosexuality, women who excelled at sport were thought to challenge femininity and therefore faced an assumption of lesbianism (Cox and Thompson 2001; Griffin 1998; Lenskyj 2003; McDonagh and Pappano 2008).

The prohibition and stigmatization of women in sport was not, however, necessarily new to just the nineteenth and twentieth centuries. In the ancient Greek Olympics, women who even attempted to view the sporting spectacle, who just wanted to watch men compete, were subject to the death penalty (Boutilier and San Giovanni 1983; Griffin 1998). In fact, the founder of the modern Olympics, Pierre de Coubertin, made his stance very clear on the issue of women in sport: women were spectators, not performers (Hargreaves 1994). Contrary to popular belief, de Coubertin did not re-establish the Olympics to promote international friendship between nations. Nor did he use the Olympics to promote harmony among people of all genders. Instead, he used the Olympics to revive masculinity and to instill in men the values that he saw in team games such as rugby (Kidd 1990).

Women, of course, were not always complicit in adhering to men's desires. They competed in "feminine appropriate" activities in conjunction with the men's events at the first modern Olympics, but these took place outside of the Olympic arena. It was not until the 1924 Olympic Games in Paris that women were permitted to compete in a status equal to that of men (Hargreaves 1994).

This was a direct result of the first wave of feminism. For example, in 1921, women formed the Fédération Sportive Féminine Internationale, which ran the Women's Olympic Games in the 1920s and continued to run them until 1934, even after women's inclusion in the main Olympics (Ferez 2012). Equality was not, of course, achieved in 1924. The number of events that women could participate in was far less than the men's.

The proceeding decades of the twentieth century saw slowly increasing equality for women's sport. For example, the first women's Olympic marathon was in 1984, the triple jump came in 1996 and both the pole vault and 20 km walk in 2000. However, women are still exempt from the longest walking event: the 50 km.

Legislation supported the quest for sporting equality. In the US, following the ongoing inequality faced by women in sport, Title IX impacted on both playing and coaching. Although it may not seem overly relevant to sport in the UK, it shows how legislation can be used to try and enforce equality. Burton-Nelson (1994: 41) describes the legislation: "Title IX, a 1972 amendment to the Civil Rights Act, forbids gender discrimination in educational institutions that receive federal funds." Title IX ensures that equality is maintained, from funding and accommodation to guaranteeing that students' interests are met (Boxhill 1995). There were, however, opponents to Title IX in the 1970s. There was concern within male sport, particularly American football, that their glory days could be numbered and they placed the blame on women (Burton-Nelson 1994).

Title IX has allowed women to enter a sporting institution in the US that had previously been a masculine privilege. The positive effect on participation rates of female athletes in the educational system has been substantial (Frey and Eitzen 1991). The figures represented by Adams, Schmitke and Franklin (2005) note that participation has increased more than 800 percent since the implementation of Title IX. The UK has no direct equivalent, although the 2010 Equality Act covers all aspects of society, including sport, with a specific focus on minority groups—such as women.

However, the gains for American women go beyond the participation figures. There has been an increase in media coverage of women's sport which has in turn created female role models who inspire young girls to take up sport (Boxhill 1993). Additionally, there have been changes within school hierarchies as noted by Adams, Schmitke and Franklin (2005: 18): "Athletic high school girls are the recipients of a form of power, prestige and status once relegated solely to cheerleaders and majorettes." There is no doubt that Title IX made an impact, although not all of its impact has been positive.

However, although women's participation rates have soared, the number of female coaches has decreased (Burton-Nelson 1994). So, although more women now have the opportunity to participate in sport, they still play for male coaches (Acosta and Carpenter 1992). Frey and Eitzen (1991: 517) quote the figures: "In 1972, 90% of women's teams were coached by women; in 1989, 47 percent were coached by women." A *Washington Post* article in 2012 stated that the percentage has reportedly decreased again, to 43 percent (Greenwell 2012). According to Griffin (1992), one reason for the lack of female coaches is because hiring males instead of females reduces the number of lesbian coaches.

Before Title IX, the inequality between male and female sport was in some cases 50:1 (Hargreaves 1994). But most US educational institutions are funded in some way or another by federal money and therefore must comply with Title IX (Burton Nelson 1994); however, many are failing. Burton-Nelson (1994: 126) wrote: "At the Division I-A level only one out of 107 schools complies with Title IX. This is Washington State University (WSU), which was forced to do so by its own supreme court." Heywood and Dworkin (2003) update these figures almost a decade later, writing that 90 percent of educational institutions were still not conforming to the measures set out by Title IX. In order to meet requirements, some institutions have taken to removing sports programs, but the legality of this has been challenged (Burton Nelson 1994).

According to McDonagh and Pappano (2008: 103), Title IX was "a weak, even meek tool," because in legislation the following words are missing: "segregation sports." Additionally, they claim that the number of exemptions also undermines the legislation. Griffin (1992) suggests that it was the *interpretation* of Title IX that was the problem and it was not until 1988 that the legislation was fully restored, and therefore allowed educational facilities to be charged with sex discrimination. However, in an analysis of court cases in the last thirty years, 32 percent involve sex discrimination (McDonagh and Pappano 2008). This is a significantly low number given that few colleges are playing by the rules.

Despite this gradual progress in the West, other parts of the world, particularly Islamic countries, have lagged far behind (Hamdi and Anderson 2015). It was not until the 1996 Olympics that attention was drawn to countries who failed to send women to the Games, mainly due to religious restrictions (Heywood and Dworkin 2003). Furthermore, it has taken until the 2012 London Olympics to have women competing in all the same sports as men (though the 50 km walk remains the exception).

The final sport to relinquish the "men only" label was boxing. At the 2012 London Olympic Games, women were, for the first time ever, able to box on the Olympic stage (Channon and Matthews 2015). However, the number of weight divisions for women was less than men's, meaning that the number of medals available to men still exceeds the number available to women. In fact, men were able to compete for 30 more medals than women could, across all events at the London 2012 Olympics.

But women's gains never come in total. Just because a woman is permitted to compete, does not mean that they are welcomed, unless they appeared to be fully female. From 1968 until 2000, the International Olympic Committee used sex testing to decide if women were able to participate (Sykes 2006). Outside the Olympic arena, the initial tests carried out by sporting governing bodies were run by gynecologists. As Burton Nelson (1994: 71) describes, "Women at major competitions were obligated to lift their shirts and pull down their pants," and then male doctors decreed if women were feminine enough to take part. However, the IOC exchanged the visual test for a chromosome test known as the "Barr body test," which examines the chromosomes of the athlete (Burton Nelson 1994). This test was discontinued in 2000, on condition of finding another method to test and control gender (Ferez 2012). However, South African runner Caster Semenya is a prime example of how female athletes are still subject to humiliating verification testing. Following her 800-meter gold medal in the 2009 Athletics World Championship, questions were raised about her gender. The International Association for Athletics Federation (IAAF) conducted tests, reportedly releasing the results to the public that she was intersex (no ovaries but undescended testicles) before even telling her. It took a year of bureaucratic wrangling before she was cleared to race again.

It is not surprising that women's bodies were (and remain) subject to gender verification; they are competing in a masculinized terrain. The medicalization of their "different than average bodies" is only one mechanism by which women are objectified and stigmatized for being athletic. The only women ostensibly capable of bridging this gap are those who forgo femininity, those socially understood (rightly or wrongly) to be lesbian (Blinde and Taub 1992; Griffin 1992; Wolter 2010). From an orthodox view, any woman playing competitive, organized team-sports is understood as presenting a masculine image; the logical conclusion is that she must therefore be a lesbian (Lenskyj 1986).

Traditionally, sports participation equating to lesbianism is problematic for heterosexual and closeted lesbian women who compete in traditional male sports, such as football and rugby. Here, they are constantly under the assumption of being homosexual (Cox and Thompson 2001). Thus, sport has historically been used as a vehicle to reinforce homophobia (Hargreaves 1994), especially by male coaches who encourage their female players to instill and nurture an aggressive attitude.

It is this association of athletic competency with a socially perceived lesbian identity which provides the political utility for Griffin's assertion of the utility of homophobia in policing gendered boundaries. Griffin (1998) suggests homophobia has been previously used as policing agent of women's gendered expression. In the case of sport, homophobia is clearly used to control women's behavior and channel them into certain "appropriate" sports: namely those that are aesthetically pleasing activities for the gaze of heterosexual males, such as gymnastics or cheerleading. The lesbian label has historically been constructed by a heterosexual majority to carry with it an extremely negative social stigma and even intimidation of physical violence (Griffin 1998). Lesbian women who played sport therefore belong to two groups that are marginalized: they are not only women, but they are deviant women (Lenskyj 2003), intruding upon men's privileged space. Within the sporting context, homophobia serves as a fierce and confrontational mechanism (Hargreaves 1994), which attempts to deny their equal participation.

Homophobia, however, hurts more than just lesbian women. Theberge and Birrell (1994) suggest that all women's participation in sport, regardless of sexual orientation, is hindered by the homophobic behavior surrounding women's sport. It causes a division between lesbians and heterosexual women, therefore preventing a joint approach of political action (Lenskyj 1991). Accordingly, the more lesbians are seen as the cause of women's sports' poor image, the deeper the rift becomes (Griffin 1992). Evidencing the severity of lesbian stigma, older research shows that some athletes prefer to be referred to as "whores" rather than "dykes" (Blinde and Taub 1992a: 162).

The lesbian label is feared by women participating in sport because, once labeled "lesbian," women are still shown to face discrimination (Fink et al. 2012). Martina Navratilova and Billie Jean King serve as historical reminders of how hostile sport can be toward lesbians; they each lost a huge proportion of their income after coming out as lesbians in tennis due to the homophobic culture at the time (Cahn 1994). Sponsors did not want to associate themselves with athletes who challenged the hegemonic societal norm of compulsory heterosexuality (Griffin 2012; Rich 1980). In connection with this, Griffin (1998: 60) notes that, "Lesbians in sport are held to a different standard of morality than heterosexual women or men in sport." This results in lesbian women facing systematic oppression when participating in sport (Hargreaves 2000). Griffin (1998), therefore, separates homophobia into six categories for more systematic analysis: *silence, denial, apology, promotion of heterosexy image, attacks on lesbians* and *preference for a male coach.*

It was only in the final decade of the twentieth century that women participated in sport without necessarily being homosexualized for their participation. Before then, sports had been divided into appropriate and inappropriate, with aesthetic sports (like gymnastics) conveying social sanctioning and heterosexualization, while invasive, contact, or sports requiring muscle mass were masculinized and thus homosexualizing for women.

At the time that the precipitous amount of research into the experiences of gays and lesbians in sport came into force—the 1990s, and the early years of the new millennium—sport had conditionally accepted lesbian women, as long as they acted in hyperfeminine ways (Anderson and Bullingham 2013; Griffin 1998). By the new millennium, sport had also conditionally accepted gay men (Anderson 2002), as long as they either participated in feminized sports (like ice dancing), or remained silent in masculinized sport through a policy of "don't ask, don't tell." This is to say that even when sports were not overtly homophobic—which they often were—the previous two decades found cultures of extreme heterosexism within sport. In these previous two decades, the 1990s and first decade of the new millennium, acting straight seemed to be the rule at hand for gay and lesbians to be socially tolerated in the sporting world.

The structure of sport

The previous section has outlined why competitive, organized sport was thrust into the cultural fore during the beginning of the twentieth century (to make boys into straight, masculine males), and how the decades preceding the twenty-first century brought hard-fought, but gradual, permission for women to also participate. It took a century before women could play sport, and a century before gay men could play openly. But, during the course of this century, the economy changed dramatically.

As stated, one of the primary reasons for the cultural indoctrination of modern sport a century ago was to 1) prepare boys for factory life; 2) prepare boys for soldiering and 3) prevent boys from becoming homosexual. But, a century later, these three factors are increasingly irrelevant. First, the West has lost most of its manufacturing jobs to overseas; gone are the days when most men needed to be tough and stoic to work in heavy industry. Instead, men work in the professional, business, service or technical industries—hardly a bastion of masculinity. Second, we live in a rapidly de-escalating military society. Gone are the days where large standing armies were required; today's military is fewer in number, more precise and uses professional soldiers. The notion of a draft is inconceivable to millennials. Finally, today, most people understand that one does not become a gay male because one did not play football. Most understand that sexual minorities, like sexual majorities, are produced by a biological, perhaps epi-genetic, road map. There is thus no longer the widespread cultural belief that boys became gay because they didn't play sport. There is no evidence—whatsoever—that homosexuality is socially constructed.

With these economic changes, scientific understandings of the origins of homosexuality, and changing cultural perspectives on homosexuality, have led to significant changes. One must ask how it is that sport, in the last few decades (and increasingly not applicable to the second decade of the twenty-first century), managed to retain its relevance. One must also ask how sport managed to maintain a hypermasculine and homophobic social attitude despite the cultural changes around it. It was not too long ago that sport was a social anchor, preventing the progress of gay and lesbian athletes. This section explores how that occurred. It shows how the structural operation of sport enabled it to remain shielded from the cultural progress outside of it. It explains how, in an era in which social institutions have radically reinvented and improved upon the understanding and treatment of gay and lesbian people, both closeted and openly gay athletes said that sport remains steadfast in its production of conservative gender orthodoxy (Anderson 2005a, 2005b).

It does so by showing that, first, sports are a near-total institution in which athletes find it difficult to escape a single-minded way of viewing sex and gender. The second is that sports are a gender-segregated institution that prevents heterosexual men from hearing the narratives of women and gay men. The third is that the institution of sport is a closed-loop system in that it lacks critical self-examination. When taken together, these factors enable sport to near-seamlessly reproduce itself as an institution of orthodox masculine expression. We now interrogate these in detail.

Sport as a near-total institution

Anderson (2005a: 66) describes sporting cultures as a "near-total institution." Goffman (1961) originally described a "total institution" as an isolated, enclosed social system designed to control all aspects of a person's life (such as a prison or mental asylum). Anderson (2005a) borrows this concept to discuss how sport holds almost as much as power as a total institution, the difference being that athletes have the freedom to quit sport, whereas a prisoner completely lacks agency. The myth of homogeneity of thought and action required to produce desirable athletic results is so strong that athletes willingly subject themselves to severe restrictions in their social lives.

The process is similar to the argument Foucault (1984) made concerning the ability of a military to transform peasants into soldiers. Foucault suggested that, through intense regimentation and implementation of a standard ideal of behavior, men can be taught to become more docile in their identity because their growing identity as a soldier is also one of subordination from agency. He said that the longer a soldier remains in the institution of soldiering, the less agency he maintains to contest it.

Much like the military, sport structures men into ranks and divisions. Athletes are obliged to dress in uniform, follow the orders of coaches without question and think in alignment with their teammates, putting team expectations first. Hence, a subtle but progressive ideology is imposed upon athletes that, like the solider, crodes their agency and restructures them as highly masculinized conformists in thought and action. The longer an athlete remains in the field of sport, the less agency s/he might have to come out.

In sport, athletes spend large amounts of time with each other: training, attending school or university, socializing and living together. In soccer, for example, Parker (1996a) discusses the living arrangements among footballers and documents how the accommodation for apprentice players was referred to as the club "digs," showing how all the boys' bedrooms and leisure space was in the same place. Interestingly, Parker (1996a) also notes how this was a very "closed space:" visitors, including parents, were restricted to communal areas only, rather than the boys' bedrooms. Such an example supports Anderson's (2005a) near-total institution, with the close-knit group creating a rigid and tightly policed bond with each other.

The immersion into the total institution can begin in early childhood. Athletes are indoctrinated into the mindset of teamsports at a very young age, influencing their identity to grow and center on their athleticism. But this also limits their social networks to mainly other athletes. Athletes befriend each other off the field, and their social lives are routinely dictated by their rigid schedule of practices and competitions and other team functions. In doing so, they must shut out other cultural options and limit whom they befriend, particularly those who do not fit the notion of orthodox masculinity.

Furthermore, athletes must publicly acknowledge the same goals and team commitment as other athletes if they are to retain their masculine and social status among peers. This involves adopting a collective worldview that tends to be narrow and restrictive, one that they maintain until adulthood. Now with centralized funding for elite athletes, some have to live in a specific region, so that athletes can train together every day and this often means house sharing with other athletes.

The consequences of coming out in this near-total institution are made worse when one considers that advancement is not solely determined by the physical ability of the athlete to perform their sport. Athletes who reflect the institution creed are deemed to be "team players," and they are selected over other athletes who may be physically equal or superior. Conversely, if they do not reflect team norms, they can be labeled a "non-team player," or a "loose cannon." In this regard, any variance from orthodox masculinity is viewed as subversive and is therefore likely to result in decreased opportunity for matriculation to the next level. Until recently, this virtually necessitated that those who aspire to the next level (or even the next game) must disengage with any public notion of a gay or lesbian identity.

This protracted disengagement from one's homosexual identity must be difficult to challenge after retiring from decades of living within this rigid institution. Just because one is removed from the athletic arena physically does not necessarily mean that one has disengaged from their athletic identity emotionally. The prospect of being stigmatized and marginalized as gay or lesbian becomes more terrifying to him or her than the daily torment of the homonegative environment s/he endures.

But, gay and lesbian athletes, like heterosexual athletes, who spend most of their free time in the near-total institution report that they also feel alienated from mainstream gay culture. This can occur because they do not have the time to escape their athletic network, or because they are too young or live too far away from an urban arena in order to seek out gay life in the bars and clubs.

Sport as a gender-segregated institution

Other than jails and mental hospitals, few other institutions segregate men and women so perfectly. While occupational sex segregation is declining in other institutions (Rotolo and Wharton 2004), formal and traditional reasoning has left teamsports a largely unexamined arena of gender segregation (Anderson 2009b). Highlighting the hegemony of this segregation, people largely support it, sometimes even framing their support in analysis of its benefit to women (Crosset 1990; Hargreaves 1994; Kidd 1990; Whitson 1990).

It is easy to understand why feminists value segregated women's sporting programs. It was not until the passage of Title IX in 1972 that American women were really given a start in the institution of sport, and many fear losing it by being pushed out by males if sports were desegregated (McDonagh and Pappano 2008). One can certainly understand the feminist desire to play sports away from men, particularly where women are protected from the violence of male athleticism (Kreager 2007). Gender segregation in teamsports is therefore confirmed by both men and women. It is then naturalized through notions of opposite phenotypes and boys' elevated levels of aggression and athletic advantage over girls. Collectively, sex segregation in sport is thus a mutually agreed-upon notion of boys' and girls' separate worlds.

Sports are segregated under the guise of providing equality of competition, even in sports where there is no physical danger to men and women competing together, or no gendered advantage (like golf or bowling). But the consequence is that sex segregation allows men to exist in a homogenous, highly masculinized, (increasingly less) homophobic and sexist arena without the voices of women to contrast their conservative understandings.

While women's sporting programs certainly have been shown to benefit women, the near-total segregation has a great number of deleterious effects for women as well. There is a disparity in the allocation of sporting resources, as women's athletics have consistently been shown to fare worse than men's. Specific to the reproduction of orthodox masculinity, however, is that structural segregation removes men from the narratives of female athletes who might otherwise enlighten them about their athleticism (Anderson 2008a).

When men and women are integrated in play, there is benefit to both sexes (Channon 2013, 2014). In the desegregated sport of cheerleading (Anderson 2008b), for example, men are able to partake in conversations with and about sex and gender—the kind of conversations they were unable to have in a homosocial, ostensibly heterosexual (and homophobic) culture such as football (see Curry 1991). Channon and Matthews (2015) show similar results in their research on mixed-sex martial arts. In this environment, they are able to socialize with and develop team cohesion with women as participants of equal agency and responsibility for the outcome of a game. They are often able to experience women as leaders (as women are most generally the team captains in cheerleading), and to even see gay men do what they do, but frequently better (because gay men often cheered in high school too). Therefore, by entering the co-ed division of cheerleading in college, these men hear the narratives of women's sexual and gender identities. We suggest that desegregating sport may thus help develop a form of masculinity that is based less on misogyny and homophobia, like Anderson's (2009a) notion of inclusive masculinities.

Sport as a decreasing opportunity structure

Athletes who emulate the institutional creed of sport are usually selected over players who break from its tenets, influencing them to adopt the gendered norms associated with orthodox notions of gendered expectations. Ewald and Jiobu (1985) show that some athletes so overly adhere to the norms of sporting culture that they disrupt family relationships, work responsibilities and even their physical health—all guided by a masculine creed of *giving their all*.

Anderson (2005a) has shown that gay male athletes largely remain closeted for these same reasons, fearing that coming out will thwart their athletic progress. Hughes and colleagues (1991: 311) describe this social deviance as *overconformity* to the sport ethic saying, "The likelihood of being chosen or sponsored for continued participation is increased if athletes overconform to the norms of sport." Of course, athletes do not see overconformity as problematic; rather, they see it as "confirming and reconfirming their identity as athletes."

Building upon Hughes and colleagues' (1991) overconformity theory, we examine the structural mechanisms that help reproduce sport as a site of orthodox notions of gendered expectations by highlighting the near-total institutional aspects of teamsports. Chiefly, sport is built upon a decreasing opportunity structure. There are millions of children with dreams of making it as a professional, but only a few thousand who actually do. Somewhere between the ages of 12 and 22, athletes are culled from the increasingly difficult progression from recreational athlete to gold medalist.

Even for those who do not consider that they will ultimately be a world champion, when athletes think in alignment with their teammates, they are given social prestige and are publicly lauded; they are honored by their institutions and celebrated by fans and community. Hughes and colleagues (1991: 311) write: "Athletes find the action and their experiences in sport so exhilarating and thrilling that they want to continue participating as long as possible." Coakley (1998: 155) later adds: "they love their sports and will do most anything to stay involved." Thus, it is understandable that, from *their perspective*, sport is a socially positive vessel.

And while we think that the reasons athletes will do almost anything to remain in teamsports are more complicated than just the thrill one receives from playing them, the point remains that athletes who withstand the selection process do so because of their outstanding athletic ability *and* their willingness to conform to the team and coach's expectations. Conversely, athletes who do not conform are sanctioned by verbal insults and are less likely to be given valued playing positions. Thus, desiring peer recognition and social promotion, athletes normally put team expectations before individual concerns, sacrificing individual agency and contributing to the reproduction of a rigid sporting culture. Of particular concern is the fact that, this virtually necessitates that those who aspire to the next level must publicly disengage with any stigmatized notion of sexual or gender ideology that is inconsistent with orthodox masculinity.

From an early age, then, athletes befriend each other on and off the field. Their social lives are routinely dictated by a rigid athletic schedule of practices, competitions and other team functions. Teamsport athletes, from this and other research, report that the further they rise through the ranks, the less freedom exists to inhabit any social space outside this network and the more their identity narrows in order to be competitive with other men (Anderson 2005a).

We suggest that this might make gender construction in teamsports different from the type of agency-laden gender construction that West and Zimmerman (1987) or other social constructionists propagate. This is because, from youth to adult-hood, males socialized into competitive teamsports follow a subtle but increasingly institutionalized gender ideology: an incipient notion of gender that slowly erodes individual agency and restructures athletes as highly masculinized conformists in thought and action. The subordination required for retaining one's sporting status, or being selected for advancement, wears away at their agency to construct opposi-tional masculinities. This is then justified by the prevalent belief that homogeneity is required in sports to produce desirable results (Sabo and Panepinto 1990), even though there is only a small and dubious relationship between a group's social cohe-sion and athletic success (Granovetter 1983; Mullen and Cooper 1994).

Sport as a closed-loop institution

Finally, sport exists as an insular institution; nepotism runs high. For every athlete who has excelled in sport, there are scores who did not make the cut. Yet these others do not go on to coach. Coaching comes from those who excelled at sport, those with at least modest sporting success stories.

However, success stories fail to recognize the statistical reality of sports. Not every kid can play professional football. Books aren't published, sponsorships aren't given and movies aren't made about those who didn't make it. Only certain stories are being told, stories that glamorize the struggle and romance of the sporting hero genre. These stories make for great entertainment, but falsely lead us to bestow upon sport meritocratic qualities that may not actually exist, or that only exist for those born with the talent and social circumstances to excel at sport.

As discussed earlier, athletes who pursue sport find that the further they advance, the more time and emotional investment they must devote in order to remain competitive. This serves to further narrow their social life, to the point in which everything revolves around sport. They grow so wrapped up in their status as an athlete that it often becomes their master identity.

But centering one's identity on athleticism carries with it great risk, particularly in such a volatile field. At any time, an injury can end a career, or the athlete can be cut from the team on a moment's notice. But whether they suddenly lose their association with their athletic identity or their body slowly ages out of competitive form, eventually athletes are forced to disengage from that master identity.

Men who drop out, are forced out or otherwise do not make the next level often find themselves detached from much of the cultural masculine power they once enjoyed—something sport psychologists call the "disengagement effect." Under such conditions, most athletes report a desire to be part of a team again, so that they can recoup some of their masculine worth. It makes sense that athletes who rode atop the masculine hierarchy would also feel the greatest loss upon dis-engaging from that status. Coaching, therefore, often becomes the avenue to get back in the game.

Sport almost always draws leaders from those who ascribed to the previous cohort's ideals. Conversely, the vast majority of those who were marginalized by sport do not go on to coach and tell their stories. Their ideas about how sport ought to operate are not heard in the athletic arena. When athletes leave the sporting arena, their perceptions of how sport ought to operate go with them. Sport is therefore a closed-loop system.

Much like the military, those who survive are promoted to leadership positions, where they reproduce hero genres to inspire a new generation. Complacency and over-conformity get one promoted. Then, only highly devoted athletes (who usually were rewarded by sport) return to coach, denying sporting experiences and narratives of those whose experiences were not so wonderful. This closed-loop system serves elite athletes. It is held in place by the hero myth, that so thrills those who patronize the sport through fandom, particularly the underdog genre. We listen to those who have made it through the abusive system tout the wonders of sport but are not privy to the stories of those whose experience was poor.

If we were to examine the institution of sport from a medical perspective, however, sport would fail to gain the mass approval it has. It would likely appear inefficient in producing significant positive results for the majority of those who experience it. Sport, undoubtedly, does *some* people some good, but the cultural myth that sport is good for everybody is wholly misguided (Anderson 2010).

Knowing that the few who gain merit in sport go into coaching, we should next note that most coaching positions, public or private, and particularly those concerning youth sports, require no training in pedagogy, sport psychology or even physical education. In fact, coaching youth sport requires no degree at all for most leagues. Whereas one needs a license to cut hair, anyone can hang a whistle around his or her neck and call him or herself a coach. Increasingly, some sports, in some countries, require a "level one" or "level two" coaching certificate. These certificates are generally earned with just a few hours of study. Thus, despite even these efforts, coaches largely learn their trade by modeling what their coach did. In other words, coaches tend to reproduce themselves because they both value the system they have progressed through, and they are not required to critically analyze the institution. Without such intervention, there is little input to evaluate or change the system.

When taken together with gender segregation, the decreasing opportunity structure and the near-total institutional atmosphere of most sports, it should not be surprising that these factors have traditionally managed to maintain and reproduce orthodox notions of gender that have been based on homophobia and misogyny. This book shows that matters are, however, changing.

Changing sport

While the structures of teamsports have mostly remained the same for over a century, emphasizing competition and obedience to authority, the culture surrounding sport has begun to shift (Anderson 2013b). Increasingly, youth are less interested in playing competitive, organized sport. In fact, research shows that youth are dropping out of these types of sports somewhere between 2 and 5 percent a year.

While that might not sound like much, over the next ten years, it could mean that youth sport rosters are reduced by up to half. Part of this concern comes from the negative, life-long impact that using the head as a weapon in sport can cause. Of particularly concern is chronic traumatic encephalopathy (Anderson and Kian 2012). For athletes not familiar with the effect of using the head to tackle, hit a ball, or inadvertently receive concussion, they are devastating. It is for this reason that the authors of this book are working to remove heading the ball in soccer, and tackling in other sports. Readers interested should read Allyson Pollock's overview of rugby injuries, *Tackling Rugby: What Every Parent Should Know About Injuries* (2014), and visit the website SportCIC.com.

In the next chapter we show that the softening of sport culture is due to more than just health concerns, however. There exists a wholesale change to masculinity among youth. As youth are less invested in being macho, there is less need to play competitive, organized sport (Anderson 2011b, 2012).

3

HOMOHYSTERIA AND DECLINING HOMOPHOBIA

Since the foundation of organized sport in the late nineteenth and early twentieth century within the Western world, sport has traditionally served as a masculine preserve. It has maintained the purpose of turning young boys toward a hegemonic perspective of male heterosexuality, one distanced from femininity and homosexuality. The construction of a dominating form of heterosexual masculinity was accomplished through multiple mechanisms, including socializing boys into the physical violence, sexism and homophobia indicative of organized, competitive sport (Anderson 2009a). Adams, Anderson and McCormack (2010) add that to construct an esteemed and "acceptable" masculine identity, it is not just necessary to display one's heterosexuality, but also to "police" the gendered behaviors of one's peers. Policing is conducted through specific discourses used to question men's heteromasculinity. Epithets such as "fags," "sissies" and "poofs" are often used to emasculate and feminize those who do not comply with supposed traditional hetero-masculine norms.

With sport's traditional function of masculinizing and heterosexualizing boys—and subsequently marginalizing effeminacy—it is unsurprising that homophobia and anti-femininity have been commonly employed among athletes in the construction of gender-normative performances (Anderson and McGuire 2010). This was particularly true of the purpose of sport (in the Western world) in the 1980s. Here, sport took on renewed importance for boys and young men as it was a central tool in heterosexualizing men in a culture that Anderson (2009a) calls "homohysteric."

Just as playing sport permitted men some cultural transgression of rigid masculinity norms (Anderson 2005a), the promotion of a feminine image allowed women playing men's sports to do so with less lesbian suspicion. Griffin (1998: 68) wrote that "femininity has become a code word for heterosexuality," just as Kimmel described that masculinity was heterosexuality for males (1994), and Lenskyj (1986) summarized that the central issues concerning women's participation in sport were that, "femininity and heterosexuality [were] seen as incompatible with sporting excellence: either sport made women masculine or sportswomen were masculine from the outset." Griffin (1998) argued that in order to limit controversy about their participation, women have been shown to promote heterosexual images (heterosexy) and use overt homophobia as a way to socially distance themselves from being thought lesbian. Even early in the twenty-first century, Cox and Thompson (2001) found that female footballers were assumed to be lesbian because of their choice to play a traditionally male teamsport. Shire, Brackenridge and Fuller (2000: 49) describe the behavior of heterosexual women within one hockey team, writing, "They joked about the lesbian women in order to reinforce their heterosexuality to others."

Thus the conditions described by Anderson of homohysteria for men in sport also existed for women in sport. Just as a culture of homohysteria presented a problem for both gay and straight men, the homohysteria of women's sport also created a problem for both lesbian and straight women. Women were understood as being pressured into presenting an image of hyperfeminine heterosexuality in order to gain and maintain public support of their new-found sporting freedoms (Lenskyj 2003). This can either be understood as a form of denial, or it might also be viewed as a survival strategy to compete without homosexual suspicion and the discrimination that comes with it (Lenskyj 1995). Either way, the silence and denial of lesbianism in sport permits stereotypes and discrimination to continue unopposed (Krane and Barber 2003).

The erasure of lesbianism through the promotion of femininity and heterosexuality is known as the "apologetic." Apologetic behavior occurs because women are participating in a male domain. Felshin (1974: 36) argues that "because women cannot be excluded from sport and have chosen not to reject sport, apologetics develop to account for their sport involvement in the face of its social unacceptability." Davis-Delano and colleagues (2009) explain that apologetic behavior occurs in numerous ways: creating a feminine image, or apologizing for on-field behavior, such as aggression (Ezzell 2009). Even in recent years, Davis-Delano and colleagues (2009) show that apologetic behavior is still evident—specifically, looking feminine, appearing heterosexual and apologizing for aggressive sporting-related behaviors. So while it seems that homohysteria is falling in men's sport, it remains rife within women's sport.

A growing body of work has documented the power of homohysteria both in understanding when homophobia regulates gendered behaviors and also for understanding the change in gendered behaviors when homohysteria decreases (Adams 2011, Adams and Anderson 2011; Anderson, McCormack and Lee 2012; McCormack 2011b; Roberts 2013). While Anderson (2009a, 2011c) developed the idea of homohysteria in relation to men's gendered behaviors, we argue that it is equally applicable to women in sport, and that although not recognized as such, a plethora of research already documents the conditions of homohysteria within female sporting cultures from the 1980s (Hargreaves 2000).

Defining homohysteria

Anderson (2009a) developed the concept of "homohysteria" to explain the power dynamics of changing homophobia on the masculinities of heterosexual men. While earlier scholarship demonstrated that high levels of cultural homophobia influence individuals to distance themselves from social suspicion of homosexuality through the avoidance of gender-atypical behaviors (Floyd 2000; Ibson 2002), there was less attention paid to how changing social norms would influence these behaviors (Anderson 2015a). Anderson used the term "homohysteria" to situate this scholarship within specific social and historical conditions, arguing that homophobia only operates this way in *homohysteric* settings. In other words, homophobia only influences gendered behaviors in particular social and historical contexts.

There are three social conditions that must be met for a homohysteric culture to exist: 1) widespread awareness that homosexuality exists as an immutable sexual orientation within a significant portion of a culture's population; 2) high levels of homophobia in that culture and 3) an association of gender atypicality with homosexuality. As each of these factors change, the level of homohysteria and the nature of gender dynamics in the culture will vary. Given that each of these factors can and do change, it is clear that there will be temporal variation within any given culture, variation across cultures and organizational variance within any given culture (McCormack and Anderson 2014a).

Homohysteria is particularly useful for understanding different attitudes toward homosocial tactility in homophobic cultures. Why can men hold hands in Iran without being homosexualized, but in America in the 1980s they would have been? Both of these cultures had high degrees of homophobia. The difference occurs because it is simply not accepted within Iran that homosexuality exists (Afary 2009)—the first condition of homohysteria mentioned earlier. Instead, homosexuality is claimed to be a Western, imperialist phenomenon (Frank, Camp and Boucher 2010). From this cultural perspective, homosexuality is considered an aberration (Zuhur 2005), and combined with extreme homophobia, homosexuality is effectively erased.

Iran and other similar cultures in Africa and the Middle East are thus highly homophobic but they are not yet homohysteric. This is why homophobia does not regulate these men's gendered behaviors. Thus, homohysteria provides an explanation for the differences between the intersections of homophobia, masculinity and men's tactility in differing contemporary cultures, explaining why homophobia retains the ability to regulate gender in one culture but not another.

Considering countries like Iran also highlights that attitudes toward homosexuality can become more intolerant as well as progressive (Plummer 2014). Homophobia is often used for political gain, and can also be seen as another form of the rejection of imperialism in particular contexts. Even so, Smith (2011: 1) highlights that while trends in homophobia occur in both directions, the global trend is "towards greater approval of homosexual behavior with 87 percent of countries moving in that direction and with the gains in approval also being larger than the declines."

Homohysteria is also contingent upon the social dynamics of organizations within any macro culture. This recognizes that levels of homophobia vary greatly even within countries, and particularly one as diverse as the US; Anderson (2005b) demonstrates this in his ethnography of competing co-educational university cheerleading associations with national reach. Both of these cultures were aware that homosexuality existed as a sexual orientation, but homophobia was only stigmatized in one. Men belonging to one cheerleading association adhered to orthodox notions of masculinity, while the other belonged to an association which supported gay rights and celebrated femininity among men. Males in the inclusive association would dance provocatively and be thrown in the air by women without censure, while the conservative teams perceived these behaviors as indicative of homosexuality and thus inconsistent with masculinity. Accordingly, within the same broader culture, and the same sport, one organizational culture was homohysteric while the other was not.

Whilst the concept of homohysteria offers a useful and historically situated conceptualization of homophobia, some argue its shortcomings. Negy (2014: 1) questions the wisdom of developing the term "homohysteria," asking, "How many terms do we need to refer to prejudice toward sexual minorities?" He also critiques unnecessary application and utility of the term, as well as the lack of empirical evidence for the construct validity of homohysteria—notably citing the lack of quantitative data to support it. This is something McCormack and Anderson (2014a) argue would strengthen the utility of the concept. Finally, Negy (2014) also argues that homohysteria has limited applicability, as it currently omits the role of women and lesbians from its theorizing (see also Worthen 2014)—something we address in this book—as well as bisexuals (see Morris, McCormack and Anderson 2014) and transgendered individuals.

Nevertheless, we maintain that homohysteria remains the most useful concept to understand the prejudice suffered by sexual minorities, and it conceptualizes greater social phenomena that other concepts—such as homophobia, heterosexism and heteronormativity—fail to incorporate. Most importantly, it historically situates the study of masculinity (Anderson 2009a).

A stage model of homohysteria

Based on the foundational arguments of homohysteria discussed above, we have developed a stage model of homohysteria that is rooted in research on masculinities in the US since the late 1800s. This model has three stages: 1) homoerasure, 2) homohysteria and 3) inclusivity. We suggest, particularly given similar developments in the UK, the US and Australia, that it may prove useful for understanding homophobia, changing masculinities and the importance of sexual minority politics in other contexts.

While we devised our stage model in relation to homohysteria, other concepts have been used to highlight three significant cultural zeitgeists in the twentieth century related to homosexuality. For example, Ghaziani (2014: 9) discusses the "closet, coming out, and post-gay eras." He argues that the closet era was defined by concealment, isolation and shame, and lasted until the mid-1940s. He defines the period between 1945 and 1997 as the coming-out era, as a period when "gayborhoods" flourished and people increasingly lived as openly gay (although not necessarily without stigma).

The third era emerged in 1997 and is known as "post-gay," characterized by a "dramatic acceptance of homosexuality and a corresponding assimilation of gays and lesbians into the mainstream" (2014: 9). There is significant similarity between Ghaziani's characterization of the twentieth century and our own, with the differences in time explained by his focus on the influence of homophobia on urban sociology and the organization of local gay neighborhoods and our focus on the influence of homophobia on gendered behaviors. We now explicate our stage model as a way of demonstrating the emergence and contemporary decline of homohysteria in American culture. Figure 3.1 provides a visual representation of this stage model. The levels of homophobia are drawn from GSS data (see Anderson 2009a; Loftus 2001).

Homoerasure

Anderson (2009a) argued that homohysteria is a product of modernity, and that the conditions for a culture to be homohysteric are the result of the discourses of gender and sexuality that emerged from the second Industrial Revolution in the West (see Cancian 1987). Recognizing that contemporary taxonomies of sexual identity are the result of specific historical, social and intellectual circumstances (Giddens 1992; Greenberg 1988), the modern understanding of gay identity is pivotal to the emergence of homohysteric cultures. There is only evidence supporting homohysteria in modern cultures, and homohysteria does not apply to cultures that have no understanding of sexual identities, such as pre-modern Western civilizations (Spencer 1995).

Prior to urbanization, the majority of the population lived in rural areas and males with same-sex sexual desire were unlikely to encounter others with similar desires. However, the migration to the cities of the second Industrial Revolution provided a population density that enabled individuals with same-sex desire to organize socially (Spencer 1995). This included the emergence of sexual subcultures of gay men (Chauncey 1994). At the same time, new forms of labor that included long working hours structured men away from their families (Cancian 1987), influencing Freud's (1905) theorizing of same-sex sexual desires as a form of gender inversion. Near contemporaneously, Westphal, Ulrichs and Krafft-Ebing sought to classify homosexual acts as belonging to a *type* of person—a gender invert.

The emergence of sexual identities was supported by developments in the public and political sphere. The 1895 conviction of Oscar Wilde for "gross indecency" was particularly important: so extensive was the media coverage around the trial of Britain's celebrated playwright that he became emblematic of the gay male identity, even though Wilde himself was bisexual. The case consolidated

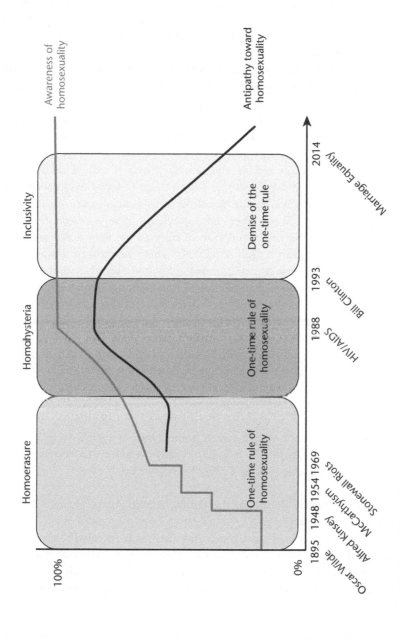

FIGURE 3.1 The shift from homoerasure to inclusivity.

the conflation of gender a-typicality with same-sex attraction: the image of the male homosexual as effeminate. It was reported that many men fled to France after Wilde's conviction (Norton 1992). Thus, the first wide-scale social recognition and awareness of same-sex sexuality as a static and relatively immutable sexual identity was accompanied by social and legal oppression of same-sex sexual acts. Ibson (2002) provides evidence that this British phenomenon also influenced American men's behaviors.

This stigmatization of same-sex sexual identities was also consolidated through the medicalization of homosexuality (Greenberg 1988). Corresponding with an increasing criminalization of male same-sex sex, doctors sought to define these acts within a medical framework as a way of consolidating their own emerging respectability as a profession. As a result, homosexuals were considered mentally ill or morally depraved (Greenberg 1988).

While sub-cultures organized around same-sex desires existed in the early twentieth century (Beisel 1998; Chauncey 1994), threat of social and legal censure kept these cultures mostly underground and the general population was unaware that such cultures existed. Where there *was* knowledge of same-sex desire, it was greatly stigmatized and the general population rejected the notion that same-sex sexual identities were legitimate (Johnson 2004). These were thus cultures of *erasure*, where homophobia was so extreme that social and legal persecution forced sexual minorities to conceal their sexual desires and identities, preventing identity politics from occurring.

In this stage of erasure, gendered behaviors are not regulated by homophobia and men did not find their behaviors policed in the way we often think of today. In the latter decades of the nineteenth century and early part of the twentieth, men exhibited a great deal of physical intimacy, posed for photos while sat on each other's laps and gently hugging, and expressed themselves emotionally in letters (see Ibson 2002). These cultures were homophobic, but not homohysteric.

Relating this to a sporting example, Treves (2015) uses the notion of homohysteria to explain the relationship between homoerasure and tennis by examining the experiences of Bill Tilden, who is largely regarded as the father of tennis, who played—and was unbeatable—in the 1920s. Treves writes:

> He was also widely known to the tennis community as having a curious propensity for young men . . . his sexual identity was complicated. He had affairs with ballboys, and was arrested and jailed twice for lewd behavior with minors. Tilden became a social pariah. He was barred from all the tennis clubs and died penniless, cast out from the sport he loved. Early biographers discounted his sexuality, even passing it off as a strange complex centered around the need to be a father.

If Tilden had fraternized with ballboys in the 1980s, there is no doubt that the media would have cased him as gay. The unwillingness to do so in the 1920s highlights a culture of homoerasure—they just didn't conceptualize that one could be gay.

A key development in the emergence of homohysteria in American culture was the publication of Kinsey's (1948) study of males' sexual practices (Anderson 2011c). Appearing during the dawn of the political context of McCarthyism, Kinsey's work presented homosexuality as a normal variation of human sexuality (Weeks 1985), claiming that 10 percent of the population was homosexual and that far more had engaged in same-sex sexual acts. Partially because Kinsey's research raised awareness of the existence of homosexuality in the US, sexual minorities were purged from public office and homosexual men were labeled "sex deviates" (Johnson 2004). The oppression of homosexuality was near-total: it was culturally stigmatized, classified as a mental illness, and criminalized with harsh sentencing. Thus, most same-sex attracted males remained silent about their desires. While this "Lavender Scare" could be conceived as evidence of a homohysteric culture, we do not classify it as such because homosexuality was effectively erased.

However, the sexual conservatism of the 1950s was contested by increasingly liberal attitudes toward sexuality in the 1960s and 1970s (Spencer 1995). Political activism regarding sexuality split into assimilationists, who supported a politics of sameness, alongside those who advocated for a more revolutionary politics that parodied masculinity and embraced gender a-typicality to contest homophobia and heterosexual privilege (Shepard 2009). Even though a growing proportion of the heterosexual population was aware of homosexuality as a static sexual identity and while societal attitudes were still largely negative, there was less overt oppression even as legal discrimination persisted (Greenberg 1988). This was because people did not readily believe or suspect that a friend or family member could be gay. During this time, sexual minorities were still perceived as belonging to sexual subcultures in particular metropolitan cities. It was only in the 1980s that Anglo-American cultures entered a phase of *homohysteria*.

Homohysteria

Despite the liberalizing trend in the 1960s and 1970s, a combination of social factors led to an upsurge in homophobic attitudes in the 1980s in the West. In the mid-1980s, high levels of homophobia (Loftus 2001) combined with a closing-down of inclusivity that had resulted from the beatnik politicking and feminist movements of the 1960s and 1970s (Hall 2013). This increase in homophobia occurred for three reasons:

1. *HIV/AIDS* made visible the notion that homosexuals were present in the population in large numbers (Shilts 1987), giving cultural credibility to Kinsey's figure of 10 percent. Iconic figures dying of AIDS-related illnesses, like Robert Reed (Mr. Brady of the Brady Bunch) and Rock Hudson, also highlighted that homosexuality existed in men who seemed to embody masculinity and heterosexuality. In this culture, homosexuality was pathologized as a danger to physical health (Weeks 1991) and AIDS phobia was exacerbated

by a media panic. As Connell (1987: 37) summarizes, these events led to "international moral panic" about AIDS. Erroneous rumors persisted that AIDS could be caught from a handshake or a sneeze. Health care professionals, schools and even airlines denied service to those with HIV/AIDs. Some undertakers refused to bury those who had died from illnesses related to the disease (Weinberg et al. 1994). The image of the effeminate homosexual was replaced by that of the emaciated one (Weeks 1991).

2. *Fundamentalist Christianity* grew increasingly concerned with and opposed to homosexuality and bisexuality, positioning them as threats to the nuclear family, while conveniently using this fear to increase donations to the church in an age in which church attendance began to decline (Chaves 1989). This corresponded with an increasingly conservative moral outlook more broadly. As Loftus (2001: 765) describes, "From the 1970s through the mid-1980s, Americans held increasingly traditional religious beliefs, with more people supporting prayer in school, and believing the Bible was the literal word of God."

3. *The Grand Old Party's Republican politicians* adopted the religious right's culture war against homosexuality, realizing that elections could be won through inspiring socially conservative Christians to vote (see Sherkat et al. 2011). These conservative politicians drew on fears of homosexuality and bisexuality and HIV to foster a moral panic about sexuality, social change and so-called traditional family values (Lugg 1998).

It was in this epoch that awareness of homosexuality as a static identity in the US was near-total and attitudinal homophobia reached its apex. Evidencing this, data from the 1987 General Social Survey (GSS) documented 77 percent of Americans stating that homosexual sex was *always wrong*, a rise from the previous decade. The equivalent British Social Attitudes Survey (BSAS) reported a similar rise to 63 percent in 1987 believing homosexuality was *always wrong*, almost 15 percent higher than when the question was first asked four years previously.

Following from the emergence of modern sexual identities and the conflation of gender and sexuality, these conditions proved to be a perfect storm for homohysteria. In this homohysteric culture, where femininity in males was conflated with homosexuality, men had to distance themselves socially and attitudinally from homosexuality (Floyd 2000; McCreary 1994). They aligned their gendered behaviors with idealized and narrowing definitions of masculinity.

Men used culturally endorsed sports to consolidate their masculine standing (Burton-Nelson 1994), and demonstrated masculinity through anger and violence, while denying fear and weakness (Kimmel 1996). They also stopped engaging in homosocial intimacy (Pollack 1998). Derlega and colleagues (1989) found undergraduate heterosexual males rated photos of men hugging as significantly more "abnormal" than photos of men standing alongside each other; conversely, they did not rate mixed-sex couples or women hugging as abnormal.

However, while HIV/AIDS led to the hysteria of the 1980s, it also served as a catalyst for identity politics and more inclusive attitudes. Given the power of social contact in improving social attitudes (Smith, Axelton and Saucier 2009), the increased numbers of openly gay and bisexual males that resulted from the visibility of HIV/AIDS began to improve cultural attitudes among heterosexual communities in the early 1990s, particularly with Bill Clinton's advocating for gays to serve in the military in 1992. This is a trend which continues today (Anderson 2014). As homophobia decreased, so did the hysteria, and homophobia gradually became less effective in policing gendered behaviors—something McCormack (2012a: 63) describes as a "virtuous circle of decreasing homophobia."

Inclusivity

The decrease of homophobia in British and American cultures accelerated in the twenty-first century (e.g. Anderson, McCormack and Ripley 2014; Baunach 2012; Clements and Field 2014; Keleher and Smith 2012). We describe a culture where people with positive attitudes toward homosexuality are in the majority, and where there is widespread recognition of homosexuality as a sexual identity, as one of *inclusivity*. This does not mean that these cultures are inclusive in general, as there may well be issues related to class, ethnicity and disability among other forms of discrimination. *Inclusivity* refers to attitudes toward gay men and lesbians, although even here heteronormativity may persist.

This cultural condition is also distinct from that of erasure for two reasons. First, the history of the UK and the US is such that there are cultural signs and reminders of the previous homohysteric culture; and second, because of the awareness of homosexuality in the culture—near total today where it was almost completely erased a century earlier. It is hard to claim that the cultures of masculinity in the early 1900s were inclusive of homosexuality (Ibson 2002), and there is significant evidence to say they were homophobic (Spencer 1995).

The key driver of decreasing homohysteria during this stage has been the improving attitudes toward homosexuality. The late 1990s and first decade of the new millennium saw the political labor of feminist and LGBT identity politics come to fruition. During this period, in which homohysteria decreased but homophobia was still used as a political tool (Harris 2006), men started to lose some of the hypermasculinity of the 1980s. One of the most visible elements of this was the emergence of the "metrosexual" (Coad 2008).

In the late 1990s, metrosexuality emerged as a counter-cultural trend among young men who cared about their appearance and had a sexualized image of themselves. McNair (2002: 157) described metrosexuality as "a homosexualized vision of masculinity, in the sense that this studied narcissism and attention to self-grooming are traditionally associated with gayness." The metrosexual was interpreted as a conscious rejection of more traditional male norms, where such expressionism was strictly censured. The metrosexual is such an important figure in understanding decreasing homohysteria because metrosexuality was used by heterosexual men as a way to engage in a softer form of masculinity without being socially perceived as gay.

At the time, scholars queried whether the metrosexual was anything more than a surface-level change, positing that men were seeking to keep their privilege in a changing social context (Demetriou 2001). It was during this time—in the 1990s and until the early 2000s—where changes were occurring, but any confidence about decreasing homophobia would have had to be tempered by recognition that sufficient time had not passed for these changing attitudes and behaviors to become consolidated. While we characterize the 1990s as inclusive, their dynamic was distinct from the decade either side of it—no longer homohysteric like the 1980s, but not the relaxed inclusivity of the new millennium (Anderson 2014; McCormack 2012a).

However, research has since shown that these shifts in masculinities the early stages of something profound. Anderson (2002, 2005a) found that openly gay men were being accepted on their sporting teams, challenging dominant forms of masculinity by being the *best* on their teams. Furthermore, he found other sporting teams where *competing* versions of masculinity held equal sway. A style of masculinity that was inclusive of gay men and valued the voice of women was valued by as many people as the once-dominant misogynistic and homophobic version (Anderson 2005b). At a similar time, metrosexuality moved from the counter-culture to be embraced in sports that were considered highly masculine (Harris and Clayton 2007a, 2007b) and among men who use make-up but perceive themselves to be part of mainstream culture (Adams 2011; Hall, Gough and Seymour-Smith 2012). These findings were supported by research showing the increasing inclusion of sexual minorities in a range of contexts (Jones and Clarke 2007; Savin-Williams 2005).

These shifts in masculinity corresponded with the sustained decrease in homophobia that continues to the present day. General Social Survey (GSS) data show the proportion of the US population condemning homosexuality has steadily declined since 1987. In a statistical analysis of this data, Keleher and Smith (2012: 1232) contend that "willingness to accept lesbians and gays has grown enormously since 1990." While more progressive attitudes toward homosexuality are partly due to generational replacement (Loftus 2001), Keleher and Smith show that all demographic groups analyzed became more tolerant, and, importantly, that all age cohorts became more tolerant at the same rate, arguing that "we are witnessing a sweeping change in attitudes toward lesbians and gay men" (2012: 1324).

Recent PEW (2013) research found that 70 percent of those born after 1980 support same-sex marriage, and 74 percent of these Americans believe that "homosexuality should be accepted by society." A May 2014 PEW poll found 66 percent of Americans say it wouldn't matter if a presidential candidate is gay or lesbian; 27 percent say they would be less likely to support a gay or lesbian candidate while 5 percent would be more likely. Highlighting the speed of social acceptance, when the same questions were asked just seven years earlier, 46 percent said they would be less likely to vote for a homosexual candidate (see also Baunach 2012). Supporting this, Smith, Son and Kim (2014) find that there is between 20.1 and 23.4 percentage point difference in people's attitudes toward homosexuality and gay rights for those under 30 compared to those over 65. They argue this is due to their cohort—their generation—and not the result of processes of ageing.

In the UK, similar trends of inclusivity have emerged. In the 2013 British Social Attitudes Survey, only 22 percent of those questioned claimed that homosexuality was *always wrong*. In 2012—a time when the introduction of same-sex marriage was being debated in the British Parliament—a poll conducted by the *Guardian* newspaper reported that 62 percent support the legalization of same-sex marriage (Clark and Sparrow 2012). Progressive results were also shown in a 2014 BBC poll, which showed that this figure was as high as 68 percent (Piggot 2014). This was significantly higher for young people, with both surveys reporting that the figure for those in support under the age of 35 was over 75 percent.

PEW (2013) research also found that 70 percent of millennials (those born after 1990) support same-sex marriage in the US, and 74 percent of these Americans believe that "homosexuality should be accepted by society." The following year they found more striking results: that 85 percent of American Catholics aged under 29 support gay equality, and 75 percent gay marriage (PEW 2013). Gallup polls also highlight that older Americans are more likely to oppose marriage equality: majorities of each under 65 cohort support marriage equality in the most recent (2015) poll.

Recent research in the *American Sociological Review* also highlights the dramatic change in attitudes toward homosexuality. In a national survey of just over a thousand people, Doan, Loehr and Miller (2014) found that almost 100 percent of heterosexuals supported legal equality for gays and lesbians. However, they also found a level of disconnect in this broader support when asked about particular laws such as marriage for same-sex couples—here 55 percent of heterosexuals supported the law. In 2015, Gallup shows that 60 percent of the American population was supportive of same-sex marriage, up five percentage points from the previous year (McCarthy 2015). Similarly, 55 percent of heterosexuals approved of gay men kissing on the cheek in public. This is something Ghaziani (2014: 252) calls "performative progressiveness," where some heterosexuals proclaim values of equality without practicing them in their lives. It is an important corrective to any argument that no inequality exists for gays and lesbians, but it is still evidence of profound change—a clear majority of heterosexuals (55 percent) support gay marriage *and* public displays of affection among gay male couples. Given this does not take differences in age cohort into account, it is reasonable to assume that young people will be even more progressive in their interactions with gays and lesbians.

Further evidencing this shift, Anderson, McCormack and Lee (2012) analyze sport team initiation rituals over a seven-year period. During this time, same-sex hazing activities were phased out in line with the decrease in cultural homohysteria. Earlier in the study, male athletes were forced to kiss one another as a form of doing something stigmatized to prove their worth, loyalty and desire to be on the team. But, by the end of the study, team members willingly engaged in same-sex kissing, not as a form of hazing, but as a mode of homosocial bonding and support (see also Chapter 10).

Evidence for the impact of decreasing homophobia is present in qualitative research, and helps understand the dissonance between attitudes and experience, showing positive effects on the lives of sexual minorities (Cohler and Hammack 2007; Ghaziani 2014; Savin-Williams 2005). This includes better representation of gay people in the media (Channon and Matthews 2015; Netzley 2010), an improving environment for gay students in schools and universities (Robinson and Espelage 2011), and more positive experiences for gay males within sports compared to a decade ago (Anderson 2011a). Highlighting the speed of change among young people, Savin-Williams (2005) argues that many gay youth are no longer defined by their sexuality, rejecting a victimhood framework of sexual minority development.

These changes have both been impacted by and helped bring about improved legal equality for same-sex couples. A 2003 Supreme Court of the United States decision found unconstitutional the few remaining states with sodomy laws on their books, and in 2013 it also ruled that Section 3 of the Defense of Marriage Act was unconstitutional. Finally, in 2015, the US Supreme Court ruled that gay marriage must be permitted across the United States. The first same-sex marriages occurred in the UK in 2014, and there are no anti-gay laws.

The development of positive attitudes toward homosexuality is influenced by a range of other factors, too: positive attitudes have seen shown to be correlated to contact with sexual minorities (Smith, Axelton and Saucier 2009), the existence of "ally groups" within organizational or institutional communities (Szalacha 2003), early childhood experiences that normalize homosexuality (Stotzer 2009) and the role of the Internet and improving media discourses of sexual minorities (McCormack 2014; Netzley 2010). Smith, Son and Kim (2014: 13) argue that "Positive attitudes towards homosexuality and gay rights are generally greater among younger adults, the better educated, those attending religious services less frequently, and women."

It is also important to stress that decreasing homophobia is an uneven social process. The visibility of gay and bisexual men is, for example, still restricted in professional sports, among senior politicians, within organized religions and among elementary and high school teachers (Anderson 2011a). Notwithstanding this variance, considerable evidence documents a markedly improved environment for sexual minorities. Weeks (2007: x) provides an overview of this improved social, political and legal context in the US and the UK, arguing that:

> The momentum is positive, and largely due to one essential feature of this new world: grass-roots agency is central to the direction we are moving in. Increasingly the contemporary world is a world we are making for ourselves, part of the long process of the democratization of everyday life.

The masculinities of men in this stage of inclusivity have changed dramatically (McCormack 2012a). In general, adolescent males no longer police their gendered behaviors to avoid being socially perceived as gay, or do so to a much lesser extent.

Because the stage of inclusivity is the contemporary zeitgeist, we discuss the effects of inclusivity in further detail below.

Explaining the shift to inclusivity

Prejudice toward sexual minorities has been one of the most persistent and tenacious forms of discrimination in attitudinal-based research (Hooghe and Meeusen 2013). A number of American conservative politicians have attempted to use anti-gay rhetoric as part of their election manifesto (Anderson 2014; Keleher and Smith 2012). Despite this, American polling data has highlighted that public acceptance of gay and lesbian relationships has risen dramatically (Fiorona et al. 2006; Hooghe and Meeusen 2013). Anderson (2009a) evidences similar acceptance trends in Britain. Furthermore, he highlights several influences playing a part of this acceptance, such as the Internet, the media, decreasing cultural religiosity (Lee 2012), a shifting economy from manufacturing to service-oriented occupations (Roberts 2013), the success of feminism, the success of gay and lesbian politics and subsequent increased number of gays and lesbians coming out of the closet (Anderson 2011a). However, as Keleher and Smith (2012: 1309) argue, "observing opinion trends is one thing; explaining them is another." The same authors' study using social attitude data draws on three potential explanations for the growing tolerance of the community in American culture—also relevant to British culture.

This research offers three rationales to explain the increased levels of tolerance. First, the life-cycle explanation incorporates a cohort shift in attitudes over time, claiming that as people age they become more conservative in their views. Social scientists first proposed this during the 1950s and 1960s, considering it to be a genuine possibility, because they lacked attitudinal data to test the model.

Limited evidence supports this idea, however. Schuman, Steej and Bobo (1985), for example, found that the attitudes of children and teenagers brought up believing in racial equality did not lose their tolerance as they grew older. Further examining the life-cycle effect, Mayer (1992) used data affecting a number of topics, and argued that any life-cycle effects must have two characteristics: they must be correlated with age, and opinions of the youngest generation must move consistently in the direction of the older generation. Only three sets of questions examined by Mayer were found to have any life-cycle effects. Analyzing attitudes toward homosexuality over a ten-year period, Keleher and Smith (2012) find similar shortcomings. However, sociopolitical events like George W. Bush's promise to constitutionally ban gay marriage during his re-election campaign elevated public intolerance to homosexuality (Nylund 2014). Nevertheless, this is, at best, an inconsistent proposition to explain the shift toward inclusivity.

An alternative rationale, which potentially explains the shift toward inclusivity, is the generational-replacement explanation (Keleher and Smith 2012). This rests on the assumption that attitudes do *not* alter over time: rather, older cohorts die off and younger cohorts come of age. Keleher and Smith (2012) use the increase in education to demonstrate this, as few people progressed further than high school in the early twentieth century, before an increase shortly after World War II. Accordingly, the number of well-educated Americans replaced poorly educated older generations, causing the average level of education to rise.

Applying this model to attitudes toward gays and lesbians, Keleher and Smith (2012) find that generational-replacement has *some* impact—21–40 percent—which accounts for a substantial but not complete explanation. Simultaneously, generational change is a fairly slow process, and cannot solely account for the rapid decrease in homophobia in Western cultures since around 2000 (Loftus 2001). But this would still support many scholars who argue that decreasing homophobia is a strong trend across young male adolescents (Anderson 2009a; McCormack 2012a, 2012b; Roberts 2013).

While social scientists typically rely on the life-cycle explanation and generational-replacement explanation to explain changes in public opinion, period effects refers to anything left over—relating to causes of opinion which affects all cohorts at the same time, producing a general shift in public opinion in the same direction (Keleher and Smith 2012). Examining nine essential variables within social attitude data—political party, ideology, religion, region of the country, region where a person grew up, gender, race, ethnicity and education—Keleher and Smith (2012) found increased tolerance toward gays and lesbians among *all* of these demographic groups. Accordingly, they write that "We are witnessing a sweeping change in attitudes toward lesbians and gay men" (2012: 1324).

Men's sport and decreased homohysteria

The sweeping change in attitudes toward gays and lesbians noted by Keleher and Smith (2012) has been replicated in numerous studies on sport. Inclusive attitudes toward homosexuality were initially documented in 2002, when Anderson conducted the first research on openly gay high school and collegiate athletes. Here, no athletes reported receiving any physical or verbal abuse when they came out, something the athletes in question were surprised about. Since then, decreasing homophobia has been empirically measured in various other social settings. When Anderson replicated his study in 2011—enabling a comparison to be made between temporal epochs—gay athletes reported even more positive experience than those from his original study. Regardless of the sport played, when athletes came out to their teammates, they were not treated with negative difference (Anderson 2011a). In his latest treatment of the subject, Anderson (2014) says that the evidence on teamsports now speaks loudly, and that to suggest that teamsport athletes are more homophobic than non-athletes is prejudice.

In football, Adams' (2011) ethnographic research among an American college football team also found inclusive attitudes toward sexual minorities, with athletes challenging orthodox notions of masculinity. Anderson (2011b) found similar inclusivity among a university-based football team in the US. Here, some members of the team expressed reservations with homosexuality—notably due to their conservative social background—but were embarrassed when asked to explain them. Adams and Anderson (2012) also highlighted a decrease in heteronormativity and increase in social cohesion when they observed first-hand an athlete's coming-out process (the researchers were in the field at the time). Similarly, in work with British academy-level soccer players, when players were asked to consider how they would feel if a player were to come out, they were equally as supportive and accepting (Magrath, Anderson and Roberts 2015). Research on openly gay male athletes in a variety of other ostensibly heterosexual teamsports, such as rugby (Anderson and McGuire 2010), male cheerleading (Anderson 2005b), American football (Anderson 2008a) and equestrian sports (Dashper 2012) concurs with this research.

Beyond solely sports players, Cashmore and Cleland (2011) show that homophobia among football fans is also in decline. Using mixed online methods, they found that 93 percent of 3,500 respondents—including 62 professional players, referees, managers and/or coaches—have no objection to the presence of openly gay players, arguing that homophobia has no place in football. An athlete's ability was the only criterion on which he is judged—their sexuality was seen as unimportant.

Nevertheless, these same fans who fiercely deny homophobia any place in football barrack players with homophobic epithets. Cashmore and Cleland (2011: 421) describe this as "counterintuitive and paradoxical." Fans interpreted this as good-natured banter, claiming exploiting weaknesses in your opponents is necessary (Cashmore and Cleland 2011). In his present research, Magrath (under review) explores the nature of this discursive regulation, finding a lack of intellectualized homophobia; instead, fans' discourse suffered cultural lag. Fans also stigmatized any chants which were perceived as *genuinely* homophobic or abusive; this included premeditated chants making reference to AIDS' link to the LGBT community (Anderson 2009a).

These findings document football culture's transition toward one of inclusivity—some fans resented the homophobia label notoriously attached to football supporters. Cleland (2015) also documents this when analyzing discussions and narratives of homosexuality on 48 online football fan forums. Interestingly, posts which contained homophobic sentiment were challenged: in replying to a message claiming that gay culture was detrimental to a "cohesive, family-based culture," one fan responded that "your views belong in a previous era," making reference to when homophobia was accepted and encouraged (Anderson 2009a). Similar challenges to homophobic comments were made in Cleland, Magrath and Kian's (under review) analysis of football fans' responses to Thomas Hitzlsperger's coming out in January 2014. Here, fans were generally supportive towards Hitzlsperger, many also positively observing the cultural shift in attitudes towards homosexuality

Complex matters for women's sport

Although research has shown significant improvements within male sporting culture, women's sport is more complex. There remain few lesbian athletes who are out in professional sport. In (1998) Clarke found only 27 names of "out" lesbian elite athletes. One of the earliest (post Navratilova and King) was Muffin Spencer-Devlin, who came out in 1996. The WNBA has had four players come out: Michelle VanGorp in 2004, Sheryl Swoopes in 2005 (although she is reportedly now engaged to a man), Seimone Augustus in 2012 and Brittney Griner in 2013. There is only one openly lesbian Division 1 basketball coach, Sherri Murell, who received national attention when her family photo was posted on the university website (Melton 2013).

Sheryl Swoopes' coming out was rather less straightforward than most. Swoopes won a full scholarship to play basketball at the University of Texas. However, she quickly left because, according to her mother, the team included lesbians, causing the team to plummet in the national rankings (King 2009).

In England, footballer Casey Stoney, who plays for Lincoln Ladies and England, recently proclaimed that, although men's football still has "prehistoric attitudes," the women's game is "more grown-up." She purports the lack of media attention has helped female players to come out. She notes: "On average there have been one or two gay players in most teams I have played for, up to three in some, but it's not caused any trouble." She notes the relaxed environment of the teams she has been involved in allows open conversations about private live are seen as normal and comfortable.

Her revelations allow an interesting insight in women's football and suggests that open and inclusive environments are more prevalent than suggested in previous research. This is at odds with the lack of openly lesbian athletes in England. We suggest that this is because the assumed prevalence of lesbians in teamsports adds an extra burden to them, whereas gay male athletes do not to men's sport. This extra burden comes in the form of guilt by association. If a male member of a team comes out, there is no threat that the rest of the team will be labeled gay. However, for women, things are very different: athletes may stay closeted to protect their teammates being labeled a lesbian. In essence, homohysteria operates here, not only through gendered performances of the apologetic, but though lesbian pollution.

On the other hand, homohysteria in women's sports is likely declining in terms of their gendered performances. Melton (2013: 27) notes that there is increasing acceptance of women's bodies being muscular: "Societal views no longer contend that the female physique needs to be delicate and dainty. Instead, women are now able to embrace muscularity." Evidence of this change can be seen in the pictures of Jessica Ennis, the face of the London 2012 Olympic Games; both pre- and post-games photos show her muscular abdominal muscles.

4

OPENLY GAY ATHLETES IN HIGH SCHOOL AND UNIVERSITY SPORT

This chapter reports on the findings from interviews with gay male athletes. We begin with interviews of 26 openly gay male athletes who came out between 2008 and 2010. We then compare their experiences to those of 26 gay male athletes who came out between 2000 and 2002, showing that the athletes in the latter cohort have better experiences after coming out, experiencing less heterosexism and receiving stronger support among their teammates.

Aside from these 52 systematically compared interviews, we highlight that Eric Anderson has both formally interviewed another 14 openly gay male athletes, and another 28 closeted male athletes. This gives 94 formal interviews with gay male high school and university athletes from the United States. This is further enhanced by other research that includes gay men who play sport from Anderson's other research projects (i.e. in fraternities or classroom settings). Finally, Anderson has informally conversed with dozens of other gay athletes. Oftentimes, these are athletes who contact him; sometimes they are athletes he reads about on Outsports.com.

We add to this data Anderson's experience of having been in the field conducting ethnography on three separate teams when a gay male athlete came out of the closet. This research allowed researchers to examine the moment of coming out as opposed to players having to recall the event. Here, we highlight how an athlete's coming out bonds the team closer together—that either the gay athletes are jocks on equal standing, or nobody is a jock at all.

There is, however, missing from this chapter, formal analysis of the experiences of openly gay male college (equivalent to US high school) and university athletes in the United Kingdom. Anderson has typically focused his research on US athletes because the US has slightly higher overall rates of homophobia. We can perhaps safely assume then that the experiences of openly gay athletes in the UK is likely equal to, or improved, compared to the US.

Collectively, the results examined in this chapter suggest that gay athletes are coming out and having positive experiences in their teams, even if problems with their administrations or coaches still exist. The results particularly highlight the impact of decreased homophobia by generation. In fact, not one of the gay male athletes Anderson has interviewed in the previous decade has had what can be considered a troubling experience in sport. Quite the opposite; they are thriving on their teams. This is because their fellow heterosexual jocks are un-bothered, and oftentimes quite delighted, to include gay men as teammates (see Chapter 4; see also Adams and Anderson 2012).

We highlight that the data we present in this research parallels the findings that one can independently glean by reading a handful of stories of gay men coming out in sport on the website Outsports.com. In monitoring the—now volumes—of stories of gay male athletes on this website over the past fifteen years, the trend is consistent, and, apart from one, they are stories of acceptance and celebration of diversity. Written by the athletes themselves, they provide powerful evidence that it is no longer fair to characterize heterosexual male athletes as homophobic—to make such a claim would be to do so without systematic evidence and to rely on outmoded stereotypes; in other words, claiming that heterosexual jocks are homophobic is prejudice.

Coming out in men's sport

In 2002, Eric Anderson conducted the first systematic research on the experiences of openly gay high school and university athletes in the United States. Almost a decade later, he updated his research so that comparisons could be made to highlight cultural progress. Overall, Anderson found considerably less heterosexism than previously existed. Meanwhile, openly gay athletes were also significantly easier to find than in his previous research—a reflection that there are many more of them.

Neil, for example, was an openly gay soccer player at a small, Catholic college in a rural Midwestern state. Recalling his experiences, he commented: "My teammates are very supportive. I think it's good that we played together for a long time. So they got to know me before I came out. But they have been amazing. Absolutely nothing has changed since I came out . . . I should have come out earlier."

Like Neil, none of the other athletes interviewed had any substantial difficulties with their teams after coming out as gay. Just as with the first study of openly gay male teamsport athletes (Anderson 2002), no gay athlete interviewed was physically assaulted, bullied or harassed by teammates or coaches.

Also, much of the internal turmoil and anxiety found with the 2002 athletes is absent from the 2010 men's narratives. Athletes in the 2010 group came out without the same struggle over whether they thought it would be appropriate or disadvantageous for them. For example Tom, a high school runner, had no real fear in coming out to his teammates: "I knew it wouldn't be a problem. Why would it be?" When Anderson expressed to him that athletes did not always think that way, he replied: "There are at least a dozen openly gay kids at my school. None of them have problems, and so I knew I wouldn't either. It just doesn't make sense to be homophobic today, everybody has gay friends. You might as well be racist if you're going to be homophobic."

Charlie, a college soccer player in California, came out through a different mechanism: he was never in the closet. "It's hard to say how they found out I was gay," Charlie said, referring to his teammates: "It said that I like men and women on my Facebook profile, but I think it was the first week [of college] when I was making out with a guy at a party. I've never bothered to be anything other than out. And nobody, I mean nobody, has cared."

Like these young men, most of the athletes interviewed did not expect that there would be homophobia from their teammates. Neil said that his teammates were "an excellent group of guys" and that he did not expect that any of them would have a problem with his coming out. "None. No. I knew they would be fine with it."

These narratives reflect a different experience than the narratives of the men in the 2002 research, where athletes sometimes viewed their sports as being highly homophobic social spaces. Back then, most (but not all) of the athletes interviewed feared violence, bullying, discrimination, and/or harassment from their teammates. Some of this is because they had heard their teammates discussing homosexuality negatively. With the 2010 group, however, none expected bullying, harassment, discrimination or violence. This, they suggested, was because their peers were not overtly homophobic, both inside and outside of sport. When Anderson asked Neil if he ever heard his teammates speaking negatively of gay men, he answered, "No. Never. Not before or after I came out." However, this result might also partially reflect the bias of a more confident group of men. Unlike previous research, these are young men who made contact with Anderson, rather than the other way round.

In the 2002 research, all the gay male athletes heard frequent use of the word "fag" and phrases such as "that's so gay." However, athletes in the 2010 study heard these less often and many athletes reported that these words and phrases were not used at all. We cover the use of homosexually-themed language more in Chapter 8.

Nullifying athletic capital

Compared to the 2002 sample, athletes in the 2010 cohort are more accepted by their teammates, who discussed their sexuality openly. Further, whereas most of the athletes in his 2002 sample had high sporting capital—meaning that almost all of them were stellar athletes who used their athletic ability to buy resistance against homophobia—the athletes in the 2010 sample did not match this characteristic. Of the 26 men he interviewed, only six reported being among the top athletes on their teams; most described their athletic performances as average. This implies that one does not need to be outstanding to come out anymore.

"I wouldn't say I was the best," Joey said. "I'm a good wrestler, but certainly not the best." John, a university swimmer, maintained that his ability had nothing to do with his positive experience being out: "Maybe being better would be good, but not because I think my teammates would be any cooler with it. I think it would just be more fun." Unlike Joey and John, Mark is one of the top players on his high school ice-hockey team: "Yeah, I'm good. But that's not why my teammates accept me. They accept me because I'm Mark. I don't think my skills have much to do with it. They liked me before I came out, why wouldn't they like me now?"

These attitudes are remarkably different than those Anderson previously documented. In the previous study, he found athletes only came out once they had achieved a particular standard of ability, and thus importance to the team. While it may be the case that athletic capital matters in homophobic settings, for the men in this particular group it was not a variable of importance. Their positive experiences appear to be largely independent of their athletic abilities.

Also related to athletic capital is muscle size. Whereas it used to be that young men, both gay and straight, desired to be buff, and being so was the only way to be thought sexual, in contemporary times young men can be considered sexy if they are either muscular, or thin. Instead, what counts is that they have a six-pack (Filiault, Drummond and Anderson 2014). This means that athleticism is less valued in youth peer culture overall.

Cohort differences in social support networks

The homosocial bond between members of sports teams bridges many arenas of their social lives. Teammates often spend large parts of their days together practicing, attending school and (in the case of most collegiate and professional athletes) living together, in what Anderson describes as a near-total institution (Anderson 2005a). This has traditionally created a rigid and tightly policed bond between team members. Accordingly, in his 2002 research, he stressed that, in this narrow social world of hyper-heterosexuality and hypermasculinity, the presence of an openly gay male athlete creates dissonance where there was once masculine homogeneity. Gay athletes reminded their teams that athleticism did not necessarily imply heterosexuality.

However, athletes in the 2010 group maintained that being out to one's peers was the same as being out to one's teammates. These athletes suggested that the delineation between friends and teammates was not a factor in their experience of being out, that it was their perception that their teammates were not more homophobic than non-athletes, and that there was not a clique or cluster of homophobic athletes at their school. Thus, compared to the earlier group, whose identities were segmented, gay athletes today maintain holistic identities.

Neil found that when he came out, it actually drew him closer to his teammates. However, he did have difficulties with staff, who were in their 40s. One of the athletic directors asked him, "Why don't you just choose to be straight?" It was, Neil said, "only adults" who had a hard time with his sexuality.

Grant had support from his friends, too. Yet, like many others, Grant feared coming out to his parents: "My dad is a major homophobe." He added:

> He's always bitching about my gay uncle. He said things like, "Bob is making an issue out of things." He won't say it in person, but after he leaves he does. It's really awkward and uncomfortable . . . I have to be careful that when my friends come over they don't say anything.

Joey attributed his teammates' silence to their parents. "I don't think they have a problem with it, actually. I think they don't want their parents to know [that Joey is gay] because *they* will have a problem with it!" Referring to the generational divide (discussed in the opening chapter), there is often a real disconnect between many of these young men and (at least some of) the adults in their lives. John said, "It's a whole different thing coming out to old people. Some will be fine with it, I'm sure, but, like, is it really worth it? They are from a generation who just don't get it." Thus, from the perspective of the athletes interviewed in this research, decreasing homophobia is an uneven social phenomenon.

The influence of coming out

Although decreased homohysteria comes via many media, political and other influential cultural factors, McCann and colleagues (2009) suggest that among the numerous ways social attitudes toward homosexuality are enhanced is social contact with sexual minorities—something known as "contact theory." They show that when the homosexuality of a friend is revealed, homophobic men are forced to quickly re-evaluate their impressions of someone they had previously viewed positively. In other words, once they understand that a friend is gay, they expe rience an "awakening of new ideas" which challenges their preconceptions of homosexuality (McCann et al. 2009: 211). This finding is something that Anderson has retrospectively accounted for concerning gay athletes (Anderson 2005a).

Pettigrew (1998) further identifies the importance of contact in reducing prejudice between heterosexuals and homosexuals. He shows that knowing a gay male helps reduce heterosexual prejudice, but that maintaining the ability to speak to him about sex provides a further reduction in personal homophobia. Thus, Anderson's research shows that discussing homosexuality with teammates is useful in reducing sexual stigma about homosexuality. This is something that was greatly improved in his (2011a) study on gay male athletes on ostensibly heterosexual male teams.

The improved experience of those in the latter cohort compared is further evidenced by the manner in which gay athletes discuss homosexuality with their teammates. All but two evaded the culture of "don't ask, don't tell" that Anderson found in half of the athletes he interviewed in his first study. In 2002, athletes reported that teammates simply did not discuss their sexuality; it was as if they did not know that their teammate was gay. Gay athletes often upheld this heteronormative standard through self-silencing—permitting heterosexism to dominate team culture and nullifying a gay identity.

Conversely, men in the 2010 sample told Anderson that their heterosexual teammates discussed their homosexuality openly. Gay athletes were asked about the types of guys they liked, and even asked about which teammates they thought were attractive. "Of course we talk about my sexuality," Mark said. "We talk about it all the time." He added:

> I think it's fair to say that I'm known as "the gay hockey player'" at my high school. I'm the only gay athlete who is out, even though I suspect a few more . . . It's funny, I'll be at a party, and meet someone new and they will be like, "Hey, I heard of you. You're the gay hockey player, huh?"

When Anderson asked Mark what type of reception he received after having these start-up conversations, he said. "Oh, it's always something positive. Like, 'that's cool, man' or whatever . . . No. I never have a problem . . . In fact my teammates will sometimes introduce me as their gay friend."

However, Joey, who is an openly gay wrestler at his high school in a state known for its Mormon religious conservatism, said that while he has no difficulties, even with his fundamentalist teammates, they do not all talk about his sexuality: "Yeah, they all know. It's just not a big deal." But, Joey added:

> I try not to make a big deal about it . . . there are a lot of [religious guys] on my team, and they never say anything about it, but at the same time I try not to put it in their faces . . . Other guys on the team talk about it, but I just think that it's an interesting mix of people on the team. So yeah, some of the guys talk about it with me, and like sometimes we make jokes when practicing, but the [religious] guys don't so much.

Anderson asked Joey if there are ever difficulties when the more conservative boys have to wrestle with him in practice. "No," he said. "They just wrestle me. It's not an issue, really. They are still my friends, we still hang out together after practice, but we don't really discuss my sexuality much." Joey's statement reflects the type of "don't ask, don't tell" narratives that existed among half of the men in Anderson's 2002 research.

However, among these men, Joey's statement is an outlier; the rest *did* talk about their sexuality to their teammates. Tim, for example, said that his swimming teammates often joke about his sexuality:

> They love it. I mean do you have any idea how much shit I get for it? Not like bad stuff, I mean, it's always guys pretending to be interested in fucking me, or guys bending over in front of me. That sort of thing. They laugh, I laugh. Everybody just has fun with it. It's like, we joke about it, daily.

Wondering whether this repartee might also be a method for venting internalized homophobia, Anderson therefore asked Tim if they had more serious conversations about his sexuality. "Not serious," he said. "Not like, 'Oh man, you're gay, wow, that's serious.' But yes, we talk about it." Tim provides an example:

> We were driving to an away meet once, and the entire time we were talking about what makes people gay and stuff like that . . . the guys thought it was cool that I was so open with it and we just talked about it for like an hour . . . We talked like that at other times, too. Like we have talked about it so much that when others [non-teammates] ask, like my teammates can just carry on answering for me. They got it down, like little gay ambassadors or something.

At the time of interview, Chris was an NCAA Division I American football player at a university in the American South, which highly esteems American football culture. He told Anderson that he was out to his teammates, his coach and friends in college. Not only was he accepted by the players, and not only do they discuss his sexuality with him, but they symbolically show their acceptance through touch as well, hugging him and giving him high-fives as they do other players:

> One time I told one of my teammates [about being gay], and I was sort of on the fence about whether he'd accept it or not . . . anyhow, so I told him in [a restaurant] and there are like students everywhere. I said, "I'm gay," and he paused just a second and then got up, came to my side of the table, gave me a big hug and said, "You're my boy. End of story." Like, ever since then he gives me longer hugs than others. It's just his way of showing love I guess.

Today, a few years after writing about "Chris" he can be recognized by his true name, Alan Gendreau. He is trying to become the National Football League's first openly gay player by trying out as a placekicker and a Google search will reveal some good stories about him.

First-hand experiences of athletes coming out

As an ethnographer of sport, Anderson has been fortunate enough, three times, for an athlete to come out during the period that he was conducting research on a team. This is a novel situation, and permitted him to measure a team's attitude toward homosexuality before and after one of their players comes out. In this section we discuss the outing of Brent, a university soccer player.

During this ethnography of a Catholic college's soccer team in the American Midwest, Anderson had interviewed six men before Brent came out to his team. When discussing homosexuality (among other topics), three of the men thought all of their teammates would accept a gay athlete, while the other three suggested a gay athlete might not be accepted by *all* members of the team. They could not, though, name any particular player they thought might have difficulty with a gay teammate. Furthermore, they all maintained that they would have no difficulty with a gay teammate themselves. This is known as the "third-person effect." Everybody on a team is gay friendly, but suspects someone else will not be.

Although two of the members of this team said that showering situations might be awkward, they did not consider this particularly troubling. Tom said, "It might be strange in the locker room, but I think you'd get used to it pretty quick." Jason added, "Like anything new, it would definitely throw you off a little. Maybe some people would struggle with it more than others. But we all adapt, that's part of being a team." Howie agreed, "It might be a little awkward at first, but I'd get over it."

None of these six players said they would blame a gay teammate for *making* them feel awkward. Instead, they suggested that they would need to overcome their personal discomfort. Tom said, "Besides if he's been closeted, he may have been checking us out already." Mark added: "I can say to you as much as I want that it wouldn't bother me one bit, and it wouldn't in the sense that I'm not at all homophobic, but I've never had that situation . . . so I know it would be on my mind. But it would just be something that I, personally, had to get over."

Finally, these six athletes also argued that an openly gay player would not negatively impact upon the team's level of cohesion. "No," Tom speculated. "Why would it lower morale? A friend is a friend, regardless of his sexuality."

However, none of this inclusivity stemmed from suspicion that there was a gay player on the team. During the first two days of observations, none asked Anderson if Brent was gay. In fact, on the second night, while sitting around a board game with eight players, Max, a freshman, was asking Brent about his trip to Amsterdam. "Did you pay for pussy?" he asked, referencing the legal trade of heterosexual prostitution in Amsterdam. Brent simply answered, "No."

Brent said that this is how he normally manages his sexuality: by offering short, direct answers that do not reveal his sexuality. It is a tactic which permits him to be heterosexualized by the heterosexist standards of his teammates. Brent's strategy seemed to work, as players were surprised to learn that he was gay.

Brent determined that he would prefer to out himself to several of the seniors first, and that Anderson should out him to the others. Thus, Brent outed himself to a number of close teammates on the third day of our research. He received favorable responses from all. For the younger players, Anderson determined that it would be best for one of his young, heterosexual research colleagues to out Brent, in order to reduce researcher effect.

While talking about homosexuality with Brent's teammate Ben, the heterosexual researcher Adi Adams asked, "How do you feel about the fact that Brent is gay?" Ben responded, "Brent is gay? You serious?" After receiving confirmation, Ben said, "That's cool. I just had no idea, that's all." And when talking in Tom's room that same night, the same question evoked, "What? Brent's gay? . . . That's fucking awesome."

Later in the evening, Anderson outed Brent to teammate Max. Referring to the discussion about Amsterdam, he said, "I thought it was funny you asked a gay guy if he paid for pussy." He responded, "Wait, you're saying Brent is gay?" "Yeah," I answered. "Oh. I didn't know that. Well, shit, I feel bad now." Max clarified, "It's no big deal. I just didn't know."

It therefore appears that the acceptance of homosexuality documented on this team is less attributable to researcher effect and more accurately reflects a majority position of positive attitudes toward gay men before we came to the team. In order to examine for this, Adi Adams and Eric Anderson inquired about exposure and attitudes toward homosexuality in the interviews of remaining players.

Here, all but three of the men knew a gay male before the start of this research. Most maintained informal relationships with gay men, but some had strong friendships, too. The common narrative was that most had a friend or family member who is gay, and they used this association to learn and then express a degree of social inclusion. Men talked about gay uncles, friends, neighbors, etc. While most reported never being homophobic, a few expressed that they learned to work through homophobia after meeting a gay man. What these men had not known, however, was that they had a gay male teammate.

The influence of open communication

As mentioned above, teammates often live within what Anderson calls a near-total institution. This is to say that they train together, live together, travel together and party together. Accordingly, they grow emotionally close to each other. Thus, men on teams generally feel free to discuss homosexuality (in-depth) with openly gay male athletes. When discussing Brent, John said: "I've known gay guys, yeah; but Brent is the first one that's part of my core of friends . . . we spend lots of time talking about all types of deep or personal things . . . and now I can ask him stuff I've never been able to ask other gay guys."

Steve states matters more bluntly: "I've always wondered whether it feels good to be fucked. I asked, and now I know. I asked Brent all kinds of stuff about gay sex. It's cool, it's totally different than what you'd talk to your straight friends about; but then again it's really not different."

While most of the 22 heterosexual men on Brent's team had some previous contact with gay men (and while their coach is a pro-gay Catholic priest), most players have not had the opportunity to ask detailed questions about homosexuality. Tim said, "My uncle is gay, yes. But you can't just talk to your uncle about what anal sex feels like, can you?" Similarly, participants found talking to us about matters of sex to be of value. For example, Howie said, "When you said he was gay, we were like, alright, whatever, that's cool. I think we talked about it [homosexuality] more those few days because you were around. And then Brent came out, so now it's here on our doorstep." Howie added, "And now we've had even more chances to talk about homosexuality with gay men, so I think people are just even more comfortable with it." Ed said, "I wasn't homophobic before I knew Brent was gay.

But knowing him has made me pretty positive about gay stuff." And when Ed is asked how knowing Brent is gay has specifically facilitated this, he answered:

> We've spent the last few nights just lying on the couch talking about sex and about what it was like being closeted . . . I've grown to understand things from his [homosexual] perspective . . . Hell, I can even tell you what kind of guys he's attracted to now. I think the more you understand something, the more you accept it.

Also reflecting on his new-found sensitivity to Brent's homosexuality, Scott said, "We were walking between classes yesterday and I just knew Brent was checking out a guy, and I just said, 'Yep, I saw him, too.'"

David is another player that is close to Brent. When asked about how his friendship with Brent has been influenced by his coming out, he said, "Yeah, Brent is great. I mean, you can talk to him about anything, and I learned a lot about homosexuality from him already. I think his coming out has really bonded us. We're great friends." Mike added: "We've both been here for four years, and I've always considered him a good friend. Things are the same as they were before I found out that he was gay, but now he can be more honest. I think that's real cool."

Mike also suggested that his perspectives on sexuality had evolved during the research period: "Talking with you [Eric Anderson] about this stuff has been awesome. I never really had anyone to talk to about that kind of stuff before." And when asked if talking about homosexuality has made him feel more endeared to Brent, he said, "Absolutely, it's like he's told us this, and he didn't have to. I just love him even more now."

Similarly, Jason recognized the potential influence that social contact with both homosexual men and pro-gay men can have, not only in reducing prejudice, but in further facilitating their existing tolerance and acceptance of homosexuality:

> I think people would be more open to homosexuality if they were around it more. It would open their eyes; make people a little more open to the possibilities . . . I mean, most of the guys here [on the team] knew gay people before they came here [to college], so we are pretty cool with it . . . but now Brent is gay, I mean now we *know* he's gay and we know him personally and stuff, and this whole thing [the research] has brought that to our attention. I think it's opened up our eyes to new levels of openness beyond how open we thought we were.

Danny added:

> I wanted to know what he [Brent] thought, being gay and all. Maybe I'm ignorant, but I asked him if it was a choice, not that that was what I believed. I just wanted to hear it from him, so I spoke to him about it a little bit. He said he knew from a young age and that he didn't just *turn* gay. It's not conclusive, but when you hear it from a gay guy directly it's gotta tell you something.

It is also significant that these men often ended discussions about the origins of homosexuality with a statement of indifference. We often heard them remark that it makes no difference what made one gay. One said, "I wouldn't treat him differently," and another asked, "Does it matter?" Trent said:

> It didn't matter to me if someone was gay before I met you guys; people are what they are. But I guess Brent is the first gay guy who I would call a true friend, and talking with you guys about this stuff has really been cool. I understand things so much better now. I feel like I can tell you guys anything.

Thus, the combination of Brent coming out publicly alongside an openly gay researcher in the field provided these players with the opportunity to partake in sexualized conversations: the type of conversations they have not been able to have in an ostensibly heterosexual, homosocial environment. The event of Brent's coming out to the team encouraged teammates to talk about their own sexual and gendered experiences, and their social experiences of other gay men they had previously met. It is also evidence of the problems of a culture where homosexuality is not discussed.

Challenging "don't ask, don't tell"

In addition to finding that these participants maintained pro-gay attitudes and that discussing homosexuality with gay men further enlightened their views on homosexuality, once Brent came out to his teammates there was an immediate change to the once heteronormative discourse used by the team. As noted in Anderson's 2002 research, about half of gay athletes existed within a "don't ask, don't tell" culture, where gay athletes and their teammates silently agreed upon a culture in which none spoke of the gay player's sexuality. Inclusive language was therefore not part of the team's communication style under "don't ask, don't tell." However, coming out publicly, and discussing homosexuality openly, seems to have warded off a "don't ask, don't tell" policy with Brent's team and others studies in more recent years.

Exemplifying the efforts of these players to discursively integrate Brent's sexuality into their conversations, while driving home from a match, Drew talks about how he thought a few of the female soccer players, who played on the field adjacent to them, were attractive. He immediately followed this statement by asking Brent, "Did you find any of the guys hot?" Brent answered, "Yeah, a few . . . I thought number nine was hot."

Another time the men determined they should not go to the normal dance club they frequent, because there was no gay club in the same area for Brent. Instead, we drove to a different venue, so that Brent and a few of the players could visit the gay club. Furthermore, when players were asked if they would support Brent's (hypothetically) bringing a boyfriend to a match, none voiced concern. Conversely, at one of the three games observed, players introduced their parents to the openly gay researcher.

While Brent's story is an exemplar to the finding of decreased heteronormativity, a significant finding in comparing the two samples of athletes is that athletes in the later study evaded cultures of "don't ask, don't tell" that characterized the experiences of athletes in the 2002 cohort. This forces us to rethink once-opined ideas about heteronormativity. For example, in 2002 Anderson argued:

> In the absence of the ability to ban openly gay athletes from sport, heterosexual athletes within teamsports, both contact and non-contact resisted the intrusion of openly gay athletes through the creation of a culture of silence around gay identities. Although publicly out, the informants in this study were victimized by heterosexual hegemony and largely maintained a heteronormative framework by self-silencing their speech, and frequently engaged in heterosexual dialogue with their heterosexual teammates. (Anderson 2002: 874)

Conversely, athletes in the 2010 group found their sexualities accepted among their teammates. With the exception of Joey, the 25 other men talked about their sexualities frequently, and none reported that their teammates tried to publicly or privately heterosexualize them. Further evidence of this can be determined by examining the narratives that openly gay athletes post on the website Outsports. com. Here, there is story after story of athletes coming out to be socially included in team activities.

However, it is important to note that these findings do not suggest that all athletes, in all sports, at all levels or locations, would have equally as supportive coming-out experiences as the men in this study. It is possible that these men evaluated their social situations well enough before coming out, helping insure a positive experience. There is a complex web of variables that most athletes use to make such decisions: team climate, social networks, the attitudes of their coach, as well a host of other identifiable and unidentifiable factors (Anderson 2005a). Thus, these results speak only to these athletes, men who have made informed choices.

Coming out on a team with a highly homophobic coach

It is fair to say that most gay male athletes do not publicly come out of the closet if they exist on teams that have highly homophobic coaches. In all of Anderson's research on the topic, he shows that the athletes take into consideration the attitudes of their coach before making their decisions about coming out. Sometimes they value their sport more than their freedom to express their sexuality, and choose to remain closeted; other times, they quit. For example, Michael (2013) shows us a case of a high school wrestling team in which all of the players were gay friendly, as were two assistant coaches, but the head coach was highly homophobic.

The solution to their difference in perspective on homosexuality was complicated by the fact that high school wrestlers are often homosexualized, because their sport involves a great deal of intimate personal contact with other males. This has the possibility of making the sport homohysteric. Thus, the players had two driving forces for reasons to espouse homophobia: (1) to prove to their peers that they were not gay, and (2) to align their perspectives with the head coach, who has control over their playing careers.

Yet, they did not. Instead, they framed wrestling as an aggressive sport of "war," a hyper-masculine venture that only the brave partake in, regardless of sexual orientation. They included their gay teammate and friend, and only asked of him not to sexualize the sport—i.e. to make comments about the attractiveness of his teammates that he was in close physical contact with. Apart from this, there was no isolation of the teammate. This rich ethnography thus highlights the power of the inclusive culture toward homosexuality that these youths inhabit.

Decreasing need for open communication in reducing homophobia

Between 2011 and 2015, Anderson conducted a three-month ethnography on a high school running team in Southern California each summer. It was during the first of the three bouts of ethnography that he met Jordan, a top-notch varsity runner. Having helped coach his team, he grew to know Jordan, an aspiring model, quite well. He did not know it at the time, but Jordan was closeted.

Before Anderson returned to Southern California in the spring of 2012 to run with the team for another few weeks, Jordan came out to him on Facebook and Anderson began mentoring Jordan in the coming-out process.

A week into Anderson's return to Southern California, Jordan determined that he was ready to come out to his team. Anderson asked to be present, directly in some cases, and within vicinity to hear but without his presence necessarily noticed, for others. This was exciting: unlike Brent, Jordan wanted to do the outing himself, and this gave Anderson the opportunity to observe.

He observed as Jordan told his coach, "Coach, there is something I want to tell you. I'm gay." The coach responded, "That's cool," and then began to talk to Jordan about the day's workout. A few days later Anderson watched Jordan come out, individually, to the rest of his varsity team as they arrived for dinner the night before a race. Here, Jordan said, "Hey, Max, I just want to tell you I'm gay." His teammates' responses ranged from, "Oh, I didn't know that," to, "Wait. What?"

What was fascinating to Anderson as a researcher, however, is that none of the athletes needed to talk about his sexuality. This was seemingly not because they wanted to deny, suppress, or hide it. This is because they had known so many other gay male friends that they had already asked all the questions about it.

The following summer, Anderson returned to run with the team again. One day while stretching, Jordan was stretching with Anderson, and engaging in banter in front of the rest of the team. The night before they had been out to a gay club together, and Anderson was making fun of the way he danced. Anderson then remarked to the other 40 athletes on the team that together Jordan and I would give gay dance lessons to the rest of the team. To this, one of the 15-year-old freshman quipped, "I think Kenneth would do a better job." Anderson took this as banter, a "burn" to insinuate that Kenneth was gay, when he was not. It was only in running with Kenneth later that day that Anderson learned Kenneth was openly gay on the team.

This was a striking revelation for Anderson. Kenneth had been out of the closet to his teammates, but there was such division between the freshmen and sophomores (years one and two), compared to the juniors and seniors (years three and four), the first group did not know that Jordan was gay and the second did not know that Kenneth was gay—it was a very large team. In his previous research, the outing of a gay male was so novel it became gossip—spreading rapidly across teams and schools. In this 2012 example, however, openly gay males were increasingly common in school settings. This means that having an openly gay male on a school-based sport team (as most sport teams in the US are) is also less novel. Increasingly, when athletes come out to their teams, they are met with some version of "So what?" This is not a begrudging form of acceptance; instead, it might suggest total acceptance (see also McCormack 2012b; Riley 2010). Evidencing this, when Anderson asked Kenneth why he didn't tell him before he answered, "I don't know. It's not really a big deal I guess."

Apparently it is not that big a deal. When Anderson returned to run with this same team in 2013, another bisexual male joined the team, another gay male came out who ran on the team a year prior, and when he said to another student, in front of a few teammates on a run, "You've never declared a sexual orientation to me, so I don't want to assume, but do you have a girlfriend?" He replied, "No. I don't. I am not bothered by that though, I'm only a sophomore. And I don't care who comes along, a girl or boy."

5

OPENLY LESBIAN ATHLETES IN HIGH SCHOOL AND UNIVERSITY SPORT

While the previous chapter outlined the positive environment faced by openly gay male athletes, there is less evidence for the experiences of lesbian athletes in Western sport. Since Griffin published her groundbreaking research in 1998, the only research to be published with primary data was: 1) that of Janet Fink and colleagues (2012), who interviewed 14 US collegiate lesbian and bisexual athletes; 2) Anderson and Bullingham (2013) who carried out 12 interviews with openly lesbian American athletes in the US collegiate system in 2002 and 2003) two interviews from lesbian women in the UK university system as part of Bullingham's research into 31 lesbian athletes in 2014.

Thus, even though there are a number of openly lesbian athletes in the British and American higher educational system, there is, unfortunately, limited up to-date research on their experiences. To rectify this, and in order to paint a more complete and current research project on the experiences of lesbian athletes in sport, Rachael Bullingham has interviewed 31 British lesbian athletes all of whom are out of the closet. Of these, two were university athletes, three were international athletes and the rest play in community-based league structures—which, unlike the US, is where most sport participation occurs in the UK

Results from these collective investigations into women's sport are positive, but the change has been less straightforward than with men. We discuss how, in the US, the administration of women's sport is less receptive to lesbian athletes. We suggest that this is primarily an effect of elevated homohysteria in women's sport, compared to men's. In the UK, however, the results are more positive, as university sport is predominately run by older students rather than an administration.

Relying on dated data

Sociologists examining the issue of lesbians in sport during the 1980s and 1990s agreed that organized teamsports were normally characterized as highly homophobic organizational cultures (Griffin 1998; Hekma 1998; Lenskyj 1986; Sykes 1998; Veri 1999). However, since 1993, homophobia has been in rapid decline (Clements and Field 2014; Keleher and Smith 2012; Loftus 2001), both within sport and society more broadly (Anderson 2009a, 2011a, 2011b, 2011c). By the new millennium, attitudes had changed dramatically—this is particularly the case for youth (McCormack 2012a).

Research on ostensibly heterosexual female undergraduate athletic teams conducted in recent years shows growing cultures of acceptance. For example, Fink and colleagues (2012) show that improvements in educationally based sports teams can provide a "safe zone" for lesbian athletes to be open about their sexuality. Melton and Cunningham (2012) also find lesbian athletes of color supported by teammates, while they show that as heterosexism declines, support for lesbians increases in sport. However, there is a "missing decade" (1999–2011) in which we can find no literature on openly lesbian athletes in the United States, or other English-speaking nations, competing in predominately heterosexual teams. The work of Anderson and Bullingham (2013) fills this void in the data, using interviews from 2002 on American collegiate athletes.

Results from the data collected in 2002 largely concur with what Anderson found in men's sport, with the notable exception of finding elevated hostility compared to men's teams (Anderson and Bullingham 2013). We suggest that this is due to heterosexual teammates' fear of being socially lesbianized because of their openly lesbian teammate/s—something Anderson describes as homohysteria (2009a, 2011c). But this is not something he finds occurring among heterosexual men in sport after a teammate comes out (2002, 2005a, 2011b). This data provides a half-way point from the research of Griffin (1998) to more current research (Fink et al. 2012).

Athletes also reported support from their teammates, and only two athletes reported any resistance to their coming out. Their coming-out stories were loud and obvious. Danielle, a college soccer player, said that she came out to her teammates while watching a movie in one of her teammate's apartments after practice. She stood up in the middle of a film and told her teammates that she was gay and she received immediate support from her teammates. She was not the only participant to receive such support.

Cynthia, a cross country runner, was preparing to go to a friend's party with her teammates. She acknowledged that her teammates seemed relaxed about going to a lesbian party so she came out to them just before they entered. Again she received support, "The girls surprised me that night, not treating me any differently than they had before . . . here I thought that they likely suspected I was lesbian, but they had no clue. This didn't change anything, though." Michelle's coming out was equally positive, she came out to her team halfway through the season:

> The rest of the season was just as it was before. There was no difference really. Then the next year we had an entirely new team . . . they have all been very cool when I mention my girlfriend, and I haven't felt any tension

or uneasiness from them . . . my coach even asks how she's doing . . . I feel very comfortable with them.

Although nine of the twelve participants expressed positive experiences, this could be due to what Anderson (2002) describes as "reverse relative deprivation." He found this occurred with the openly gay male athletes when they compared themselves to people who had had overtly negative experiences. Thus, when Danielle said, "I've been extremely lucky," or Cynthia said, "The girls surprised me that night, not treating me any different," they reveal the possibility that they expected things would be worse after coming out. Therefore, they could be experiencing reverse relative deprivation and may still be experiencing homophobia in more covert ways. This suggestion also highlights a weakness with our data; there was no ethnographic component, so we rely solely on participants recalling their experiences.

The second point, raised by Michelle, is that the coming-out process is never over for openly lesbian athletes in collegiate sport. Educationally based sport teams lose about 25 percent of their teammates each year, and gain about 25 percent in new members. Therefore, athletes must come out to new teammates. However, this study does not investigate how the coming-out process changes as athletes adopt more senior positions within the team. It is possible that new players accept the openly lesbian teammates because they are simply adopting the ethics held by the majority of their teammates. This, at least, is what Anderson (2011a) found in a follow-up study to his research on gay male athletes. But this is in itself evidence of progress, as lesbians experience more positivity than demonstrated in previous research.

Overt hostility

As with Hekma's (1998) research on gay and lesbian athletes, and Anderson's (2002) study of gay male athletes, overt homophobia was less apparent than researchers might have predicted. However, unlike Anderson's (2002) study of 26 openly gay males, two athletes did report overt hostility. They reported that at least one player on their team had called them a "dyke" with intent to marginalize them. This is a contrast to gay athletes, as none of them had experienced being called a "fag" with any ill intent (we examine the effect of homophobic language in Chapter 8; see also McCormack 2011a).

One athlete, Amy, reported a particularly negative experience. Amy, who played softball, acknowledged a lack of acceptance from her teammates when she came out. She recalled an incident that occurred after training when her coach had kept her behind to express disapproval of her short haircut. When she finally returned to her car, she found that all four of her car tires were flattened, her back window was smashed, and her windshield cracked, with a note left on her windshield that said "die dyke." Although Amy had no evidence to support her claim that her teammates had inflicted the damaged, she claimed that nobody else would have known it was her car. She reported the damage to her coach, who had kept her behind when the incident occurred. The coach replied, "Well, what do you expect when you tell people that sort of thing?"

This was not the only evidence that Amy presented to suggest her lack of acceptance. On her first overnight trip with her teammates, she also experienced overt homophobia. Four women were assigned to a room, each with two double beds (standard practice in many American sporting teams). However, no athlete would share a bed with Amy, instead preferring to sleep on the floor. Discussing this situation, Amy said, "Let's just say that I got a really good night's sleep." The same situation occurred on subsequent trips. Amy said, "There was either someone on the floor or three people in one bed, every night." This example shows stark contrast to gay male athletes' who did not have problems sharing beds with straight teammates. For example, in Anderson's 2005 book, *In the Game: Gay Athletes and the Cult of Masculinity*, he profiles the story of two straight men who were sharing a room with one gay teammate. The straight male athletes each feared that if one of them did not share a bed with the gay teammate, he would think them homophobic. Not wanting this, they then argued over who would get to sleep next to the gay athlete. Each of the two straight athletes wanted to, because each feared that if they were not the one to do so, they would be thought homophobic. Their solution was to push both beds together and put the gay athlete in the middle.

The behavior of teammates, combined with the lack of support from her coach, eventually led to Amy leaving the team. She felt "run off" by her teammates. Two other athletes experienced hostility as well.

Monique, a college basketball player, said she was called "dyke" frequently by her teammates. However, this direct hostility was framed in a surprisingly positive attitude. She said, "No real hostility came from them." Interestingly the use of the word "real" was a reflection on other more physical reflections from university life. She was sexually assaulted by a member of the men's football team (we are unclear where on campus this occurred): "One of the guys picked me up and gave me the nastiest kiss on the back of my neck. I used all of my strength to fight him off, but I couldn't. He asked, 'Still lesbian now?'"

Despite this assault, Monique didn't file charges. She said that another lesbian friend had filed charges with the school over a similar incident by a football player and nothing had happened to the perpetrator (Crosset, Benedict and McDonald 1995). She did, however, tell her coach, who discussed the situation with the football coach, and the harassment ceased, yet remained unpunished. Thus, use of the word "real" becomes contextualized. Her teammates' homophobia was insignificant compared to the actions of the football player.

The link between athletic capital and coming out

Athletic capital was found to be very important for gay male athletes in Anderson's (2002) study of openly gay male athletes. He found that 22 of the 26 had high athletic capital, compared to only five of the 16 closeted athletes studied. This was also true of the 2002 research (Anderson and Bullingham 2013) on lesbian athletes. Seven of these twelve players described themselves as the top player on their team. It can therefore be suggested that they, collectively, had a better experience than they would have if they were not stellar athletes: the more athletic capital one had in this era, the better one was treated after coming out (Anderson 2005a).

An alternative explanation could be that lesbian athletes of average athletic ability drop out of sport earlier, a factor that Hekma (1998) found with community-based gay and lesbian athletes. While the authors acknowledged that this sample size meant more generalized conclusions, it is clear that more research needs to be conducted in this area.

The coach's attitude

Griffin (1998) has previously suggested that the coach's attitude is likely to be a significant influence in the type of experience an openly lesbian athlete will have on her team. In women's sport, coaches have not only been seen to be demonstrating homophobic behavior and language, but also they have implemented measures to ensure that athletes conform to a hyperfeminized image (Blinde and Taub 1992a; Kane and Lenskyj 1998; Mennesson and Clement 2003; Anderson and Bullingham 2013). Perhaps the most infamous example of this comes from the now-fired Penn State women's basketball coach, Rene Portland, who maintained a team policy of "No drinking, no drugs, no lesbians" (Osborne 2007: 481).

Evidencing the power of a coach to shape team culture, Anderson and Bullingham (2013) note how levels of acceptance vary across different levels of sport. In their 2002 research, Angela reported that while her college coach was very supportive of her being a lesbian, this was not the case with her high school coach:

> My coach knew I was gay, but never suspected it with my girlfriend, her other star. So I guess she began hearing stuff and called my girlfriend into their office and basically asked her was all this true. My girlfriend denied it at the time. The worst part, however, was that my coach then began to make her feel bad about the whole thing, and telling her that she was glad it wasn't true because a "nice girl from a nice family" couldn't dare be like that. It just made her feel bad for being with me.

Telling the coach is one of the biggest challenges lesbian athletes face, and many in the 2002 research avoided going through this process. Denise, for example, was out to all the players on her team, but none of them told their coach. When asked why, she responded, "He's an older gentlemen of the Catholic belief and he's pretty set in his ways."

However, other coaches have been shown to be supportive of their lesbian athletes. Kelly's coach was incredibly supportive. Highlighting this, she recalled one event, a party, when her coach approached young men and asked "So what are your intentions with my daughter?" He then approached the female date Kelly had brought and said the precise same thing in the exact same tone.

Kelly was not the only athlete to have a positive experience. Cynthia remembered her coach enquiring about her girlfriend: "Whether he knew it or not, he validated my relationship with her, and let me know that he can acknowledge who I am with some level of comfort."

Some athletes experienced negative recruiting (when coaches warn players about lesbian players or coaches on rival teams) when searching for a university. Jennifer recalled being told, "Oh you don't want to go to that school, the coach is a lesbian." However, the coaches who used negative recruiting did not realize that she had chosen the team *because* the coach was a lesbian. She said, "It was important for me to go somewhere where I would really feel comfortable talking to my coach." Unfortunately, her expectations were not met. Her coach affirmed that she was a lesbian, but actively dissuaded players from coming out because she was concerned with negative recruiting.

Heterosexism

In 2002, the most evident form of homophobia was in the form of a "don't ask, don't tell" climate. Jennifer can again be used as an example: while her coach was also a lesbian, nobody on the team was prepared to talk about it. Griffin (1998) refers to athletes and coaches in this position as "in the glass closet," when everyone knows there are lesbians on the team but their presence is shrouded in silence.

Lesbian athletes interviewed in 2002 were, on the whole, complicit in reinforcing and the continuation of this climate. However, they tried to justify their lack of open discussion: "Sport is not the appropriate place for such discussions," or, "Well, it's none of their business." In Jennifer's case, her coach was actively encouraging her to remain quiet and she said, "My coaches have these rules for what I can do and what I can't do." Her coaches' influence was evident she said: "Me and my girlfriend would be walking down campus holding hands, but as soon as we get near the P.E. department, we split up." Jennifer's coach was so concerned with negative recruiting and the team getting a "bad name" that she enforced what Griffin (1998) describes as a "conditionally tolerant" climate on the team (see Chapter 8).

Rhonda, a softball player, also had a lesbian coach, although her coach tried to suggest it was a non-issue:

> While I was on the team, I was out to everyone, considering I dated a girl on the team and everyone knew about it. Although I was out and everyone knew, oddly enough my coach, who was a lesbian, tried to act like it was a non-issue. I never really agreed with that mentality.

In today's climate, it could be mooted that the coach was trying to normalize her sexuality. However, in 2002, it is more likely that she did so out of the cultural mandate of heterosexism, which labels any discussion of homosexuality as being "in your face" (Ripley et al. 2012). This is best evidenced by Rhonda:

> The worst experience was my first year. The team became very discriminatory towards myself, both as a person and a player on the team. While on a road trip in New Mexico, I was basically excluded from any activities that were not a team function. I began to feel very isolated and when I talked to my coach about it, her advice was to try and not be with my girlfriend so much around them. She basically told us to separate. Thing is, had we just been "best friends" none of this would have happened. I got to the point where I almost wanted to leave the team.

Cathy, an athletics sprinter, was also ostracized by teammates, but met no overt homophobic behavior: "I get excluded from certain things that are going on . . . and that's just the way it is. Sometimes when my teammates see me eating in the cafeteria with my friends, they won't come sit with us because they don't want to eat at the lesbian table."

Denise also noted a culture of "don't ask, don't tell" when she referred to her teammates. She noted the lack of conversations about her sexuality with teammates and friends: "The fact that I'm gay doesn't seem to make a difference to her, although we never really talk about it either." She concluded:

> The most positive thing I can think of is that I wasn't shunned. I was accepted. Although at times it felt like a "don't ask don't tell" kind of thing, it was okay. I can see how the subject of one being a gay person can make a straight person uncomfortable, especially if your changing [in the locker room] with her.

Silence has been acknowledged as a form of homophobia (Griffin 1998), or at least an operation of heterosexism, so while some may see the partial openness as addressing the issue, it does not lead to an open and inclusive environment. Silencing of homosexual athletes reinforces cultural heterosexual hegemony (Sykes 1998), where lesbian athletes are prevented from discussing relationships and social lives in the same way as heterosexual athletes.

Within the findings of the 2002 study on lesbian athletes, coupled with the recent work of Cunningham and colleagues (2014), Griffin (2012), Fink and colleagues (2012) and Melton and Cunningham (2012), it could be suggested that lesbian women face more hostility than gay men in sport. This is due to the homo-hysteric process of cultural lesbianization: whereas an openly gay male athlete does not bring homosexual suspicion to his teammates, an openly lesbian athlete does. This double standard exists because female athletes are stereotypically linked to homosexuality for women.

While this research filled a gap in literature during a period of culturally declining homophobia, it was clear that more research needed to be conducted.

While Anderson (2011a) updated the results on openly gay athletes, it was not until 2012 that Fink and colleagues published an updated article on lesbians in collegiate sport. Both updated studies found significant improvement in the experiences of lesbian athletes.

More contemporary research

Fink and colleagues (2012) examined openly lesbian athletes competing in the American collegiate system. In a larger study of openly lesbian athletes competing in a variety of settings, two university students in the UK were interviewed. The results from these studies have shown a more positive outlook for lesbian athletes. The culture of "don't ask, don't tell" appears to have been replaced with one of inclusivity and acceptance (see also Anderson 2014).

The two university athletes that took part in the 2014 study acknowledged acceptance and approval when they came out. One athlete was a first-year student, Jasmine, who came out to her team soon after joining by telling her teammates that her girlfriend had bought her a new lacrosse stick. While she has been fully accepted onto her team and her girlfriend is welcome to all occasions, she notes some negatives. She gives examples of banter where they are discussing athletes' behavior on a night out, and she felt left out. However, she puts this down to not joining in with the university drinking culture, rather than her sexuality. The only negative story related to us was this:

> So, in the drinking game, "Never have I ever," there will be stuff like, "I never ever orgasmed during sex," and I'll be like, "Well, yeah," so I'll drink. And then like a few of my heterosexual counterparts will [drink], and then they'll be like, "Oh no, Jasmine, that doesn't count." . . . I feel like my sex counts, but so they will specify penetrative sex and you are like, "Well, why would you specify that?" And that actually happened and I was confused by that.

Unlike previous research, she does challenge her heterosexual teammates, and ask them why it doesn't count, although this conversation was not prolonged as her teammates were intoxicated.

By contrast, the other university athlete, Holly, waited until her second year, and until she had a girlfriend, before she came out to her team. This was due to a negative role model who was in the year above her. Holly described how she remained closeted, as she did not want to be associated with the older player who was promiscuous with both men and women. She explains:

> I felt a lot more comfortable, and obviously every year—because it is university sport—we get a massive intake of first years every year. So, for a lot of people who join the club, their first impression is that I am out and gay and happy and proud about it. And none of them ever had a problem with it. So I felt kind of silly in retrospect, but I haven't given everyone in my

6

OPENLY LESBIAN AND GAY MALE ATHLETES IN RECREATIONAL SPORT

Although a plethora of research documents the experiences of high school, university and elite gay male athletes (Anderson 2002, 2011a; Cleland, Magrath and Kian under review; Kian and Anderson 2009; Kian, Anderson and Shipka 2015), and inclusive attitudes of ostensibly heterosexual athletes (Adams 2011; Adams, Anderson and McCormack 2010; Adams and Anderson 2012; Anderson 2005a, 2005b, 2011b; Anderson and McGuire 2010; Magrath 2015, 2016; Magrath, Anderson and Roberts 2015), limited research exists documenting the experiences of gay male athletes in recreational sport. The situation is similar for women's sport: the majority of research focuses predominantly on collegiate female athletes (Griffin 1998; Fink et al. 2012). To address this gap in the research, this chapter focuses on recreational athletes.

Twentieth-century homophobia

Using retrospective accounts of their experiences in sport from a decade or more ago, Bullingham (2015) found that there was a mixed bag for British lesbian athletes. Just as Anderson and Bullingham's (2013) work on American collegiate lesbian athletes showed that there was acceptance and inclusion for some in 2002, but hostility for others, this retrospective research on British lesbian athletes suggests that a decade or more ago, there was also some hostility toward lesbian athletes in recreational sport in the UK.

Those who had troubles a decade ago primarily experienced verbal bullying. They were called names like "dyke" or "lesbo." Yet, we do not want the reader to think that when the athletes were targeted by homophobic abuse a decade ago, they were passive victims: those who told stories of last-decade's homophobia challenged it. Mia said:

first year that opportunity to prove to me that I didn't need to prevent coming out at first. But, equally, I had such a good time in my first year in the sport, and I wasn't ever worried about people judging me, because I didn't tell them—so I almost don't regret it because it meant that I did have a really good experience, like, guaranteed.

Holly went on to discuss how she has been fully accepted by her teammates, and that she had provided support to younger athletes. She concludes her story by saying:

The only negative thing . . . [was] not to be comfortable straight away, and then, maybe, just the kind of normal fielding of questions that you always get when you know otherwise you might say I have a girlfriend. Whereas, when you say you have a girlfriend and you are a girl you have to then field the twenty questions that come at you just about your sex life or your love life . . . I still see that as a slightly negative experience because I slightly resent having to answer the same questions.

Both Holly and Jasmine described their experiences as wholly positive at the end of the interview. Interestingly, the small examples of negativity experienced by these two athletes were related to sex, rather than their coming-out experiences. Unlike some of the stories in the research conducted on American collegiate sport, both athletes came out by discussing their girlfriends as opposed to a big event (Anderson and Bullingham 2013).

Although these are only two athletes (out of 31) participating in university sport, their stories are similar to the work of Fink and colleagues (2012). They described a positive environment that athletes in the American collegiate system are currently competing within. They explain that athletes are no longer willing to remain hidden in order to gain equality and acceptance (Fink et al. 2012). Perhaps the only negative is the lack of change in the administration that athletes are competing under.

Someone said something to me about being a dyke and I took the piss out of her. I said, "Are you calling me a water system that protects Holland from being flooded?" and she went "Er, what?" because it was a bit too intelligent for her!

Faye recalled an event that happened to her (over a decade ago), when she was at university:

Some lads used to walk past the team at practice and give a bit of gob to the girls. But one day our captain just stopped the game and went over and had a word with them. She said, "Look you need to be a bit more respectful to my players because they are here to play football. They are not here to be hollered at by you. We don't do it to you." We didn't have any problems with them after.

The only athlete that did not challenge homophobic comments was Ruth. In her first season of play (over a decade ago) the team captain made homophobic remarks:

I was quite taken aback, because I just didn't expect it from her. I just sort of was quiet. I should have said something. I think because the captain is quite outspoken and speaks her mind anyway, you know people maybe just go along with it. I didn't. It was on my mind to challenge her, but I didn't.

Despite these few incidents of homophobia, the present-day realities of lesbian athletes playing recreational sport in the UK were better. This was even the case with coaches (who tend to be older than teammates). Of the 28 recreational athletes interviewed, 24 athletes simply replied "no" or "never" when asked if their coach ever used homophobic language. The others said that they could not recall any. Faye explained how her male coach created a relaxed atmosphere on the team toward sexual diversity, which allowed for banter about sexuality in a positive way. Homophobia, she said, would not be tolerated today.

The twenty-first-century climate for lesbian athletes

While older research only describes recreational sports climates as either hostile or conditionally tolerant (Hargreaves 2000; Kauer and Krane 2006; Anderson and Bullingham 2013; Davis-Delano 2014), Bullingham's (2015) research shows open and inclusive environments across a range of sports throughout England. The participants in her research described being friends with heterosexual teammates on and off the field; and they argued that their sexualities did not matter. Cathy explained, "I count my heterosexual teammates as more than teammates. I count them as friends. They ask about how my partner is doing; they ask how I am doing; they are caring." These findings mirror Fink and colleagues' (2012) results on American lesbians in collegiate sport, who showed that supportive teammates help with positive change.

In Bullingham's research, the inclusivity toward lesbian athletes was not dependent on the number of lesbians on a team, either. Heterosexual teammates were not concerned with how many of their teammates were gay. This, we argue, reflects decreasing cultural homohysteria around women's sport: today's heterosexual female athletes do not worry about being thought lesbian for having openly lesbian teammates. In Bullingham's research, Claudia (who was the only out lesbian on her team) said, "It is the straightest club that I have every played for. But it's also very welcoming." Angelica discussed a similar scenario, "Of all the rugby teams I've played for, this one is the straightest. But nobody cares that I'm lesbian. We are all in the state of being grown up enough to deal with that."

Similarly, a number of openly lesbian athletes in Bullingham's (2015) research were out of the closet alongside other teammates. Despite the presence of these out athletes, they did not receive any backlash from their heterosexual teammates. Their teammates did not ask them to hide or silence their sexuality. Instead, their straight teammates seemed unconcerned whether people thought they were lesbian or straight.

Highlighting the lack of homophobia on their teams, some athletes were more open about their sexuality with their teammates than they were with their colleagues at work. Jennifer explained her positive experience in sport: "Yeah and probably more so than anywhere like work or anything else. I feel really comfortable being myself." Tamara had a similar experience: "I don't even bat an eyelid. Like at work you'd always think twice."

When questioned about homophobia on their teams, the lesbian athletes were unable to locate any. Some found describing their acceptance difficult to verbalize, as they had not experienced any negativity. Acceptance was seen as normal; comments like "I get treated like any other person" were common throughout Bullingham's research. Mia, for example said:

> I keep getting picked to be on teams, and I haven't been pushed away. I haven't been sworn at or anything like that. I haven't been isolated. I think you are more likely to be isolated for being a douche or being grumpy than being lesbian.

The welcoming environment for lesbian athletes was extended to partners, too. Thus, unlike previous research on lesbian athletes in 2002 (Anderson and Bullingham 2013), inclusion of lesbian partners was normal for these British athletes. They described how their partners were not only asked about, but they were invited to social events and welcomed into the team. Brooke (the only lesbian player on her team) recounted a story from a sports tour:

> When we were on tour, the people I shared a room with probably spoke to my girlfriend more than I did. Any time she rang they wanted to chat with

her. They would run and answer the phone and talk her about what we'd done in the day, and then pass me over after they had a chat with her.

Bullingham then asked how she felt about her teammates speaking to her girlfriend and if she found it strange: "No, I liked it! Because, not that I would have any reason for them not being OK with it, but it is a very clear overt way of showing their support and you know their acceptance of it."

Who comes out and how

Although his initial research showed that only gay male athletes with high athletic capital were able to come out to their teams (Anderson 2002), Anderson's later (2011a) research does not find this. When Bullingham examined for the concept of athletic capital among lesbians in recreational sport in 2014, there was no relationship to one's coming out, either.

Tamara said, "There doesn't seem to be a correlation between talent and sexuality or the way you are treated, everyone is just welcomed." Although most of the openly lesbian athletes Bullingham studied suggested that they were in the starting line-up, no players said they were the best in the club, and only two alluded to the fact that they rated themselves highly. With athletic capital nullified, it does not appear that one needs to be good at sport to come out and be treated well in sport.

The coming-out process for lesbian athletes appears to have changed in recent years, too. Anderson and Bullingham (2013) found athletes make big statements when they came out, like sitting the team down for "a talk." Yet, athletes in Bullingham's (2015) research appear to have changed their approach to coming: they normally just dropped it into conversation.

Highlighting the level of inclusivity found in England, Lily said, "I don't recall even coming out. I was just out when I came to the team. It's not an issue for them." Similarly, Mel said, "I didn't have a coming-out party, with balloons or anything!"

The data we use to make these claims is not just limited to the data that Bullingham gathered. Outsports.com gives gay and lesbian athletes the opportunity to tell their stories, too. Here, numerous athletes suggest that there was no big event when they came out.

Perhaps the biggest contrast that Bullingham's research uncovered in comparison to the older literature on lesbian athletes was that being out of the closet was deemed being easier than being in. This was not the case with older research (Blinde and Taub 1992a; Cahn 1994; Griffin 1998; Wright and Clarke 1999; Lenskyj 2003). Participants in Bullingham's research reflected upon their feelings of what it was like before they came out of the closet. Here, they spoke of feeling "ashamed" or being "angry all the time," when they were in the closet. Their internal angst rubbed off on their teammates and friends, too. This caused interpersonal difficulties. Lily, who took three years to tell her friends, explained how being closeted negatively impacted her friendships, saying that she pushed friends away when she suspected that they suspected she was lesbian. Fortunately, after she came out, she regained those friendships.

Trailblazing lesbian athletes

Trailblazers are the first athletes to come out of the closet on their team, thus their experiences will depend on whether other athletes join them in coming out. Perhaps the best example of a trailblazer in sport is Martina Navratilova. Her reception in professional tennis was so negative and damaging that, rather than encouraging others out of the closet, it ensured that elite athletes remained firmly closeted. The same process applies in recreational sport: if an athlete comes out and is accepted, then more athletes are likely to come out. Fink and colleagues (2012: 90) noted the importance of trailblazers in the coming-out process for those competing in collegiate sport: "In essence, these trailblazers provided a window into what would be on the other side (after they had come 'out')."

The importance of trailblazers in recreational sport was also shown for the lesbian athletes in Bullingham's research. Heather said: "I think that the fact that there were out lesbians, and I could see that they were being accepted by other players on the team, kind of made it a lot easier for me."

Caroline and Angelica also noted the positive effect that trailblazers had on them. Caroline said that it was easier because someone else being out of the closet first proved that it was a safe environment. Cathy said, "It 100 percent made it easier . . . because there were literally, you know, people in the same boat as you." Angelica gave a more humorous response that referenced a character from *Little Britain*, a popular British comedy from the early 2000s: "I wasn't the only gay in the village." Finally, Grace said, "If you have already got somebody who is openly gay on the team, there is that underlying feeling that it is accepted."

This was not the case for all athletes, however. Some did not rely on the experience of other lesbian athletes to gauge how they would be treated—they just assumed they would be treated equally. Lily described how trailblazers had "no effect" on her decision to be open with her teammates. Mia agreed: "No, not in the slightest," while Lorna simply replied, "No" to trailblazers having any effect on her decision. These responses were made because these athletes could not conceive that their teammates would be homophobic, even without openly lesbian athletes on a team.

Gay men's sports clubs

There is a vast, sometimes complicated, but nonetheless rich network of gay and lesbian sporting teams across the globe. This book is not about those leagues—instead, we focus on the experience of gay and lesbian athletes on ostensibly heterosexual leagues. However, it is important to note that these gay clubs have cultural visibility, and are important to many athletes. For example, in the UK, supported by key stakeholders, such as the Gay Football Supporters Network (GFSN), and in part by the Football Association (FA), there has been a large-scale increase in the number of gay men's football leagues and teams. The growth of gay sport subculture—influenced by pioneering gay football clubs (such as Village Manchester and Stonewall FC)—has helped challenge commonly held beliefs and stereotypes associated with homosexuality. As Jones and McCarthy (2010: 170) argue, "Gay football has grown as an entity, with the various teams as focal points for strong community ties."

The necessity for these clubs originally came from perceived or real hostility toward sexual-minority athletes in mainstream sport. Hekma (1998), for example, found mainstream sport clubs hostile toward gay and lesbian participation in the Netherlands, in the 1990s. Ostensibly, it is this which is as the core of a decision for people to choose gay sport clubs. Yet athletes also choose gay or lesbian sports because they are a homosocial environment. Gay men and lesbians often like being around their "own kind." This desire for homosocial activity extends to gendered preference as well. Thus, there tend to be gay and lesbian sporting programs, as separate entities. In this capacity, lesbian and gay (and to a lesser extent bisexual and transgendered) sport can facilitate a recreational alongside a social need. Gay sport leagues can serve as a place for finding others to date, or just have sex with, outside of the bar scene. Here, players consume one of the primary advantages of teamsport: the idea that it crafts a group of people as friends in order to accomplish a certain task (Anderson 2010).

But these clubs are not without issue. In his excellent documentary on the topic, *The Brighton Bandits*, Ian Macdonald features a gay sports team that experiences tension between the players who just want to play, and are unconcerned with performance, and players who desire to win—to beat other gay and straight sport teams.

But the desire for gay sports clubs to win has led to a paradoxical event. Jarvis (2015) notes how gay sports clubs have recently been infiltrated with a number of heterosexual athletes, many of whom have challenged traditional homosexual stereotypes, and exhibit inclusive attitudes towards homosexuality. In the United States, leagues have even had to adopt rules concerning how many heterosexuals they let play on a gay team. Some losing teams have accused winning teams of stacking the deck with straight athletes.

Highlighting this, and illustrating a national problem, the 2008 Gay Softball World Series was fraught with controversies, as many teams were alleged to have flouted the rules which restricts teams to only two straight players per team. One such club—San Francisco's D2 team—blamed this distraction for their defeat by the LA Vipers.

The policing of "who can play" also raises questions of what classifies as being gay, lesbian, or bisexual. Whereas heterosexual sport, or "mainstream" sports for a lack of a better term, do not ban gay and lesbian athletes and thus do not have to define what it means to be gay or straight, gay teams do ban (or limit) the number of straight athletes and they must therefore define this. What counts as a gay player on a team? Does a bisexual player count only as half a gay player for a quota? What if one is just a little bit bisexual?

On the one hand, this sounds infuriating; however, if gay men have gathered around sport as a mechanism to meet other gay men, having straight men present can dilute that. The scenario is reminiscent of Eric Anderson's experience with the LGBT weekly society at the university where he did his PhD. It was common for sociology professors to assign students to observe a social group's meeting (to study them). Having one observer among 15 participants might not be an issue, but eventually, the number of heterosexual observers grew, making gay and lesbian people less likely to attend. One meeting saw seven heterosexual observers and one sexual minority. At this point, it was determined to ban heterosexuals from the meetings. Of course, this would limit someone from attending who internally knew/suspected he was gay, but still publicly identified as heterosexual. In other words, the attempt to make policy around this was a mess; likewise, not making policy around this was problematic.

The same is occurring with gay clubs and spaces. As homophobia declines, heterosexuals enjoy going to gay bars. Thus, the popular London venue GAY is now more straight than gay. Gay and lesbians spaces are being overrun by open-minded and accepting heterosexuals. Gone are the days when a gay man can hit on a guy in a gay bar and only have to fear whether the other man was attracted to him or not. Now, he must fear whether he is even gay. Anderson has even seen a straight man grow upset with a gay man for hitting on him—in a gay bar.

Despite these problems, recent research on gay sports clubs shows that gay and lesbian athletes in recreational sports do not suffer from homophobia from the straight teams they compete against. In her (2014) article focusing on two teams who compete solely in gay football leagues—Dublin Devils FC and Glasgow Saltire Thistle FC—Teresa Willis documents how attitudes toward these athletes were generally positive. Drawing on stereotypes related to gay men, many of their opponents were surprised with the physicality shown by these gay footballers. What is significant here, however, and what differs from most research on collegiate athletes, is that these athletes hail from cities not known for their gay-friendliness.

Willis (2014) documents a number of paradoxes associated with gay male sport. Gay athletes have often been feminized by peers for failing to embody a masculine identity, and, when they don't participate at all, it is assumed that they participate in more feminine terrains, such as gymnastics, ice-skating and cheerleading (Anderson and McCormack 2010; Willis 2014). Many of the athletes interviewed by Willis were concerned with challenging common stereotypes associated with male homosexuality—such as femininity and weakness. Similarly, gay male footballers in Jones and McCarthy's (2010) study comment on their desire to present a challenge to the straight community about stereotypical perceptions of gay men.

However, Willis (2014) notes how their participation in football perhaps shores up the more orthodox form of masculinity commonly associated with sport. In other words, whilst the presence of gay men in a masculine domain challenges stereotypes, it also reinforces orthodox masculinity, or, as she puts it: "The way they do this is often by displaying, adopting or embodying the kind of masculinity that by its very nature has sought to exclude them" (2014: 5).

Some of the athletes within this research even acknowledged that the presence of gay leagues may not be "the best forums for directly challenging stereotypes, [but] they do provide an important function for team members" (Willis 2014: 9). Indeed, Anderson (2002) interprets this as a form of self-marginalization, as gay athletes refuse to challenge dominant notions of masculinity associated with mainstream sport. Interestingly, despite their participation in a gay football club, many of these men were against the idea of a gay league forming in Ireland, believing that competing against non-gay teams in a mainstream league will be more successful in eradicating homophobia.

The Gay Games and World Outgames

Although not the focus of this book, it is also important to acknowledge the influence of gay mega-sport events—specifically, the Gay Games and the World Outgames. Based on the mainstream Olympics, the Gay Games first established in 1982, due to the work of Tom Waddell, a gay American athlete. The Gay Games is currently the world's largest sporting event for LGBTIQ (Lesbian, Gay, Bisexual, Transgender, Intersex and Queer) participation, and frequently overtakes the Olympics in pure numbers of participation. This is particularly because the Olympic Games limit the number of competitors to 10,500, whereas the Gay Games' model is one of almost unlimited participation.

Although the Gay Games is grossly under-researched, Caroline Symons's (2010) seminal monograph—which draws upon oral histories and participation observation—documents the social, cultural and political history surrounding the need for and purpose of this event. Principally, it is important to understand that these gay mega-sporting events no long exclusively exist because of homophobia in straight spaces; instead, they facilitate the culture of sexual minorities, and serve as a festival and cultural celebration.

The World Outgames serves a similar purpose to the gay community. Following the decision by the Federation of Gay Games (FGG) to remove the Gay Games from Montreal in 2006 because of issues of size and finance, Montreal continued to organize their event without sanction from the FGG: the World Outgames was born.

The first event, Montreal 2006, usurped participation numbers of the Gay Games, with over 18,000 participants involved in the inaugural event. This was the largest sporting event to take place in Canada since the 1976 Olympic Games.

Because of the divide between these two sporting bodies, there is continued political wrangling. Mark Tewksbury's (2010) text *Inside Out: Straight Talk from a Gay Jock* offers an insightful analysis. Here, he outlines how few athletes were concerned with the political tensions. Recalling the decision of the FGG to remove the Gay Games from Montreal, he writes:

> Very few LGBT athletes had firsthand experience of how the Federation [of Gay Games] operated, and most didn't care about the business and political side of the movement. All they knew was that they had life-changing

experiences at the games, and by the time the press conference took place announcing yet another deficit, most of the athletes were already on their way home. Few saw the devastation that was left within the local LGBT community (2010: 129).

After this split, the Gay and Lesbian International Sport Association (GLISA) was formed, and the World Outgames and Gay Games compete for the greater number of competitors for each of their events.

While the politics of this is out of the scope of this book, we leave this chapter by reminding readers of a salient fact: if there is enough of a market for two mega-sporting events to compete for sexual-minority athletes to attend, we've come a long way.

7
OPENLY GAY AND LESBIAN ELITE ATHLETES

In this chapter, we first address the lack of representation for gay and lesbian athletes at the professional level of sport. We highlight the oxymoronic concept at play: whereas gay men are highly under-represented in professional sport, partially because they are less interested in playing competitive, contact sports and perhaps because they are less powerful than heterosexual men, lesbian athletes are both interested in these types of sports, and perhaps more powerful than heterosexual women. Lesbian athletes are both attracted to sport, and potentially benefited by a more masculine biology that helps them succeed in it. This chapter examines why, then, there is poor representation of lesbian athletes in professional sport.

Acknowledging that it is difficult for us to conduct interviews with openly gay professional athletes for this book, we include three interviews at the end of this chapter. But to bolster our arguments, we necessarily draw on published media accounts. Here, we show that professional athletes who come out of the closet, in either American or British sports, and regardless of the sport, are experiencing social inclusion. Collectively, male athletes have come out and played in rugby union, rugby league, American football, soccer, basketball, Olympic boxing, cricket, weight lifting and a host of more individual and more feminized sports.

In women's professional sport, athletes have come out in basketball, tennis, field hockey, soccer, softball and many other sports.

Still, there are gaps in this roster. There are a number of sports that have not yet had an openly gay player in them. For men, hockey, baseball and tennis are a few; for women, rugby union, cricket and other sports have yet to have a professional athlete come out. Given the over-representation of lesbian athletes playing in sport, compared to what we argue is an under-representation in men's, we argue that in some ways, lesbian athletes have further to travel toward public openness than gay male athletes.

In addition to examining the experiences of openly out athletes in professional sport, we also take a more comprehensive approach to the topic of study. We do this by examining the relationship between professional gay athletes and sport through exemplars related to changing media narratives and Internet fan forums. Here we show that fans of professional men's sport are largely desiring to be inclusive; and we show that the media has changed its perceptions on gay men in sport, too. We conclude by suggesting that there are complicating factors for coming out at this level of play, but that athletes are nonetheless slowly emerging from their professional closets.

The missing men in professional sport

Highlighting the shift of increasingly positive and inclusive attitudes of sporting teams, it can be argued that sport is no longer overtly, and perhaps even covertly, a homophobic culture. At the professional level, this is perhaps best exemplified by the different reactions faced by openly gay English soccer player Justin Fashanu, and openly gay players Anton Hysén (who came out in 2011) and Robbie Rogers (who came out in 2013).

In 1990, having learned that he was to be outed by *The Sun* newspaper in the UK, Fashanu came out, and was harassed and bullied by his family, teammates and fans. His mistreatment was so awful that it is generally accepted it was a contributing factor to his suicide a few years later. However, when one compares that with Anton Hysén (who plays for Torslanda IK in Sweden, and is son of former Liverpool player, Glenn Hysén) and Robbie Rogers (who plays for the LA Galaxy), the improvement to soccer culture is evident. Both of these players were celebrated and supported by their teammates, the media and fans. Add to this the accepting attitudes of both contemporary British soccer fans (Cashmore and Cleland 2012), and footballers from two Premier League academies disclosing that they would have no issues with an openly gay male athlete coming out on their team (Magrath 2016; Magrath, Anderson and Roberts 2015), the variance in culture over these twenty years is evident.

Nevertheless, one of the continuing issues in Europe is the lack of openly gay professional football players—the continent's biggest sport. This is a similar issue in the top four American sport leagues (American football, baseball, basketball and ice hockey), which we use here as an exemplar to make a point about the dearth of openly gay players in the highest-profile sports.

At the writing of this book, using game-day rosters as the criteria, there are 3,496 men in the four major North American sporting leagues: National Football League (NFL, 32 teams, 53 players in each team); Major League Baseball (MLB, 30 teams, 25 players in each); National Basketball Association (NBA, 30 teams 12 players in each) and National Hockey League (NHL, 30 teams and 23 players in each). Assuming the proportion of gay athletes is similar to the proportion in the general population, and using a measure of 2.8 percent of the US population being a gay male (Laumann 1994), we should observe approximately a hundred gay men at this level of sport. Yet, while there have been a few (Michael Sam in the NFL and Jason Collins in the NBA) there is actively playing only one – Robbie Rogers, for the Major League Soccer team the LA Galaxy.

While the recent outings of some of these high-profile names/cases are encouraging, taking in a larger picture over the previous forty years, these leagues have had only another nine men (or so) who are publicly known to be gay by coming out after retiring: six in American football (Jerry Smith, David Kopay, Roy Simmons, Esura Tuaolo, Wade Davis and Kwame Harris), two in baseball (Glenn Burke and Billie Bean) and one in basketball (John Amaechi). To this date, there have been none who have come out in the North American sport of hockey, either while playing or in retirement, although Anderson did interview one player for his book *In the Game: Gay Athletes and the Cult of Masculinity* (2005).

If one does the math on these American figures, it indicates that only about 0.03 percent of professional contracts have been signed by men ever known to be gay. Similar patterns hold for major European soccer leagues and, perhaps surprisingly, even other individual sports such as tennis and boxing. In all cases, we know of exceptionally few gay athletes. This value, 0.03 percent, is significantly lower than homosexuality estimates in the general population, which average about 2.8 percent. No statistical techniques are needed to confidently assert that this is more than a sampling error. An explanation is warranted.

Anderson (2005a) has previously highlighted multiple rationales for the lack of openly gay athletes in professional sport: first, gay men in these leagues remain silent about their sexuality because of homophobia—the "homophobia" hypothesis, and second, gay men choose not to play these types of sports—the "non-participation" hypothesis. Yet there may be other reasons for the lack of proportional-representation of gay men in professional sport.

Magrath (2016) contends that there may also be a third reason: the "international" hypothesis. Using football as an example, Magrath argues that players are often contracted to travel to countries governed by strict and archaic laws around homosexuality (Frank, Camp and Boucher 2010)—such as Russia and Qatar, the hosts for the 2018 and 2022 FIFA World Cups. Being an openly gay player, for example, might not be perceived as a difficult position if one only plays in the UK or other Western European countries. However, if one is contractually obliged to travel and compete in highly homophobic countries, ones that assign the death penalty for homosexuality, it can represent a problematic proposition. Similarly, at the top level of the game, increased migration (Giulianotti and Robertson 2009) has resulted in players from all over the world competing for Europe's top clubs— including those from countries where homosexuality remains illegal. It is perhaps for this reason, or at least a contributing factor, that the lack of openly footballers is a continued issue in Europe's top leagues and might be a compounding factor for Olympic and other internationally competing athletes.

Finally, Ogawa (2014: 295) maintains that the aforementioned hypotheses are "an untenable way of understanding the silence among all athletes." He suggests a "non-participation" hypothesis, but it perhaps is more accurately understood as an "inability" hypothesis. Here, it is argued gay men might just not be physically demonstrative enough to play sport to the point of equal representation to the percent of gay men in culture at the professional level of combative sports. He doesn't discount that some gay men are capable of playing at the elite level—evidence shows that they do exist here—but he suggests that at the tail end of a muscular/athletic distribution, a small biological difference can exaggerate the effect. There is evidence for this proposition, too. A very large body of academic work suggests that, as a whole, gay men are slightly different than straight men: gay men are smaller, thinner and less muscle-bound. In other words, the research shows that gay men's bodies are slightly more feminized than straight males (Bailey 2003). We note here that this might very well be the opposite for lesbian women, who might be physically more masculine and thus are over-represented in teamsports.

Unfortunately, the media, as well as cultural discussions, only attributes one of these hypotheses as being responsible for the lack of representation of gay men in sport at the professional level—the homophobia hypothesis. For example, in soccer, Cashmore and Cleland (2011: 421) describe the lack of openly gay players as "a culture of secrecy." For many, this ostensibly seems the obvious answer: people assume that if 2.8 percent of the general population is gay, then 2.8 percent of the NFL player population must also be gay. However, we argue that gay men exist in finite supply. If gay men are over-represented in theatre, music, dancing, art and a host of feminized sports, that necessarily reduces the numbers of gay men in other activities. Hence, there is logical evidence for the selection hypothesis: gay men are not as attracted to competitive teamsport as straight men, instead opting for other recreational and sporting activities. We thus argue that a more balanced perspective holds that the absence of the openly gay athlete at the professional levels of most teamsports exists because of a variety of reasons, including all four of these hypotheses.

Historically, the homophobia hypothesis was evidently effectual; this is why players have come out after retiring. The selection hypothesis is also true: gay men are drawn to other activities and leisure pursuits in the first place; and for those who start sport young, once gay men come out in sport, they tend to drop out before university (Zipp 2011). Once at university, Anderson (2005a) suggests that university-level athletes drop out after coming out because they find a life of gay friends, clubbing and sex more appealing than sport. The international hypothesis has face-value validity, too. It may not be the hypothesis that keeps the majority in the closet, but it must certainly be a complicating factor. Finally, there is evidence showing that the inability hypothesis is also at play in this equation, particularly in sports that require extreme strength. Differing hypotheses might best explain individual sports, too. For example, the inability hypothesis might make more sense in American football, but the homophobia/international hypothesis more sense in football (soccer).

We next note that the homophobia hypothesis really should be divided into two categories. The first is related to direct, overt, intolerant attitudes toward homosexuality, and the second to complicating factors based less in difference than hostility. Just because the entirety of attitudes among members of one team might be inclusive, if the coach, or even one member of the team is not, it might be enough to scare an athlete enough from coming out. Even if an entire team is supportive, with a supportive coach, if an athlete fears that members of other teams might not be supportive, this too might be enough to keep one closeted. Hence, the homophobia hypothesis can operate even with only a drop of homophobia in a lake of otherwise gay friendliness.

The second aspect to the homophobia hypothesis is that gay athletes might remain silent because of not wanting to be perceived as different. Athletes predicate their master identities as that of sportsmen. Athletes live together, go to school together, train, travel and compete together. Coming out to even gay-friendly teammates is difficult when one is different than the others. Athletes fear that their difference will interrupt the homosocial camaraderie, that they will be treated differently. Also, athletes know that while their teammates might be "true friends," they are also competition for selection to the next level of play in a rapidly decreasing opportunity structure (Roberts, Anderson and Magrath forthcoming). Athletes therefore perceive any difference, or distraction, as possibly impeding their progress (Magrath 2016).

Athletes are also afraid to come out of the closet because of the age of the gatekeepers of their sport. Older men, those whose adolescence was in the 1980s or earlier, serve as their managers: when stakes are high, one over-conforms to norms in order to be selected. In other words, one must not only play well, but must exhibit all of the other emotional and personal characteristics that the coaches desire if one is to be selected for the next level of play. Athletes fear that coming out will result in deselection.

Finally, we highlight what we might consider a fifth hypothesis: the "selective hypothesis." This hypothesis maintains that gay and lesbian professional athletes do come out at the professional level of sport, but that oftentimes they only come out to their close teammates and not the media (Anderson 2005a). Just because the media is not aware of one's sexuality does not mean that one is not gay. American football player Kwame Harris is an example of such an athlete. He was only outed after he was arrested for physically assaulting his boyfriend. Further evidence comes from the fact that, in this book, we report upon a professional female athlete who is out to her team, but not the media.

It is, of course, reasonable that readers might speculate about our trustworthiness when we say that we have interviewed a professional athlete who has not come out publicly. We build some credibility in this matter, however, by reminding readers that it was Anderson who broke the Alan Gendreau story, writing anonymously about this NCAA Division I American football team player in the deep South, who was out to his team but not out to the media. At the time the story broke, Gendreau did not want to be bothered with being seen as different in the eyes of his teammates for the news flurry that would inevitably hit. Anderson received emails from disbelievers about the story he published on Outsports.com, from readers suggesting that he had just made the story up. However, this player did eventually come out.

When one takes both forms of the homophobia hypothesis into play with the other four hypotheses that we've provided in this chapter, it's evident that there are a lot of reasons why gay men are under-represented in elite, competitive team-sport. Collectively, however, before we can rule out the homophobia hypothesis, we need to see a generation of young men who have grown up with inclusive attitudes toward homosexuality take to the seats of power within sport. We are, today, far from this.

Exemplifying a generational divide on this issue, following the award of the 2022 World Cup to Qatar, FIFA President Sepp Blatter claimed that due to the illegality of homosexuality in Arabic states, gay athletes and fans should abstain from any sexual activity. His sentiment seems reasonable to him, yet unthinkable to today's emerging players. It will thus take a generation or two; for those playing today to take seats of power within the institutions before the entirety of sport will be inclusive. Only then, might we start to more fully explore which of the other hypothesis are most responsible for the dearth of gay men in professional sport (notice that we still think gay men will be under-represented in combative teamsports in the future).

The missing women in professional sport

It is oxymoronic that there is a dearth of openly lesbian women who are publicly out at the professional level of sport, because ostensibly it seems that lesbians are highly over-represented in women's sport. In other words, there is no shortage of lesbians in sport, but there does seem to be a shortage of openly lesbian athletes who are out in professional sport.

It is thus ironic that there are more openly gay male professional rugby players in the United Kingdom (namely, one) then there are openly lesbian rugby players competing at the highest level. When examining this question, it is immediately evident that the inability hypothesis is void: lesbian women are clearly capable of playing professional sport. We also note that lesbian women seem to be attracted to sport as a form of socialization. Although we can find no academic reference for this, it seems that when gay men were organizing in the 1970s, they took to the bars—something their sex may have afforded them the financial luxury of doing. But while men controlled the indoor social spaces, lesbian women took to sport to meet others. This is not to say that there were no lesbian bars, but then, as now, there are far more gay bars that cater specifically for men than women. There are also more apps that cater to gay men than lesbian women. It thus seems plausible that sport has been heavily populated by lesbian athletes not only because they are good at it, and perhaps because they are naturally gifted (as a collective) at it compared to straight women, but also because they select it for social reasons.

Yet, there is also a disadvantage for women playing sport. It comes in the form of heterosexual power. Heterosexual women who excel at sport challenge femininity, and therefore face an assumption of lesbianism (Griffin 1998; Cox and Thompson 2001; Lenskyj 2003; McDonagh and Pappano 2008). Those who are financially invested in making professional women's sport profitable perhaps find this counterproductive to helping sport grow at a professional (and recreational) level for women. This has meant that female sport has consciously been promoted in a heterosexy style. Lesbian women are cajoled into acting feminine, and denying or hiding their lesbian desires publicly so that sport might be made more appealing to heterosexual women—soccer moms. For example, we highlight that during the 1998 Women's World Cup title match against China, the US women's team was heavily heterosexualized and described as mothers. Whereas sport programs normally post the player's name at the bottom of the television screens with career statistics, for one player at least the programmer posted "mother of two." Can you imagine seeing such a "stat" posted for a male soccer player? This highlights the intent to heterosexualize the sport.

Another reflection of the desire to portray sport as the domain of heterosexual women occurred when two of the biggest female sport celebrities came out in the sport of tennis, Martina Navratilova and Billie Jean King, in the early 1980s. Their reception was one of hostility and resulted in a loss of earnings (Hargreaves 1994). King lost all her endorsements in under 24 hours. When she was outed, she took an apologetic stance by posing for a magazine with her husband (Hargreaves 2000; Griffin 1992).

Some argue that the lack of female visibility for out players in professional sport today is somewhat affected by these early and horrific examples. The hostility that both players faced could be seen as a contributing factor for those who wanted to come out. If trailblazers are accepted onto the team, then others are more likely to follow (Fink et al. 2012). In King's and Navratilova's case, the opposite was true, and it took until 1999 for another female tennis star, Amelie Mauresmo, to come out. She was met with some hostility, but not the level seen by her predecessors (Forman and Plymire 2005).

One of the most high-profile cases of a lesbian coming out has been WNBA superstar Sheryl Swoopes. She came out in 2005, in a less straightforward manner than most. After winning a full scholarship to play basketball at the University of Texas, she quickly left due to her mother's concerns that the team included lesbians King 2009. This shows one of the differences faced by men and women, women can be "guilty by association" (Blinde and Taub 1992b: 526). If a male member of a team comes out, there is no threat that the rest of the team will be labeled gay; however, for women, things are very different. This then becomes a matter of homohysteria.

Other high-profile athletes have also recently come out to a positive reception. Soccer player Casey Stoney, capped over a hundred times by England, officially came out in 2014. However, this was pre-empted by the news that her partner, Megan Harris, also a footballer, was expecting twins. Despite coverage being generally positive, she tweeted that she had received a letter explaining the health hazards of being a lesbian.

Similarly, Kate and Helen Richardson-Walsh are two field hockey players in the UK who came out as a couple when they announced their impending marriage. Little media attention was paid to these athletes, though the coverage received was generally positive. Interestingly, all these athletes came out during an important life event: expecting children or marriage. Some may argue that this forced them to come out: both, for example, had to update their shirts to include their married surname.

While this list is not complete—there are many more openly lesbian athletes than this—we highlight that while there are a greater numbers of lesbian athletes competing at a high level, many lesbian athletes, perhaps most, still do not come out of the closet. Despite the fact that recent examples have had a positive reception, this has not resulted in a large-scale increase of out lesbian athletes.

We thus argue that another hypothesis must exist for women: the "protection" hypothesis. Here, women avoid coming out of the closet in order to protect their sport from being socially downgraded through promotion of the lesbian label. In a recent newspaper article, King has since stated that she did not come out sooner because she wanted to protect the professional women's tennis tour, which had started shortly before her announcement. With women's sport growing in popularity both on and off the field, players could still deem remaining closeted to be a form of protection for themselves and their sport.

Openly lesbian athletes in professional British sport

For this research, we were lucky enough to be able to interview three lesbian athletes who were all Olympic-class, and who were also out to their teams.

The athletes interviewed were asked about their coaches' attitude and language during their time as an international athlete. Out of the three international athletes interviewed, one, Angie, suggested that her coach never used homophobic language but he knew players well enough to engage in banter. Angie did note that if outsiders over heard these conversations they may be perceived as homophobic. She said "Yeah, in the environment it was I would say so. I don't know if some of the newer players might because we knew the coach that did it: we knew him quite well by now." However, as players, they know that there is no intent to harm and therefore the language is accepted as banter within the team.

Although Kerry explains that her coaches have never used homophobic language, she felt that the relationship with them needed time. She has two coaches and needed to have open and honest conversations with both, as they were not sure how best to support her. She noted that one coach had an open conversation with her about her sexuality so that she was able to provide appropriate support and use inclusive language. She recalled the conversation with her coach:

> [The coach said:] "I really don't know much about, you know, what being gay means. Can I ask you a whole range of questions? You know, because I want to understand and I want to be able to support you better. So what language should I use, what do I need to think about?" I think she was very honest about the fact that she had never thought about it before.

This allowed the athlete and the coach to have an open conversation. However, Kerry's male coach took longer to address her sexuality. He eventually had a conversation with her:

> Eventually, we knew we had to have that conversation and I need to have that conversation with him. Don't assume because I am gay, I don't have periods, or because I'm gay I, you know, don't worry about what my hair looks like!

Kerry insinuated that having these conversations was simply due to lack of contact with openly gay or lesbian athletes by the coaches. There was overwhelming support from coaches at the grass-roots level, and for Kerry and Angie at international level, but there was an exception.

Sally explained that her coach had used "gay" on two occasions and she challenged him about his use of language. As McCormack (2011a: 670) explains, if there is "pernicious intent," this language can be deemed homophobic. This could have been the case for Sally as she acknowledged that the administration was not overly supportive. This was not the only incident where Sally felt uncomfortable. Two of her coaches, on different occasions, talked to her about people they knew who were gay in a manner which she perceived as homophobic. She said, "People who try to convince you that they are not homophobic because they know someone gay."

International athletes face a dilemma when considering their sexuality. Elite athletes have a fear of losing sponsorship. Kerry noted that athletes' fear of losing sponsorship becomes "an unspoken myth" that athletes are unprepared to test. She noted that unless you have a conversation with the sponsor, no judgment can be made. While Navratilova lost all her sponsorship in the 1980s (Hargreaves 1994), Mauresmo had clothes specifically designed to show off her muscles by her sponsor, Nike. However, the assumption that sponsors will be open and inclusive is dismissed. Sally noted that both the administration and the sponsor were keen on a "certain type of person." Thus, it appears that the changes may not be as straightforward as anticipated.

Additionally, international athletes also have to face the media. Angie, an international athlete, explained that her team were told in a press meeting to "dismiss" any questions that were asked by journalists on sexuality. She said:

> We set up a meeting about it before a competition because the media lady anticipated that we might get some questions about it [sexuality]. She directed us to dismiss it, essentially: "I don't want to talk about it," but one of girls was actually, "If I get asked I'm going to say, because I'm happy in my relationship and I'm not going to hide it." There are a couple of people that are like that but the majority I would say are similar to me.

Although Angie was not one of the players to speak up, she described how it was not something that should have been said by the press liaison. She said the meeting was awkward and described the tension in the room, as athletes were being told effectively to hide their sexuality. Angie said that no players were asked about their sexuality in any interviews. She did explain that some players had received negative messages on Twitter, "a couple girls had some Twitter trolls." However, she explained the majority of messages and interviews had been positive and supportive.

While it appears that the players are accepting of their teammates, the sporting administrations seem less open to change. Sally describes the lack of acknowledgment within her administration: "I think it is something they deliberately don't publicize, that there are gay people in their sport." Sally was reluctant to talk about the administration of her sport, as she was concerned about any potential repercussions. Although athletes are competing in a more open and inclusive environment, it appears that the administration of sports are changing more slowly and more research needs to be conducted in this area.

International athletes must travel in order to attend competitions and training camps. This can be a concern for lesbian athletes traveling to countries where homosexuality is illegal. Kerry explained, "We went on a training camp to Russia and I wouldn't go, I refused to go." Her coach ensured her safety on the trip and tried to encourage her to participate and they had long conversations about her attendance. She said that safety was not the issue but "it is about standing up and representing the other people who don't have that voice." She also has worn rainbow items of clothing when she has played teams from countries that outlaw homosexuality in an individual protest. She described it as "a little protest" and noted that she did this despite "breaking rules" of her sport to do so.

International athletes often have close relationships with their team members because of the amount of training and traveling time they spend together. Kerry acknowledged the importance on her teammates knowing about her sexuality:

> I can't imagine how it would be to be in that pressured environment and not be able to pick up Skype and speak to my wife. To talk about how "I had a really crap game today and I think I'm rubbish," and to get that support. I can't imagine how difficult that must be to not be able to access that in the same way everyone else does. It must be horrendous. I don't know how you can possibly achieve in that environment.

While Sally and Angie discussed the significance of the lack of support from some, they *did* outline that they had the support of their teammates, which was important to their success.

None of the international athletes had experienced homophobia. Angie explained, "I've not experienced any [homophobia] at all." Sally noted a similar experience "No I've not had anything negative . . . not one thing." Kerry noted that she had experienced some apprehension from some of her teammates' husbands:

> I used to share a bed most Monday nights because we went training late on Monday and early on Tuesday, so, to save costs, we just rented a room.

We had a double room and we'd share a bed; initially her husband was quite nervous about that, and I think she had some anxieties. We were able to talk about and get over—once you've experienced something that normalizes it. Then the fact that she was sharing a bed with a lesbian is another issue, but you get over that really quickly, and he now will proudly tell everybody his wife shared a bed with a lesbian one night a week for two years. But a lot of my team say that by meeting me and by exposure to me it has broken down a lot of the myths and stereotypes they had about lesbians.

Kerry has shown that being open on her team has broken down stereotypes and she has also had other players speak to her in confidence about their sexuality. She has had a different experience to Sally and Angie as she was the only open lesbian on her team when she started playing. Sally and Angie acknowledged that there were other players who were open on their team, which resulted in them not having to challenge stereotypes as they were not alone.

This research has shown that elite athletes are competing in an open environment, comparable to that at other levels of sport. However, it is acknowledged that they have faced more challenges than recreational athletes. No national governing bodies responded to the request to speak to these athletes and they were approached via social media, suggesting the administration is still willing to be silent about lesbians within their sports. Angie and Sally both had other openly lesbian players on their teams, but no other players came forward to share their experiences. This could be for a number of reasons—such as lack of time. The interview with Kerry took over a month to arrange and Sally rearranged her interview on three separate occasions all because of timing constraints. However, it could also be because athletes do not want to talk about sexuality in sport. Significantly more research is needed within this area of sport.

Professional gay and lesbian athletes in the media

When Sheryl Swoopes came out of the closet as the Women's National Basketball Association's top-rated player, hardly anyone took notice. While the event made headlines, it was not picked up by mainstream papers as an important story. In comparison, when Michael Sam came out as a college player trying to make the NFL, it was headline news not only in sport papers, but in mainstream old and new press. When Jason Collins came out as a journeyman NBA player, he met President Obama.

What accounts for this difference between the celebrations of gay male versus the dismissal of lesbian athletes? On the one hand, we suggest that it reflects the homohysteria of women's sports. If we don't celebrate and promote lesbian athletes, it prevents women's sport from developing a further lesbian label. But there is another reason.

On the whole, we socially over-value men's teamsports, and we are collectively unbothered or even unaware that professional women's sport exists. Highlighting our collective disinterest in women's sport, we ask the reader a few questions: does professional American football exist for women? Professional rugby? Professional field hockey, ice-hockey, soccer, basketball or softball? We all know that professional football, rugby, ice-hockey, soccer, basketball and baseball exist for men, but not even the authors of this book know if they do for women.

Our lack of cultural interest in women's sport might be in part because they are understood as being less significant compared to men's sports: men outperform women in almost all of the sports that we culturally celebrate. This ability difference is then used as a reason to avoid reporting on women's sport in the popular press (both old and new). Highlighting this, in 2006, Lapchick, Brenden and Wright surveyed more than three hundred US daily newspapers, and found that men comprised 95 percent of sport editors, 87 percent of assistant sport editors, 93 percent of columnists, 93 percent of reporters and 87 percent of copy editors/designers in sport departments. These numbers ensure that it is men's sports that are written about.

Bruce (2015) shows that even four decades since the passage of Title IX in the US mandating equal opportunity for women in sport, media coverage for women still lags far behind that of men's sports. She shows that sportswomen still account for only 10 percent of everyday media coverage, with their visibility only rising during mega-sports events such as the Commonwealth and Olympic Games (Bruce 2015). In some cases, coverage of women's sports on television is lower now than twenty years ago, although some events—netball in New Zealand, basketball in the US and Grand Slam tennis tournaments—receive substantially more attention than in years gone by.

When women do receive media coverage, it normally refers to their "the-girl-next-door" sex appeal which promotes the athletes' heterosexuality (Kane and Lenskyj 1998; Lines 2001; Wensing and Bruce 2003). According to Lines (2001), only in stories promoting an athlete's bravery or courage is the "girl-next-door" label used. Griffin (1998: 53) describes the different ways the media can portray athletes: "(1) the sexy beauty queen, (2) the wholesome girl next door, (3) the cute little pixie, (4) the bitchy slut, (5) the wife and mom." Griffin (1998) explains that throughout the history of women's sport, athletes have had to fit one of these categories in order to gain media coverage, and therefore more income.

All of these results lead us to conclude that when it comes to women's sport, the media is not much interested in their physical performances, probably because their viewership is not interested in their physical performances. Men are generally not interested in watching women's sport in the same way that women are interested in watching professional men's sport; and that those who run and control the institution of sport (men) are chiefly interested in men's sport. We doubt matters will change. What the media is interested in, however, is heterosexual sexiness, scandals and stories of women bettering men. It is no wonder, then, that the media is not that interested in covering lesbian women in sport: it does not promote a heterosexual image; it is no longer scandalous, as it was when Billie Jean King came out, and rarely do female athletes compete against male athletes.

While the media has not changed its coverage of women's sport, it has, however, changed the approach it takes to reporting upon gay men in sport. Recent research suggests that sport media plays a significant role in contributing to cultural change of inclusivity toward male homosexuality in the way they present and discuss these issues (Anderson and Kian 2012; Anderson 2009a; Kian, Anderson and Shipka 2015).

Representing the heart of this changing cultural representation is David Beckham, and how the shift in attention towards men's looks and appearance has led to a resistance to the traditional hegemonic value of male teamsports that has long been associated with working-class masculinity (Boyle and Haynes 2009; Vincent, Hill and Lee 2009). Up until Beckham, the media presented orthodox masculine traits, and avoided any debates concerning a shift in masculinity, as well as a wider discussion of sexuality in football (see Cleland, Magrath and Kian under review), or in sport more broadly (as shown in academic studies on media framing of masculinities and gender—see Harris and Clayton 2007a, 2007b).

Finally, the mainstream media, alongside social media, play an important role in shaping cultural perceptions of gay and lesbian athletes. Most people have little knowledge of them, unless they hear of it from a major media source. It is thus illustrative to examine how the media portrays professional athletes who are out of the closet—not only because this portrayal shapes attitudes toward gay and lesbian athletes more broadly, but because it also shapes public attitudes about sexual minorities. Accordingly, in the subsections that follow we present as case studies four media-analysis events of the outings of two openly gay male and two openly lesbian professional athletes.

Individual media case studies

John Amaechi

By most standards, John Amaechi was a mediocre professional basketball player who received little media coverage during a five-year NBA career in which he played for the Cleveland Cavaliers, Orlando Magic and Utah Jazz. After his rookie season with the Cavaliers, Amaechi's NBA career was interrupted by his two-year stint of playing professionally for teams in France, Italy, Greece and Britain. After attaining his most professional success with the Magic and Jazz, Amaechi retired from professional basketball in 2003 after his NBA contract was traded from the New York Knicks to the Houston Rockets, but he was not invited to play for either team.

Although a largely unknown basketball player, Amaechi received worldwide media attention in 2007 after he revealed his sexual orientation as gay. It began when Amaechi's publicist, Howard Bragman, said that his client is gay and Amaechi officially came out four days later during an interview on the ESPN television show *Outside the Lines*. This strategic outing kicked off a speaking tour to promote the release of his autobiography, *Man in the Middle*, and some very well-paid speaking engagements.

It is significant to note that the media attention given to Amaechi's announcement had subsided significantly—that is, until former Miami Heat star point guard Tim Hardaway made a series of homophobic remarks about Amaechi during a radio interview three days after Amaechi came out. "I hate gay people, so I let it be known," Hardaway told WAXY-AM in Miami. "I don't like gay people, and I don't like to be around gay people. I'm homophobic. I don't like it. It shouldn't be in the world or in the United States" (Banks 2007). After Hardaway's comments, several major newspaper columnists wrote about the current place and status of gays in sport.

Amaechi's decision to leave the closet shortly after retiring from basketball is particularly interesting for several reasons. First, he was the first former NBA player to declare he is gay. Basketball has long been considered one of the most masculine teamsports in US culture (Baroffio-Bora and Banet-Weiser 2006; Rader 2004). Thus by their mere presence, openly gay men in professional basketball challenge orthodox notions of masculinity (Anderson 2002).

Also, the NBA has long been dominated by African Americans (Andrews 1999). In addition to the elevated rates of homophobia within the African-American community (see Chapter 10) (King 2004; Waldner et al. 1999), basketball players are deemed among the highest role models within US black culture (Hoberman 1997). This creates a form of double hegemony for black athletes, who are expected to uphold orthodox standards of achieved variables (toughness, stoicism and sacrifice) as well as the ascribed variable of heterosexuality. The consequences of breaking either of these orthodox conscriptions might be higher for black athletes than white.

By analyzing the international print media coverage concerning Amaechi's coming out, and Hardaway's ensuing homophobic comments, Kian and Anderson (2009) highlighted the changing nature of the relationship between sport, the sport media complex and the issue of gay athleticism.

Sport reporters rejected the domineering, homophobic behaviors and attitudes of orthodox masculinity, even though some attributed this attitude toward others, particularly basketball players. Taken with accounts of athletes, who are increasingly shown to value emotional intimacy (Pringle and Markula 2005), racial diversity (Anderson 2008c) and homosexuality (Anderson 2005b; 2008a, 2008b), they are more likely to alter the meanings associated with homophobic discourse (Wilson 2002). Collectively, these studies lead to the conclusion that there is a very rapid shift in what is considered an acceptable, desirable and even hegemonic status among teamsport athletes in the US. New research (Kian et al. 2015) also shows that the sport media today is gay friendly.

Part of this may be attributable to sport being increasingly viewed as a workplace environment. Accordingly, the often unwritten non-discrimination policies that apply to many other employers also apply to sport. But we suggest it mostly has to do with the changing culture within sport. Ethnographies of American and British athletes (Anderson 2014) all show that an inclusive, less homophobic, form of masculinity is on the rise. Therefore, this may be a case in which the dominant society's more inclusive attitudes influence sporting men's gendered accounts, instead of it being the other way around.

Kian and Anderson (2009) also suggest that narratives produced by African-American sport writers are helping to reverse elevated rates of homophobia that exist within US black culture, and are often strengthened through sport (Cohen 1999; Harper 1996). It is significant that prominent African Americans in the sport industry are beginning to stand alongside some key black religious and political leaders (including Barack Obama) in calling for an end to the elevated rates of homophobia that exist within the African-American community.

Thomas Hitzlsperger

Retired footballer Thomas Hitzlsperger made history on January 8, 2014 when he came out with through the German newspaper *Die Zeit*. The public revelation by Hitzlsperger, who played professionally for clubs in his native Germany (where he also won 52 caps for the national team), and Italy, in addition to his contracts with three different English Premier League clubs, quickly became a major news story. He became the first player in the English Premier League to have come out since its inception in 1992, and only the second openly gay player in English professional football—after Justin Fashanu.

Building on previous research which has documented football fans' acceptance and inclusivity of an openly gay footballer (Cashmore and Cleland 2011, 2012; Cleland 2013), Cleland, Magrath and Kian (under review) further address the intersection of masculinity, homophobia and gendered behavior on the Internet. In doing so, they investigated the attitudes, opinions and views of over 5,000 football fans actively involved in 35 football message boards across the UK as well as 978 comments submitted in response to an article in the *Guardian* newspaper that immediately reported on Hitlzsperger's decision (Christenson 2014).

Unofficial football club websites and message boards have provided disparate fans with an opportunity to engage in asynchronous communication (i.e. the opportunity to debate and respond to posts outside of real time) with fellow fans at any time of the day. Indeed, the availability of remote Internet access on mobile devices has provided added opportunities for fans to engage in virtual conversations. Given the anonymity afforded by football message boards and social media platforms (including sites like Twitter), not surprisingly they are increasingly being used by a minority of posters as a platform for hate speech (such as homophobia, racism, sexism and anti-Semitism). For football message boards, however, it has become a common feature to find how registered users effectively self-police these sites where discriminatory virtual discourse is often challenged, dismissed or resisted (Cleland 2013; Millward 2008).

Whereas message boards in the UK and US have been utilized as a source for debate amongst a number of sports scholars (Clavio 2008), very few have actually looked at the discourse surrounding sexuality for evidence of homophobia (Kian et al. 2011; Cleland 2013). In fact, both of these studies found significant differences in the discourse on fan message boards. For example, in their analysis of homophobic language on one American football fan message board (rivals. com), Kian et al. (2011: 694) explain that, despite the prevalence of homophobia, it went largely uncontested and led them to state how the "performance of hegemonic masculinity seemed to be mutually reinforced or policed by subsequent postings, possibly meaning that the main board serves as a haven for men trying to attain masculine capital and acceptance from like-minded peers." On the other hand, in his analysis of over 3,000 anonymous posts on 48 football message boards from across the UK on fans' views towards the presence of a gay footballer, Cleland (2013) found that despite the presence of heteronormativity and orthodox views, posts that are deemed to contain pernicious homophobic intent are rejected by the vast majority of posters who demonstrate inclusive discourse and support for any gay player. Given that this latter focus was on a hypothetical situation, the online reaction to the coming out of a high-profile footballer like Hitzlsperger provided a new dimension to football, masculinity and sexuality research.

Across 5,000 forum posts and 978 Guardian comments, the online discourse provided further support to those scholars also finding more inclusive representations of sexuality and masculinity within football (Adams 2011; Adams, Anderson and McCormack 2010; Cashmore and Cleland 2011, 2012; Cleland 2013, 2014; Magrath, Anderson and Roberts 2015). Cleland, Magrath and Kian's (under review) findings illustrate how men engaging in football message boards and comments sections of national newspapers no longer need to construct their own masculinity by opposing homosexuality through their actions and use of language (as argued by Kimmel 2008; Plummer 2006).

As suggested by Berila and Choudhuri (2005) and Anderson (2009a), heterosexual men are becoming less obsessed by historic definitions of masculinity and, instead, are using the Internet to present their own notions of masculinity and sexuality. For those fans that continue to express homophobic views, the culture of football has almost turned full circle. Rather than gain power through the use of language and actions with homophobic intent, it is actually homophobia that is stigmatized by the vast majority of fans who effectively self-police those views that fall outside of the collective majority across the increasing number of online platforms available to engage in virtual conversations. Concurring with the arguments put forward by Adams (2011) and Cleland (2013), as decreasing homophobia is increasingly being found in the culture of football, this has had a positive impact on the gendered behavior of heterosexual boys and men, particularly on the Internet.

Although the culture of football is often perceived as one that has remained traditionally heteronormative and homophobic, the findings reflect Thorpe's analysis of masculinities in snowboarding when she states masculinities "are multiple and dynamic; they differ over space, time, and context, and are rooted in the cultural and social moment" (2010: 202). In later writing, even Connell (2012) now refers to a more expressive, egalitarian and peaceable form of "modern" masculinity. Thus, the findings question the views of Clayton and Humberstone (2006: 297) who argue that football "epitomises the notion of sport as a male preserve, and basks in the philosophy of dominant masculinities and male ideology." They also challenge Plummer's (2006: 122) analysis of sport, where he argues that "homophobia is deeply implicated in the gender order and its influence on contemporary masculinities and male identity is comprehensive."

Amelie Mauresmo

Whilst men's sport is progressing as increasingly liberal, matters are different for women's sport. Women's sport has a well-documented history of sexism, heterosexism and homophobia (Cahn 1994; Griffin 1998; Lenskyj 1986). Homophobia and sexism certainly endure in women's sports, largely as a result of homohysteria. In highlighting this, we point to elements of the Mauresmo story, which read as a "lesbian panic."

On January 26, 1999, French female 19-year-old tennis player Amelie Mauresmo upset the world's highest-ranked player, Lindsey Davenport, in the semi-finals of the Australian Open Championships. Following the conclusion of the match, in her press conference, Davenport commented that "A couple of times, I thought I was playing a guy," as well as referencing Mauresmo's broad shoulders and power. Shortly after, the world's second-ranked tennis player, and Mauresmo's opponent in the final, Martina Hingis, echoed Davenport's sentiment, joking that, "She's [Mauresmo] here with her girlfriend. She's half a man."

These comments from the top two tennis players were national news in a number of Australian newspapers. The final was then played under heightened media scrutiny. Although Hingis won the match, and the competition, comfortably, Mauresmo's time in the media spotlight was not over. Shortly after the match, Mauresmo told a *New York Times* reporter that she had intended to discuss her sexuality, even before the competition began, commenting that she did not "want to become a symbol or the focus of attention, but . . . she did not want to dance around the subject throughout her career" (Clarey 1999: 10).

Mauresmo's experience became an object of scrutiny in the media. Of course, Mauresmo was not the first strong female tennis player to have incited what Forman and Plymire (2005: 121) describe as "lesbian panic." We earlier discussed the hostile experiences of trailblazers Billie Jean King and Martina Navratilova. But the Mauresmo story does not read as a total marker of the progress of lesbians in sports, the way the abovementioned analysis of the men's stories do. This is because, as the authors of this study (Plymire and Forman 2005) argue, in Mauresmo's case, the press was unable to dispense with two deeply held cultural assumptions—first, that muscles are masculine and therefore athletic prowess is inherently masculine, and second, that masculinity among women is a sign of lesbianism. She was, however, reported in the media as being brave for coming out. Therefore, she seemingly represents a better brand of tennis player and/or lesbian than those who enact homophobic utterances and/or those who fail to come out of the closet.

Sheryl Swoopes

Sheryl Swoopes is perhaps the most prominent figure to have played in the WNBA. Not only has she played in the WNBA, but she has been to the Olympics representing the US and has won three gold medals. Her ability led her to claiming the six-time WBNA All Star, and defensive player of the year on three separate occasions. Her prominence in the sport attracted lucrative corporate sponsorship with Nike and she became the first female athlete to have a shoe name after her: 'Air Swoopes.' She now coaches at Loyola University in Chicago, having retired from playing in 2011.

In 2005, Swoopes came out in an interview with *ESPN Magazine*. Here she said, "I can't help who I fall in love with. No one can." Her partner was a former coach from a team that Swoopes had represented. They had been together for eight years even though Swoopes had previously been married to a man and had a child. Throughout the article, Swoopes discussed the challenges she faced coming out and the effect of her religious background.

After coming out, Swoopes embraced the LGBT community. She became the face of the lesbian cruise-ship company Olivia, and took on various fundraising opportunities within the LGBT community. Unlike the cautionary tale of Navratilova, Swoopes attracted corporate sponsorship. Swoopes also declared that she felt that the "don't ask, don't tell" culture of women's sports had faded in recent years.

Throughout the numerous media interviews, Swoopes maintained the same stance: she was not born gay and her relationship with a woman was a choice. This goes against the narratives that most sexual minorities maintain, that their sexuality is of biological design. She refused to label herself as bisexual throughout interviews, but she did refer to herself as gay. The fluidity of her sexuality became apparent when she announced her engagement to a man in 2011. This is not entirely unusual; research shows that women's sexualities are much more apt to fluidity—to change over time—than men's (Diamond 2002).

Interestingly, her engagement to a man in 2011 failed to gain substantial news coverage. The athletic director of Loyola College, a Catholic University, argued that it is the ability of the person that matters to the university, rather than their relationship status. This is a significant statement from the athletic director of a Catholic university.

Although her initial reception when she came out seemed positive in the popular press, and although the popular press largely ignored her marrying a male, the LGBT community was, perhaps, more judgmental. Swoopes received some negative press from the LGBT community after she married a man. Shewired. com notes how some in the LGBT(Q) community called Swoopes a "lie-sexual" because of her engagement to a man. There was a sense of betrayal by the lesbian community. She went from being the poster girl of lesbian athletes in the WNBA, as well as the face of a lesbian cruise ship company, to heteronormative.

Unfortunately, the Christian community used Swoopes to promote their argument of homosexuality being a disease, or a choice, and that it was thus curable and preventable, despite the fact that there is no scientific data that supports the contention that homosexuality is socially produced (LeVay 2010). There is no evidence whatsoever that sexuality can be a choice. Thus, it is likely that Swoopes is actually bisexual. When she was in a relationship with a woman, she called herself lesbian, and with a man, straight.

This highlights the erasure of bisexuality in the press and the academic world. We, the authors of this book, are equally guilty of erasing bisexuality from this text by not examining the specific and different experiences that bisexuals maintain in sport.

8

IMPACT OF TEAM CLIMATE AND LANGUAGE ON GAY AND LESBIAN ATHLETES

Introduction

In this chapter, we use Pat Griffin's taxonomy of three climates—informed with Anderson's (2009a) concept of homohysteria—in order to conceptualize the experiences of openly gay and lesbian athletes. Supporting this, we draw upon academic sports research undertaken during periods of high homohysteria to exemplify Griffin's taxonomies.

We then progress to discuss the complex terrain of homosexually-themed language. Numerous scholars have attempted to conceptualize homosexually-themed language—many of whom are discussed throughout this chapter—but we draw upon the work of McCormack (2011a), who historically situates this language, comparing it across different cultural zeitgeists. We also highlight various limitations with this conceptualization, for instance, that it may not always provide an exhaustive model for understanding language, particularly factors such as banter.

Hostile team climates

Pronger (1990) highlights how boys in Western cultures needed to use sport in order to prove their heteromasculinity, stigmatizing gay athletes as pariahs. In this homophobic environment, Clarke (1998: 145) describes gay men "largely as deviant and dangerous participants on the sporting turf." Pronger (1990) shows how gay athletes were frequently the last to be picked for teams, despite boasting fine athletic prowess. One example concerns teams being selected during a physical education class, and one team captain claiming his team only had "five and a half members" instead of six, as the final team member was gay. Even if an athlete was not openly gay to his teammates, the presence of a hyperheterosexual (Hekma 1998; Wolf-Wendel, Toma and Morphew 2001) and macho culture created an unwelcoming environment for gay athletes. Within this environment, Parker (1996b) argues that heterosexuality is taken for granted; alternative forms of masculine representation are stigmatized as deviant.

This has been cemented by those exhibiting a dominant form of masculinity, who are generally referred to as "jocks" (Anderson 2014). These men have been responsible for the harassment of subordinate social groups, such as "nerds," or "geeks" (Connell 1989). Most significantly, jocks also engaged in similar behavior against gays—or those suspected of being gay—despite them valorizing those at the top (Anderson 2014). To be gay, or thought of as gay, was deemed unacceptable, leading Anderson (2005a) to suggested that sport is a good place for a closeted man to hide his sexuality. Evidencing this, Anderson (2015b) writes that when kids in a school started a Gay-Straight Alliance in 1993, football players responded by starting a heterosexual club, picketing the gay club with signs which read "no faggots." Accordingly, Sabo and Runfola (1980: 43) wrote: "Within the highly masculine world of sport, the threat of homosexual stigmatization is ever present . . . It is no mere coincidence, therefore, that the cultural image of the jock is the polar opposite of that of the homosexual."

Unsurprisingly, scholars who conducted research around this time found extreme forms of homophobia toward those who were gay or perceived to be gay (Bryant 2001; Clarke 1998; Pronger 1990; Wolf-Wendel, Toma and Morphew 2001). Hekma (1998: 2) wrote that "gay men who are seen as queer and effeminate are granted no space whatsoever in what is generally considered to be a masculine preserve and macho enterprise," whilst Wolf-Wendel, Toma and Morphew (2001: 47) wrote that heterosexual athletes were "unwilling to confront and accept homosexuality." Such was the power of homophobia at this time, Pronger (2000) argued, that no scholarly research existed which shows mainstream sport to be a welcoming environment for sexual minorities. Put simply, sport was a hostile place for gay men.

In women's sport, lesbian athletes suffered similar discrimination, and concealed their sexual identities by not coming out or, as Griffin (1998: 253) summarizes, "maintain deep cover at all times." Accordingly, this creates problems for all women, as homophobic attitudes are not challenged, and all are controlled by the lesbian label (Drury 2011). Conceptualizing this, Griffin (1998) developed a taxonomy of climates that lesbians can move through, starting with *hostile*, moving through *conditionally tolerant*, to *open and inclusive*. These can be conceptualized using Anderson's (2009a) concept of homohysteria (see Chapter 3).

Within a hostile climate, Griffin (1998: 93) writes that "lesbian participation is prohibited." Accordingly, lesbian women use silence as a survival strategy (Lenskyj 2003): breaking this silence by coming out is described by Hargreaves (2000: 95) as a "heroic quest." Evidencing this, research on specific sports has uncovered that particularly hostile environments have been found to be highly homophobic and therefore lesbians have had problems expressing their sexuality (Mennesson and Clement 2003). In the American collegiate system, two of twelve athletes interviewed by Anderson and Bullingham (2013) reported homophobic language being used by players on their team. Additionally, the authors found that one player had their car vandalized and covered in homophobic abuse (Anderson and Bullingham 2013). Although these examples show hostile environments, all are either dated and/or did not take place in the United Kingdom.

Oppression faced by sexual minorities during this time led Rich (1980) to theorize the "compulsory heterosexuality" framework. She wrote that any form of non-heterosexuality is perceived "on a scale ranging from deviant to abhorrent" (1980: 632). This was developed to explain how women are forced to adhere to particular heterosexual and feminine ideals, thus avoiding lesbian suspicion (Sartore and Cunningham 2009). Given the high levels of homohysteria at the time, Connell (1995) suggests that this framework was also compulsory for men.

The most frequent way homophobia was shown was through the use of homophobic discourse or through violence (Pollack 1998). Although abusive language may not be directed toward anyone in particular, it can still be hurtful to gay men and women (Hekma 1998), and is pivotal to maintaining a culture of hostility. Homophobic slurs or "queer-bashing" (Pronger 1990) have been commonplace in both male and female locker rooms and sporting settings where men and women have failed to live up to orthodox forms of masculinity and femininity (Anderson 2002; Griffin 1998). This is outlined in more detail later in this chapter.

Tolerant team climates

In hostile climates, openly gay athletes are expected to remain in the closet in order to hide their identity. This was particularly the case for the highly homohysteric culture of the 1980s (Anderson 2009a; see Chapter 3). But, since the early 1990s, attitudes towards homosexuality began to improve (Loftus 2001), and although it took a while for this to reflect in sport, things slowly began to change.

In 2002, Eric Anderson conducted the first research on openly gay athletes, finding that many of his sample had had positive coming-out experiences, many regretting not coming out sooner. However, because Anderson (2002) could only find openly gay athletes who were examples of athletic excellence—the best on their teams—it appeared that the ability to come out was dependent on maintaining high sporting, and therefore high masculine, capital. In other words, athletes were accepted by heterosexual peers only "as long as one plays the sport well." There was also a strong heterosexist culture of "don't ask, don't tell," in which gay athletes and teammates colluded in silencing the voices of gay men, something that these gay athletes were unable to recognize, even defending its use.

Griffin (1998) also documents this for women's sport: what she conceptualizes as *conditionally tolerant*. Here, the closet remains evident but is made of glass: lesbians "keep their identities 'secret' but everyone knows who they are" (Griffin 1998: 100). Rowe (1990: 154) also discusses the concept of "glass walls," portraying them as "impenetrable" and describes their function in the business world as aiding "occupational segregation" for minority groups. Plymire and Forman (2001) state that people involved in women's sport are compelled by strong cultural codes of heterosexuality to effectively swear to silence, keeping lesbians closeted to ensure that the media still covers events and that fans still come and watch.

It can be argued that silencing may reflect a covert way of addressing the issue, just like those who favor race-neutral policies championed affirmative action. However, silencing may also reflect a covert institutional and cultural heterosexual hegemony (Sykes 1998), in which lesbian athletes are denied from speaking as freely about their personal life as heterosexual athletes. Silencing mostly reflects a covert form of hegemonic oppression that often leads the athletes to feel that they should not discuss their sexuality, despite the fact that discussions of heterosexuality are all around them (Anderson 2002, 2005a).

Within a conditionally tolerant climate, the issue is not lesbian participation but rather their visibility within sport; lesbians are allowed to participate providing they subscribe to a set of rules (Griffin 1998). Described earlier as "don't ask, don't tell," Anderson and Bullingham (2013) found that athletes defended its use claiming that sport was not the right forum for discussion on sexuality. This is also evident with Bullingham's (2015) research, in which lesbian athletes commented on their experiences of "don't ask, don't tell." Interestingly, one of these athletes—whose coach was also lesbian—talks of her coach attempting to normalize her sexuality by pretending it was a non-issue. It is, of course, possible that her coach may have done so out of the cultural mandate of heterosexism. Within a conditionally tolerant environment, lesbian athletes must conform to a set of rules which includes silencing their sexuality (Anderson and Bullingham 2013).

The reason for the lack of recognition of the data comes from what Anderson calls the theory of *reverse relative deprivation*. Also discussed in Chapter 5, reverse relative deprivation occurs when with the "absence of severe expected intolerance, [gay athletes'] sense of how well things went may have been artificially boosted" (Anderson 2005a: 90). Athletes reflect on their experiences, comparing themselves to those less fortunate than themselves. Even though some athletes had lost friends, or had members of the team who would no longer speak to them, they still described their coming-out experiences as "pretty good" (Anderson 2005a: 90). Athletes failed to notice that they were in fact in a conditionally tolerant environment, but, because they expected hostility, they felt they were in an overtly positive environment. As Anderson (2002: 870) describes, "Most of the time, however, the gay athletes failed to recognize that their identities were being denied, and they often took part in their own oppression by self-silencing and partaking in heterosexual dialogue". Anderson discovered during his interviews that athletes were expecting outcomes such as physical assault or being removed from the team, but still described their experience as positive.

The existence of reverse relative deprivation has been found in interviews with both gay and lesbian athletes. In their research with lesbian athletes in the American collegiate system, Anderson and Bullingham (2013: 11) concluded that "Although they have not been fully accepted onto their teams, because [most] had not be dismissed or severely ostracized, they described their experience as a positive one—matters could have been much worse."

Open and inclusive team climates

Since Anderson's initial research on openly gay athletes, an increasing body of research focusing on the relationship between sport and homosexuality has documented the continued decrease of homophobia (Anderson 2009a; Clements and Fields 2014; Keleher and Smith 2012). Using similar sampling methods, Anderson (2011a) has tracked a positive shift in the acceptance of gay male athletes since his initial research. In 2002, Anderson discovered gay athletes participating in a conditionally tolerant climate. Almost a decade later, he found openly gay athletes competing in a more inclusive environment: athletes faced no hostility after coming out, nor was this determined by their athletic capabilities. Accordingly, he also found a reduction of "don't ask, don't tell".

This culture of inclusivity has been mirrored in a number of other sporting environments. For example, an increased number of studies have focused on the positive and inclusive attitudes of ostensibly heterosexual athletes in a variety of teamsports (Adams 2011; Adams and Anderson 2012; Adams, Anderson and McCormack 2010; Anderson 2011b; Magrath 2015, 2016; Magrath, Roberts and Anderson 2015). Further evidencing the changing cultural conditions for gay men in sport, Adams and Anderson (2012) monitored the effect of a gay player coming out in an American soccer team. He was not shunned, nor abused: instead, the response was one of inclusivity, and even strengthened these athletes' closeness.

These positive findings have also impacted the expression of heterosexual masculinity (Anderson 2014). With the reduction of cultural homophobia has come an increased number of gendered behaviors which were once stigmatized (Anderson 2009a; Anderson and McCormack 2015; McCormack 2012a). The impact of diminished cultural homophobia on heterosexual athletes is also documented in Chapter 9.

Research on female athletes' capital is limited, but Hargreaves (2000) argued that the situation described above is a long way off for lesbian athletes. Griffin (1998: 161), though, was more positive, noting that "The winds of change can be heard in the comments of some young lesbian athletes." Anderson and Bullingham (2013) found that all the lesbians interviewed in 2002 were valuable to the team, with seven calling themselves the most valuable player. This insinuates that the situation for women, and lesbian athletes, is somewhat different. Whilst this research was undertaken in 2002, and only published recently, times have changed since then. In her doctoral research on lesbians in sport, Bullingham (2015) found that the average lesbian athlete was no better than the average heterosexual athlete.

Griffin (1998) conceptualizes this positivity as *open and inclusive*. When an open environment has been achieved, women have been able to express their identity freely—some women use the sporting environment as a safe zone. Because of the high representation of lesbians within sport (Lenskyj 2003), athletes have found a lesbian community within sport that allows athletes to provide support for each other (Cahn 1994; Griffin 1998). Trailblazers can spark the process of more athletes coming out; trailblazers are described as athletes who are the first to come out on their team. As Fink and colleagues (2012: 90) describe, "In essence, these trailblazers provided a window into what would be on the other side [after they had come out]." The importance of trailblazers is also noted by Hargreaves (2000: 146), who describes an openly lesbian athlete as someone who "becomes a special symbol of resistance and promise." Griffin (1998) describes how high-profile athletes can bring about changes in values and provide education for others.

The changes in the sporting environment can be seen in the posts on the website Outsports.com, too. Here, openly gay male and female athletes frequently post blogs about how they have come out (Anderson 2011b). Summarizing his decade of research in England, the US, Australia and Canada, Anderson (2012: 41) writes: "1) We can no longer assume homophobia based on team sport affiliation; and therefore, 2) We can no longer assume homophobia based on simply being a young male—the relationship between masculinity and youth is changing."

Despite a plethora of research on gay male athletes, Bullingham's (2015) research on openly lesbian athletes in England, and Fink and colleagues' (2012) examination of the American collegiate system, there is a distinct lack of research on openly lesbian athletes in the United Kingdom. But team climate is not the only way one can monitor levels of acceptance and inclusivity—this can also be assessed through the use of language.

Homosexually-themed language

Understanding meanings and dynamics of language is significant as it represents the primary method through which ideas and social norms are both conveyed and consolidated (Cameron and Kulick 2003; Kiesling 2007). Typically, discussions of homosexually-themed language are simplified into being merely homophobic or non-homophobic—often leading to exaggerated perceptions of homophobia, due to assumptions that hearing colloquial homosexually-themed language equates to homophobia (McCormack 2011a). But, this oversimplifies the nature of homosexually-themed language when a much more complex range of forces are at work. Thus, critically reviewing old conceptualizations of homophobic language, McCormack (2011a: 664) presents a new model for understanding what he terms "homosexually-themed language." Significantly, he situates this language using Anderson's (2009a) concept of homohysteria (see Chapter 3).

McCormack's (2011a) engagement with literature highlights two requisite features which must be apparent for something to be considered homophobic: *pernicious intent*—referring to the use of language which attempts to degrade or marginalize a person by use of the association with homosexuality—and *negative social effect*—referring to emotional trauma suffered by the LGBT community because of this language. Whilst these two factors are essential in determining if language is deemed homophobic, an ongoing debate is the assumption that this homophobic language is said within a homophobic environment (McCormack 2011a).

Some scholars have documented this homophobic culture (Burn 2000; Giulia-notti 1999; Plummer 1999; Pronger 1990), whilst some have merely *assumed* the presence of a homophobic environment upon hearing homosexually-themed language (see Jackson and Dempster 2009; Smith 2007). Given that much of the research on homophobic language was undertaken when Anglo-American cultures were decidedly homophobic (Loftus 2001), it is perhaps a reasonable assumption. Contemporarily, however, this has become problematic due to a marked decrease in cultural (Anderson 2009a; Clements and Field 2014; Keleher and Smith 2012; McCormack 2012a, 2012b; Savin-Williams 2005; Weeks 2007) and sporting (Adams 2011; Anderson 2011a, 2011b; Anderson and McGuire 2010; Cashmore and Cleland 2011; Magrath, Anderson and Roberts 2013; Magrath 2016) homopho-bia. Homosexually-themed language has therefore become a more complex terrain.

Accordingly, McCormack (2011a) proposes that a third requisite must also be met for language to be considered homophobic: *homophobic environment*—the link-ing of environment with effect and intent helps to historically contextualize the conceptualization of homophobic language which accurately captured the social dynamics of the 1980s and 1990s (Anderson 2005a; Griffin 1998). This can some-times, however, be a difficult requisite to meet, as homophobia cannot always be proved nor discounted. Think, for example, how one can conceptualize numerous football fans engaging in a homosexually-themed chant/song without conducting arduous survey research. The traditional framework for understanding homopho-bic language is illustrated below in Figure 8.1.

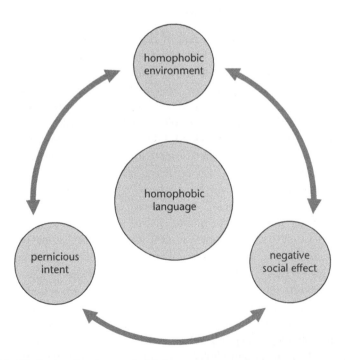

FIGURE 8.1 Understanding homophobic language.

Whilst this remains a useful conceptualization, more recent research has uncovered complexities not explained under the requisites of homophobic language. *Fag discourse* is a concept introduced by C.J. Pascoe (2005) in her ethnographic research in a California high school; this refers to settings where the word "fag" is used, and will have negative social effect, but has mixed meanings: some will use it with pernicious intent and some won't. For example, Pascoe (2005: 336) states that "some boys took pains to say that 'fag' is not about sexuality," and argued that it has nothing to do with sexual preference at all. Pascoe's research was unique, however, in that the word "fag" was used as a pernicious insult that regulated only gender, not same-sex identities (see Figure 8.2).

Some scholars, however, fail to incorporate the subtle changes in intent and effect of language, and labeled fag discourse as part of the traditional framework of homophobic language (Bortolin 2010; Kimmel 2008). McCormack (2011a) argues this was because pernicious intent was still sometimes present and the social effect was often negative. Consequently, it is easy to read high levels of homophobia in the schools Pascoe studied, and the changes in the use of language were overlooked (McCormack 2011a). High levels of homophobia would have been an appropriate assumption in the 1980s and 1990s, when the word "fag" was used as a derogatory term for homosexuality in a broader culture of extreme homophobia (Anderson 2009a). It would not, however, be accurate in all cultural contexts.

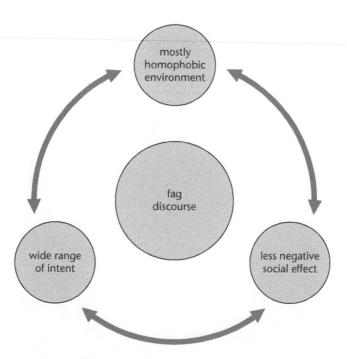

FIGURE 8.2 Understanding fag discourse.

Gay discourse, first introduced by McCormack and Anderson (2010a), refers to how language used by rugby players had "a homosexual theme but was not homophobic as described by the frameworks above [homophobic discourse and fag discourse]" (McCormack 2011a: 669). Here, respondents espoused pro-gay attitudes and had openly gay friends, but continued using phrases such as "that's so gay." Thus, McCormack and Anderson (2010a) apply Ogburn's (1957) cultural lag to contextualize the players' discourse in a culture of decreasing homophobia. Figure 8.3 maps how the meaning attached to discourse changes as cultural homophobia decreases.

Engagement with the word "gay" is significant here, because these men claimed the word had two independent meanings: sexuality and that something was "rubbish." This is consistent with Lalor and Rendle-Short (2007), whose research documents how the term has developed into a homonym—a word with two discrete meanings. Rasmussen (2004: 304) also notes complicated understanding with the phrase: "It does not *always* have to be read as homophobic, it can also be ironic, self-referential, habitual, or even deployed without a 'knowing' relation to gayness as sexual signifier." Despite this research, the phrase "that's so gay" is still interpreted as homophobic (see Woodford et al. 2012; Lu 2012). A recent YouGov poll in the UK recently attracted criticism as 49 percent of 3,000 young people (18–29) believe it an acceptable phrase to use. However, like McCormack (2011a), many of those surveyed argued that understanding context was a significant

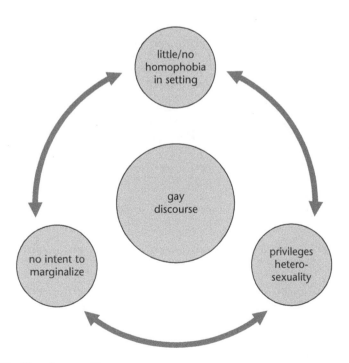

FIGURE 8.3 Mapping gay discourse.

factor in understanding this language. In the same report, 75 percent rejected use of "faggot," and 50 percent the word "lezza."

Investigating a semi-professional British soccer team, Adams, Anderson and McCormack (2010) also illustrate *masculine challenging discourse*—used frequently by coaches to portray football as a "man's game" and to motivate players—and *masculinity establishing discourse*—a way of regulating the masculinity of these players should they stray from these rigid boundaries.

Building on gay discourse, *pro-gay language* explains how homosexually-themed language is used as a form of social bonding when men greeted each other, using phrases such as "Hey, gay boy" (McCormack and Anderson 2010a) McCormack (2011a: 671) critiques previous interpretations of gay discourse, arguing that this language "could continue to privilege heterosexuality because of the framework of homosexual stigma that used to exist in rugby." McCormack (2011a) therefore argues that the authors were falling back on the same assumption of context that they accused others of by labeling "that's so gay" as homophobic—a position aided by the lack of openly gay athletes to judge the use of this language (McCormack 2011a).

McCormack (2012a) explores the social effect of homosexually-themed language between gay and straight students and argues that it has a positive effect as it is used as a means of bonding students together in socio-positive ways. Examples of this include when an openly gay student was working with heterosexual friends, one of whom was doodling in his book. The heterosexual student then looked up and asked, "Is this pretty gay what I'm doing?" The openly gay student then laughed and agreed, stating, "Yeah, it's pretty gay." Similarly, when a gay student was playing catch, one of his heterosexual friends let the ball slip out of his hand, traveling only a short distance. The gay student then shouted, "You're gayer than me!" jokingly drawing upon stereotypes of gay men being unable to play sport competently (Anderson 2005a). McCormack (2012a) describes how this was a regular occurrence within established friendship groups, and appeared to both bond the students together and remove any negativity associated with these words.

A second form of pro-gay language is also documented from McCormack's (2012a) research, which occurred where heterosexual male students casually address their close friends as "lover" or "boyfriend." Students enacted this language out of homosocial affection, without any discernible attempt to consolidate their heterosexual standing (McCormack 2011a). Furthermore, it is also interpreted as a way of demonstrating emotional intimacy and tactility. Importantly, students did not think that employing such terms with other males would arouse homosexual suspicion and homosexualize them (McCormack 2012a).

A model of homosexually-themed language

Drawing together various conceptualizations of homosexually-themed language, McCormack (2011a) presents an empirically grounded model, recognizing that language is historically situated. Accordingly, he applies Anderson's (2009a) concept of homohysteria (see Figure 8.4). It is important to note, though, that the use of language is complex, and although this is the most conclusive model through which to judge homosexually-themed language, no phrase is necessarily part of the same category (McCormack 2011a). It is, however, the most useful framework to judge other forms of language.

One example of this is what McCormack (2012a) refers to as "heterosexual recuperation." This is conceptualized as "A heuristic tool for understanding the strategies boys use to establish and maintain heterosexual identities without invoking homophobia" (2012a: 90). Although there are not exhaustive methods as to how boys can manage their sexual identities, McCormack (2012a) delineates between two common forms of heterosexual recuperation: "conquestial" and "ironic." Both are used by boys when they fear their heterosexuality is threatened.

First, conquestial recuperation incorporates the ways in which boys boast of their heterosexual desires or conquests (Mac an Ghaill 1994). McCormack (2012a) provides an example of conquestial recuperation where students were discussing a house party which they had recently attended, at which one of them left early to have sex with his girlfriend. When this student was jokingly mocked for leaving, he replied, "I'm the one who got laid last night." The other students replied by commenting, "Fair point. I can't ever imagine turning down sex. I mean, I want it *all* the time" (McCormack 2012a: 91). Although heterosexuality was often consolidated through this medium, McCormack (2012a) argues that the attitudes of these boys towards women was improved compared to other literature (see Chambers, Tincknell and Van Loon 2004; Dunning and Sheard 1979; Elias and Dunning 1986; Robinson 2005).

Second, the more frequent method of heterosexual recuperation is described by McCormack (2012a) as "ironic recuperation." Here, boys recuperate their heterosexual identities by participating in close physical contact, where men and boys ironically proclaim same-sex desire to consolidate their heteromasculine standing. Crucially, they argue that this is a way that heterosexual men prove their masculinity *without* being homophobic. They also suggest that this is necessary because, unlike gay men who are socially accepted to be gay upon proclamation, the same does not hold true of heterosexual men (McCormack 2011a).

Another significant element of homosexually-themed language concerns that of *banter*. Although banter does not need to incorporate any element of sexuality, it can be incorporated in any of the previous conceptualizations of homosexually-themed language outlined here. However, it is worthy of further examination because of its presence in most sporting settings. Previous research has highlighted that banter has been used to reinforce heterosexual discourse (Hargreaves 2000), whilst others have documented sexism, misogyny and elevated competitiveness (Adams, Anderson and McCormack 2010; Gill, Henwood and McLean 2005; Lyman 1987; Renold 2004). However, banter can also be used as a way of showing acceptance and tolerance toward gay and lesbian athletes (Bullingham 2015; Magrath 2016; McCormack 2011a). For Baxter (2004), engaging and sharing jokes allows the construction of relationships with

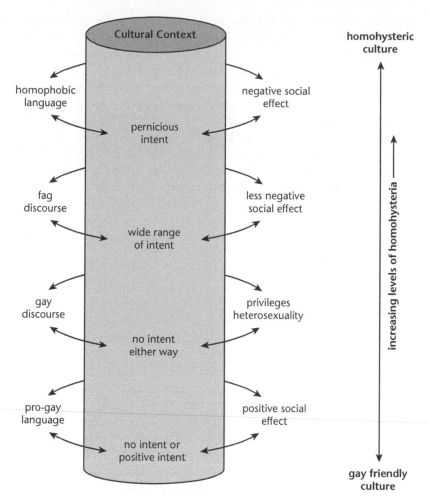

FIGURE 8.4 A model of homosexually-themed language.

one another, whilst it can also contain "the playful exchange of teasing remarks" (Hein and O'Donohue 2014: 6).

The presence of banter in men's and women's sport, whilst acknowledged, has received little academic attention. However, in women's teamsports, Bullingham (2015) notes how banter can be used as humor, to ease tension, or break potential awkwardness among teammates. Magrath (2016) also finds that banter is used to construct and consolidate friendship among mate teammates. In his research on Premier League football academies, he notes that banter has a potentially paradoxical relationship because it can act as a medium to cathartically express emotion in a competitive environment, where boys effectively compete against each other to secure a contract in professional football. But, this banter could also *facilitate* this competitive environment, too.

Applying Anderson's (2009a) concept of homohysteria—the cultural fear of being homosexualized—is useful in understanding the context of all forms of homosexually-themed language. In Figure 8.2, it can be seen how McCormack (2011a) applies homohysteria to understanding homosexually-themed language. Homohysteria historically situates levels of homophobia, and theorizes how varying levels can impact upon the stratification and construction of masculinities. Supporting this changing cultural context, Anderson (2002) determined that half of the athletes he interviewed judged levels of homophobia on their team through the amount of homophobic language their teammates used. This half of the 2002 sample suggested that the phrase "that's gay" and the use of the word "fag" were indicative of homophobic attitudes among those who used them: the other half argued that this was not the case. However, when he replicated this study in 2011, none of the sample judged the level of their teammates' homophobia through use of this homosexually-themed language. One of the participants in the latter study makes salient this contextual shift:

> Gay doesn't mean gay anymore. And fag doesn't mean fag. You can't say that because someone says "that's so gay" or "he's a fag" that they are homophobic. I guess they could be, but you know when someone is using those words as a homophobic insult and when someone's not. (Anderson 2011a: 258)

Like Neil, and in contrast to 2002, all the players in the 2011 sample who heard use of the words "gay" and "fag" argued that these phrases were not homophobic. Supporting this, Jones and McCarthy argue that this kind of discourse is "deemed to be different from 'real' homophobic comments," and that the men they had interviewed from a gay football team had "come to expect such banter" (2010: 168).

In a highly homohysteric culture, there is an elevated stigma attached to homosexuality, resulting in boys and men using homophobic language to consolidate their own heterosexual identity and masculine standing (Plummer 1999). Consequently, when homosexually-themed language—or homonegative discourse (Bullingham, Magrath and Anderson 2014)—is employed within this setting, it demonstrates homophobia, as it is used with pernicious intent and has a negative social effect. The policing of gender and sexuality through the medium of discourse has been documented by a number of scholars (Hekma 1998; Parker 1996b; Plummer 2001; Thurlow 2001).

Fag discourse occurs in settings which are less homohysteric, and although many will have pro-gay views, language may still be used with pernicious intent. Indeed, use of fag discourse can cause negative social effects, including regulation of acceptable gendered behaviors because the intent of the language is not always clear (Anderson 2002).

Gay discourse incorporates settings of low homohysteria where young men show no concern if they are socially perceived as gay. Phrases such as "that's so gay" may be used as expressions of dissatisfaction—which may privilege heterosexuality. But, significantly, it is not employed with the intention of marginalizing gay people. Accordingly, this language suffers cultural lag: despite the inclusive perspectives of participants, their discourse lags behind. Despite this, attempts have been made by an increasing number of athletes to eradicate remarks such as "that's so gay" and "you're gay," once dismissed as acceptable "trash-talk" (Nylund 2014). American basketball player Grant Hill's recent involvement in an NBA campaign to take a stand against homophobia highlights such resistance towards the utility of such phrases (Nylund 2014).

Building on this further, pro-gay language occurs within a near-complete or total absence of homohysteria, exposing a gay-friendly culture (McCormack 2012a). Here, homosexually-themed discourse bonds students by demonstrating emotional intimacy or inclusion of gay students, and the stigmatizing of homophobia, thus maintaining the reproduction of a gay-friendly culture. While some of the theorizing of homosexually-themed language here does not specifically refer to sport, it nonetheless remains useful in explaining how language varies in different cultures, different contexts and different epochs. Of course, language remains a complex and multi-faceted issue, perhaps more so in sport—epithets and phrases often differ from a person's attitudes (Cashmore and Cleland 2011; McCormack and Anderson 2010a).

9

THE IMPACT OF DIMINISHED HOMOPHOBIA ON STRAIGHT ATHLETES

There has been a wholesale cultural change toward sexuality among today's youth. Sexual activities that were once highly stigmatized (like pre-marital sex, hooking up, oral sex, anal sex and group sex) are now commonplace and socially acceptable sexual activities for youth (Anderson 2010, 2012b; Branfman, Stiritz and Anderson forthcoming; Scoats, Joseph and Anderson forthcoming). This chapter examines another impact of decreasing sexual stigma, the impact of declining homophobia, and the impact it has, not on gay men, but on straight athletes and non-athletes (Anderson and McCormack 2015; McCormack and Anderson 2010a) alike. The impact is greatest for men, but is also true of women.

To this effect, a steady flow of research has been conducted on straight male athletes' behavior, which shows evidence of increased tactility and affection, whereas there is a dearth of research on heterosexual women and if diminished homophobia has had an equally liberating effect. Therefore, this chapter predominately focuses on the actions of straight men.

Increased physicality between millennial males is paralleled by emotional closeness. In times of high homohysteria, men must be emotionally restrictive with one another (Williams 1985). But as homohysteria continues to decrease, men and boys are more emotionally open with one another, developing what Anderson (2014) theorizes as a "bromance"—essentially a love affair between close friends but without sex. These are borne out of strong and deep emotional relationships as boys bond through activities such as shopping, playing video games, exercising and eating out (Anderson 2014). Here, they disclose secrets and emotions establishing a closer friendship, allowing stronger forms of emotional support.

Love and support for other men

Research from decades ago shows that most males were not emotionally intimate with each other (Lewis 1978; Williams 1985). For example, Olstad (1975) suggested that, although men report more same-sex friendships than women did in the 1970s, these friendships were not close or intimate. In his study of Oberlin College students (a very liberal institution), males had more male best friends than female best friends. Yet these males tended to place greater confidence in, consulted more about important decisions, and spent more time together with their best female friends than with their best male friends. With a nationally representative sample, Joseph Pleck (1975) showed that 58 percent of all males questioned had not told their best male friend that they even *liked* him. This is something that grew worse in the mid-1980s, where "like" became a euphemism for love and was edged further from friendship vocabulary (Williams 1985).

In the development of gender and sexuality politics for Generation X, sport played a central role. For Generation X, organized, competitive teamsports were almost universally described as locations where heterosexual men battle for masculine dominance in Western cultures. In order to achieve the most socially valued form of masculinity, men had to repress fear, weakness, intimidation or pain (Giulianotti 1999). This has particularly been true of sports that are intertwined with school systems (Gerdy 2002), where one's teamsport life flows into one's non-sporting social life. Here, failure to live up to the esteemed cultural construction of masculinity has traditionally resulted in males being subject to physical and discursive methods of subordination, not only on the field, but among peers in school as well (Mac and Ghaill 1994). More recently, however, more progressive attitudes are being esteemed among young men in sport.

Highlighting this, Anderson (2014) notes that ostensibly heterosexual men are increasingly valuing strong, same-sex friendships, often over romantic relationships with women. This is frequently visible upon examination of Facebook posts and text messages between friends. For example, one informant explained that he was preparing to travel for a two-week holiday to Spain with his best friend. When asked if he was concerned about being together so long, he responded: "No mate, we're too close for that," and that his girlfriend wouldn't be jealous because "She knows how close we are. She's gotta share me."

This is not isolated: for example, in research on English working- and middle-class, white sixth-form students (equivalent to US high school seniors), McCormack and Anderson (2010b) show that the style of men's masculinity most esteemed among these youths approximates inclusive masculinities. They show that a decrease in homophobia simultaneously permits an expansion of heteromasculine boundaries so that boys are able to express emotional intimacy without being homosexualized.

Matters have been the same across multiple research projects (Magrath 2016; McCormack and Anderson 2014b; Roberts, Anderson and Magrath under review). Anderson (2008c), for example, shows how members of a fraternity shared anxieties and troubles, secrets and fears. This emotional bonding had been constructed so tightly that it remained acceptable for men to cry in each other's presence, something which occurred with surprising frequency. Nowhere was this more the case than the final fraternal event before senior fraternity members graduated. Here, brothers each were given an opportunity to say something about their time in the fraternity. Almost all cried in giving their speech, or in hearing of the narratives of another.

There is no claim here that men have the same emotional spectrum as women to cry—research shows that women cry eight times more frequently than men (Becht et al. 2001)—but they have significantly improved upon their freedom of expression from where the literature said men were concerning emotionality in the 1980s (Askew and Ross 1988). Men in Becht and colleagues' (2001) study cried 6.5 times per year.

Thus, multiple levels of emotional bonding are apparent here, ranging from men who have a harder time expressing themselves, to men who cry and talk emotionally with their friends. These studies found no judgment for those who related to each other in ways that the gender literature associates more with the social mechanisms through which women bond (Diamond 2002), including crying, in the research conducted by Anderson and colleagues. Even among men who were unable to cry, or unwilling to open up emotionally, none stigmatized, homosexualized or in any other way look disparagingly upon those who did.

Within another university-based football team, Anderson (2011b) highlights how, when a member of the team felt abandoned as his best friend had been spending a lot of time with a new girlfriend, other team members consoled him. Contrary to previous research, which shows how men have been unable to show emotional distress (Pollack 1998), this team responded by listening intently, continually expressing concern for his emotional state. When asked about his situation, the player discussed having spoken openly with his best friend about the situation, even crying with him (Anderson 2011b). Indeed, support for friends has also extended to the social acceptance of crying.

Supporting these findings, Schrack-Walters and colleagues' (2009) qualitative analysis of men's participation in athletics suggests that the development of communal and emotional effects is becoming increasingly more important between men on sports teams, and finds that comments from athletes were laden with emotional intimacy. When these researchers heard men "express very high levels of affection for each other, none of the athletes qualified their statements using a heterosexual standard of acceptability" (Schrack-Walters et al. 2009: 92). Importantly, their data suggests that representing male athletes as monolithic "jock" individuals is an unfair representation of the experiences and gendered identities of all male athletes.

Thus, the emotions of love and support that young men express for each other, combined with sacrifice, are more akin to a love affair than a traditional male friendship. They are what young men today call a "bromance."

Bromance

As a consequence of fearing homosexualization, or not being socially perceived as masculine, American males have not traditionally had close male friends (Komarovsky 1974; Pleck 1975). Morin and Garfinkle (1978) suggested the fear of being labeled homosexual interferes with the development of intimacy between men: that they have not known what it means to love and care for a friend without "the shadow of some guilt and fear of peer ridicule" (Lewis 1978: 108). Men have been so alienated from each other that Jourard (1971) showed that self-disclosure, a vital component of emotional intimacy, was utterly lacking between males. Instead, young men knew that they had a friendship with another male when they did stuff together (Seiden and Bart 1975). Conversely, matters have been different for women. Women have maintained that they have a friend when they share emotions and, particularly, secrets together.

However, young men today do both. They make friends relatively easy, through doing things/stuff together (like sports, video games, drinking, exercising, shopping or eating), but they also have the opportunity to quickly form strong, deep emotional relationships based on emotional disclosure with one another.

This intimacy, the intimacy shown between heterosexual boys, both in the United States and the United Kingdom, is oftentimes self-labeled a "bromance." One athlete described a bromance as "like we are dating but really aren't." The "really aren't" part of this statement likely serves as a way of signifying that the relationship is emotionally deep, as it would be with a female, but that there is no sexual attraction. Simply described, a bromance is a love affair between two friends which omits sex.

These bromances have been documented in multiple studies investigating the contemporary nature of men's relationships (Anderson and McCormack 2015; Magrath 2016; McCormack 2012a; McCormack and Anderson 2014b). Finding evidence of the bromantic nature of contemporary adolescent male friendships is not difficult: all one has to do is log onto Facebook and befriend some of these men, for the love that young men show for one another today extends beyond their own private conversations. Social media, particularly Facebook, is bursting with florid emotions of young straight men showing their love for each other. They do this in multiple ways.

First, it is very common for young straight men to list that they are in "a relationship" with their best male friend. Ostensibly, this has the ability to publicly homosexualize one. It is not, for example, clear to those outside their immediate friendship network as to whether the "relationship status" means that one is in a homosexual or heterosexual same-sex love affair. Yet, because these young men live in a culture of inclusivity, this does not matter to them. For those who know the sexuality of the Facebook user offline, the act serves as a form of ironic heterosexual recuperation (McCormack and Anderson 2010a), but unlike heterosexual recuperation studies among men in their school settings (where their sexuality would be known to all), doing it on Facebook puts out a message to one's Facebook friends that one might not be straight. It is, at minimum, flirting with the privileging of homosociality over heterosexuality.

Another way that young men show their love is by listing their friends on Facebook as family members. Here, either they put down that their friends are "brothers," or they designate them with some other relationship or family label.

Again, to those outside their immediate networks, nobody would necessarily know that one was not a blood relative.

Finally, and most significantly, heterosexual youth today express their love for their male friends with hearts, and touching emotional statements to each other. These messages are free for all of their hundreds of Facebook friends to see. Thus, in posting messages of love to one another on Facebook, they are not afraid to be thought gay for their expressiveness; instead, they revel in it. Declarations of love and support posted on Facebook walls, as well as the posting of photos along with emoticon hearts are all commonplace activities.

Kissing other men

Multiple studies examining adolescent males have documented the significant growth of kissing on the lips among British undergraduate, school-aged and men in their twenties (Anderson, Adams and Rivers 2012). Eighty-nine percent of the young heterosexual men interviewed in the UK have, at least once, briefly kissed another heterosexual male on the lips (Anderson, Adams and Rivers 2012). These results did not include kissing one's father, kissing other men on the cheek (which occurs with regular frequency anyway) or kissing other men through team sport initiation rituals or hazing ceremonies (Nuwer 2001). Similar research was conducted on Australian men, showing that 29 percent had kissed another male in this fashion (Drummond et al. 2014). Research conducted on men in the US found the number to be 10 percent on the lips, and 44 percent on the cheek (Anderson, McCormack and Ripley forthcoming).

It can be hypothesized that kissing behaviors are increasingly permissible in Western cultures due to rapidly decreasing levels of cultural homohysteria, as well as the decrease of restricted physical and emotional boundaries of traditional heteromasculinity in educational settings. Accordingly, this has gradually assisted in the erosion of prevailing heterosexual hegemony—something Anderson (2014) describes as "the one-time rule of homosexuality."

The one-time rule of homosexuality

Heterosexuality has traditionally maintained hegemonic dominance in North American and Western European cultures, where privilege is unequally distributed according to one's perceived masculinity and sexuality (Anderson 2005a). That is, straight men with the highest degree of masculine capital tend to be rewarded, while those who break norms of heterosexual masculinity face prejudice and discrimination (Katz-Wise and Hyde 2012). In light of these harsh interpersonal consequences, heterosexual men and boys often fear being labeled as gay (Pollack 1998).

There are several ways in which men have traditionally avoided the stigma associated with being labeled as gay. Because male homosexuality is widely conflated with femininity (Johnson et al. 2007), heterosexual boys and men wishing to avoid stigma often act in distinctly non-feminine ways. For example, they generally do not work (Williams 1995) or play (Adams 2011) in feminized domains and they avoid engaging in feminine behaviors (Kimmel 1994), in order to uphold the perception that they are both heterosexual and masculine (i.e. heteromasculine).

Aside from engaging in overtly heteromasculine behavior, the concealment of discrete instances of and desires for same-sex physical intimacy may also help men to avoid being labeled as gay. This is because, in North American and Western European cultures, any intimate display with a same-sex partner is conflated with a homosexual identity (Parker 2009). In line with this logic, Almaguer (1993: 253) suggested that American and Western European cultures historically carry "a blanket condemnation of all same sex behavior . . . because it is at odds with a rigid, compulsory heterosexual norm." Lancaster (1988: 116) similarly argued "Even homosexual desires [in absence of behavior] stigmatize one as homosexual."

Borrowing from theories of racial hypodescent in which anyone with even a single drop of African ancestry was labeled as black (Harris 1964), Anderson (2008b) refers to the total behavioral avoidance of same-sex physical intimacy as the "one-time rule of homosexuality." According to the "one-time rule," men must avoid performing even a single act of same-sex sexual intimacy, or even having any same-sex sexual desire, in order to be considered heterosexual. This widespread norm precludes men from engaging in fairly extreme forms of same-sex intimacy (e.g. recreational sex with other men), but also from more moderate forms of physical homosocial tactility (e.g. kissing on the lips or cheek), if they wish to avoid being labeled as gay.

The presence of heterosexual men kissing on the lips represents slippage, an erosion of the one-time rule. The men in all the studies mentioned, regardless of whether they are located in the UK, Australia or America, are not thought gay for their kissing. Surprisingly, this slippage to the total hegemony of what it once meant to be heterosexual began not with those who opposed the orthodox masculinity of jocks, but it emerged from the jocks themselves.

Interpreting kissing

Statistical analysis indicates that the athletes in these studies engaged in significantly more kissing behaviors than non-athletes. This is likely as a result of both the fact that they maintain high degrees of heterosexual capital, and because sport promotes increased camaraderie and emotionality. Darren, a sixth-form student, said, "Kissing happens all the time in football [soccer]. Loads of guys kiss on the lips after scoring a goal; you'll see it on TV, too." Andy, who is a judo player, reported it also occurs in his sport. Will, a hockey player, commented that all athletes do it: "It's just part of sport now, isn't it?" Confirming this, Gary Neville's celebratory kiss on the lips of teammate Paul Scholes in 2010 caused much media attention. The *Guardian* even claimed that "by kissing Paul Scholes, Gary Neville declared war on homophobia" (MacInnes 2010: 67).

All of the men on the soccer team at another university said they had kissed. Grant said, "Yes. I kiss guys on the pitch. Guys I don't even know. And I'm not the only one." Grant added that he also kisses men on recreational teams, including men he is not close to. He said, "The first time it happened to me, I was 17, and I scored a goal. This guy ran over to me—some guy I didn't even know—and he just grabbed me and kissed me." When asked why kissing occurs in sport, he answered, "It's the energy of the moment. It's something that happens in moments of high emotion. It's normal in sport." These responses were mirrored by a number of athletes: the rationale, location and meaning behind these kisses did not substantially vary between them.

Several informants suggested that same-sex social kissing occurred among men in their community-based sports clubs, too. For example, when Alex (who played cricket for a community club) was asked about kissing, he responded, "Yeah, we go out with all the older cricket lot, and they are always kissing each other." He indicated, however, that he only kisses players that are his age. "Some of the older guys kiss each other, too; but I only kiss my mates." Ryan also stated that while players on his team range from 16 to 35, kissing only occurs among those aged around 26 and under. While this does not serve as systematic evidence of kissing occurring with regular frequency in other sport settings, it suggests that research on kissing in other locales and among other demographics of men would be interesting.

Those who did not kiss suggested that it was primarily because they did not socialize in these types of gatherings. There was also a context of it being more the jocks and lads that kissed, compared to less social or popular men. Andrew said, "No. I don't do that. I don't really go out. I don't have *those* kind of friends." Matt commented, "I know everybody does it, but I just don't have many friends here. I spend most of my time with my girlfriend . . . but I don't have a problem with it." This sentiment was reflected among the sixth-form students who did not kiss, too. As Jon said, "The athletes do that, yeah. But I'm not an athlete, and I don't go to their parties . . . but if I was part of that scene, I wouldn't be upset if another guy kissed me."

Of the 25 men who have not socially kissed in the British research (Anderson, Adams and Rivers 2012), none were opposed to it. Ricky joked:

> When I tell my mates what this interview was about, and they find out that I've not kissed a guy, you know what's going to happen? [referring to his belief that one of his friends would kiss him] . . . I'm not bothered by it . . . I'll let you know if it does, so that you can change your statistics.

Anderson received a text message from him later that night, reading, "I'm in the majority now."

One factor the men in this study shared was that they did not consider their kissing a sexual act. Instead, participants likened these types of brief kisses to a strong embrace or other exuberant ways of showing affection for a close friend, at appropriate times. Tim said, "It's no more a sexual act than kissing your father," and Tom argued, "It's like shaking hands. Well, it's more than that, but it's the same attitude."

For these young men, this type of kiss has been socially stripped of sexual significance. Whereas kissing a male friend on the lips would once be coded as a sexual
act, the symbolic meaning of kissing has been differently interpreted by the participants. Here, kissing was consistent with a normal operation of heteromasculine
intimacy. Highlighting this, when Pete was asked about which friends he kisses
and which he does not, he answered, "I wouldn't kiss just anyone. I kiss my good
mates." He continued, "You kiss a friend because there is no fear of being rejected;
no fear of being knocked back." And when Pete was asked about how he measured
who was worthy of being kissed, he said, "It's not that there is a system to who gets
it or not. Instead, it's a feeling, an expression of endearment, an act that happens to
show they are important to you."

A number of other men spoke of loving their friends ("mates"), too: kissing became a symbol of that platonic love. Mark said, "They [the kisses] happen
because you are the guy's mate. It's an, 'I love you, mate' type of kiss." Tim
agreed, "Kissing others guys is a perfectly legitimate way of showing affection
toward a friend." Ollie, a third-year engineering student, added, "You do it sometimes when out having a laugh with your mates, yeah. But I suppose it's also a
way to show how much we love each other, so we do it at home, too." When
asked if these kisses were performed any different in private, he said, "Not really.
No . . . You are more likely to pose for a camera when out and to perhaps play it
up. But the meaning is the same. It means you love him."

Contrary to heterosexual men having to physically and emotionally distance
themselves from one another, these informants seemed to appreciate emotional
intimacy. For those we interviewed, a same-sex kiss has been stripped of its homosexualizing significance and been re-coded as a symbol of platonic, heteromasculine
affection (McCormack and Anderson 2010b). A brief kiss, for the majority of these
British men, is now a heterosexual symbol of homosocial intimacy. Real close
friends, however, might do even more.

Many of the students said that they also engaged in *sustained* kissing with other
men. Of the 145 heterosexual men interviewed by Anderson, 48 said that they
have (and sometimes regularly) engaged in provocative displays of same-sex kissing,
which they described as being part of the repertory of jocular banter among friends.
This extended kissing may be enacted for shock value, even though data suggests
that this type of intimacy between heterosexual young men is now so common
that it does not seem to elicit the desired effect.

Overall, 12 (55 percent) of the 22 sport-related students and six (24 percent)
of the 25 non-sport-related students said they had engaged in a sustained kiss with
other men. By way of contrast, 17 (32 percent) of the 53 students interviewed exit-
ing the library and one of the seven graduate students reported similarly. At the
other university, 10 (63 percent) of the 16 soccer players, and two (9 percent) of the
22 sixth form students, said they had engaged in sustained kissing with another male.

Key to this form of intimacy, and relevant to this work, is the fact that these men
demonstrate a shared understanding that while they were not erotically attracted to
the men they kissed, they used kissing as a means of establishing intimacy, a close

bond of friendship. It is this type of shared meaning that permits sustained kissing (within a semi-public sphere) to remain acceptable within a heterosexual framework, regardless of how those outside their network understood this meaning.

The shared understanding that kissing does not have to be erotic permitted the young men in our study to avoid being thought gay for kissing—at least within university and college culture. This was sometimes even the case when engaging in sustained kissing with *gay* men. Some informants recalled kissing a gay friend "for fun," whilst other suggested he'd engaged in prolonged kissing with gay friends "just for laughs."

Sustained kissing is usually performed on nights out, when informants were under the influence of alcohol (see Peralta 2007; Roberts, Anderson and Magrath under review), particularly in England, where the legal age of alcohol consumption is 18—lower than in the US. A number of sixth-form students explain that kissing frequently occurs alongside alcohol consumption, because alcohol creates a social environment conducive for men to engage in sustained banter.

This is not, however, a universal phenomenon. Many informants explain that men did not kiss *because* of alcohol, and display no form of regret for their actions when sober, and nobody chastises anyone for being gay. Instead, these actions are widely celebrated. Some merely expressed that their desire to kiss one another was characterized by love for their friends.

Cuddling and spooning other men

Declining homophobia does not just restrict heterosexual men to kiss one another. Desiring to know the frequency of bed sharing, Anderson and McCormack (2015) interviewed 40 British heterosexual male students, finding that 39 of the 40 had slept in a bed with another male. These men oftentimes cuddle with the men they share beds with, too. McCormack (2012a) found the same occurring among sixth-form students in England, too. Anderson (2014) thus hypothesizes that sleeping with other men represents an act of homosocial, but not homosexual, physical and emotional intimacy between two (or more) ostensibly heterosexual males.

Sharing beds

Bed sharing that occurs between young men is sometimes "relatively" without contact, particularly before boys go to university. Guys go out drinking together, or just stay over at each other's places, and sleep in the same bed as a matter of convenience to avoid sleeping on a hard floor. Sleeping together is also helpful, particularly in England, where it is colder. Most British people do not run their heating at night, living in what Americans would consider very cold houses.

It is important to remember, however, that even when two men just "sleep" together in the same bed, it doesn't mean that there is no physical contact between them. Unlike American hotel beds, British beds are much smaller: what Americans call a "queen"-size bed, the British call "king"-sized. And nearly all students do not have this size bed in their rooms. The standard bed in university is called a "single." Americans will recognize this size as a bunk bed. It is just 36 inches wide (less than a meter). Beds in student homes are not much bigger, and most students also have a single bed (36 inches wide) or, if lucky, a double (54 inches wide). Rooms are small in the UK, thus the beds are too. Accordingly, almost any bed sharing necessitates not just some, but a good degree of, physical contact from one's sleeping partner.

Despite this, sleeping together in bed is normal for undergraduates in the UK. Tom provided an example of how one might end up doing such: "One time me and all my mates went out, and I ended up walking home to my best friend's and stayed at his because I couldn't be bothered to walk the rest of the way to mine." When Anderson asked what he did, he responded: "I asked if I could stay at his." Tom said that his friend said, "Yes," so he walked into his friend's house (who lived at home with his parents), entered his room, took his shirt and trousers (jeans) off, and that his friend (who was sleeping when he texted) opened up the covers to invite him in. Together the two men slept in their underwear until the next morning, though he was unsure if they had spooned or cuddled as he was drunk.

Most university athletes describe this sort of behavior as normal. "It's just what we do," one said, whilst another said: "There is nothing gay about it, we just love each other, and I tell him that so why wouldn't we sleep together?"

When asked how good a friend one has to be before one is comfortable sharing a bed. Stephen indicates that they do not need to be a close friend. Accordingly, he tells me he is unable to count how many times he has done it. "Just all the time," he said. Unlike Stephen, however, Anthony has only shared a bed a few times with a guy. "Just out of convenience," he told me. Anthony is therefore more judicious about whom he shares a bed with: "Only ever close mates where we are very comfortable with each other." These interviews therefore suggest that there is variance in how often guys sleep together, and this variance has to do not only with how comfortable one is sleeping with lesser-than friends, but also, and more importantly, variables to do with drinking and homosociality.

Interviews with undergraduates make clear that there is also no limit regarding the frequency one can sleep in a bed with the same male. One might think, for example, that if two men elected to sleep in the same bed with another male every night of the entire university year, others might suspect there was more going on than just sharing a bed. This does not, however, appear to be the case for Tom and Pete.

Tom and Pete share a bed and a room, in a house with three other rooms, and three other roommates. "We share a room to save money," Tom tells me. "But then again Pete is also my best friend. I love him. Why wouldn't I want to sleep with him?" I asked Tom if he worries people think he's gay for it. "Not at all, why would they?" he responded. "And do you cuddle?" He answered, "Yeah, like proper spoon," he said. "He's my best mate. It's a pleasure." He elaborated. "We have shared beds loads of time last year, and we thought why not save money and just share a room [bed] this year." By all accounts the arrangement has worked out well—not only have the two men saved a good deal of money on rent, but they independently indicate that they like sharing a bed, presumably for the same reason Abraham Lincoln shared a bed with James Speed for seven years—homosocial intimacy is enjoyable. Pete and Tom's bed sharing does, however, raise questions about how one navigates sexual desires, erections and issues of masturbation.

Threesomes

In recent research on heterosexual men having male-male-female threesomes, Scoats, Joseph and Anderson (forthcoming) interviewed thirty heterosexual, British, undergraduate men about threesomes, their friendships and the one-time rule of homosexuality. The prevalence of general threesome experience was that, after a year-and-a-half at university, ten out of the thirty had had a threesome. Although threesomes did not appear to be a dominant fantasy or component of undergraduate men's sexual lives, all but five were open to having one.

The rich sexual marketplace of the university appears to provide a good opportunity for this type of sexual exploration. Half of these men had a female-female-male (FFM) threesome, and the other a male-male-female (MMF) threesome. Still, all but five said they would have a male-male-threesome if the opportunity arose. These results indicate that the semi-sexual, same-sex interaction that comes with these threesomes (i.e. watching a friend ejaculate) is culturally normalized for these adolescent men. In this socio-historical context, the men were open to MMF threesome sex as yet another different and unique experience to partake in, as part of the thrill of consuming an alternative sexual practice.

The authors of the research therefore contextualize a MMF threesome as a homosocial rather than a homosexual experience. A MMF threesome is often viewed as something to be done before one dies, an experiment, and a means to bond with another male friend. Although participants did not demonstrate much interest in interacting sexually with another male in a MMF threesome, the majority did express a desire for the other man to be one of their bromances—one participant actually turned down a MMF threesome opportunity because it was not with his bromance. The capacity for men to have bromances may be a facilitating factor in men being open to MMF as being comfortable nude in the presence of another man, and explicit awareness of other male's sexual behaviors are often fostered within a bromance (Anderson 2014).

Cuddling other men

Of the 39 heterosexual undergraduate British men interviewed who had slept in the same bed as another male, 37 say that they have also cuddled with another male. Cuddling occurs in two locations: in bed and on the couch. Cuddling on the couch tends to occur during a nap or while watching a movie with a friend. Both types of cuddling are prolific among these men, and both types of cuddling seem to increase as one ages from school, to college/sixth form, and then into university life.

There are, of course, many variations on "cuddling," so defining it is important. For the purpose of this chapter, cuddling is counted as anything from one guy resting his head on another guy's shoulder while watching a movie, to purposeful spooning, where two men lie next to each other and one wraps his arms around the other and holds him tight. Both types are commonplace among undergraduates, but interviews with the university men indicate that the latter is less common for men before university. Some undergraduate men have cuddled more friends than they can remember, and others can recall each particular time. When I ask Sam, he says:

> It is very common for us to go out [late], and then the next day after class receive a text from someone saying something like "Do you want to come and nap," or often we'll just be watching a movie and I'd just put my head on whoever was next to me.

Matt discussed what I would describe as a typical sleeping/cuddling arrangement. He said his best friend, Connor, is his most frequently cuddling partner:

> I feel comfortable with Connor and we spend a lot of time together. I happily rest my head on Matt's shoulder when lying on the couch or hold him in bed. But he's not the only one. The way I see it, is that we are all very good and close mates. We have a bromance where we are very comfortable around each other and don't see anything wrong with sleeping in the same bed, or even showing that love in a club [dancing with and kissing other guys] or even just at uni during the day.

When Jarrett was asked about sleeping with other males he said, "I have literally done most things with a guy." He added:

> Me and my mates are pretty close, like emotionally. We let each other know everything so we always have a big hug when we leave . . . when a couple mates [from back home] came to stay at uni we had to share beds too, like two per bed. We always have a quick snuggle before sleeping.

Without being prompted, Jarrett repeatedly stressed the amount of cuddling he and his mates engage in: "We're always cuddling, my lot. We're all comfortable with each other." Others highlight that cuddling occurs during the day, too. Max said:

> I probably could talk a lot about this topic, actually. Cuddling is a standard part of my uni life, really. We, very often, have hangover cuddles and naps together. I have even done it today, actually. I really enjoy it! Seriously, I do it all the time.

When asked what a hangover nap is, it became clear that after a group of friends go out clubbing together, they divide up where they are going to sleep. Those who have "pulled" a woman have first choice of bed, and the others then sleep with their mates. But the next day, it is common to have friends over to just lie around, watching TV, playing video games and recovering from the previous night's drinking. This is where cuddling "feels good." "If your mate has a headache you can like massage his head, or you just lie there together holding each other and laughing about how awful you feel," Max said.

Cuddling also occurs in smaller, non-drunken events. Here, guys will give each other "a cuddle" which might be an extended hug, or a smudging of heads together. Smaller gestures serve as a way to show physical affection for a mate and they are important because they occur in public as well as private. One of my heterosexual graduate students summed it up best. He said that perhaps your friend is working hard on a paper, so you "come up from behind him, maybe give him a little kiss and a cuddle just to show you care."

An example of public cuddling comes from 16–18-year-old soccer players of an English Premier League who often go to the movies together, where they lie in the bean bags in the front row (Magrath, Anderson and Roberts 2015). They lie in them, together, like a giant game of Twister. This might be a new phenomenon and more research would be required to determine this, but at face value it seems that guys began cuddling in their rooms after drinking, which then extended to cuddling without alcohol, which then permitted other forms of cuddling (head on shoulder) in schools, the way McCormack (2012a) shows with sixth formers, and then perhaps the most recent advancement is cuddling in venues where others outside of their peer groups are present, like movie theatres.

While men do not always spoon when sharing a bed, it seems more frequent than not that when two undergraduates begin to sleep together there is at least a "quick cuddle" before going to sleep. This means that one guy throws an arm around another and squeezes, or maybe wraps a leg around his leg. Perhaps they let out a squirming giggle as a way to show that they are sort of mocking gay sex, or ironic heterosexual recuperation (McCormack and Anderson 2010a).

Yet cuddling for warmth and affection, without feigning homosexuality, is also quite normal. Here, men spoon, one lying on his side, holding the next on his side: one in front (little spoon) held by one at back (big spoon). Anderson examined the participants interviewed to see if there was a system of who gets to be the big spoon and who the little. But there does not seem to be. "It's just whatever," Anthony told me. Others confirmed. John said, "No, you don't talk about that, there are no rules or anything. Whatever happens, happens."

Thus, it appears that because the men are ostensibly both heterosexual, there is no issue of power at play in this cuddling arrangement; unlike their spooning with girlfriends, where the men are expected to be the big spoon, one is not emasculated for being the little spoon. Stephen said, "You switch sometimes. You know, one guy rolls over so you roll over and now it's your turn to hold him."

The closeness of two bodies, regardless of sexual orientation, raises issues of sexual arousal and erection, particularly given that some males wake with erections. When asked Sam about whether he fears getting an erection while sleeping with a mate he responded, "No. There are no worries about boners." He was then asked whether that meant he's not worried he will get one, or whether it meant that if he gets one it's not a big deal. "Of course you get them," he said; "every morning. It's not a problem."

Like the others, Jarrett said that he has no fear of getting an erection. "I've woken up with one before. We all have." He elaborated that if one is "fully awake" they make a joke of it: "All the boys piss themselves, maybe saying something like 'happy to see me or whatever.' We love it." He continued, "We're all close. We don't care about little things like that." Asked if he's ever felt another guy's erection poking him, he replied, "Yeah, it's not a problem. It happens, doesn't it?"

This method of dealing with erections might best be examined through the previously mentioned "ironic heterosexual recuperation" (McCormack and Anderson 2010a). Here, we show that by playing up to be gay, or joking about same-sex desires, heterosexual boys, ironically, are actually proclaiming that they are straight. It is a form of banter which is mutually understood to occur because there is trust in the fact that one's friends are what they say—heterosexual.

Other men are equally direct about erections. Stephen said: "It's 2013, we don't give anyone shit anymore." In fact, he suggests that there are no limitations in cuddling as to where guys touch each other. When asked, "Are there limitations as to where you can touch or hold?" He answered, "Never! Sometimes you grab his cock, sort of as a joke, particularly if he's got a semi going." Here, Stephen again illustrates how ironic heterosexual recuperation works. When I asked Stephen why he grabs another guy's cock he said, "It just relieves the tension." Accordingly, grabbing another guy's erect cock serves as a way of saying: I know you have a hard-on but it's no big deal. Stephen added, "It's not like you're going to wank him." He added, "You can rest your hand on his leg, or his hand, or wherever. There are no limitations." Sam said that he does the same: "Yeah, we hold hands loads."

Another undergraduate was asked, "So if you're lying on the couch, snuggling, and you are holding hands, is the hand-holding banter/a joke, or is that genuine affection?" "Banter," he first answered before saying, "Like we love each other to pieces, though. We don't have to hold hands to show each other that. We always tell each other we love each other, too." He later told me, "but you only hold his hand because you love him. Banter is how you show love." Asked if when the banter ended, the hands remained held, he answered, "Of course." It then became clear that when one holds another male's hand, he often initiates it with banter (i.e. "Hey, honey I'm gonna hold your hand now"). The other male returns the banter (ironic heterosexual recuperation) and then they just hold hands.

Cuddling gay male friends

Cuddling is not automatically limited to heterosexual male friends, either. Both gay men and straight men tell me that cuddling is sometimes part of their friendship behaviors. James, who is gay, tells me that he cuddled with a straight male friend: "He's just a friend, not like a best friend, and it only happened once so far.

But yeah, we slept in the same bed. No big deal." He was asked if he engaged in other forms of cuddling or physically tactile behaviors with straight males. "Yeah, I guess," he answered. "I sat on my friend's knee the other day, is that what you mean?" He told me that these types of behaviors are pretty common among his straight friends: "They don't treat me any different, if that's what you're asking about?"

For another gay male, Charles, these behaviors are so normal that he thinks that they are of little interest or value to me. When he told Anderson about being held by one of his straight mates for a few minutes before falling asleep on the same couch after a party he said, "I was really drunk, and so was he. And it was a group of us in the room, so maybe my story wouldn't be so great?"

Andrew found that cuddling served as a mechanism to help his straight mates bond with him. Supporting Anderson's notion that inclusive masculinities proliferate at his university, he said:

> So I had two friends [who were also his flatmates] who I would say embraced lad culture as if it was a big joke. So sort of like anti-lads. Like they would talk about women, drink and such. However, when face to face with women they treated them with respect. It was all for show indoors. I guess that helps set their personalities a bit in perspective. They both have had girlfriends, brought girls home. When drunk I see them looking at girls. And they knew I was gay and that I thought they were attractive.

Andrew said that one night early in his freshman year one of these guys came into his room to chat. After talking about what they like, sexually, Andrew said that he likes cuddling with guys after sex. At this point, his roommate said, "I love cuddling." His friend took Andrew down to the bed, and spooned with him, while they continued to chat. This opened the door for other straight men in his flat to cuddle with him, too. In describing his two closest friends in the dorm (of eight people) he said, "So for one I was big and the other I was little spoon. Sometimes we did three-way spoons."

As with the homosocial straight men's cuddles, Andrew said, "But none of it was sexual, we literally just chatted as if it was normal, nothing out of the ordinary." He added, "But yeah, this would happen every other week for a year." He said, "One of my roommates came to my fancy dress party dressed as a spoon," assumedly a way of publicly owning his spooning with a gay male.

Finally, just as straight men told me that they, as a matter of course, gain erections while sleeping with other males, matters were obviously no different for Andrew. He told me that one time the cuddling just became too sexual for him. "With all three of us in our underwear, in a three-way spoon, me in the middle, it was really just too much. I got too turned on and just had to leave." He said that the two straight boys laughed about it, seemingly taking pride in the fact that they had turned Andrew on, and they continued to cuddle each other after he left the room.

Relaxing the straight male anus

The sexual and gendered lives of young, heterosexual males are in rapid flux (Anderson, Scoats and McCormack forthcoming; McCormack, Wignall and Anderson forthcoming; Ripley et al. 2011) millennial men are rapidly casting off traditional sexual and gendered views (Anderson 2012b, 2014). Research into straight men also shows that the diminishment of the one-time rule of homosexuality means that straight men are more open to their own anal pleasuring than ever before. In research on American undergraduate men, Branfman, Stiritz and Anderson (forthcoming) provide the first ever data on the prevalence of heterosexual men's anal receptivity to fingers and toys.

Whereas research from the last few decades showed that straight male's anuses being penetrated or even stimulated (i.e. if a female partner rims him) constructed the ass/anus as a queered body part that caused the male dissonance, the majority of respondents did not consider receptive anal play the exclusive domain of gay men; nor did they see anal play as a sign of gayness or failed manhood. In fact, we show that 24 percent had experienced anal sex, and few men associated heterosexual men enjoying anal sexual experiences as homosexualizing.

The American difference

When it comes to cuddling, like in every other aspect of homosocial love, American teenagers lag behind the British. For example, in 2013, Eric Anderson interviewed (over Facebook) ten members of a high school boys cross country team that he coached in California over the summer. They indicate that they have few sleepovers, but when they do, the friend sleeps on a couch or the floor. This greatly varies compared to ten British males of the same age that he interviewed. Garrett, who is 16 and American, said that he isn't allowed to sleep over at friends' houses because his dad doesn't trust him: "He thinks I'd do stupid shit to get in trouble." Still, Garrett said that if he could sleep over at a friend's, and his best friend did want to sleep in the same bed, he would have no problem with that. Still, he wouldn't cuddle.

It would be hard to describe Garrett as homophobic—not only did he socialize alone with Anderson during the research process, but he actively advocates for gay rights on his Facebook profile, and has several gay male friends. Ultimately, he doesn't really have an answer as to why he wouldn't want to cuddle with his best friend, but homophobia is not a possible answer. Nor does it stem from a lack of ability to show affection to other males. Like others on this team, Garrett is highly expressive with his emotions, letting his friends know that he loves them. His Facebook wall is full of expressions to his friends about loving them.

Joseph, 18, is an American athlete who has slept at a friend's house "a few times." Still, he has never slept in the same bed with another male on one of these sleepovers. When I asked where he sleeps, he said, "I'm comfortable anywhere, so usually like on a couch or the floor or something." And when I asked Tim if he would sleep in the same bed if his best friend were to ask him to, he said,

"I'd maybe say no. I don't know. I've never been in that situation before." Despite this fear of physical affection, Joseph is clear to state that he expresses his love for his best friends in person. When I asked him if he tells his best friend that he loves him, he responded, "All the time."

These cultural differences can be attributed to the Anglo-American disparity—what teenagers do in the United States compared to the United Kingdom homohysteria. Evidencing this, Tony, 18, another runner who has been highly vocal about his pro-gay stance, said that while he's only spent the night at a friend's house "a couple of times" in his four years of high school, he has never slept with a friend in the same bed. Like the others interviewed, he's highly expressive about his affection for his friends verbally, but does not sleep in the same beds or cuddle with them. When asked why he has not slept in the same bed with a friend he answered, "I don't know. I wouldn't be comfortable with it."

So we essentially have two sets of teenagers—one British, the other American— both with highly positive attitudes toward gay males, and both of whom express their affection verbally and through digital media, like Facebook. Yet in the UK teenagers readily sleep in the same bed with their friends, and usually cuddle/ spoon as part of that, and in the US the friend sleeps on the floor. This illustrates the power of homohysteria to shape cultural behaviors, even after the meanings of those behaviors have been lost.

In other words, this is a matter of cultural lag (see Ogburn 1957). The teenagers in America interviewed don't know why they do what they do; it is an artifact of men from a previous generation who avoided sharing a bed with another male because it was a sign of homosexual desire. Or more aptly put, refusing to share a bed, or cuddle a friend, was a way of saying, "I'm not gay." Yet, three of the men I interviewed here are regular members of the Gay-Straight Alliance at their school, and thus do not fear homosexual suspicion. A cultural lag of homohysteria seems the only viable explanation.

Still, research on university American undergraduates shows that men do sleep together, perhaps not as often, and with considerably less cuddling, but they do willingly share beds. There is a lack of data on American undergraduate athletes to assess what percent of them are cuddling. This should form the basis of future research.

Finally, one of the men interviewed on the American cross country team was just 15, yet he (the youngest of the Americans interviewed) does sleep over at his friend's house. Here, he tells me that he sleeps on the couch, usually with another male. Sometimes, he said, legs or arms will touch. He is gay. So perhaps the cultural lag of homohysteria is already dissipating.

A culture of overt support from heterosexual teammates does not mean that the presence of a gay male on the team might not disrupt the normal, homosocial operation of an otherwise homogenous team. Masculinity studies have long determined that heterosexual masculinity is a front which is essentially granted by other men (Kimmel 1994). Here, males seek the approval of other males, both identifying with and competing against them in order to raise their heteromasculine capital (Anderson 2005a).

Using images from Ibson's (2002) *Picturing Men*, Anderson (2009a) demonstrates the changing nature of physical intimacy, and the gradual awareness of homosexuality as a static sexual identity which led to elevated forms of cultural homophobia. Anderson (2009a: 82) comments that Ibson's work details images of athletes from before the 1920s, as well as

> [f]riends, servicemen, brothers, collegiate and prep school boys in many settings lavishly dressed, provocatively undressed, arms wrapped around each other, embracing, lying in piles, sleeping in the same beds, holding hands and sitting on each other's laps in order to show their affection for one another.

The images Ibson (2002) displays highlight an increasing rigidity, with later pictures showing limited physical contact between boys and men. Indeed, in periods of high homohysteria, demonstrations of physical intimacy are relegated to playing teamsports—soft tactility (hand-holding, soft hugging, caressing, or nonsexual kissing) is culturally prohibited, and results in homosexualization.

Homosociality and homosexual camaraderie for men

Physical interactions between friends and fellow teammates have also occurred in alternate ways. Much of this also includes the playful, direct, overt and sometimes ironic establishment of one's heterosexuality through sexualized discourse and banter, which oftentimes includes men feigning gay sex with one another (Diamond, Kimmel and Schroeder 2001). Anderson (2014) argues that mock gay sex is the predominant way for heterosexual young men to show banter with one another.

Here, young heterosexual men—normally in private spaces like parties, hotel rooms and, most frequently, locker rooms—pretend to be sexually attracted to one another. In jest, they complement each other's bodies, or make jokes about being sexually attracted to their teammates. They might, for example, comment that one looks good in that towel, or smack one's arse as a gesture of artificial homosexual attraction. Still, it is highly common for homosocial groups of young straight men to pretend to give each other oral sex, and there is also a great deal of mock anal sex in these interactions (Schroeder 2002), as well as boys lying atop one another, often wearing nothing but a pair of shorts. Some men also pretend to masturbate together, often under the sheets. All these activities also involve screaming and moaning in imaginary ecstasy (Anderson 2014).

This type of behavior is documented in both interview and ethnographic research among adolescent, heterosexual team sport players on sex-segregated teams (Anderson 2005b, 2009a; Anderson and McGuire 2010; Flood 2008; Magrath, Anderson and Roberts 2015). Adams and Anderson's (2012) ethnographic research of a university football team showed that before, during and after one of its players had publicly come out, mock gay sex operated between gay and straight men, with the purpose of including gay men, and showing their support

(Anderson 2005a). Exemplifying this, in a forthcoming article, Anderson shows that among a group of fifty adolescent boys he coaches in California (with three openly gay teammates), straight athletes feign sexual interaction with gay athletes as a symbolic gesture of acceptance.

Interactions of mock gay sex can be interpreted in different ways. One might, for example, view it as a homophobic mocking of gay men, while others might prefer to view it as a method for ironically showing that one is not gay in a culture of homohysteria (Anderson, Adams and Rivers 2012). Anderson (2014) suggests that many argue that the various forms of homosocial love between two straight men is not a genuine act of friendship or love, but merely a means to mock gay men. Some scholars view it as a mechanism for the degradation of women (Sedgwick 1985; Dunning and Sheard 1979), although is perhaps unsurprising given the era in which this previous research was undertaken. Anderson (2014) further states that many of the men he interviewed who regularly engage in homosocial love are insulted when asked if their behavior is intended to mock gay men. Pretending to fuck a gay male friend is, ironically, a way of saying, "I'm straight, but I celebrate your difference." Therefore, perhaps the most apt view can be explained by McCormack's (2012a) discussion of ironic heterosexual recuperation in Chapter 8.

Homosociality and homosocial camaraderie for women

The matter is slightly different for women's sports. Unlike the 'one-drop' rule which is associated with straight men becoming gay after just one experience, for women, it is slightly different. In teamsports, one lesbian on the team can infect the team in a slightly adapted use of the one-drop rule. In this case, imagine one drop of orange squash put into a glass of water making the whole glass become orange. This is the effect that one lesbian has on a team they cast suspicion onto their teammates (Hargreaves 2000). Griffin (1998) examines how heterosexual athletes therefore distance themselves from lesbians in teams so as not to cast suspicion upon themselves. However, she also acknowledges that without heterosexual allies, changes within women's sport will not occur, as there is a divide between heterosexual and homosexual players.

In a study of 31 openly lesbian athletes, this distancing effect and the one-drop rule appear to have diminished. This can be seen by the number of heterosexual teammates going out to gay and lesbian bars. Some athletes noted how previously the team had previously split on nights out so that the heterosexual teammates did not have to go to gay bars. However, it now appears that athletes enjoy socializing with their teammates regardless of their sexuality. Susan suggested that her teammates "love it" in gay bars and this was not unusual. With the idea that associations with lesbian teammates could cast suspicion on their own sexuality, it could be assumed that heterosexual athletes would not want to enter into gay bars.

However, this was not the only change: it appears as though the behavior of athletes has also changed. One participant, Brooke, notes that her heterosexual teammates openly discuss their crushes on other players. They also acknowledge jealously when one of their teammates has an attractive opponent. Brooke notes "[They] say something along the lines, 'Oh, make sure you give her some contact.'" This was one of numerous stories that this particularly player had about the behavior of her heterosexual teammates.

Conversations about bodies also show that there is a change in culture in women's sport. One rugby player noted that some of her heterosexual teammates "comment on each other's boobs or bums or something like that so it is really good fun." This sort of behavior shows that the fear of the lesbian label is no longer evident, as commenting on other players in the shower could amount to homosexuality. It appears as though the distancing effect of heterosexual athletes has been diminished in line with the decline of cultural homophobia. However, it is clear that there needs to be more research carried out on heterosexual women to discover if the same effects as we've seen in men can be found.

10
COOLING DOWN

Organized sport emerged at a particular historical moment in the West—a time in which society was gradually recognizing that homosexuality existed as an immutable, unchangeable characteristic, and a time in which women were beginning to campaign for equality. This led to a turn-of-the-twentieth-century moral panic, when society feared that young men were becoming weaker, softer, more feminine and, thus, homosexual.

It was this moral panic which, among other reasons, helped to justify sporting activity for young males. Sports were not only culturally promoted because they were perceived as being able to build positive attributes in young boys' lives that would be useful as they became workers in an industrial economy, as well as being useful in war (i.e. teaching the "value" of sacrificing oneself for the team and being complicit to authority). But sports were erroneously presumed capable of turning young men away from softness, weakness and femininity, which were conflated with homosexuality. This, combined with masses migrating from rural areas to cities, gave sport a robust start.

By the turn of the twentieth century, sport had emerged as a near-compulsory activity for young boys. Women, on the other hand, were considered both incapable of taking part in sports, and pathologized out of playing them. This was perhaps a strategic ploy to combat the first wave of feminism at the time. This is why we say that sport was designed against gay men and women. However, sport would not remain immune to the "intrusion" of those that it was designed against.

The last decades of the twentieth century saw an insurgence of women demanding and playing competitive sports. Our institutions of education began to facilitate their gender-segregated play (oftentimes through legal force). Yet, despite lesbians being attracted to competitive sport, the total control of coaches over athletes (that is required if one wants to make a team, stay on a team, and be promoted within the field of sport), exasperated by a culture which promotes sports so thoroughly that athletes negate their agency and subscribe to even an oppressive team ethos, meant that sport was made accessible to heterosexual women only. Lesbian women played, and their presence was undeniable, but they remained so invisible that Griffin called it, "A silence so loud it screams" (1998: 139). Accordingly, few women came out while actively playing sport, and hardly any men.

Research into the experiences of gay and lesbian athletes in sport

Until recently, there was little academic research exploring the relationship between mainstream sport and homosexuality. This was perhaps a dual effect of the high homophobia of the twentieth century, which kept gay and lesbian athletes closeted, and thus unable to be studied, and perhaps a lack of research interest, as there have historically been exceptionally few openly gay male athletes (from any level of sport) and even fewer openly lesbian professional athletes to study.

The first substantial research project on the topic for men, by sociologist Brian Pronger (1990), had to be conducted solely with closeted athletes because he could find no openly gay athletes to interview. Among those he interviewed, Pronger cited a culture of verbal harassment about homosexuality, such that gay men were afraid to emerge from their closets.

While there was similar work on the homosexualization of female athletes in sport (i.e. Blind and Taub 1992) and the stigma against lesbians among straight female athletes, the first major work on the experience of openly lesbian athletes came with Pat Griffin's (1998) work. She found that, despite the fact that there were a number of sports overly represented by lesbians, there was still a great deal of homophobia and heteronormativity at play.

Unfortunately, Griffin's groundbreaking work represents the last empirical research on the topic of lesbians in ostensibly heterosexual sport, until Anderson and Bullingham (2013) published their work (using data collected in the early 2000s) on the experiences of openly lesbian high school and college athletes in the United States. Here, they showed that while homophobia was decreasing, there was no universal pattern for the treatment of openly lesbian athletes. Some were accepted onto their teams, while others were met with hostility. How good an athlete was at their sport appeared to have influence on who came out, just as it did in Anderson's earlier (2002) research on gay men. Heterosexism was also prominent. Teammates were often okay knowing that a teammate was lesbian, but they did not want to hear about it, and they certainly did not want to see it.

By the time that sociologist Eric Anderson, in 2000, began his research into the experiences of male athletes who were out of the closet, cultural matters had improved to the point that some were beginning to come out. Anderson published the first ever research on openly gay male athletes in 2002. Of the 26 American collegiate athletes studied from across the spectrum of teamsports offered in high schools and universities, it was found that they largely reported positive coming-out stories and acceptance among teammates. The caveat of importance to this research was, however, that only athletes who were the best on their teams were coming out. While this hinted at social progress toward the inclusion of gay men in sport, all of the athletes reported that they were anxious about telling their teammates that they were gay, as they perceived sport to be a homophobic institution. This is best theorized as a culture of fear. They were concerned with being socially excluded, verbally abused and physically assaulted, even though none of this happened after coming out. In fact, coming out was much easier than anticipated, and these same athletes framed their experiences as positive. When asked if they would have changed anything, most mentioned how they had wished to come out to their teammates earlier.

However, the gay athletes' experiences of coming out in the first two years of the new millennium were not wholly positive. The majority of the athletes we interviewed included stories of heteronormativity. Principally, this came in the form of a mutually agreed upon "don't ask, don't tell" policy. Here, straight male athletes said that sport was not the place to bring one's personal life into, and gay male athletes agreed. Yet the policy was applied unequally. This was an unofficial policy in which heterosexual athletes were open and free to discuss their girlfriends and explicitly talk about heterosexual activities, but gay athletes were not extended the same liberty to discuss their boyfriends or gay sex. When this was pointed out to the gay male athletes, they largely claimed that they did not want to make a big deal of their homosexuality or *force it upon* their heterosexual teammates. Despite this silencing, gay male athletes of the time saw their experiences as largely positive, precisely because they expected them to be awful: if one expects to get an F on a test and instead receives a C, it's a relief, compared to if one expects to get an A and instead receives a C.

Anderson followed up this initial (2002) research by interviewing yet more openly gay male athletes, as well as interviews from closeted and ex-professional athletes. This cumulated data was analyzed in his (2005a) publication of *In the Game: Gay Athletes and the Cult of Masculinity*. Here, he found that athletes still feared coming out, even though none were abused after coming out. Importantly, he also wrote about how homophobia appeared to be decreasing rapidly in the wider culture. He theorized that as this progressed, eventually, sport would either have to change its attitude toward the existence of openly gay and lesbian athletes, or it would be viewed as an archaic relic of an outdated and unpopular way of thinking.

The above-mentioned books and articles are not exhaustive of all of the research published on the experiences of gays and lesbians in sport. There is, for example, a good deal of research published on the experiences of sexual minorities in gay and lesbian organized sporting leagues. Jarvis (2006) for example, has looked at the experiences of gay men's softball as well as—uniquely—the experiences of 12 heterosexual men's participation in gay sports clubs (Jarvis 2015); Symons (2010) has traced the history of the Gay Games; Wellard (2006) has examined a gay men's tennis team; Owen (2006) a gay men's rowing team; Price and Parker (2003) a gay men's rugby team and both Jones and McCarthy (2010) and Willis (2014) have examined the extent of gay men's football. Yet, none of these examine the experiences of gay and lesbian athletes in otherwise heterosexual leagues. In other words, they have not examined gay men or lesbians in school-based or university-based sports.

Stigmatizing homophobia, not homosexuality

In retrospect, Anderson (2005a) was correct. The intervening decade between his 2005 research and this book's publication has seen tremendous social progress on cultural attitudes toward all aspects of homosexuality. On June 13, 2013 PEW research found that 70 percent of those born after 1980 support same-sex marriage, and 74 percent of these Americans believe that "homosexuality should be accepted by society." A host of other academic and pollster research shows that homophobia is no longer socially acceptable in Anglo-American culture. This is particularly true of youth (the age demographic that is of concern to openly gay and lesbian athletes).

Supporting this, Smith, Son and Kim (2014) find that there is between a 20.1 and 23.4 percentage point difference in people's attitudes toward homosexuality and gay rights for those under 30 compared to those over 65. They argue this is due to their cohort—their generation—and not the result of processes of ageing.

In the UK, similar trends of inclusivity have emerged. In the 2013 British Social Attitudes Survey, only 22 percent of respondents claimed that homosexuality was *always wrong*, down from 64 percent in 1987. In 2012, the *Guardian* newspaper reported that 62 percent of British citizens supported the legalization of same-sex marriage (Clark and Sparrow 2012), and this was before the gay marriage law passed in the UK. By 2014, a BBC poll showed that this figure was as high as 68 percent (Piggot 2014). This was significantly higher for young people, with both these surveys reporting that the figure for those in support under the age of 35 was over 75 percent.

Gay marriage—which is now just called marriage—was made legal in the United States the next year, 2015. Showing support for this, an *ABC News/ Washington Post* opinion poll (Langer 2013) shows support for gay marriage across the US was at 58 percent a few years ago. We would expect to see a significant bump in that figure after the Supreme Court ruled in favor of gay marriage. As things stand, the polls highlight a shift of 26 percentage points since 2004, and that the number of people who think homosexuality is a choice has decreased from 40 percent to 24 percent, while those who think it is "just the way they are" has increased from 49 percent to 62 percent. Again, the statistic of importance concerns youth, as PEW found that 70 percent of millennials (those born after 1990) support same-sex marriage in the US, and 74 percent of these Americans believe that "homosexuality should be accepted by society." The following year they found more striking results: that 85 percent of American Catholics under the age of 29 support gay equality, and 75 percent support gay marriage (PEW 2013).

The most recent academic research on attitudes toward homosexuality is startling. Research in the *American Sociological Review* also highlights the dramatic change in attitudes toward homosexuality. In a national survey of just over a thousand people, Doan, Loehr and Miller (2014) found that almost 100 percent of heterosexuals supported legal equality for gays and lesbians. This is reflected in other academic research, too. In the US, Keleher and Smith (2012: 1324) show that *all* demographic groups have become increasingly tolerant of homosexuality since 1991, arguing that "we are witnessing a sweeping change in attitudes toward lesbians and gay men." Clements and Fields (2014: 541) document a similar shift in the UK, showing that attitudes toward homosexuality have rapidly improved since the early 1990s, and "accelerated following the millennium, especially during the second half of the first decade of the 2000s." With this rapid, and increasing, cultural support for gays and lesbians, the question we had before embarking upon the research in this book was this: was Anderson right? Did sport (i.e. those who play and maintain the games institutionalized within Anglo-American culture) bend to also include gay and lesbian athletes?

Gay and lesbian athletes in high school, university and community sporting leagues

The research in this book contributes to two bodies of knowledge. The first concerns that of sport, but the results are also significant for the social movement of gay and lesbians more broadly. Fundamentally, if gays and lesbians can play openly in otherwise heterosexually dominated sport, if they are welcomed and celebrated too, then it shows that one of the pillars of hypermasculinity, homophobia and misogyny is not immune to rapid social change. Given that the US military (the last to hold out of the 28 NATO countries in permitting gay soldiers) now also permits gay and lesbians to serve openly, sport is often viewed as a last holdout for homophobia among Western institutions (along with fundamentalist religious churches).

The results of our research paint a positive portrait of the experiences of gay and lesbian athletes, at high school-, university- and community-based levels of sport. We cannot, however, speak to the conditions of youth coming out in grade school-based sports (and we later speak to professional sports players). This is for several reasons: those who remain highly afraid of coming out, or those who do not yet know they are gay, are not able to be interviewed. Furthermore, it would be more difficult (perhaps impossible) to get ethical approval to discuss this with youth under 16. Thus, apart from one article on Outsports.com about a young tennis player (and a subsequent interview with him) and his positive coming-out story, there is just no data for us to draw conclusions from.

Considering sport at the other levels of analysis, we preface our findings about gay and lesbians with an important caveat—declining homophobia is not an even social process. Overt homophobia is declining (or non-existent) in some locales, and perhaps less so in others. Whereas we would be hard pressed to believe that homophobia is on the rise in the United States, the United Kingdom or most other Western countries, we do not suggest that homophobia is absent in all geographical locations within these countries.

Our research is also limited in a number of obvious and not so obvious ways. For example, our research is necessarily limited to studying those who have already come out. We cannot study those who do not want to tell us that they are gay or lesbian. This makes finding closeted gay and lesbian athletes difficult (but not impossible). Still, we have not interviewed closeted athletes for this research. This is for two reasons.

First, the last research on closeted gay male athletes (Anderson 2005a) showed that gay athletes had a great deal of fears before coming out, but that once they did, those fears did not materialize. We do not believe that the substantial nature of 'fear' in coming out has changed much. There is thus little reason to research a phenomenon that is likely to have not changed. The same is true of research on lesbian athletes who remain closeted (Griffin 1998). We know the basic reasons why closeted athletes do not come out in sport: homophobic coaches, teammates, or administrators; fears that word will get back to parents, or just fears that they will not be viewed as one of the "boys" (or "girls") anymore. For a more nuanced discussion of the fears athletes maintain in coming out, we recommend reading Eric Anderson's (2005a) or Pat Griffin's (1998) works.

Second, we have taken the strategic decision to interview athletes who are out of the closet because it is those athletes who will provide the best data as to our general understandings of identity management and homophobia in culture more broadly. Our research is thus based in an area where we expect to see change: the experiences of openly gay and lesbian athletes.

Our findings were mostly positive. In some incidents, extremely heart-warming levels of acceptance and celebration of sexual diversity were evident. Whereas athletes used to believe that sport had elevated levels of homophobia compared to society as a whole, today's athletes see their sports teams as safe spaces for gay men. Whereas the gay athletes of the 1980s and 1990s needed to be athletically superior to open up about their sexuality, today's gay athletes don't need a cloak of athletic capital to protect them from victimization. The openly gay athletes that we found for interview were not statistically over-representative of being central to the outcome of their team's success, either; consequently, they held considerably less athletic ability compared to those a decade earlier. This implies that gay or lesbian athletes no longer feel that they need to be the best on their teams in order to have a successful coming out.

Our research also suggests that, when a gay or lesbian athlete opens up about their homosexuality today, their teammates value the disclosure of a personal matter in a similar way to close friends sharing secrets. They feel privileged, honored and trusted with the disclosure. Accordingly, many teammates respond by also disclosing personal information.

There is also a great deal of evidence that one's coming out draws teammates closer together, that coming out as gay or lesbian on a team can promote a team's level of cohesion (Adams and Anderson 2012).

Further, openly gay and lesbian athletes today largely evade the conditions "don't ask, don't tell" on their teams. They openly talk about partners, discussions of homosexual sex and chat about who they think is attractive. They are often encouraged into these conversations by their heterosexual teammates. This open discussion about sexuality not only affords heterosexual athletes a chance to learn about a previously taboo subject, but also creates a culture of inclusion for gay and lesbian athletes.

The positive experiences of gays and lesbians in sport is supported by a considerable degree of research into the attitudinal disposition of teamsport athletes and their views on homosexuality. Here, cultural homophobia has impacted those within sport as much (perhaps more) as those outside of sport. Longitudinal surveys in the UK, for example, show year after year of incoming athletes to a university maintaining positive dispositions toward gay and lesbian athletes (Bush, Carr and Anderson 2012). Collectively, we argue that it is no longer acceptable to assume that athletes are homophobic. Saying otherwise would be to do so without systematic evidence. This is what we call prejudice.

But despite this, there is still an assumption that many heterosexual athletes continue to harbor homophobic attitudes. In fact, many researchers hear the results that we present here in academic conferences and say to us, "but what about . . . ?" They follow this question with whether we have studied this among BME groups, or lower-class, or school-leavers or [insert demographic here], with the expressed assumption that these groups will not yield the same progressive results if studied. Thus, what they are really doing is assuming higher rates of homophobia, without evidence. We answer this question by asking "Are you telling me that Asian people are more homophobic than white people?" Finally, others assume homophobia because they have retained an emotive example of extreme homophobia. For example, at one conference in Cardiff, Wales, a full professor said, "I don't believe homophobia is declining, what about Matthew Shepard?" Our response was that his horrific murder occurred twenty years ago and 9,000 miles away. Finally, a 50-year-old academic once said, "I can't believe that football fans are not homophobic, I grew up in Northern Ireland and my family were always homophobic at matches." The point is, academics (particularly) feel free to assume homophobia, without recognizing that they are being prejudiced.

Gays and lesbians in professional sport

The story of these progressive sporting attitudes is significantly different from athletes of only a couple of decades ago. The decreasing levels of cultural homophobia have afforded gay athletes the ability to be open, accepted and highly esteemed in contemporary sports teams. Regardless of their athletic ability, they are normally welcomed, valued and oftentimes popular team-members in sports across modern Anglo-American society.

This might seem at odds with the fact that few openly gay men exist at the professional levels of certain sports. But examining this level of sport is counterproductive to understanding what is occurring at the level of sport where millions play. Nonetheless, addressing the most popular professional sports (of which only 3,500 play in the US), the research highlights that there is no evidence that competitive, professional teamsport athletes maintain higher rates of homophobia than men in the general population. We doubt female athletes are more homophobic than female non-athletes, too. Evidence from surveys taking on female athletes in the UK (Bush, Carr and Anderson 2012) shows homophobia to be non-existent.

Furthermore, there is a trickle of gay men coming out at this level of sport. Since the beginning of the second decade of the twenty-first century, athletes have come out at an accelerated rate, including within professional sports: soccer (Robbie Rogers), American football and then the Canadian Football League (before removing himself from play for undisclosed reasons) (Michael Sam), basketball (Jason Collins), rugby union (Gareth Thomas), rugby league (Keegan Hirst), cricket (Stephen Davies), boxing (Orlando Cruz), power lifting (Chris Morgan). Famous lesbian athletes include: Casey Stoney (soccer), Britany Griner (basketball), Kate and Helen Richardson-Walsh (field hockey), Megan Rapinoe (soccer), Michele Van Gorp (basketball).

Finally, there is an endless tide of heterosexuals in professional sport not only accepting gay men in sport, but oftentimes campaigning for it: think of former rugby union international Ben Cohen (see Chapter 7) for evidence. One only needs to examine the website Outsports.com for more examples.

Still, when most think of "homophobia in sport," they think of men's sport, and they think of professional sport. And while there are some who are out in these sports, they are not statistically representative of the population, which is about 3 percent gay male (Laumann 1994). This is for four reasons. First, gay men in these leagues may sometimes remain silent about their sexuality because of (real or imagined) homophobia. There is little (if any) modern evidence of this. Second, gay men choose not to play these types of sports in the first place. There is considerable evidence for this when one considers the over-representation of gay men in music, the arts, theatre, film and dance, and other, feminized, sports.

Third, athletes may fear coming out publicly because of repercussions in non-Western countries where harsh laws exist against homosexuality, such as Russia and Qatar, the hosts for the next two FIFA World Cups in 2018 and 2022. Fourth, and finally, gay men might just not be physically demonstrative enough to play sport to the point of equal representation to the percent of gay men in culture at the professional level of combative sports. This speaks to biological differences between gay and straight males (LeVay 2010). In addition to physiological differences supporting this contention (Bailey 2003), it might help to suggest why lesbian athletes are highly over-represented in sports. It may very well be that those who are attracted to men (regardless of sex) are less apt, and those who are attracted to women (of either sex) are more apt at the types of sport that we culturally value.

While no conclusive evidence exists for any of these hypotheses, evidence suggest that the lack of representation of gay men in football, basketball, baseball and hockey might be a combination of all three. For example, gay American high school students are more likely to self-select out of macho sports than straight (the non-participation hypothesis); gay men are strongly over-represented in other activities like dancing, ice-dancing, diving, theatre, art, music, etc. (the non-participation hypothesis), and this over-representation necessarily means that gay men must be under-represented elsewhere. Once in sport, they may elect not to come out to the press because of international problems.

Despite the fact that there exists no evidence in any Western country to suggest that teamsport athletes are more homophobic than men in the general population, gay men might nonetheless fear homophobia. This is perhaps as a result of the media broadcasting any incident of homophobia and exaggerating the perception of homophobia. This is also because it is easier for people to retain a negative news story than a positive one. It is also because, in the UK, the high-profile case of Justin Fashanu is still widely known, despite the fact that his suicide was over two decades ago.

It is not just teamsport athletes, we argue, that have lost their homophobia. Research on fans shows that they are becoming more inclusive, too. Cashmore and Cleland's (2011) pioneering research on football fans shows that 93 percent of 3,500 respondents have no objection to the presence of openly gay players, arguing that homophobia has no place in football. Rather, a footballer's ability was seen to be the only criterion on which he is judged—sexuality is deemed unimportant.

Cleland (2013) also documents this inclusion when analyzing discussions and narratives of homosexuality on 48 football fan message boards. Interestingly, posts which contained homophobic sentiment were rejected. Similar challenges to homophobic comments were made in Cleland, Magrath and Kian's (under review) analysis of football fan responses to Thomas Hitzlsperger's coming out in January 2014. Here, fans were generally supportive towards Hitzlsperger, many also positively observing the cultural shift in attitudes towards homosexuality.

We are thus encouraged by recent news events like the widely reported story of Michael Sam trying out for and making the NFL (though ultimately being cut) as an openly gay draftee before then playing for the Canadian Football League, or Jason Collins being picked up for another season of play after coming out. Our research into these events, alongside the watershed moment of the coming out (after retirement) of NBA player John Amaechi in 2004, suggest that the sport media is no longer entrenched in portraying the gay male athlete as a pariah, as a 1998 issue of ESPN's *Outside the Lines* episode once did. Casey Stoney came out to the media after seeing the positive reaction that diver Tom Daley had received. Kate and Helen Richardson-Walsh came out whilst playing on the same international team and again received positive coverage.

Furthermore, there have been a large number of social activist organizations that have promoted inclusion for gay and lesbian athletes in professional and other levels of sport. In the US, for example, You Can Play, The LGBT Sports Coalition, It Gets Better, GO! Athletes, as well as Nike's Be True campaign, may have made a difference. We cannot empirically say that they have—for there are no studies extant—but the existence of these highly visible campaigns is likely to have had some level of impact.

More directly related to policy, the Women's Sport Foundation (in both countries) and the National Center for Lesbian Rights in the United States have helped provide legal counsel for lawsuits to promote equality, and the NCAA has adopted a trans-inclusion policy and developed materials to help member schools create a more inclusive environment in their athletic departments. There have been a number of institutional proclamations of equality from professional sports teams, and other stakeholders of sports, too.

In the UK, the Justin Campaign and the Gay Football Supporters Network (GFSN) formed to fight the battle against homophobia in football. Perhaps the campaign that caught the most attention has come from the nation's leading gay rights association, Stonewall, with their Rainbow Laces campaign. The campaign was however, controversial, because they asked teams to wear rainbow laces to show support for LGBT rights, without consultation. The initiative, sponsored by a betting company, met resistance for a number of non-homophobia-related reasons. Thus, Stonewall also serves as an example of a how an activist organization can be counter-productive to gay rights when they are not sufficiently informed. They have, on a number of cases, given pause to gay rights with misinformed or inaccurate campaigns—something which occurs when a group is ideologically and not scientifically led. Another example comes from Stonewall's poor understanding of the relationship between homophobia and homosexually themed language.

Homosexually themed language

In their research on homophobia, Stonewall considers the phrase "that's so gay" as evidence of individual homophobia. This exemplifies a gay rights organization being out of touch with those for whom they advocate. In recent years, scholars have known that the phrase no longer is intended to imply antipathy toward homosexuality among the youth who use it. The use of language is complex. Accordingly, a more nuanced perspective on the use of this language comes from the work of Mark McCormack (2011a), who draws on Anderson's (2009a) concept of homohysteria—the cultural fear of being homosexualized—to understand the context of all forms of homosexually themed language. He suggests that in a highly homohysteric culture, there is an elevated stigma attached to homosexuality, resulting in boys and men using homophobic language to consolidate their own heterosexual identity and masculine standing. Consequently, when homosexually themed language is employed within this setting, it demonstrates homophobia, as it is used with pernicious intent and has a negative social effect.

However, in absence of homophobia and homohysteria, the same phrase is better understood as gay discourse. Here, the phrase "that's so gay" may be used as an expression of dissatisfaction—which in turn may privilege heterosexuality—but it is not employed with the intention of marginalizing gay people. The same word can even be morphed into pro-gay language, where it has no negative intent and positive social effects. When, for example, a straight male friend says to his best gay male friend, "Hey, gay boy," it serves as a way to ironically show that he loves him.

Softening heterosexuality

The fact that gay athletes have valued experiences in competitive sport necessarily indicates that their heterosexual teammates have positive beliefs about homosexuality. However, in line with the principle of homohysteria, this beneficially affects more than just gay and lesbian athletes—it also affects heterosexual athletes. This is because homophobia has served as the primary policing agent of heterosexuality. Among men, femininity was and still is associated with homosexuality and masculinity associated with lesbianism. In a culture that is both aware of homosexuality and with strong antipathy toward it, this leaves heterosexuals scrambling to prove that they are not gay—an impossible task. Instead, heterosexuals attempt to prove, and reprove, repeatedly, their heterosexuality by aligning all aspects of their gendered lives with the "appropriate" gendered terrain. This has been shown to limit occupational choices, entertainment, fashion, food and clothing choices, too. Of course, homohysteria has bifurcated the sporting world into acceptable male and female sports as well.

Little research has examined the impact of decreasing homohysteria on the lives of heterosexual women (Anderson and Bullingham 2013; Bullingham 2015; Worthen 2014), and this is a topic that certainly requires more researcher attention. A great deal of literature has, however, examined the impact of decreasing homohysteria on the lives of young heterosexual men, and particularly heterosexual male athletes. The body of this research can be found in Anderson's (2014) book *21st Century Jocks: Sporting Men and Contemporary Heterosexuality*.

The collective body of this research shows that young straight males are today physically tactile with each other. This is to say that they are not afraid to touch each other's bodies, to hug and even cuddle in bed (Anderson and McCormack 2015). Boys today are more emotionally open with one another, developing bromances that are valued more than their heterosexual romances (Robinson and Anderson forthcoming). Young straight men have been shown to kiss one another in non-sexual, but nonetheless endearing ways in increasingly high percentages: 89 percent in the UK, 39 percent in Australia and 10 percent in the US. By the time this book is published, the US and Australian numbers will be much higher, as homohysteria continues to decline.

All of this is to say that young straight men are vastly different in their gendered performances than their fathers were. Gone is the hypermasculine, violent, misogynistic, stoic masculine posturing. Instead, young straight men are better-dressed digital hippies. They espouse love for one another, and symbolically cement that love through their physical behaviors and written statements of love on Facebook.

Yet the majority of this research, in both the US and the UK, has been conducted on white, middle-class men. There is growing examination of the phenomena in the UK with white, lower-class men. But the vast majority of research on this topic has examined white men. The reasons for this are numerous, but it is important to note that we do not yet, academically, know if the lives of black, Asian, Hispanic or other non-white US or UK citizens reflect those of the white men studied. We have no idea if decreasing homohysteria also positively impacts upon women's gendered performances, permitting a greater range of masculinized behaviors. Also, we know even less about the lives of gay and lesbian athletes of color.

Missing athletes of color

We have not strategically set out to locate white athletes to interview. Race was not a qualifying factor for our collective works. However, nearly all of the openly gay and lesbian athletes we interviewed were white. Part of this is due to the lack of ethnicities other than white in the UK. According to the 2011 census, in England, approximately 1 percent are of Chinese origins, 3 percent black, and about 6 percent Asian (which includes India). Given that this represents a large number of first-generation people and that homosexuality is less acceptable in their home countries, it seems plausible that race and religion are responsible for part of the lack of findings. However, for the lesbian women we interviewed, this is also complicated by the position of our universities, which are in an area of the country that is about 97 percent white.

In the United States, there is a lack of representation in our studies of black and Asian men, particularly. While the first openly gay NFL and NBA players are black, along with the WNBA's Sheryl Swoopes, there—appears—to be a lack of representation among high school and college athletes. Part of this might be due to elevated rates of black homophobia in America.

Most studies find that black men maintain elevated rates of homophobia compared to white men (Baunach and Burgess 2010), something that Southall and colleagues (2009, 2011) found when comparing the attitudes of white versus black football players in the American South. This differential has been theorized to reflect disproportionately higher rates of blacks in lower economic classes and, as a way to raise their own worth by saying, "at least I am not gay" (Froyum 2007). Poorer black gay athletes might therefore feel compelled to remain closeted, so as not to disadvantage what they believe to be their route out of poverty (Anderson 2005a). This means that heterosexual black men very rarely interact with black gay men. Furthermore, gay culture, gay support systems and much of what can be described as a gay male identity have been established in a culture that presumes whiteness and elevated class status (Green 2007). Finally, Baunauch and Burgess (2010) show that one reason for the elevated rates of homophobia among black college students is that, whereas whites are more likely to improve their attitudes about gays and lesbians after meeting a gay or lesbian—something known as "contact theory" (Allport 1954), black men seem somewhat immune from the effect of this contact.

Recent research in the United Kingdom has also shown this. In Magrath's (2015) research on 60 British academy football players, 17 identified as Christian.

Despite the fact that 86 percent of the British population is white, 11 of those 17 were black. This research is the first to examine the intersection of race, religion and homophobia using inclusive masculinity theory. It found that the black players did indeed maintain more conservative attitudes than the white players, including the rejection of same-sex marriage. However, their religious beliefs were usurped by their strength of friendships with hypothetically gay friends. In other words, they rejected biblical rhetoric in favor of friendships.

The black American population is not immune from the broader social changes toward homosexuality, either. Keleher and Smith (2012) show that while black Americans remain more intolerant of homosexuality than whites, they have still improved their attitude toward homosexuals by 14 percent between 1991 and 2010.

Future directions

Comparing the experiences of black and white athletes does, however, prove fruitful for helping us understand where to look for discrimination in future research on gay and lesbian athletes. Anderson and McCormack (2010) compared the history of black and gay athletes, showing that they follow a similar trajectory—just that gay athletes are decades behind. This comparison proves useful in suggesting areas for future research.

For example, as black athletes are shown to self-segregate out of the "thinking positions" and into the "speed" positions (Coakley 1998; Eitzen 2001), we may find that gay athletes also self-segregate out of the macho sports and into the individual (less aggressive) sports, and that they may only come out in select sports.

Where it has been shown that in order for a black man to make the team he must be better than a white athlete, we may similarly find that in order for an openly gay athlete to be picked by the professional (or collegiate) leagues, he will need to be better than his heterosexual teammates. Research on openly gay athletes has found this to be accurate so far (Anderson 2002, 2005a). So we might therefore be able to predict that it will be a long time before there are "average" openly gay athletes selected onto professional teams, just as there were few average black players until recently (Smith 2000).

Moreover, whereas black men were once thought to lower team morale and cohesion on competitive teamsports (Anderson 2005a), we should examine how gay men are viewed by their teammates today. While the interviews we conduct suggest that a teammate's coming out promotes team cohesion, it would be useful to do a pre- and post-coming-out test using the *Group Cohesion Questionnaire*.

Adding to this analysis, just as black athletes are stacked into certain positions in sport (where they are less important to the outcome of the game (Eitzen 2003; Schneider and Eitzen 1986)) we might find that gay athletes are also stacked. For example, because they are mostly white, it is likely that gay men will be stacked into positions that require less physical aggression, and into positions more central to the outcome of the game.

Finally, just as black athletes have had a difficult time making it to the ranks of coaches, managers, media members and referees (Rasmussen, Esgate and Turner 2005; Walker 2005), gay athletes might also have a hard time making it to these ranks after their playing careers end.

Until now, it has been methodologically impossible to conduct such investigations—there simply have not been enough openly gay athletes to work with. However, it is our hope that this book will inspire a new generation of scholars concerned with equality in sport to make these empirical comparisons.

REFERENCES

Acosta, R. Vivian and Linda. J. Carpenter. "As the Years Go By—Coaching Opportunities in the 1990s." *Journal of Physical Education, Recreation & Dance* 63, no. 3 (1992): 36–41.

Adams, Adi. "'Josh Wears Pink Cleats' Inclusive Masculinity on the Soccer Field." *Journal of Homosexuality* 58 (2011): 579–96.

Adams, Adi and Eric Anderson. "Exploring the Relationship between Homosexuality and Sport among the Teammates of a Small, Midwestern Catholic College Soccer Team." *Sport, Education and Society* 17, no. 3 (2012): 347–63.

Adams, Adi, Eric Anderson, and Mark McCormack. "Establishing and Challenging Masculinity: The Influence of Gendered Discourses in Organised Sport." *Journal of Language and Social Psychology* 29, no. 3 (2010): 278–300.

Adams, Mary Louise. *Artistic Impressions: Figure Skating, Masculinity, and the Limits of Sport.* Toronto: University of Toronto Press, 2011.

Adams, Natalie, Alison Schmitke, and Amy Franklin. "Tomboys, Dykes, and Girly Girls: Interrogating the Subjectivities of Adolescent Female Athletes." *Women's Studies Quarterly* 33, no. 1/2 (2005): 17–34.

Afary, Janet. *Sexual Politics in Modern Iran.* Cambridge: Cambridge University Press, 2009.

Allport, Gordon. *The Nature of Prejudice.* Cambridge, MA: Addison-Wesley, 1954.

Almaguer, Tomas. "Chicano Men: A Cartography of Homosexual Identity and Behavior." In *The Lesbian and Gay Studies Reader,* edited by H. Abelove, M. A. Barale and D. A. Halperin. 255–73. New York: Routledge, 1993.

Anderson, Eric. *Trailblazing: America's First Openly Gay High School Coach.* Fountain Valley, CA: Identity Press, 2000.

Anderson, Eric. "Openly Gay Athletes. Contesting Hegemonic Masculinity in a Homophobic Environment." *Gender & Society* 16, no. 6 (2002): 860–77.

Anderson, Eric. *In the Game: Gay Athletes and the Cult of Masculinity.* Albany: State University of New York Press, 2005a.

Anderson, Eric. "Orthodox & Inclusive Masculinity: Competing Masculinities among Heterosexual Men in a Feminized Terrain." *Sociological Perspectives* 48 (2005b): 337–55.

Anderson, Eric. "'I Used to Think Women Were Weak': Orthodox Masculinity, Gender Segregation and Sport." *Sociological Forum* 23, no. 2 (2008a): 257–80.

Anderson, Eric. "'Being Masculine is Not about Who You Sleep with . . .': Heterosexual Athletes Contesting Masculinity and the One-Time Rule of Homosexuality." *Sex Roles* 58, no. 1–2 (2008b): 257–80.

Anderson, Eric. "Inclusive Masculinity in a Fraternal Setting." *Men and Masculinities* 10, no. 5 (2008c): 604–20.

Anderson, Eric. *Inclusive Masculinity the Changing Nature of Masculinities*. London: Routledge, 2009a.

Anderson, Eric. "The Maintenance of Masculinity among the Stakeholders of Sport." *Sport Management Review* 12 (2009b): 3–14.

Anderson, Eric. *Sport, Theory and Social Problems*. London: Routledge, 2010.

Anderson, Eric. "Updating the Outcome: Gay Athletes, Straight Teams and Coming out at the End of the Decade." *Gender & Society* 25, no. 2 (2011a): 250–68.

Anderson, Eric. "Inclusive Masculinities of University Soccer Players in the American Midwest." *Gender and Education* 23, no. 6 (2011b): 729–44.

Anderson, Eric. "The Rise and Fall of Western Homohysteria." *Journal of Feminist Scholarship* 1 (2011c): 80–94.

Anderson, Eric. "Shifting Masculinities in Anglo-American Countries." *Masculinities and Social Change* 1, no. 1 (2012a): 20–60.

Anderson, Eric. *The Monogamy Gap: Men, Love and the Reality of Cheating*. Oxford: Oxford University Press, 2012b.

Anderson, Eric. "A Need to Review Peer Review: The Regnerus Scandal as a Call to Action." *Journal of Gay and Lesbian Mental Health* 17, no. 3 (2013a): 337–51.

Anderson, Eric. "i9 and the Transformation of Youth Sport." *Journal of Sport and Social Issues* 37 (2013b): 97–111.

Anderson, Eric. *21st Century Jocks: Sporting Men and Contemporary Heterosexuality*. Basingstoke: Palgrave, 2014.

Anderson, Eric. "Adolescent Masculinity in an Age of Decreased Homohysteria." *Boyhood Studies: An Interdisciplinary Journal* 7, no. 1 (2015a): 79–93.

Anderson, Eric. "Inclusive Masculinity Theory." In *Exploring Masculinities: Identity, Inequality, Continuity and Change*, edited by C.J. Pascoe and T. Bridges. Cambridge: Oxford University Press, 2015b.

Anderson, Eric and Mark McCormack. "Comparing the Black and Gay Male Athletes: Patterns in American Oppression." *The Journal of Men's Studies* 18, no. 2 (2010): 145–58.

Anderson, Eric and Rhidian McGuire. "Inclusive Masculinity and the Gendered Politics of Men's Rugby." *The Journal of Gender Studies* 19, no. 3 (2010): 249–61.

Anderson, Eric and Adi Adams. "'Aren't We All a Little Bisexual?': The Recognition of Bisexuality in an Unlikely Place." *Journal of Bisexuality* 11 (2011): 3–22.

Anderson, Eric and Edward M. Kian. "Examining Media Contestation of Masculinity and Head Trauma in the National Football League." *Men and Masculinities* 15, no. 2 (2012): 152–73.

Anderson, Eric and Rachael Bullingham. "Openly Lesbian Team Sport Athletes in an Era of Decreasing Homohysteria." *International Review for the Sociology of Sport*, no. Online First (2013): http://irs.sagepub.com/content/early/2013/06/12/1012690213490520 (accessed November 15, 2015).

Anderson, Eric and Mark McCormack. "Cuddling and Spooning: Heteromasculinity and Homosocial Tactility Among Student-Athletes." *Men and Masculinities*, 18, no. 2 (2015): 214–30.

Anderson, Eric, Mark McCormack, and Harry Lee. "Male Team Sport Hazing Initiations in a Culture of Decreasing Homohysteria." *Journal of Adolescent Research* XX, no. X (2011): 1–22.

Anderson, Eric, Adi Adams, and Ian Rivers. "'I Kiss Them Because I Love Them': The Emergence of Heterosexual Men Kissing in British Institutes of Education." *Archives of Sexual Behavior* 41 (2012): 421–30.

Anderson, Eric, Mark McCormack, and Matthew Ripley. "Sixth Form Girls and Bisexual Burden." *Journal of Gender Studies* (2014): 1–11.

Anderson, Eric, R. Scoats, and M. McCormack. "Metropolitan Bisexual Men's Relationships: Evidence of a Cohort Effect." *Journal of Bisexuality* 15, no. 1 (2015): 21–39.

Andrews, David L. "Whither the NBA, Whither America." *Peace Review* 11, no. 4 (1999): 505–10.

Askew, Sue and Carol S. Ross. *Boys Don't Cry: Boys and Sexism in Education.* Buckingham: Open University Press, 1988.

Bailey, J. Michael. *The Man Who Would Be Queen: The Science of Gender-Bending and Transsexualism.* Washington, DC: Joseph Henry Press, 2003.

Bancroft, Jessie Hubbell. *Games for the Playground, Home, School and Gymnasium.* Createspace Independent Pub [orig. Macmillan], 1909.

Bandy, Susan J. "From Women in Sport to Cultural Critique: A Review of Books About Women in Sport and Physical Culture." *Women's Studies Quarterly* 33, no. 1/2 (2005): 246–61.

Banks, Lacy J. "Gay-Bashing Hardaway out of Nba Bash: Stern Cuts Ties; Amaechi Swamped with Negative E-Mails." *Chicago Sun-Times*, February 16, 2007.

Baroffio-Bota, Daniela and Sarah Banet-Weiser. "Women, Team Sport, and the WNBA: Playing Like a Girl." In *Handbook of Sports and Media*, edited by A. A. Raney and A. Bryant. 485–500. Mahwah, NJ: Lawrence Erlbaum Associates, 2006.

Baunach, Dawn Michelle. "Changing Same-Sex Marriage Attitudes in America from 1988 through 2010." *Public Opinion Quarterly* 76, no. 2 (2012): 364–78.

Baunach, Dawn M., Elisabeth O. Burgess, and Courtney S. Muse. "Southern (Dis) Comfort: Sexual Prejudice and Contact with Gay Men and Lesbians in the South." *Sociological Spectrum* 30, no. 1 (2010): 30–64.

Baxter, Leslie A. "Relationships as Dialogues." *Personal Relationships* 11, no. 1 (2004): 1–22.

Becht, Marleen C., Ype H. Poortinga, and A. J. J. M. Vingerhoets. "Crying across Countries." In *Adult Crying: A Biopsychological Approach*, edited by A. J. J. M. Vingerhoets and R. R. Cornelius. New York: Routledge, 2001.

Beisel, Nicola K. *Imperiled Innocents: Anthony Comstock and Family Reproduction in Victorian America.* Princeton, NJ: Princeton University Press, 1998.

Berila, Beth and Devika Dibya Choudhuri. "Metrosexuality the Middle Class Way: Exploring Race, Class and Gender in Queer Eye for the Straight Guy." *Genders* 42 (2005): 1–33.

Blinde, Elaine M. and Diane E. Taub (1992a). "Homophobia and Women's Sport: The Disempowerment of Athletes." *Sociological Focus* 25, no. 2: 151–66.

Blinde, Elaine M. and Diane E. Taub. "Women Athletes as Falsely Accused Deviants: Managing the Lesbian Stigma." *The Sociological Quarterly* 33, no. 4 (1992b): 521–33.

Bortolin, Sandra. "'I Don't Want Him Hitting on Me': The Role of Masculinities in Creating a Chilly High School Climate." *Journal of LGBT Youth* 7, no. 3 (2010): 200–223.

Bourdieu, Pierre. *Masculine Domination.* Stanford, CA: Stanford University Press, 2001.

Boutilier, Mary A. and Luncinda. F. SanGiovanni. *The Sporting Woman.* Champaign, IL: Human Kinetics Publishers, 1983.

Boxhill, Jan. "Title IX and Gender Equity." *Journal of the Philosophy of Sport* no. 1 (1993): 23–31.

Boyle, Raymond and Richard Haynes. *Football in the New Media Age.* London: Routledge, 2009.

Brailsford, Dennis. *Sport, Time and Society: British at Play*. London: Routledge, 1991.

Branfman, J., S. Stiritz, and Eric Anderson. "Relaxing the Straight-Male Anus: Decreasing Homohysteria around Anal Eroticism." *Sexualities* (in press).

Bruce, Toni. "Assessing the Sociology of Sport: On Media and Representations of Sportswomen." *International Review for the Sociology of Sport* 50, no. 4–5 (2015): 380–84.

Bryant, Michael. "Gay Male Athletes and the Role of Organized Team and Contact Sports." Unpublished master's thesis. Seattle Pacific University, 2001.

Bullingham, Rachael. "Changing Times: Discovering How Openly Lesbian Athletes Navigate Team Sport." Unpublished doctoral thesis, University of Winchester, 2015.

Bullingham, Rachael, Rory Magrath, and Eric Anderson. "Sport and a Cultural Shift Away from Homohysteria." In *Routledge Handbook of Sport, Gender and Sexuality*, edited by Jennifer Hargreave and Eric Anderson. London: Routledge, 2014.

Burn, Shawn Meghan. "Heterosexuals' Use of 'Fag' and 'Queer' to Deride One Another. A Contributor to Heterosexism and Stigma." *Journal of Homosexuality* 40, no. 2 (2000): 1–11.

Burton-Nelson, Mariah. *The Stronger Women Get, the More Men Love Football*. New York: Avon Books, 1994.

Bush, Anthony, Eric Anderson, and Sam Carr. "The Declining Existence of Men's Homophobia in British Sport." *Journal for the Study of Sports and Athletes in Education* 6, no. 1 (2012): 107–20.

Cahn, Susan. *Coming on Strong: Gender and Sexuality in Twentieth-Century Women's Sport*. London: Harvard University Press, 1994.

Caldwell, Mayta A. and Letitia Anne Peplau. "Sex Differences in Same-Sex Friendship." *Sex Roles* 8, no. 7 (1982): 721–32.

Cameron, Deborah and Don Kulick. *Language and Sexuality*. Cambridge: Cambridge University Press, 2003.

Cancian, Francesca M. "The Feminization of Love." *Signs* 11, no. 4 (1986): 692–709.

Cancian, Francesca M. *Love in America: Gender and Self-Development*. Cambridge, MA: Cambridge University Press, 1987.

Cashmore, Ellis and Jamie Cleland. "Glasswing Butterflies: Gay Professional Footballers and Their Culture." *Journal of Sport and Social Issues* 35, no. 4 (2011): 420–36.

Cashmore, Ellis and Jamie Cleland. "Fans, Homophobia and Masculinities in Association Football: Evidence of a More Inclusive Environment." *The British Journal of Sociology* 63, no. 2 (2012): 370–87.

Caudwell, Jayne. "Women's Experiences of Sexuality within Football Contexts: A Particular and Located Footballing Epistemology." *Football Studies* 5, no. 1 (2002): 24–45.

Chambers, Deborah, Estella Tincknell, and Joost Van Loon. "Peer Regulation of Teenage Sexual Identities." *Gender and Education* 16, no. 3 (2004): 397–415.

Chandler, Timothy and John Nauright. "Introduction: Rugby, Manhood and Identity." In *Making Men: Rugby and Masculine Identity*, edited by John Nauright and Timothy Chandler. 1–12. London: Frank Cass, 1996.

Channon, Alex. "Enter the Discourse: Exploring the Discursive Roots of Inclusivity in Mixed-Sex Martial Arts." *Sport in Society* 16, no. 10 (2013): 1293–308.

Channon, Alex. "Towards the 'Undoing' of Gender in Mixed-Sex Martial Arts and Combat Sports." *Societies* 4, no. 4 (2014): 587–605.

Channon, Alex and Christopher R. Matthews. *Global Perspectives on Women in Combat Sports: Women Warriors around the World*. Basingstoke: Palgrave Macmillan, 2015.

Channon, Alex and Christopher R. Matthews. "'It Is What It Is': Masculinity, Homosexuality, and Inclusive Discourse in Mixed Martial Arts." *Journal of Homosexuality* 62, no. 7 (2015): 936–56.

Chauncey, George. *Gay New York: Gender, Urban Culture and the Making of the Gay Male World 1890–1940*. New York: Basic Books, 1994.

Chaves, Mark. "Secularization and Religious Revival: Evidence from US Church Attendance Rates 1972–1986." *Journal for the Scientific Study of Religion* 28 (1989): 464–77.

Christenson, Marcus. "Thomas Hitzlsperger Announces He Is Gay in Newspaper Interview." *Guardian*, January 8, 2014: http://www.theguardian.com/football/2014/jan/08/thomas-hitzlsperger-gay-announces-homosexual (accessed November 15, 2015).

Clarey, Christopher. "Runners-Ups Revelation Likely to Test the Waters." *New York Times*, 1999, 31.

Clark, Tom and Andrew Sparrow. "Three in Five Voters Back Gay Marriage, New Poll Shows." *Guardian*, December 26, 2012.

Clarke, Gill. "Queering the Pitch and Coming out to Play: Lesbians and Physical Education in Sport." *Sport, Education and Society* 3, no. 2 (1998): 145–60.

Clavio, Galen. "Demographics and Usage Profiles of Users of College Sport Message Boards." *International Journal of Sport Communication* 1, no. 4 (2008): 434–43.

Clayton, Ben and Barbara Humberstone. "Men's Talk: A (Pro)Feminist Analysis of Male University Football Players' Discourse." *International Review for the Sociology of Sport* 41, no. 3 (2006): 394–416.

Cleland, Jamie. "Association Football and the Representation of Homosexuality by the Print Media: A Case Study of Anton Hysén." *Journal of Homosexuality* 61, no. 9 (2014): 1269–87.

Cleland, Jamie. "Discussing Homosexuality on Association Football Fan Message Boards: A Changing Cultural Context." *International Review of the Sociology of Sport* (2013): doi: 10.1177/1012690213475437 (accessed November 15, 2015).

Cleland, Jamie, Rory Magrath, and Edward M. Kian. "Masculinity and Sexuality in Association Football: An Online Response by Fans to the Coming out of Thomas Hitzlsperger." *British Journal of Sociology* (under review).

Clements, Ben and Clive D. Fields. "Public Opinion toward Homosexuality and Gay Rights in Britain." *Public Opinion Quarterly* 78, no. 2 (2014): 523–47.

Coad, David. *The Metrosexual: Gender, Sexuality and Sport*. New York: SUNY Press, 2008.

Coakley, Jay. *Sport in Society: Issues and Controversies*. 6th ed. Boston, MA: McGraw-Hill, 1998.

Cohen, Cathy J. *The Boundaries of Blackness: Aids and the Breakdown of Black Politics*. Chicago, IL: University of Chicago Press, 1999.

Cohler, Bertram J. and Phillip L. Hammack. "The Psychological World of the Gay Teenager: Social Change, Narrative, and 'Normality'." *Journal of Youth and Adolescence* 36, no. 1 (2007): 47–59.

Connell, Raewyn W. *Gender and Power*. Cambridge: Polity Press, 1987.

Connell, Raewyn W. "Cool Guys, Swots and Wimps: The Interplay of Masculinity and Education." *Oxford Review of Education* 15, no. 2 (1989): 391–403.

Connell, Raewyn. *Masculinities*. Cambridge: Polity, 1995.

Connell, Raewyn W. "Masculinity Research and Global Change." *Masculinities and Social Change* 1, no. 1 (2012): 4–18.

Cox, Barbara and Shona. Thompson. "Facing the Bogey: Women, Football and Sexuality." *Football Studies* 4, no. 2 (2001): 7–24.

Crosset, Todd W. "Masculinity, Sexuality, and the Development of Early Modern Sport." Chap. 3 In *Sport, Men, and the Gender Order*, edited by Michael A. Messner and Don F. Sabo. 45–54. Champaign, Illinois: Human Kinetics Books, 1990.

Crosset, Todd W., Jeffrey R. Benedict, and Mark A. McDonald. "Male Student-Athletes Reported for Sexual Assault: A Survey of Campus Police Departments and Judicial Affairs Offices." *Journal of Sport & Social Issues* 19, no. 2 (1995): 126–40.

Cunningham, George B., Andrew Pickett, E. Nicole Melton, Woojun Lee, and Kathi Miner. "Psychological Safety and the Expression of Sexual Orientation and Personal Identity." In *Routledge Handbook of Sport, Gender and Sexuality*, edited by Jennifer Hargreaves and Eric Anderson. London: Routledge, 2014.

Curry, Timothy. "Fraternal Bonding in the Locker Room: A Profeminist Analysis of Talk About Competition and Women." *Sociology of Sport Journal* 8, no. 2 (1991): 119–35.

Dashper, Katherine. "'Dressage Is Full of Queens!': Masculinity, Sexuality and Equestrian Sport." *Sociology* 46, no. 6 (2012): 1109–24.

Davis-Delano, Laurel R. "Sport as Context for the Development of Women's Same-Sex Relationships." *Journal of Sport & Social Issues* 38, no. 3 (2014): 263–85.

Davis-Delano, Laurel. R., April Pollock, and Jennifer Ellsworth Vose. "Apologetic Behavior among Female Athletes." *International Review for the Sociology of Sport* 44, no. 2–3 (2009): 131–50.

Demetriou, Demetrakis Z. "Connell's Concept of Hegemonic Masculinity: A Critique." *Theory and Society* 30, no. 3 (2001): 337–61.

Denison, Jim and Kitchen, Alistair. "Out in the Fields." (2015) Available from: www.out onthefields.com (accessed November 15, 2015).

Derlega, Valerian J., Robin J. Lewis, Scott Harrison, Barbara A. Winstead, and Robert Costanza. "Gender Differences in the Initiation and Attribution of Tactile Intimacy." *Journal of Nonverbal Behavior* 13, no. 2 (1989): 83–96.

Diamond, Diane, Michael S. Kimmel, and Kirby, Schroeder. "'What's This about a Few Good Men?': Negotiation Gender in Military Education." *Research on Men and Masculinities Series* 11 (2001): 231–52.

Diamond, Lisa M. "'Having a Girlfriend without Knowing It': Intimate Friendships among Adolescent Sexual-Minority Women." *Journal of Lesbian Studies* 6, no. 1 (2002): 5–16.

Doan, Long, Annalise Loehr, and Lisa R. Miller. "Formal Rights and Informal Privileges for Same-Sex Couples: Evidence from a National Survey Experiment." *American Sociological Review* 79, no. 6 (2014): 1172–95.

Drummond, Murray J. N., Shaun M. Filiault, Eric Anderson, and David Jeffries. "Homosocial Intimacy among Young Australian Undergraduate Men." *Journal of Sociology* Online First (2014): doi: 10.1177/1440783313518251 (accessed November 15, 2015).

Drury, Scarlett. "'It Seems Really Inclusive in Some Ways, But . . . Inclusive Just for People Who Identify as Lesbian': Discourses of Gender and Sexuality in a Lesbian-Identified Football Club." *Soccer & Society* 12, no. 3 (2011): 421–42.

Dunning, Eric and Kenneth Sheard. *Barbarians, Gentlemen and Players: A Sociological Study of the Development of Rugby Football*. Oxford: Martin Robertson, 1979.

Eitzen, D. Stanley. *Sport in Contemporary Society: An Anthology*. New York: MacMillian, 2001.

Eitzen, D. Stanley. *Fair and Foul: Beyond the Myths and Paradoxes of Sport* (2nd ed.). Oxford: Rowman & Littlefield, 2003.

Elias, Norbert and Eric. Dunning. *Quest for Excitement: Sport and Leisure in the Civilising Process*. London: Wiley-Blackwell, 1986.

Epstein, Debbie and Richard Johnson. *Schooling Sexualities*. Buckingham: Open University Press, 1998.

Ewald, Keith and Robert M. Jiobu. "Explaining Positive Deviance: Becker's Model and the Case of Runners and Bodybuilders." *Sociology of Sport Journal* 2, no. 2 (1985): 144–56.

Ezzell, Matthew B. "'Barbie Dolls' on the Pitch: Identity Work, Defensive Othering, and Inequality in Women's Rugby." *Social Problems* 56 (2009): 111–31.

Felshin, Jan. "The Triple Option . . . For Women in Sport." *Quest* 21 (1974): 36–40.

Ferez, Sylvain. "From Women's Exclusion to Gender Institution: A Brief History of the Sexual Categorisation Process within Sport." *The International Journal of the History of Sport* 29, no. 2 (2012): 272–85.

Fink, Janet, Laura J. Burton, Annamarie Farrell, and Heidi M. Parker. "Playing It Out: Female Intercollegiate Athletes' Experiences in Revealing Their Sexual Identities." *Journal for the Study of Sports and Athletes in Education* 6, no. 1 (2012): 83–106.

Fiorona, Morris P., Samuel. J. Abrams, and Jeremy. C. Pope. *Culture War? The Myth of Polarized America.* New York: Pearson, 2006.

Flood, Michael. "Men, Sex, and Homosociality How Bonds between Men Shape Their Sexual Relations with Women." *Men and Masculinities* 10, no. 3 (2008): 339–59.

Floyd, Kory. "Affectionate Same-Sex Touch: The Influence of Homophobia on Observers' Perception." *The Journal of Social Psychology* 140, no. 6 (2000): 774–88.

Forman, Pamela J. and Darcy C. Plymire. "Amélie Mauresmo's Muscles: The Lesbian Heroic and Women's Professional Tennis." *Women's Studies Quarterly* 33, no. 1/2 (2005): 120–33.

Foucault, Michel. *The History of Sexuality, Volume 1: An Introduction.* London: Penguin, 1984.

Frank, David J., Bayliss J. Camp, and Steven. A. Boucher. "Worldwide Trends in the Criminal Regulation of Sex 1945 to 2005." *American Sociological Review* 75, no. 6 (2010): 867–93.

Freud, Sigmund. *Three Essays on the Theory of Sexuality.* London: Hogarth, 1905.

Frey, James. H. and D. Stanley Eitzen. "Sport and Society." *Annual Review of Sociology* 17 (1991): 503–22.

Froyum, Carissa M. "'At Least I'm Not Gay': Heterosexual Identity Making among Poor Black Teens." *Sexualities* 10, no. 5 (2007): 603–22.

Gerdy, John R. *Sport: The All American Addiction.* Jackson: University of Mississippi, 2002.

Ghaziani, Amin. *There Goes the Gayborhood?* Princeton, NJ: Princeton University Press, 2014.

Giddens, Anthony. *The Transformation of Intimacy: Sexuality, Love and Intimacy in Modern Societies.* Cambridge: Polity, 1992.

Gill, Rosalind, Karen Henwood, and Carl McLean. "Body Projects and the Regulation of Normative Masculinity." *Body and Society* 11, no. 1 (2005): 37–62.

Giulianotti, Richard. *Football: A Sociology of the Global Game.* Cambridge: Polity Press, 1999.

Giulianotti, Richard and Roland Robertson. *Globalization and Football.* London: Sage, 2009.

Goffman, Erving. *Asylums: Essays on the Social Situation of Mental Patients and Other Inmates.* New York: Anchor Books, 1961.

Granovetter, Mark. "The Strength of Weak Ties: A Network Theory Revisited." *Sociological Theory* 1 (1983): 201–33.

Green, Adam I. "On the Horns of a Dilemma: Institutional Dimensions of the Sexual Career in a Sample of Middle-Class, Urban, Black, Gay Men." *Journal of Black Studies* 37 (2007): 753–74.

Greenberg, David F. *The Construction of Homosexuality.* Chicago, IL: University of Chicago Press, 1988.

Greenwell, M. "Title IX Was Great for Female Athletes. And Terrible for Female Coaches." *Washington Post*, July 26, 2012: http://www.washingtonpost.com/opinions/title-ix-was-great-for-female-athletes-and-terrible-for-female-coaches/2012/07/26/gJQAAFK1BX_story.html (accessed November 15, 2015).

Griffin, Pat. "Changing the Game: Homophobia, Sexism and Lesbians in Sport." *Quest* 44 (1992): 251–65.

Griffin, Pat. *Strong Women, Deep Closets.* Leeds: Human Kinetics, 1998.

Griffin, Pat. "LGBT Equality in Sports: Celebrating Our Successes and Facing Our Challenges." Chap. 1 In *Sexual Orientation and Gender Identity in Sport: Essays from Activists, Coaches, and Scholars*, edited by G. B. Cunningham. 1–13. College Station, TX: The Center for Sport Management Research and Education, 2012.

Guttmann, Allen. *From Ritual to Record: The Nature of Modern Sports*. New York: Columbia University Press, 1978.

Hall, Lesley. A. *Sex, Gender and Social Change in Britain since 1880*. London: Palgrave MacMillan, 2013.

Hall, Matthew, Brendan Gough, and Sarah Seymour-Smith. "'I'm Metro, Not Gay!': A Discursive Analysis of Men's Accounts of Makeup Use on YouTube." *Journal of Men's Studies* 20, no. 3 (2012): 209–26.

Hamdi, N. and Eric. Anderson. "Lesbian Life in Tunisian, Muslim Sport." *Journal of Homosexuality* Online First (2015).

Hargreaves, Jennifer A. *Sporting Females*. London: Routledge, 1994.

Hargreaves, Jennifer A. *Heroines of Sport*. London: Routledge, 2000.

Hargreaves, Jennifer A. and Eric Anderson, eds. *Routledge Handbook of Sport, Gender and Sexualities*. New York: Routledge, 2014.

Harper, Phillip B. *Are We Not Men? Masculinity Anxiety and the Problem of African-American Identity*. New York: Oxford University Press, 1996.

Harris, John and Ben Clayton. "David Beckham and the Changing (Re)Presentations of English Identities." *International Journal of Sport Management and Marketing* 2, no. 3 (2007a): 208–21.

Harris, John and Ben Clayton. "The First Metrosexual Rugby Star: Rugby Union, Masculinity, and Celebrity in Contemporary Wales." *Sociology of Sport Journal* 24, no. 2 (2007b): 145–64.

Harris, Marvin. *Patterns of Race in the Americas*. New York: Greenwood Press, 1964.

Harris, W. C. "'In My Day It Used to Be Called a Limp Wrist': Flip-Floppers, Nelly Boys, and Homophobic Rhetoric in the 2004 US Presidential Campaign." *Journal of American Culture* 29, no. 3 (2006): 278–95.

Hartmann, Heidi. "Capitalism, Patriarchy and Job Segregation." *Signs: A Journal of Women in Culture and Society* 1, no. 3 (1976): 137–69.

Hein, Wendy and Stephanie O'Donohoe. "Practising Gender: The Role of Banter in Young Men's Improvisations of Masculine Consumer Identities." *Journal of Marketing Management* 30, no. 13–14 (2014): 1293–319.

Hekma, Geert. "'As Long as They Don't Make an Issue of It . . .': Gay Men and Lesbians in Organised Sports in the Netherlands." *Journal of Homosexuality* 35, no. 1 (1998): 1–23.

Heywood, Leslie and Shari L. Dworkin. *Built to Win: The Female Athlete as Cultural Icon*. Sport and Culture Series. edited by T Miller and M. A. Hall. Vol. 5. London: University of Minnesota Press, 2003.

Hoberman, J. (1997). *Darwin's Athletes: How Sport Has Damaged Black America and Preserved the Myth of Race*. Boston, MA: Houghton Mifflin.

Hooghe, Marc and Cecil Meeusen. "Is Same-Sex Marriage Legislation Related to Attitudes towards Homosexuality?" *Sexuality Research and Social Policy* 10, no. 4 (2013): 258–68.

Hubbard, Katherine and Richard O. de Visser. "Not Just Bi the Bi: The Relationship between Essentialist Beliefs and Attitudes About Bisexuality." *Psychology and Sexuality* Online First (2014): doi: 10.1080/19419899.2014.987682 (accessed November 15, 2015).

Hughes, Robert, Jay. Coakley, A. Yiannakis, and M. Melnick. "Positive Deviance among Athletes: The Implications of Overconformity to the Sport Ethic." *Contemporary Issues of Sociology of Sport* 8 (1991): 307–25.

Ibson, John. *Picturing Men: A Century of Male Relationships in Everyday Life*. Washington, DC: Smithson Books, 2002.

Jackson, Carolyn and Steven. Dempster. "'I Sat Back on My Computer . . . With a Bottle of Whiskey Next to Me': Constructing 'Cool' Masculinity through 'Effortless' Achievement in Secondary and Higher Education." *Journal of Gender Studies* 18, no. 4 (2009): 341–56.

Jarvis, Nigel. "Ten Men Out: Gay Sporting Masculinities in Softball." In *Sport, Sexualities and Queer Theory*, edited by J. Caudwell. 62–75. London: Routledge, 2006.

Jarvis, Nigel. "The Inclusive Masculinities of Heterosexual Men within UK Gay Sports Clubs." *International Review for the Sociology of Sport* 50, no. 3 (2015): 283–300.

Johnson, David K. *The Lavender Scare: The Cold War Persecution of Gays and Lesbians in the Federal Government*. Chicago, IL: University of Chicago Press, 2004.

Johnson, Kerri L., Simone Gill, Victoria Reichman, and Louis G. Tassinary. "Swagger, Sway, and Sexuality: Judging Sexual Orientation from Body Motion and Morphology." *Journal of Personality and Social Psychology* 93, no. 3 (2007): 321.

Jones, Louisa and Mac McCarthy. "Mapping the Landscape of Gay Men's Football." *Leisure Studies* 29, no. 2 (2010): 161–73.

Jones, Owen. "Footballer Thomas Hitzlsperger Has Made a Brave and Commendable Move in Announcing He Is Gay." *Independent*: http://www.independent.co.uk/voices/comment/owen-jones-footballer-thomas-hitzlsperger-has-made-a-brave-and-commendable-move-in-announcing-he-is-gay-9046774.html (accessed November 15, 2015).

Jones, Roger and Gill Clarke. "The School Experiences of Same-Sex Attracted Students in the 14- to 19-Year-Old Secondary Sector in England: Within and beyond the Safety and Tolerance Framework." *Journal of Gay & Lesbian Social Services* 19, no. 3–4 (2007): 119–38.

Joseph, Lauren and Eric Anderson. "The Influence of Gender Segregation and Teamsport Experience on Occupational Discrimination in Sport-Based Employment." *Journal of Gender Studies* Online First (2015).

Jourard, Sidney M. *The Transparent Self*. Princeton, NJ: VanNostrand, 1971.

Kane, Mary Jo and Helen J. Lenskyj. "Media Treatment of Female Athletes: Issues of Gender and Sexualities." Chap. 12 In *Media Sport*, edited by L. A. Wenner. 186–201. London: Routledge, 1998.

Katz-Wise, Sabra L. and Janet S. Hyde. "Victimization Experiences of Lesbian, Gay and Bisexual Individuals: A Meta-Analysis." *Journal of Sex Research* 49, no. 2–3 (2012): 142–67.

Kauer, Kerrie J. and Vikki. Krane. "'Scary Dykes' and 'Feminine Queens': Stereotypes and Female Collegiate Athletes." *Women in Sport and Physical Activity* 15, no. 1 (2006): 42–55.

Keleher, Alison and Eric R.A.N. Smith. "Growing Support for Gay and Lesbian Equality since 1990 ". *Journal of Homosexuality* 59 (2012): 1307–26.

Kian, Edward M. and Eric. Anderson. "John Amaechi: Changing the Way Sport Reporters Examine Gay Athletes." *Journal of Homosexuality* 56 (2009): 799–818.

Kian, Edward M., Galen Clavio, John Vincent, and Stephanie D. Shaw. "Homophobic and Sexist yet Uncontested: Examining Football Fan Postings on Internet Message Boards." *Journal of Homosexuality* 58, no. 5 (2011): 680–99.

Kian, Edward M., Eric. Anderson, and Danny Shipka. "'I Am Happy to Start the Conversation' Examining Sport Media Framing of Jason Collins Coming out and Playing in the NBA." *Sexualities* Online First (2015): doi: 1363460714550915 (accessed November 15, 2015).

Kidd, Bruce. "The Men's Cultural Central Sports and the Dynamic of Women's Oppression/Men's Repression." In *Sport, Men and the Gender Order: Critical Feminist Perspectives*, edited by M. A. Messner and D. F. Sabo. Champaign, IL: Human Kinetics Books, 1990.

Kiesling, Scott. F. "Men, Masculinities, and Language." *Language and Linguistics Compass* 1, no. 6 (2007): 653–73.

Kimmel, Michael S. "Masculinity as Homophobia: Fear, Shame and Silence in the Construction of Gender Identity." In *Theorising Masculinities*, edited by H. Brod and M. Kaufman. 119–41. Thousand Oaks, CA: SAGE Publications, 1994.

Kimmel, Michael S. *Manhood in America*. New York: Free Press, 1996.

Kimmel, Michael S. Guyland: The Perilous World Where *Boys Become Men*. New York: Harper Collins, 2008.

King, C. (2004). *Offside Racism, Playing the White Man*. Oxford: Berg.

King, Samantha. "Homonormativity and the Politics of Race: Reading Sheryl Swoopes." *Journal of Lesbian Studies* 13, no. 3 (2009): 272–90.

Kinsey, Alfred C., Wardell B. Pomeroy, and Clyde E. Martin. *Sexual Behaviour in the Human Male*. Philadelphia, PA: W. B. Saunders, 1948.

Komarovsky, Mirra. "Patterns of Self-Discourse of Male Undergraduates." *Journal of Marriage and the Family* 36, no. 4 (1974): 677–86.

Krane, Vikki "We Can Be Athletic and Feminine, But Do We Want To? Challenging Hegemonic Femininity in Women's Sport." *Quest* 53 (2001): 115–33.

Krane, Vikki, and Heather Barber. "Lesbian Experiences in Sport: A Social Identity Perspective." *Quest*, no. 55 (2003): 328–46.

Kreager, Derek A. "Unnecessary Roughness? School Sport, Peer Networks, and Male Adolescent Violence." *American Sociological Review* 72, no. 5 (2007): 605–724.

Kring, Ann M. and Albert. H. Gordon. "Sex Differences in Emotion: Expression, Experience and Physiology." *Journal of Personality and Social Psychology* 74, no. 3 (1998): 686–703.

Lalor, Therese and Johanna Rendle-Short. "'That's So Gay': A Contemporary Use of Gay in Australian English." *Australian Journal of Linguistics* 27, no. 2 (2007): 147–73.

Lancaster, Roger N. "Subject Honor and Object Shame: The Construction of Male Homosexuality and Stigma in Nicaragua." *Ethnology* 27, no. 2 (1988): 111–25.

Langer, Gary. "Poll Tracks Dramatic Rise in Support of Gay Marriage." *ABC News*: http://abcnews.go.com/blogs/politics/2013/03/poll-tracks-dramatic-rise-in-support-for-gay-marriage/ (accessed November 15, 2015).

Lapchick, R., Brenden, J., and Wright, B. (2006). *The 2006 Racial and Gender Report Card of the Associated Press Sports Editors*. Orlando: University of Central Florida, 2006.

Laumann, Edward O. (ed.). *The Social Organisation of Sexuality: Sexual Practices in the United States*. Chicago, IL: University of Chicago Press, 1994.

Le Saux, Graeme. *Left Field: A Footballer Apart*. London: Harper Collins, 2007.

Lee, Lucy. "Religion: Losing Faith?" In *British Social Attitudes Survey*, Volume 28, edited by A. Park, E. Cleary, J. Curtice, M. Phillips and D. Utting. London: Sage, 2012.

Lenskyj, Helen J. *Out of Bounds: Women, Sport and Sexuality*. Toronto: Women's Press, 1986.

Lenskyj, Helen J. "Common Sense and Physiology: North American Medical Views on Women and Sport, 1890–1930." *Canadian Journal of History of Sport* 21, no. 1 (1990): 49–64.

Lenskyj, Helen. J. "Combating Homophobia in Sport and Physical Education." *Sociology of Sport Journal* 8 (1991): 61–69.

Lenskyj, Helen J. "Sport and the Threat to Gender Boundaries." *Sporting Traditions* 12, no. 1 (1995): 47–50.

Lenskyj, Helen J. *Out on the Field*. Toronto: Women's Press, 2003.

LeVay, Simon. *Gay, Straight, and the Reason Why: The Science of Sexual Orientation*. New York: Oxford University Press, 2010.

Lewis, Robert. A. "Emotional Intimacy among Men." *Journal of Social Research* 34, no. 1 (1978): 108–21.

Lilleaas, Ulla-Britt. "Masculinities, Sport and Emotions." *Men and Masculinities* 10, no. 1 (2007): 39–53.

Lines, Gill. "Villains, Fools or Heroes? Sports Stars as Role Models for Young People." *Leisure Studies* 20 (2001): 285–303.

Loftus, Jeni. "America's Liberalization in Attitudes towards Homosexuality, 1973 to 1998." *American Sociological Review* 66 (2001): 762–82.

Lowerson, John. *Sport and the English Middle Classes 1870–1914*. Manchester: Manchester University Press, 1993.

Lugg, Catherine. A. "The Religious Right and the Public Education: The Paranoid Politics of Homophobia." *Educational Policy* 12 (1998): 267–83.

Lyman, Peter. "The Fraternal Bond as a Joking Relationship: A Case Study of the Role of Sexist Jokes in Male Group Bonding." In *Changing Men*, edited by M. S. Kimmel. 149–63. Newbury Park, CA: SAGE, 1987.

Mac an Ghaill, Mairtin. *The Making of Men: Masculinities, Sexualities, and Schooling*. Buckingham: Open University Press, 1994.

MacInnes, Paul. "When Men's Lips Meet." *Guardian*, April 18, 2010: http://www.the guardian.com/commentisfree/2010/apr/18/men-kiss-scholes-neville-homphobia (accessed November 15, 2015).

Magrath, Rory. "'It's Not Homophobia, Just Banter': The Discourse of Gay-Friendly Football Fans." Under review.

Magrath, Rory. "The Intersection of Race, Religion and Homophobia in British Football." *International Review for the Sociology of Sport* Online First (2015): doi: 10.1177/1012690215597651 (accessed November 15, 2015).

Magrath, Rory. *Masculinity in the Beautiful Game: Inclusive Masculinities in Contemporary Football*. London: Routledge, 2016.

Magrath, Rory, Eric Anderson, and Steve Roberts. "On the Door-Step of Equality: Attitudes Toward Gay Athletes Among Academy-Level Footballers." *International Review for the Sociology of Sport* 50, no. 7 (2015): 804–21.

Mayer, William. *The Changing American Mind: How and Why American Public Opinion Changed between 1960–1988*. Ann Arbor, MI: University of Michigan Press, 1992.

McCann, Pol Dominic, Victor Minichiello, and David Plummer. "Is Homophobia Inevitable? Evidence That Explores the Constructed Nature of Homophobia, and the Techniques through Which Men Unlearn It." *Journal of Sociology* 45, no. 2 (2009): 201–20.

McCarthy, Justin. "Record-High 60% of Americans Support Same-Sex Marriage." Gallup poll, May 18, 2015: http://www.gallup.com/poll/183272/record-high-americans-support-sex-marriage.aspx (accessed November 15, 2015).

McCormack, Mark. "Mapping the Terrain of Homosexually-Themed Language." *Journal of Homosexuality* 58 (2011a): 664–79.

McCormack, Mark. "The Declining Significance of Homohysteria for Male Students in Three Sixth Forms in the South of England." *British Educational Research Journal* 37, no. 2 (2011b): 337–53.

McCormack, Mark. *The Declining Significance of Homophobia: How Teenage Boys Are Redefining Masculinity and Homophobia*. New York: Oxford University Press, 2012a.

McCormack, Mark. "The Positive Experiences of Openly Gay, Lesbian, Bisexual and Transgendered Students in a Christian Sixth Form College." *Sociological Research Online* 17, no. 3 (2012b): 5.

McCormack, Mark. "The Intersection of Youth Masculinities, Decreasing Homophobia and Class: An Ethnography." *The British Journal of Sociology* 65, no. 1 (2014): 130–49.

McCormack, M. and E. Anderson. "The Re-Production of Homosexuality-Themed Discourse in Educationally Based Organised Sport." *Culture, Health and Sexuality* 12, no. 8 (2010a): 913–27.

McCormack, Mark and Eric Anderson. "'It's Just Not Acceptable Any More': The Erosion of Homophobia and the Softening of Masculinity at an English Sixth Form." *Sociology* 44, no. 5 (2010b): 843–59.

McCormack, Mark and Eric Anderson. "Homohysteria: Definitions, Context and Intersectionality." *Sex Roles* 71, no. 3–4 (2014a): 152–58.

McCormack, Mark and Eric Anderson. "The Influence of Declining Homophobia on Men's Gender in the United States: An Argument for the Study of Homohysteria." *Sex Roles* 71, no. 3–4 (2014b): 109–20.

McCormack, Mark, Eric Anderson, and Adi Adams. "Cohort Effect on the Coming Out Experience of Bisexual Males." *Sociology* 48, no. 6 (2014): 1207–23.

McCormack, Mark, L. Wignall, and Eric Anderson. "Identities and Identifications: Changes in Metropolitan Bisexual Men's Attitudes and Experiences." *Journal of Bisexuality* 15, no. 1 (2015): doi: 10.1080/15299716.2014.984372 (accessed November 15, 2015).

McCreary, Donald R. "The Male Role and Avoiding Femininity." *Sex Roles* 31, no. 9–10 (1994): 517–31.

McDonagh, Eileen and Laura. Pappano. *Playing with the Boys: Why Separate Is Not Equal in Sports*. Oxford: Oxford University Press, 2008.

McNair, Brian. *Striptease Culture: Sex, Media and the Democratization of Desire*. New York: Psychology Press, 2002.

Melton, E. Nicole. "Women and the Lesbian Stigma." Chap. 1 in *Sexual Minorities in Sports*, edited by M. L. Sartore-Baldwin. 11–30. London: Lynne Rienner Publishers, 2013.

Melton, E. Nicole and George. B. Cunningham. "When Identities Collide: Exploring Minority Stress and Resilience among College Athletes with Multiple Marginalized Identities." *Journal for the Study of Sports and Athletes in Education* 6, no. 1 (2012): 45–66.

Mennesson, Christine and Jean-Paul Clément. "Homosociability and Homosexuality: The Case of Soccer Played by Women." *International Review for the Sociology of Sport* 38, no. 3 (2003): 311–30.

Michael, B. "'Just Don't Hit on Me and I'm Fine': Mapping High School Wrestlers' Relationship to Inclusive Masculinity and Heterosexual Recuperation." *International Review for the Sociology of Sport* (2013): doi: 1012690213501168 (accessed November 15, 2015).

Miller, T. M. (2001). *Sportsex*. Philadelphia, PA: Temple University Press.

Millward, Peter. "The Rebirth of the Football Fanzine: Using E-Zines as a Data Source." *Journal of Sport and Social Issues* 32, no. 3: (2008): 299–310.

Miracle, Andrew W. and C. R. Rees. *Lesson of the Locker Room: The Myth of School Sports*. Amherst, NY: Prometheus, 1994.

Morin, Stephen and Ellen. M. Garfinkle. "Male Homophobia." *Journal of Social Issues* 34, no. 1 (1978): 29–47.

Morris, Max and Eric Anderson. "Charlie Is So Cool Like: Inclusive Masculinities and Popularity on YouTube." *Sociology* Online First (2015): doi: 10.1177/0038038514562852 (accessed November 15, 2015).

Morris, Max, Mark McCormack, and Eric Anderson. "The Changing Experiences of Bisexual Male Adolescents." *Gender and Education* 26, no. 4 (2014): 397–413.

Mrozek, Donald J. *Sport and American Mentality 1880–1910*. Knoxville: University of Tennessee Press, 1983.

Mullen, Brian and Carolyn Copper. "The Relation between Group Cohesiveness and Performance: An Integration." *Psychological Bulletin* 115, no. 2 (1994): 210–27.

Negy, Charles. "Homohysteria: Useful Construct? Or an Unnecessary Splitting of Hairs?" *Sex Roles* Online First 71, no 3 (2014): http://link.springer.com/article/10.1007% 2Fs11199-014-0386-4# (accessed November 15, 2015).

Netzley, Sara Baker. "Visibility That Demystifies: Gays, Gender and Sex on Television." *Journal of Homosexuality* 57, no. 8 (2010): 968–86.

Norton, Rictor. *Mother Clap's Molly House: The Gay Subculture in England, 1700–1830.* London: GMP Publishers, 1992.

Nuwer, Hank. *Wrongs of Passage: Fraternities, Sororities, Hazing and Binge Drinking.* Bloomington: Indiana University Press, 2001.

Nylund, David. "Transmitting Softer Masculinity: Sports Talk Radio and Masculinity." In *Routledge Handbook of Sport, Gender and Sexuality*, edited by J. Hargreaves and E. Anderson. 454–60. London: Routledge, 2014.

Oakley, Ann. *Gender on Planet Earth*. Cambridge: Polity Press, 2002.

Ogawa, Scott. "100 Missing Men: Participation, Selection and Silence of Gay Athletes." In *Routledge Handbook of Sport, Gender and Sexuality*, edited by J. Hargreaves and E. Anderson. 291–99. London: Routledge, 2014.

Ogburn, William. F. "Cultural Lag as Theory." *Sociology and Social Research* 41, no. 2 (1957): 167–74.

Olstad, Keith. "Brave New Men: A Basis for Discussion." In *Sex/Male/Gender/Masculine*, edited by J. Petras. Port Washington, NY: Alfred, 1975.

Osborne, Barbara. "'No Drinking, No Drugs, No Lesbians': Sexual Orientation Discrimination in Intercollegiate Athletics." *Marquette Sports Law Review* 17, no. 2 (2007): 481–501.

Owen, Gareth. "Catching Crabs: Bodies, Emotions and Gay Identities in Mainstream Competitive Rowing." In *Sport, Sexualities and Queer Theory*, edited by J. Caudwell. 129–44. London: Routledge, 2006.

Park, Roberta J. "Sport, Gender and Society in a Transatlantic Victorian Perspective." *The International Journal of the History of Sport* 24, no. 12 (2007): 1570–603.

Parker, Andrew. "Chasing the 'Big Time': Football Apprenticeships in the 1990s." Unpublished doctoral thesis: University of Warwick, 1996a.

Parker, Andrew. "The Construction of Masculinity within Boys' Physical Education." *Gender and Education* 8, no. 1 (1996b): 141–58.

Parker, Richard. G. *Bodies, Pleasures, and Passions: Sexual Culture in Contemporary Brazil.* Nashville, TN: Vanderbilt University Press, 2009.

Pascoe, Cheri Jo. "'Dude, You're a Fag': Masculinity and the Fag Discourse." *Sexualities* 8, no. 3 (2005): 329–46.

Peralta, Robert L. "College and Alcohol and the Embodiment of Hegemonic Masculinity among European American." *Sex Roles* 56, no. 11–12 (2007): 741–56.

Pettigrew, Thomas F. "Intergroup Contact Theory." *Annual Review of Psychology* 49, no. 1 (1998): 65–85.

PEW. *Growing Support for Gay Marriage: Changed Minds and Changing Demographics.* Washington, DC: PEW Research Center, 2013.

Piggot, Robert. "Gay Weddings: Fifth of Britons Would Turn Down Invitation." *BBC News*, 2014.

Pleck, Joseph. "Issues for the Men's Movement: Summer, 1975." *Changing Men: A Newsletter for Men Against Sexism* (1975): 21–23.

Plummer, David. *One of the Boys: Masculinity, Homophobia and Modern Manhood.* New York: Harrington Park Press, 1999.

Plummer, David. "The Quest for Modern Manhood: Masculine Stereotypes, Peer Cultures and the Social Significance of Homophobia." *Journal of Adolescence* 24, no. 1 (2001): 15–23.

Plummer, David. "Sportphobia: Why Do Some Men Avoid Sport?" *Journal of Sport and Social Issues* 30, no. 2 (2006): 122–37.

Plummer, David. "The Ebb and Flow of Homophobia: A Gender Taboo Theory." *Sex Roles* 71, no. 3–4 (2014): 126–36.

Plymire, Darcy C. and Pamela J. Forman. "Speaking of Cheryl Miller: Interrogating the Lesbian Taboo on a Women's Basketball Newsgroup." *NWSA Journal* 12, no. 1 (2001): 1–21.

Pollack, William. *Real Boys: Rescuing Our Sons from the Myths of Boyhood*. New York: Henry Holt and Company, 1998.

Pollock, Allyson. *Tackling Rugby: What Every Parent Should Know*. London: Verso Books, 2014.

Price, Michael and Andrew Parker. "Sport, Sexuality, and the Gender Order: Amateur Rugby Union, Gay Men, and Social Exclusion." *Sociology of Sport Journal* 20, no. 2 (2003): 108–26.

Pringle, Richard and Pirkko Markula. "No Pain Is Sane after All: A Foucauldian Analysis of Masculinities and Men's Experiences in Rugby." *Sociology of Sport Journal* 22, no. 4 (2005): 472–97.

Pronger, Brian. *The Arena of Masculinity: Sports, Homosexuality, and the Meaning of Sex*. London: GMP Publishers Limited, 1990.

Rader, Benjamin G. *American Sports: From the Age of Folk Games to the Age of Televised Sports* (5th ed.). Upper Saddle River, NJ: Prentice Hall, 2004.

Rasmussen, Mary R. "'That's So Gay!': A Study of the Deployment of Signifiers of Sexual and Gender Identities in Secondary School Settings in Australia and the United States." *Social Semiotics* 14, no. 3 (2004): 289–308.

Rasmussen, Ricky, Anthony Esgate, and David Turner. "On Your Marks, Get Stereotyped, Go! Novice Coaches and Black Stereotypes in Sprinting." *Journal of Sport & Social Issues* 29, no. 4 (2005): 426–36.

Renold, Emma. "'Other' Boys: Negotiating Non-Hegemonic Masculinities in Primary School." *Gender and Education* 16, no. 2 (2004): 247–66.

Rich, Adrienne. "Compulsory Heterosexuality and Lesbian Existence." *Signs: Journal of Women in Culture and Society* 5, no. 4 (1980): 631–60.

Rigauer, Bero. *Sport and Work*. New York: Columbia University Press, 1981.

Riley, Bettina H. "GLB Adolescent's 'Coming Out'." *Journal of Child and Adolescent Psychiatric Nursing* 23, no. 1 (2010): 3–10.

Ripley, Matthew, Eric Anderson, Mark McCormack, and Ben Rockett. "Heteronormativity in the University Classroom: Novelty Attachment and Content Substitution among Gay-Friendly Students." *Sociology of Education* 85, no. 2 (2012): 121–30.

Roberts, Steve. "Boys Will Be Boys . . . Won't They?: Change in Continuities in Contemporary Young Working-Class Masculinities." *Sociology* 47, no. 4 (2013): 671–86.

Roberts, Steve, Eric Anderson, and Rory Magrath. "Inclusive Masculinity in a Man's Game: Continuity, Change and Complexity in the Performance of Masculinity Among Elite Adolescent Footballers." *British Journal of Sociology* (under review).

Robinson, Joseph P. and Dorothy L. Espelage. "Inequities in Educational and Psychological Outcomes Between LGBTQ and Straight Students in Middle and High School." *Educational Researcher* 40, no. 7 (2011): 315–30.

Robinson, Kerry H. "Reinforcing Hegemonic Masculinities through Sexual Harassment: Issues of Identity, Power, and Popularity in Secondary Schools." *Gender and Education* 17, no. 1 (2005): 19–37.

Robinson, S. and E. Anderson. "To Love Another Man: Expanding Homosociality Under the Rubric of 'The Bromance'." *Journal of Adolescent Research*, forthcoming.

Rotolo, Thomas and Amy Wharton. "Living across Institutions: Exploring Sex-Based Homophily in Occupations and Voluntary Groups." *Sociological Perspectives* 46, no. 1 (2004): 59–82.

Rowe, Mary P. "Barriers to Equality: The Power of Subtle Discrimination to Maintain Unequal Opportunity." *Employee Responsibilities and Rights Journal* 3, no. 2 (1990): 153–63.

Russell, David *Football and the English: A Social History of Association Football in England, 1863–1995*. Preston: Carnegie, 1997.

Sabo, Donald. F. and Ross. Runfola. *Jock: Sports and Male Identity*. Englewood Cliffs, NJ: Prentice, 1980.

Sabo, Donald F. and J. Panepinto. "Football Ritual and the Social Reproduction of Masculinity." In *Sport, Men and the Gender Order*, edited by M. A. Messner and D. F. Sabo. Champaign, IL: Human Kinetics, 1990.

Sartore, Melanie L. and George B. Cunningham. "Gender, Sexual Prejudice and Sport Participation: Implications for Sexual Minorities." *Sex Roles* 60, no. 1–2 (2009): 100–113.

Savin-Williams, Ritch C. *The New Gay Teenager*. London: Harvard University Press, 2005.

Schneider, J. J. and D. S. Eitzen. "Racial Segregation by Professional Football Positions, 1960–1985." *Sport Science Review*, 70 (1986): 259–62.

Schrack-Walters, Andrew, Kathleen A. O'Donnell, and Daniel L. Wardlow. "Deconstructing the Myth of the Monolithic Male Athlete: A Qualitative Study of Men's Participation in Athletics." *Sex Roles* 60, no. 1–2 (2009): 81–99.

Schroeder, K. "Military Masculinities." Unpublished doctoral thesis: University of Chicago, 2002.

Schuman, Howard, C. Steeh, and L. Bobo. *Racial Attitudes in America: Trends and Interpretations*. Cambridge, MA: Harvard University Press, 1985.

Scoats, R., L. Joseph and Eric Anderson. "'I Don't Mind Watching Him Cum': Heterosexual Men, Male-Male-Female Threesomes, and the Erosion of the One-Time Rule of Homosexuality." *Sexualities*: forthcoming.

Sedgwick, Eve Kosofsky. *Between Men: English Literature and Male Homosocial Desire*. New York: Columbia University Press, 1985.

Seiden, Anne and Pauline Bart. "Woman to Woman: Is Sisterhood Powerful?". In *Old Family/New Family? Interpersonal Relationships*, edited by N. Galzer-Malbin. 189–228. New York: D. Van Nostrand, 1975.

Shepard, B. "History, Narrative and Sexual Identity: Gay Liberation and Postwar Movements for Sexual Freedom in the United States." In *The Story of Sexual Identity: Narrative Perspectives on the Gay and Lesbian Life Course*, edited by P. L. Hammack and B. J. Cohler. 23–48. New York: Oxford University Press, 2009.

Sherkat, Darren E., Melissa Powell-Williams, Gregory Maddox, and Kylan M. de Vries. "Religious, Politics, and Support for Same-Sex Marriage in the United States, 1988–2008." *Social Science Research* 40, no. 1 (2011): 167–80.

Shilts, Randy. *And the Band Played On: People, Politics and the Aids Epidemic*. New York: St. Martin's Press, 1987.

Shire, Joanne, Celia H. Brackenridge, and Mary Fuller. "Changing Positions: The Sexual Politics of a Women's Field Hockey Team 1986–1996." *Women in Sport and Physical Activity* 9, no. 1 (2000): 35–64.

Smith, E. (2000). "Stacking in the Team Sport of Intercollegiate Baseball." In *Racism in College Athletics: The African American Athlete's Experience*, edited by D. Brooks and R. Althouse. 65–84. Morgantown, WV: Fitness Information Technology.

Smith, Jeffrey. "'Ye've Got To 'ave Ball to Play This Game Sir!' Boys, Peers and Fears: The Negative Influence of School-Based 'Cultural Accomplices' in Constructing Hegemonic Masculinities." *Gender and Education* 19, no. 2 (2007): 179–98.

Smith, Sara J., Amber M. Axelton, and Donald A. Saucier. "The Effects of Contact on Sexual Prejudice." *Sex Roles* 61, no. 3–4 (2009): 178–91.

Smith, Tom W. *Attitudes towards Same-Gender, Sexual Behavior across Time and across Countries.* Chicago, IL: NORC, 2011.

Smith, Tom W., Jaesok Son, and Jibum Kim. *Public Attitudes towards Homosexuality and Gay Rights across Time and Countries.* Chicago, IL: NORC, 2014.

Southall, Richard M., Mark S. Nagel, Eric Anderson, Fritz G. Polite, and Crystal Southall. "An Investigation of Male College Athletes' Attitudes Toward Sexual-Orientation." *Journal of Issues in Intercollegiate Athletics* Special issue (2009): 62–77.

Southall, Richard M., Eric D. Anderson, Mark S. Nagel, Fritz G. Polite, and Crystal Southall. "An Investigation of Ethnicity as a Variable Related to US Male College Athletes' Sexual-Orientation Behaviours and Attitudes." *Ethnic and Racial Studies* 34, no. 2 (2011): 293–313.

Spencer, Colin. *Homosexuality in History.* Orlando, FL: Harcourt Brace, 1995.

Sprecher, Susan and Constantine Sedikides. "Gender Differences in Perceptions of Emotionality: The Case of Close Heterosexual Relationships." *Sex Roles* 28, no. 9–10 (1993): 511–30.

Stotzer, Rebecca L. "Straight Allies: Supportive Attitudes Towards Lesbians, Gay Men, and Bisexuals in a College Sample." *Sex Roles* 60, no. 1–2 (2009): 67–80.

Sykes, Heather. "Turning the Closets Inside/Out: Towards a Queer-Feminist Theory in Women's Physical Education." *Sociology of Sport Journal* 15, no. 2 (1998): 154–73.

Sykes, Heather. "Transsexual and Transgender Policies in Sport." *Women in Sport and Physical Activity* 15, no. 1 (2006): 3–13.

Symons, Caroline. *The Gay Games: A History.* New York: Routledge, 2010.

Szalacha, Laura A. "Safer Sexual Diversity Climates: Lessons Learned from an Evaluation of Massachusetts Safe Schools Program for Gay and Lesbian Students." *American Journal of Education* 110, no. 1 (2003): 58–88.

Tewksbury, Mark. *Inside Out: Straight Talk from a Gay Jock.* New York: John Wiley & Sons, 2010.

Theberge, Nancy and Susan Birrell. "The Sociological Study of Women in Sport." In *Women and Sport: Interdisciplinary Perspectives*, edited by D. M. Costa and S. R. Guthrie. Champaign, IL: Human Kinetics, 1994.

Thorpe, Holly. "Bourdieu, Gender Reflexivity, and Physical Culture: A Case of Masculinities in the Snowboarding Field." *Journal of Sport and Social Issues* 34, no. 2 (2010): 176–214.

Thurlow, Crispin. "Naming the "Outsider Within": Homophobic Pejoratives and the Verbal Abuse of Lesbian, Gay and Bisexual High-School Pupils." *Journal of Adolescence* 24, no. 1 (2001): 25–38.

Treves, I. "An Analysis of the Absence of Openly Gay Male Tennis Players." Unpublished: Princeton University, 2015.

Veri, Maria J. "Homophobic Discourse Surrounding the Female Athlete." *Quest* 51 (1999): 355–68.

Vincent, John, John S. Hill, and Jason W. Lee. "The Multiple Brand Personalities of David Beckham: A Case Study of the Beckham Brand." *Sport Marketing Quarterly* 18, no. 3 (2009): 173–80.

Waldner, L. K., A. Sikka, and S. Baig. (1999). "Ethnicity and Sex Differences in University Student's Knowledge of AIDS, Fear of AIDS, and Attitudes Toward Gay Men." *Journal of Homosexuality*, 37(3), 117–33.

Walker, Marlon A. "Black Coaches Are Ready, Willing . . . And Still Waiting: By All Accounts, There Is No Shortage of Qualified Black Coaches to Lead Division 1 Teams, So Why Are There So Few?" *Black Issues in Higher Education* 22, no. 6 (2005): 26–30.

Weeks, Jeffrey. *Sexuality and Its Discontents.* London: Routledge, 1985.

Weeks, Jeffrey. *Against Nature: Essays on History, Sexuality and Identity*. London: Rivers Oram Press, 1991.

Weeks, Jeffrey. *The World We Have Won*. London: Routledge, 2007.

Weinberg, M. S., Williams, C. J., and Pryor, D. W. (1994). *Dual Attraction: Understanding Bisexuality*. Oxford: Oxford University Press.

Wellard, Ian. "Re-Thinking Abilities." *Sport, Education and Society* 11, no. 3 (2006): 311–15.

Wensing, Emma H. and Toni Bruce. "Bending the Rules: Media Representations of Gender During an International Sporting Event." *International Review for the Sociology of Sport* 38, no. 4 (2003): 387–96.

West, Candace and Don H. Zimmerman. "Doing Gender." *Gender & Society* 1, no. 2 (1987): 125–51.

White, Phillip G. and Anne B. Vagi, "Rugby in the 19th-Century British Boarding-School System: A Feminist Psychoanalytic Perspective." Chap. 5 In *Sport, Men, and the Gender Order*, edited by M. A. Messner and D. F. Sabo. 67–78. Champaign, IL: Human Kinetics Books, 1990.

Whitson, David. "Sport in the Social Construction of Masculinity." In *Sport, Men and the Gender Order*, edited by M. A. Messner and D. F. Sabo. Champaign, IL: Human Kinetics Books, 1990.

Williams, Dorie Giles. "Gender, Masculinity-Femininity, and Emotional Intimacy in Same-Sex Friendship." *Sex Roles* 12, no. 5–6 (1985): 587–600.

Willis, Teresa. "Kicking Down Barriers: Gay Footballers, Challenging Stereotypes and Changing Attitudes in Amateur League Play." *Soccer & Society* Online First (2014): doi: 10.1080/14660970.2014.961717 (accessed November 15, 2015).

Wilson, Brian. "The "Anti-Jock" Movement: Reconsidering Youth Resistance, Masculinity, and Sport Culture in the Age of the Internet." *Sociology of Sport Journal* 19, no. 2 (2002): 206–33.

Wolf-Wendel, Lisa, Douglas Toma, and Christopher Morphew. "How Much Difference Is Too Much Difference? Perceptions of Gay Men and Lesbians in Intercollegiate Athletics." *Journal of College Student Development* 42, no. 5 (2001): 465–79.

Wolter, Sarah. "The Ladies Professional Golf Association's Five Points of Celebrity: 'Driving' the Organization 'Fore-Ward' or a Snap-Hook into the Next Fairway?" *International Journal of Sport Communication* 3 (2010): 31–48.

Woodford, Michael R., Michael L. Howell, Perry Silverschanz, and Lotus Yu. "'That's So Gay!'": Examining the Covariates of Hearing This Expression among Gay, Lesbian and Bisexual College Students." *Journal of American College Health* 60, no. 6 (2012): 429–34.

Worthen, Meredith G. F. "The Cultural Significance of Homophobia on Heterosexual Women's Gendered Experiences in the United States: A Commentary." *Sex Roles* 71, no. 3–4 (2014): 141–51.

Zipp, John F. "Sport and Sexuality: Athletic Participation by Sexual Minority and Sexual Majority Adolescents in the U.S." *Sex Roles* 64, no. 1–2 (2011): 19–31.

Zuhur, Sherifa. "Gender, Sexuality and the Criminal Laws in the Middle East and North Africa: A Comparative Study." *Women for Women's Rights* (2005): 1–76.

INDEX

DATE DUE